WITH CONSCIOUSNESS OF GUILT

WITH CONSCIOUSNESS OF GUILT

THE SEXUAL PREDATOR AMONG US

Ernest Dorling

Writer's Showcase presented by *Writer's Digest*
San Jose New York Lincoln Shanghai

With Consciousness of Guilt
The Sexual Predator Among Us

Published by Writer's Showcase presented by *Writer's Digest*
an imprint of iUniverse.com, Inc.

For information address:
iUniverse.com, Inc.
5220 S 16th, Ste. 200
Lincoln, NE 68512
www.iuniverse.com

ISBN: 0-595-13592-7

Printed in the United States of America

Dedication

To the Police who investigate, and the lawyers who prosecute, the sexual predators among us. Your selfish dedication to seeking justice for victims everywhere defines who you are in life and not just what you do for a living.

Contents

Foreword

This story is about Sam Consiglio, a man with a history of committing sexual assaults on women. I first met Sam when I was nine-years old. For about six years, we were almost inseparable. Unbeknown to me or our other friends, Sam began assaulting women about the age of 13. With the help of his father, he was able to avoid being charged with his early offenses. Sam and I subsequently grew apart, not so much because of distance, but because of Sam's criminal activity and his assaults on women. Over the years, the more I learned about Sam and how he successfully manipulated the judicial system that had been the epicenter of my own career, I realized just how fallible this system is. I'd seen this system break down before but never so often as it had with someone like Sam. I also realized that Sam had become more than just a jail-house lawyer, he'd become a seasoned veteran of the judicial system and knew how to work it to his advantage as well as most attorney's I'd worked with. I also learned of the many mistakes my overzealous colleagues made in their sincere efforts to incarcerate Sam. Because of the mistakes made by the police or because of some quick deal made by an overworked prosecutor to negotiate a plea to some lesser offense, Sam remained free to victimize other women.

When I first set out to write this book, like so many other first time writers, I had no real appreciation for the magnitude of the work ahead of me. The professional and academic articles I had written didn't begin to prepare me for the journey ahead as I began my research into the criminal life of a sociopath and serial sex offender. During the almost two years I researched Sam's life of crime, I read through thousands of pages of trial transcripts, police reports, newspaper articles, witness interviews and medical reports, and interviewed police officers, attorneys and victims of his manipulations. During this time, I often asked myself, why write such a book? In virtually every case, books published under the classification "True Crime" involve some type of sensational murder. While this story doesn't involve such an act, the more I researched Sam and his violent acts against women, the more I realized, Sam's journey through the criminal justice system is a story that demands to be told. And while this story isn't about a sensational murder, it is about a sexual predator who commits a crime equally as grisly, the crime of rape. While a murder does indeed kill leaving the victims friends and family to grieve, the sexual predator often allows his victim to live so they can forever relive the moment they were violated as they try and rebuild their life. Some never do of course, while others move on. In both cases, the victims live the rest of their lives with that dark experience burned forever in their memory.

I wanted to accomplish several things in writing this book. First, I wanted to reveal the inner workings of the judicial system, especially as it related to the crime of rape. While the approach prosecutor's take to deal with sexual crimes vary, I hoped to show how victims of sexual assaults, along with witnesses and police officers are sometimes treated and what they must often endure during judicial proceedings. Second, I wanted to reveal to the reader, the efforts those who investigate and prosecute sexual offenders undertake to uncover the truth. In this case, I've relied on the transcripts of Q&A sessions between investigators, prosecutors and Sam in order to reveal the efforts made to uncover evidence as those charged with extracting the truth try and deal with a sociopath. In some cases, I've summarized trial testimony because of repetitiousness or irrelevant detail. In others situations, I've used the actual language and testimony to depict the many facets of a trial or other judicial proceeding to present the many emotions and sometimes deception offered by the witnesses, victims and the defendant when called upon to testify. Third, I wanted to try and get into the mind of a sexual predator and sociopath. To do so, I relied on medical reports as well as personal interviews with Sam. I interviewed Sam on eight separate occasions, recording each of the interviews. On each occasion, Sam was eager to tell his story discussing freely his past assaults on women, why he did it, what he felt at the time and how the police failed to convict him. Finally I hoped to demonstrate that sexual attacks, especially against women, could sometimes be avoided. As the reader will see, there are actions we can all take to reduce our chances of being a victim.

The story of Sam Consiglio is true. No last names of any victims were used in this book. In most cases, to protect an individual's identity, the first names of victims have been changed. The names of witnesses, police officers, prosecutors and other attorneys are real.

Acknowledgements

With Consciousness of Guilt could not have been written without the support and contribution of several people. I want to thank Susan Hejlik whose editorial assistance painfully reminded me to stick to investigative research. Many thanks to my friend Flora Defillipo, PhD. for her valuable insight into the mind of the sociopath and with her editorial comments related to the psychological evaluations outlined in the book. I want to thank Dick Cole, PhD., for taking time away from conducting his doctoral research to review the manuscript and provide valuable editorial comments. Thanks to Dean Caldwell, PhD., for being a true academic mentor. Your support and continued encouragement to follow through with this project kept me going at times that were difficult.

Special thanks to Tom and Loretta Sieffert for meeting me on a cold February afternoon in Michigan so that I might better understand how it is some people always find good in others no matter what they may have done in the past.

A very special thanks to Al Arena, a dedicated legal advocate for generously sharing his time and insight into what goes into defending someone charged with a sex offense.

I want to thank the members of the Police Writer's Club whose support and mentoring encouraged me to stay the course and finish this project.

And to my wife, Linda. I would have never finished this without your editorial comments, patience and support.

Introduction

…Superficially the sociopath excels in social situations…. On the other hand, those who become better acquainted are soon aware of his immaturity, superficiality, and chronic inability to make a success of his own life…. He becomes a true disappointment to those who were charmed to expect more, to those who began to believe in him, to those who continue to see his potential, to those who still hope for him.

Richard M. Suinn, Fundamentals of Behavior Pathology

His emotional reactions are simple and animal-like, occurring only with immediate frustrations and discomfort. However, he is able to simulate emotional reactions and attachments when it will help him to obtain what he wants from others. His social and sexual relations with others are superficial but demanding and manipulative.
The simple psychopath's main characteristic is an inability to delay the gratification and biological needs, no matter what the future consequences to himself or to others.

Robert D. Hare, Psychopathy: Theory and Research

The chains that bound his hands and feet whenever he was in the courtroom, had been removed out of the jury's view. Seeing him that way could be viewed as prejudicial. For days, he appeared to enjoy the same freedom of movement as those who were now about to reveal his fate. But he wasn't free to leave or even move about the courtroom. Like most everything else in his life, it was just a facade.

But regardless of the jury's decision, he wouldn't be free, not yet. Instead, he would be returned to his cell to continue his fight for freedom, a fight he'd become obsessed with. Like a seasoned combat veteran with the means to resist, he'd always fought and never surrendered. And now, he would do so in spite of his challenger's brutal attacks on his character. In his mind he knew he was a good person who could never have done the things described by the most formidable adversary he'd ever encountered.

The summer of 1991 had just ended. With the arrival of fall, even more attractive weather was on the horizon for Southern California. The weather was almost perfect; it virtually always is in San Diego. But inside the sparsely furnished courtroom in the San Diego County Courthouse the temperature was climate controlled all year around. It didn't matter what the weather outside was like to Sam Consiglio as he sat inside the artificially lit county courtroom. Instead of enjoying the cool ocean breeze that swept in off the Pacific Ocean, Sam stared intently at San Diego Superior Court Judge Frank A. Brown. After two weeks of testimony, Brown had been the first to learn of the jury's decision. When Sam rose to hear the verdict, he was convinced that the twelve men and women he had sat with in the meagerly furnished courtroom had voted to exonerate him of any guilt on charges that he had raped the young woman from the homeless shelter. After all, he had been in this position many times before. He knew when he would be acquitted of a crime. Whether he was guilty or not was irrelevant. But he also enjoyed being in a courtroom. It was his stage, a place to be someone else if even for a short time. Because in reality, he'd become a volatile misfit, never really fitting in anywhere.

Women, of course, were always an obsession with Sam. And it was this obsession that brought him, for the second time in as many months, to a San Diego courtroom charged with raping a woman. The other occasion involved a street prostitute he had persuaded to perform oral sex on him after convincing her he was a local vice-cop. Sam threatened to arrest the girl if she didn't provide him with free sexual favors. The charge of "rape by oral copulation by trickery" was so ludicrous to Sam that he represented himself at his arraignment. He was convinced that the charge was a sham, dreamed up by a vindictive prosecutor, and that no court would ever be so foolish as to convict on such a ridiculous offense. Sam considered the charge so laughable that during his preliminary hearing, he considered asking the judge, "Who among us hasn't used trickery at one time or another to get a blowjob?" As if there was any other way, he said later. Still, being with a woman, any woman under most any circumstances, and dominating them was his passion.

Sam stood silent, convinced that he was going to be freed. While he had experienced this event many times, each encounter with a judge and jury brought with it a feeling of intense fear that his freedom would be taken away. But Sam never outwardly displayed that fear. Instead, as he had so often, he displayed a mask of normality, appearing peculiarly calm, almost vacant, as if no one at that moment in time existed but him. In the minute or so it took for the judge eto receive the verdict and hand it back to the clerk, Sam appeared strikingly cool and sure of himself. But inside, his knees shook and he began to sweat as he felt a wave of dizziness come over him. As the judge handed the single sheet of paper revealing the verdict back to the clerk to be read, Sam thought about his father, wishing he could have been in the courtroom to support him just one more time. He also thought about his past and how he had found himself in judge Brown's courtroom on October 21, 1991.

"I'm a nice guy who has done some bad things, okay. But the person inside me is a nice person. I think I was 13 when I was first charged, although, it wasn't rape. I was at the shopping center at Harper and 13

Mile Road in St. Clair Shores, Michigan. I would approach women and make small talk with them. Then, I would grab them and...."

Chapter 1

Irresistible Charm, But No Shame For Wrong Doing

I met Sam Consiglio the same year Senator John F. Kennedy narrowly defeated Richard Nixon for the presidency of the United States. The first artificial satellite, Tiros I, capable of taking pictures of the earth's weather systems was sent into orbit by the U. S. Scientists from the National Aeronautics and Space Administration said that the satellite was a proto-type of those expected to provide 24-hour weather coverage of the entire nation in a few years. In that same year, a U-2 reconnaissance plane flown by Francis Gary Powers was shot down over Russia. The U-2 flights were designed to take pictures of Soviet military installations during the height of the cold war. The Food and Drug Administration announced that the birth control pill would go on sale in the U.S. the following spring. Lucy and Desi Arnez filed for divorce, and Clint Eastwood starred in a weekly television series called "Rawhide". The year was 1960.

I was 9 years old. My family had just moved from Detroit to one of its fastest growing young suburbs, St. Clair Shores, just over 10 miles northeast of the Detroit city limits. But for a 9–year old it may as well have been a con-tinent away. The school year was already eight weeks old when I entered the fourth grade at Elmira Elementary. Elmira was considerably different than the private Catholic school I had attended. Elmira had less discipline. There were no nuns and priests patrolling the corridors punishing you for not feeling guilty about something. The school had a dirt playground and ball field, instead of the paved parking lots where I had grown accustomed to playing. Most of the kids in the class had been together for several years. This new school was a foreign environment for me. I was the new kid, an outsider. Fortunately, or so I thought, I was seated next to Sam Consiglio, another outsider who also had recently moved to the neighborhood.

Sam and I were the same age, although I was older by two weeks. We enjoyed playing sports but neither of us was athletic. Most days we looked forward to school but were never accused of aspiring to academic excellence. Like many of our transplanted friends, we were angry at having been moved and forced to leave our other friends behind. We were much too young to realize that our blue-collar parents were doing the best they could to provide a better life for us than they had had growing up. So, Sam and I immediately became friends. We both came from large families, seven children in his, while I was the oldest of five.

Sam was the middle child. He had two older brothers, Joe and Jerry and a sister, Grace, who was a year older. Sam also had two younger brothers, Louie and Jim, and a younger sister, Virginia. Sam was named after his father, Sam Consiglio Sr., a full-blooded Sicilian who claimed to have strong Catholic ties and who adhered to a philosophy that dictated traditional established roles of the time. This meant that women were for cleaning the house, having babies, preparing dinner, and sex, although not necessarily in that order. The more sex his sons were able to engage in, the better. But heaven help the man who touched any of "Big" Sam Consiglio's daughters. Chastity was the basic theme of the Consiglio household as far as its women were concerned.

Sam Sr., or "Big Sam" as he was commonly called, lacked a formal education. As a laborer, he was able to work his way into a position of authority as a civil servant with Macomb County, the government body that oversaw the expansion of St. Clair Shores and all the other developing towns in the county. Big Sam was a "jack of all trades" working directly for a politician named Tom Welsh. Considered by many to be a hard line Democratic political boss, Welsh exercised control over the office that issued permits for land development. In the 1960's, as Macomb County was experiencing extraordinary development, much of the undeveloped land required drainage construction to control the water flow before actual construction could begin. In the 1960's, these "wetlands" made Drainage Commissioner Tom Welsh, one of the most powerful and influential figures in the county. Big Sam worked directly for Welsh. He had no particular job, or at least none that any of us really knew about, but he did almost everything associated with the office of Drainage Commissioner at one time or another.

By most standards, Big Sam was perceived to be a violent man. He was stocky and intimidating, seldom calm about anything. He was often excitable but could, when necessary to impress neighbors and friends, become calm and serene in order to demonstrate that he was just like them, a regular middle class guy. He was also quick with his hands, often hitting his wife, Lucy, in front of the children. He wasn't afraid to hit one of his daughters either, if he thought she had it coming.

"He used to beat my mom a lot," Sam said. "I guess the first incident I recall was when I was 7 or 8 years old. Grace had gotten a haircut without asking my Dad first. He was bitching for a week. One day, I came in the house with Grace and Virginia, and my dad is beating my mother. My mother was so big, almost 400 pounds. She couldn't get up. She couldn't get out of the chair. He just kept hitting her. He had broken her nose and she was bleeding pretty badly. I ran next door to call the police. As I was grabbing the neighbors' phone, I turned around and my Dad was coming in the house. I pissed my pants; it was embarrassing. I ran under the kitchen table, guessing that was a good hiding spot. Fortunately, our neighbor calmed him down. That's probably the most scared I've been in my life."

Big Sam didn't confine his anger to his wife and his daughters. On occasion, he would hit his own father, who by the time I met him, was in his 70's and could barely walk without the support of a hospital walker or cane. Sam's grandfather lived in one of the two bedrooms in the small house Sam's father purchased after moving from Detroit. That left one bedroom for Big Sam and Lucy. Sam and his four brothers slept in a makeshift bedroom in the attic, while his two sisters slept on a sleeper sofa in the living room.

I had only known Sam for a short time the day his mother sent him to the store for a can of tomato sauce. Spaghetti was an almost daily staple at the Consiglio house and running out of spaghetti sauce was inexcusable. That day, Sam's grandfather was eager for his daughter-in-law to get his dinner to him. When Sam and I arrived at his house with the can of sauce, his grandfather threw the can back at us because we had gotten the wrong type. He claimed we had tricked him because the woman on the can was facing in the wrong direction. While Sam's mother began to cry, Sam and I ran from the house just trying to get away as quickly as we could. I remember Sam saying that his grandfather was a "no-good son of a bitch who was ruining their home." At the time, Sam was 10 years old.

It was common for the old man to get angry and call his daughter-in-law Lucy a "puttana," Italian for whore. At other times, he would get mad and spit on her. Because of Lucy's size, it was impossible for her to run or escape from the abuses of the old man. All she could do was cry and complain to her husband when he came home from the long hours imposed upon him by the political boss of Macomb County. Sometimes, Big Sam would get mad enough to slap his father for his abuses. The old man would begin to cry and Big Sam would feel guilty, turning the blame on himself and his wife.

"I didn't like seeing my dad beat on my grandpa like that, that wasn't right. I mean that was his old man," Sam said. "He should have put him in a home or something. There was just a lot of violence when I was a kid. I'm not blaming that on anything. That's why I spent so much time away when I was a kid. It was my escape, my way out."

It was a couple of years later when the old man who had accompanied his son and daughter-in-law on their honeymoon, became so senile that Big Sam, with tears in his eyes because he blamed himself for his fathers fate, was forced to place him in a nursing home.

Sam was 13 when the police confronted his father with the news that his son had grabbed several women by the breasts at a local shopping center. Big Sam took his son into the bedroom and asked if it was true. Sam confessed. Shocked and angry, Big Sam asked his son why he did it. "I just don't know why I did it, I have no idea why," Sam said.

Big Sam convinced the police it was just a childish prank. The police made out a report and warned Sam not to do anything like that again. Sam agreed to never "grab" women by the breasts again. It's possible, that by a strict definition of the agreement he made with the police and his father that day, he may actually have kept his word. Sam never told me about the incident and I never heard of it until over 20 years later.

Sam's two older brothers, Joe and Jerry, spent as much time away from the house as possible. Both witnessed many of their father's abuses and they, like Sam, often found solace outside the home. Joe, the oldest, was athletic and participated in high school sports. As soon as he graduated from high school, he left home and joined the Navy. Joe was six years older than Sam. Contrary to Italian tradition, almost as if they came from Irish backgrounds, the two were never very close. Jerry, just three years older than Sam, was certainly the best looking of the Consiglio boys. As a thin meticulous dresser, with dark wavy hair, Jerry was the target of dozens of young girls' affections as he progressed through his junior and senior high school years. Because of his good looks and charm, Jerry was frequently observed in the company of very attractive young girls. Sam witnessed much of this activity and was often overcome by a case of hero worship for his older brother.

"By the time I came along, I had to work," Sam said. "I got tired of hearing my Dad complain. My mom was always bitching about money. I got so sick of hearing about it that I went to work to try and help out somehow. Joe and Jerry never had to do that. They could do whatever the fuck they wanted to."

Sam went to work when he was 13. As a teenager, he worked at a small grocery store earning sixty cents an hour. It wasn't much but it was something, Sam would say. "At least I didn't feel guilty, but my mom, she had a way of making people feel guilty." But what Sam wanted most desperately, was to please his father.

In the summer of 1965, Tom, a school friend, and I found work building a boat dock on Lake St. Clair. It was hard work, but we were able to stay cool during the warm summer working in waist deep water. Our employer, a successful corporate attorney pretended to demonstrate that he knew a little about construction while we pretended to prove that we could handle tools. The pay, about a dollar an hour, was good for a 14 year old in 1965. It was certainly better than the previous summer when Sam and I had worked on the back of Gino's small truck selling fresh fruits and vegetables in the neighborhood. About four hours work netted us fifty cents and two loaves of bread. We gave the bread to our mothers and kept the fifty cents. We'd pool our money and on Friday nights, sneak off and order a large Pepperoni pizza in order to avoid eating the fish sticks the Catholic Church had mandated our parents feed us in order to demonstrate that we were good Christians.Sam stopped by the lake from time to time, mostly when our employer was gone and we were left alone to do some manual labor. Aside from wondering how the dock construction was progressing, Sam's visits were designed to learn what everyone would be doing later in the evening. At 14, we were consumed with learning more about girls and most evening activity centered on some plan to meet them. Usually the plan met with little success, but we kept scheming nonetheless.

In 1965, prior to the advent of MTV and before Brittney Spears wannabe's roamed the country, parents seemed to impose greater restrictions on their daughters. Young, teenage girls were not out very late. This ultimately contributed to their protection, especially from young boys who were starting to experience the consequences of their hormones. Nonetheless, like most of our other friends, we were constantly engaging in conversation about sex and sharing stories as to how close each of us were coming to actually experiencing a sexual act with someone other than ourselves.

I remember it being a cool and overcast day, not particularly hot for mid-August, as we approached the end of our summer vacation. Sam had stopped by the house on the lake where Tom and I had been working alone for most of the day. Our employer was away on business and he had left us a series of tasks he hoped we would be able to finish before he returned the following day. That afternoon, our employer's niece, who looked several years older than her age of 15 was at the house visiting while Tom and I worked on the dock. Tom and I were talking to her when Sam came by. He quickly joined in the discussions and began trying to impress her with his tough, somewhat vulgar and authoritative language. Adding to Sam's difficulty was the fact that he was big, fat by some standards but certainly not sloppy fat, just big.

Sam's demeanor and appearance immediately turned off the young girl. Tom and I were both smitten and we, too, tried unsuccessfully to impress her. As we stood in the yard talking not earning our dollar an hour she was quickly able to see through all of us and went into the house. Tom and I went back to work and said good-bye. We all agreed to meet later that night.

Within minutes, Tom and I heard screaming coming from inside the house. We raced inside and found Sam in the upstairs bedroom on the bed and on top of the girl. Tom, who was taller and stronger, was able to help me pull Sam away from the girl who had begun crying. She watched from the bedroom window as Sam ran from the house. She noticed he was wearing a blue windbreaker jacket with the name "Consiglio" in large bold white letters written across the back. Hours later, the police confronted Sam and charged him with assault with intent to commit rape.

"She was stuck up," Sam said. "I tried to talk to her and she was kind of like shunning us. I got mad. I just remember walking into her house and she started screaming. Nothing happened, except I scared the hell out of her and I think in her mind, she thought she was going to get raped. In my mind, had she not screamed, if she would have been intimidated by me and not screamed the way she did, I probably would have had sex with her, it would have been rape."

"I remember my father feeling sad," Sam said. "I got his attention. He was concerned about me. As a kid, I started realizing this is how you get their concern up. That's where my dad was screwing up."

Sam's father hired Donald Ricard, an attorney in St. Clair Shores, to represent his son on the charges of assault with intent to commit rape. Ricard had enjoyed a staunch reputation as a proven trial lawyer. He was the type of lawyer that people called when they needed the best representation they could get. This often occurred when defendants knew they were guilty. But Ricard didn't come cheap. "Tom Welsh called me and asked me to help the family out," Ricard said. "I knew Tom (Welsh) very well and sort of took the case as a favor. I didn't charge them very much."

Ricard was successful in negotiating a short stay for Sam in a youth home. No trial or judicial procedure, in the traditional sense, took place and Sam was remanded to the Boys Training School in Lansing, Michigan for four and a half months. Sam would have been entering the 9th grade.

In May 1967, Sam and I were completing the 10th grade at St. Clair Shores High School. Like many of our friends, we were turning 16, and one by one, each of us became obsessed with getting our drivers' license. There were a couple of older guys in the crowd who already had their licenses, like Al. Al was a guitar player with the Servells, one of the more successful high school bands. With Al, we had some mobility. Everyone seemed to have a part-time job, providing us with some limited means of self-sufficiency. Al had the band; other friends worked for their parents, who had small businesses, and Sam and I worked at the snack bar of a local department store cooking hamburgers and making sandwiches. On most days, we would hitchhike to and from work because of a lack of alternative transportation. I earned $1.25 an hour that year, and time and half if I worked on Sundays. But Sam considered this minimum wage to be insufficient for his needs, so, he found ways to almost double his income on any given night. Mostly, he failed to record every transaction. Instead, he charged the customer whatever the amount was due, opened the register to deposit the money but didn't record the transaction. At the end of the shift, we were often alone to lock up the snack bar. We pulled the register receipt and dumped all the cash in a moneybag, locked it, and dropped it in a cabinet for the daytime manager. Sam kept track of the amount he charged customers without registering the money on the cash register and removed an equal amount before putting the rest of the money in the locked bag. On most nights, he was able to double his hourly rate of pay.

Another part of the job required that we take large containers of trash that accumulated throughout the day to the rear of the department store. On occasion, Sam removed one or two of the latest albums released by our favorite groups and hid them in the bottom of the trash containers. After the store closed, he retrieved them. Many of us reaped the benefits of Sam's boldness, but there was often a fee. Of course, Sam's price was always significantly lower than the best sale price the store offered. With Sam, the latest albums were always on sale.

At the end of the school year, I was faced with two traumatic events; I had failed 10th grade science, and my family was moving to Fort Lauderdale, Florida. I was devastated about moving and leaving the friends I made and with whom I hoped to be graduating. While summer school was not something I was looking forward to, it provided me with the opportunity of a lifetime. I was able to live the summer with a friend of the family who was in the process of divorcing his wife. I attended summer school, worked, and had the type of summer most 16 year-olds only dream of. During that time, I spent hours dreaming of ways that might keep me from ever moving to Florida.

In the summer of 1967, I lived virtually unsupervised and attended summer school with Sam and other friends. During that summer riots continued to break out in many cities throughout the country. Detroit was no different, and many of its neighborhoods burned while looting took place in front of the police and television cameras. Once, we tried to get close to see the action first hand, but were turned away by members of the Michigan National Guard. When the Detroit riots ended, 31 people had died and 700 were arrested.

In 1967, 135,000 people watched Barbara Streisand give a free concert in New York's Central Park. The Beatles released "Sergeant Pepper's Lonely Hearts Club Band" and Israel reclaimed the walled Old City of Jerusalem after a six-day war with the Arab Nations. A new car cost $2,724 and the average price of a three-bedroom home was $14,425. Gas was 33 cents a gallon. In 1967, Thurgood Marshall became the first black in the history of the United States to be appointed to the Supreme Court.

Of course, most of us were oblivious too much of this. Our interests were focused on the new Beatles album, earning money, and finding girls, although not necessarily in that order. Some of us, however, did begin to pay a small amount of attention to the war in Vietnam, especially when General Westmoreland received permission from President Johnson to increase the troop strength in that country to over half a million men and women.

I never knew so much independence and freedom as I did that summer. The small apartment was used mainly for sleeping, sometimes eating, and for some great poker games. Not just small games among older boys, but weekend marathons lasting sometimes two days, with virtually non-stop action. It was not uncommon to find some of my friends sleeping on the couch waiting for a seat to open up in the game. My guardian, John Pearson, who was a friend of my family, usually chaired the game and brought along one or two members of the local UAW (United Auto Workers) where he held a political position for over 10 years. Al was a regular member of the poker club as were other members of his band. Sam and his father rarely missed a game. Beer was often served, but with the condition that it was consumed on the premises and no one could drink more than John or Big Sam allowed. The rule was almost never violated since it was well known that Big Sam was quick with the fist, and no one was immune to a slap or a punch in the stomach when it came to the rules associated with our poker playing.

The games usually took place every other weekend and consisted of the typical quarter-half-dollar bets. Success and failure was usually measured in terms of winning or losing $40. When the apartment was free, that is when John wasn't using it to entertain some female acquaintance (usually one that required an exchange of money), my friends and I would take advantage of the privacy it afforded to continue our own sexual evolutionary process. We'd go to movies, have parties and sometimes just take up a collection to fill the gas tank of whoever was able to lure their parent's car away for the night and ride around for the evening. No one seemed to establish any long-term relationships that summer. If anyone had a girlfriend for over a month, it was considered a major event. By the summer of 1967, Sam, like most everyone turning 16 that year, had never been sexually intimate with a woman.

It was July 28, 1967. I had gone to school that summer morning as I did every day, walking with Sam and talking about everything other than school itself. As we approached LakeShore High, Sam turned and said he wasn't going in. I tried persuading him to come, but no one other than his father could really persuade him to do anything. He had no interest in school, insisting that he really didn't care that day. I knew long before that Sam would probably never graduate with us on time, and this certainly reinforced my suspicions. Academically, Sam was always a laggard. While most of us talked about post high school plans that included college, joining the service or entering one of the auto factories, Sam seemed to have no concrete ideas as to what he might do with his life.

That day Sam walked the short distance from the high school to the shopping center at Thirteen Mile Road and Harper in St. Clair Shores. It was the same shopping center where, several years before, he had walked up behind at least five different women and grabbed them by the breasts.

As he roamed the small strip mall, Sam watched a young woman whom he recalled later as being extremely attractive, load groceries into the trunk of her car. It was early in the afternoon. The day was clear and bright, the type of day people hope for in order to take advantage of the many outdoor activities reserved for the all too short Michigan summers.

As the woman in her early 20's with dark blond hair opened her car door, Sam walked up behind her and put his hands over her mouth and eyes. She remained calm and did as she was instructed. She was not only frightened for herself, she was terrified for the safety of her two young children sitting in the back seat of the car.

"I never really planned it," Sam said. "I didn't know how things were going to work out. I really wasn't sure what I wanted to do. She was very co-operative. She was very intimidated. I really didn't care at that point that it was in the middle of the afternoon. I figured people pull robberies in the middle of the afternoon; they don't care. She got in the car and moved past the steering wheel. I still had my hands over her eyes and she offers to blindfold herself and so I let her do that. I was trusting that she was going to do it right but she did it so that she could see me. She blindfolds herself and she gives me the keys out of her purse and I drive the car a little over a mile to a vacant lot behind a church. At the time, I'm thinking, this woman's being so cooperative because this is what she wants; she really wants to do this. I believe that. Once we get to the field, she undresses herself. Right after I penetrated her, she begins to cry. Tears were coming from her eyes. I had the blindfold off and she could see me. I asked why she was crying. She said, because I'm married and a Catholic."

The young woman continued to cry as Sam assaulted her. She cooperated with him as he instructed, hoping not to anger him more. As she cried, she begged Sam not to hurt her children. The sexual act itself didn't take long for Sam, especially since he never ejaculated. It was Sam's first time with a woman. Before he left his victim terrified and crying in her car, Sam gave one of the children a dollar because he felt sorry for them.

"I just ran and ran straight to my house," Sam said. "I was sick afterwards, very sick because I realized what I had done. It sunk into me on the way while I was running. My heart was beating real fast and it just sunk into me what I had done and I said fuck it; that's the end of my world. I thought no one's going to let me get away with this."

Sam didn't want to get away with raping this woman. He didn't want to go to jail for the rest of his life either. But that's exactly what he feared was going to happen. "I was really sick about what I did to that lady because those tears really hurt me, it just had a bad effect on me," Sam said.

When Sam arrived at my house later that afternoon, he was breathing heavily and appeared excited. He told me what he had done, leaving out the fact there were two kids in the car. At first, I considered it another one of Sam's tall tales since he was always fabricating stories in an attempt to impress people.Later that afternoon, the St. Clair Shores police came to my apartment looking for Sam. The victim reported the attack to the police. And because of his past history, the description she provided of her assailant led them directly to Sam. I told the police the story Sam had related to me a couple of hours earlier. I knew then, that Sam's story was true. "In a way, I was kind of relieved when I was arrested, but I didn't want to go to jail for the rest of my life," Sam said.

He didn't. Prosecutors tried to have him bound over and prosecuted as an adult, but failed. Donald Ricard, who once again was retained by the family to represent Sam, successfully argued to keep the case in the juvenile courts. "The courts weren't waiving jurisdiction for 16 year olds back then as easily as they do now," Ricard said. Sam was never prosecuted on the charges relating to the sexual assault on this young housewife. Instead a hearing before a juvenile judge, after prior agreements negotiated by lawyers for both the state and Sam, settled on recommendations that he would be sent to the Lafayette Clinic in Detroit for evaluation, and then sent to the Boys' Training School in Lansing, Michigan.

On August 14, 1967, Sam was admitted to the Lafayette Clinic. He spent just under two months there undergoing a series of psychological tests and analyses during which time he was examined by teams of psychiatrists. Dr. Jeffrey W. Wilson, a second-year resident at the clinic who examined Sam, wrote in a discharge statement, "The patient appears to be somewhat infantile despite a facade of worldliness. However, this is also a very angry boy. He is one who demands gratification immediately from all and this need is never satisfied. His close relationship with his mother resulted in a fairly strong identification with her and the adoption of the 'sissy like' behavior as a child. The oral dependency personality of himself, as well as his parent's, is evidenced by the gross problem of all being overweight. His performance has not been nearly as outstanding as has been that of his siblings, and he has developed a somewhat poor self-image. Failures in romantic attempts and in school have intensified his feelings of inadequacy. His father is a man whom he would like to have seen leave the house and suggested that he do so when the father was talking of suicide and holding a gun. Yet he is a man whom he responded to like an infant when the father lost his temper and the patient cowered and urinated. He is also a man with some difficulties in the sexual sphere and who seems to be vicariously acting out his desires to sexually have other women through the patient's activities. For example, the father has often been seen watching the patient during dates and frequently questions the patient on the possibility of his having done something wrong sexually with a woman. The patient's impulse control is poor and, he has never been disciplined adequately by himself or his parents. While in the hospital, the patient became involved in all of the various adolescent milieu programs. He responded quite well in all these areas. He was quite popular with peers and was elected president of the ward. He was somewhat manipulative. He was seen in individual and group psychotherapy. An attempt was made at achieving some degree of insight although it is felt that the patient receives only a mild amount in this regard."

"At one point, the doctor told my father I would spend the rest of my life in and out of jail," Sam said. "My father became enraged, arguing with the doctor, telling him he was wrong. I thought he was going to hit the doctor when he told my dad that I acted the way I did because of my mother's obesity and his violent behavior."

Dr. Wilson concluded his report by diagnosing Sam as a Sociopathic Personality Disturbance, with Sexual Deviation. The prognosis, Dr. Wilson wrote, was "guarded." He recommended that Sam be returned to the court and that treatment could best be carried out in a group setting for boys of a similar age, with a similar sociopathic problem, where strict limits would be enforced and long-term facilities would be available. Sam was returned to the Boys' Training School in Lansing.

Big Sam never forgave himself for agreeing to send his son to the school. He thought the experience contributed to his son's problems instead of helping to correct them.

"My father thought my life would have been different had he not agreed to send me to the Boys' Training School. He told me 'I sold you out.' He thought I should have been able to get away with assaulting this woman, especially after he learned that she was reluctant to testify. He thought my life would have been better had I not gone to the Boys' school. I told him that he didn't make a mistake doing that. My father had some warped thinking," Sam said.

Sam spent just less than a year at the Boys' Training School before returning home to live with his parents shortly after his seventeenth birthday. Within days of Sam being arrested for rape, I flew to Fort Lauderdale and joined the rest of my family. From the time I left Michigan in 1967, I would only see Sam five times over the next 20 years.

Chapter 2

Misdemeanors, Just Misdemeanors

Following Sam's release from the Boys Training School on June 22, 1968, Donald DePalma, an after care worker for the Department of Social Services, told authorities, "society hasn't heard the last of Sam. He began this behavior at age 12. The kid just can't keep his hands to himself. In my opinion, he is a criminal sexual psychopath."

When 17 year-old Sam returned home, it was clear that he had no interest in going back to school. Instead, he took odd jobs working at the concession stand at a department store and delivering pizzas. On the afternoon of August 22, exactly two months after his release from the Boy's Training School, Sam was driving on the Groesbeck Highway in Mt. Clemens when he noticed a woman in her early 20's driving slowly. He thought she was lost.

"I see this really gorgeous woman, I mean really gorgeous," Sam said. "I knew she was lost so I pulled up next to her and told her to pull over. I asked if she was lost and she asked me where the Hillcrest Country Club was."

Sam told her to move over and he would drive her there. "I was giving her directions," he said. "I mean I was being really nice to this woman and I'm checking her out. But there was something about her attitude. She told me to get in my own car. She made me mad. I had done this two previous times with two different women, almost identical to this. She had an attitude problem. It was just like I snapped and I slapped her. That was it, that's how it happened."

Sam slapped the woman hard, using his open hand, just the way he had seen his father slap his mother so many times before. As he grabbed her by the throat, she quickly let out the clutch forcing her car to jerk backward. Sam lost his grip and seizing the moment, she sped away. As she fled, the woman who had simply asked the wrong person for directions took a moment to notice the license number of the car Sam was driving.

He was quickly charged with assault and battery. Now, the judicial system would treat Sam as an adult.

Free on bail, Sam continued to work at various odd jobs while living with his parents and younger brothers and sisters. In early December, just four months after his first adult arrest and with the charges of assault and battery pending, Sam entertained himself by reading the personal column of the Macomb County Daily newspaper. That's how he found Jane. She was 24 and had an 18-month-old daughter. Jane had no real means of support so she was living at the Riverfront Motel in Clinton Township, hoping to find a more permanent place for her and her daughter. To find such a place, Jane took out an ad in the Macomb newspaper looking for an apartment or a house. Late on the afternoon of December 9, 1968, Jane received a telephone call from a man who identified himself as John.

"There was this ad in the Macomb Daily," Sam said. "This girl says that she is getting evicted from her apartment, she lost her apartment and she's living day to day in a motel. She was having a rough time; she needed help. So I called her up and pretended I was Mr. Rich Guy from Grosse Point." Grosse Point had always enjoyed a reputation of being an affluent suburb of Detroit where young executives of the giant automakers made their homes.

Sam told Jane he had a house for rent in Mt. Clemens and another one in Warren. He offered to take her to look at both places that night. Jane was excited and actually believed someone was finally going to help her.

"It worked, the bullshit worked, she agreed to see me," Sam said.

Sam arrived at the motel at about 9 o'clock that evening introducing himself as John. Jane wrapped her daughter in a large pink blanket with a white border and placed the baby in the back seat of Sam's old four-door Ford. Jane got in the front seat with "John." "I was bullshiting with her," Sam said. "I mean, I'm driving this old Ford, smoke coming out the back, it should have been a give away but she thinks I'm from Grosse Point. After an hour of driving around, I ask her how much she needs. She says `I don't know.' So, I ask her, would three hundred do you? She says `yeah, that's nice.' So I mean, I worked hard on this broad you know."

Sam and Jane drove around for a little over an hour, engaging mostly in small talk before Sam pulled into an office parking lot. He turned off the engine, reached over and began to kiss her, but she pulled away. When she did, Sam threatened to knock her out and hurt her baby. Afraid for herself and her daughter, Jane surrendered and did what Sam ordered. "At that point, she knew what was going to happen, it was inevitable. She was very intimidated, very afraid of me and I knew that. I was able to figure that out and take advantage of it."

Sam ordered Jane to remove her sweater then he pulled her skirt up around her waist. He grabbed her underwear, pulled them off and threw them into the backseat of the car. He then ordered her to lie on the seat. Sam unzipped his pants and began penetrating Jane with forceful thrusts while her baby lay quietly in the back seat.

"She was scared to death of me, it was definitely rape, but not the kind of rape where you beat somebody," Sam said. "Anytime there is resistance, I get scared and leave. If she had started screaming, I'd be out of there because there was never a time when I beat someone and raped them."

After assaulting Jane, Sam allowed her to get dressed and told her he was taking her back to the motel. On the drive back to the motel, Jane looked at Sam and said, "You must be sick."

"I must not be too sick because I'm in the service," Sam replied. This was Sam's meager attempt to make Jane think he was a member of the Air Force stationed at a local military base.

As Sam and Jane entered the parking lot of the motel, she tried to grab the keys from the ignition. Sam grabbed her wrist and slapped her arm away. Frightened and fearing for her life after unsuccessfully attempting to get the keys away from her attacker, Jane jumped from the car as it was moving, forgetting that her baby was still in the back seat. Jane ran to the manager's office, yelling for him to call the police. Sam quickly stopped the car, took the baby from the back seat and placed her on the ground. As he fled from the motel parking lot, Jane and the apartment manager were only able to get a partial license plate number.

"She was pretty smart," Sam said. "She wanted to nail me. At one point, she asked if she could look in my glove compartment. You know what she's doing that for? She wants to see my registration. I said, no."

When the police arrived at the motel, Jane was in a state of shock and near hysteria. She was taken to the hospital. The medical report said it appeared the victim had been raped, noting there were bruises present and a "milky substance" in her. Jane told investigators that her assailant claimed if she went to the police, his father would get him out, because he belonged to the Mafia.

On December 23, 1968, Sam pleaded guilty to assault and battery, a misdemeanor, for slapping the young woman whom had simply asked for directions on Groesbeck Highway. He was sentenced to 90 days in the county jail, and fined $100. Unhappy with the sentence, Sam's attorney requested and was allowed by the judge to withdraw the plea, asking instead for a jury trial.

Sam left the courtroom and returned home to live with his parents. Big Sam continued to blame anyone and everyone other than his son for Sam's problems, especially women who had lodged complaints against him.

"My dad always put the blame on them," Sam said. "He would say, 'she shouldn't have called the police, it was her fault, she caused it.' It made me feel like I was some kind of hero or something, like I did the right thing."

Sam enjoyed the Christmas holidays with his family. He continued to maintain his innocence; innocence his father and mother wanted desperately to believe.

Sam was convinced that 1969 was going to be a much better year for him. With the New Year just ahead, he was confident he would be able to put his past behind him. That confidence eroded in less than two weeks.

On January 5, 1969, a young woman entered her car after shopping for post-holiday bargains. She watched as a man got out of a car nearby.

"You have an oil leak," he told her.

As she started to get out of the car to see the problem for herself, the man pushed her back into the car. He ordered her to slide over or he would strangle her. Fortunately for the terrified woman, the store manager witnessed what was happening and scared the man away. Unfortunately, the manager was able to obtain only a partial license number of the man's car as it sped out of the parking lot.

The manager helped the young woman back into the store and together they contacted the St. Clair Shores Police Department. Within hours, the police arrested Sam and charged him with one count of assault. Unable to post a $5,000 bond, Sam was transported to the Macomb County Jail and held pending an arraignment.

The following day, the Clinton Township Police learned that Sam had been arrested in St. Clair Shores on a sex related charge. Detectives assigned to investigate Jane's case asked her to examine a series of photographs to see if the man who had raped her was among them. She immediately pointed to the photograph of Sam Consiglio.

When questioned about Jane's attack, Sam denied any involvement. He became very agitated and emotional, telling the detectives, "women are pigs and they deserve anything they get." The police quickly discontinued their questioning.

Sam spent the next four months in the Macomb County Jail, working as a trustee as he awaited trial. Within two months, Big Sam filed a petition with the court seeking to have his son admitted to the Pontiac State Hospital for psychiatric examination.

On May 5, 1969, just 12 days before his 18th birthday the assault charges filed against Sam by the St. Clair Shores Police related to the woman with the alleged oil leak were dismissed due to insufficient evidence. "They had the wrong guy on that one," Sam said. "But I was in jail long enough for Jane to pick me out. Had I not been falsely accused of that arrest, I never would have been caught on this one."

On June 3, Sam was admitted to the Pontiac State Hospital as a result of a court order sought by Big Sam. "My son is 18 years old," Big Sam told Dr. Amor Bouraoui, a member of the hospital staff. "Ever since he was about 14 years old, he has been involved in numerous assaults upon women. Since he was 16 years old, he has been officially charged in the courts with rape, assault with intent to do great bodily harm, and assault and battery. His two confinements at the Boy's Training School and also outpatient psychiatric treatment after his release seem to have done him no good. I have been unable to reason with him about these things. He is highly emotional and upset and I fear he will snap completely if he does not get treatment in a hospital."

Dr. Bouraoui noted that Sam was completely attentive and spoke freely about his past and questionable behavior during the evaluation.

"I don't know why I do sexual offenses. I rape, I attempted to rape twice and I did bodily harm. I can't understand myself," Sam told Dr. Bouraoui, as his mood became excited and tense.

When Dr. Bouraoui asked Sam, "How does your future look to you?" Sam looked directly at the doctor and said, "The future later, will look beautiful."

Sam told Dr. Bouraoui that he wanted to return to the Boys Training School.

When asked if he could have any three wishes, Sam told Dr. Bouraoui, "I have a girl friend, I wish to marry her; I want to see my mother and father happy and I want to stay away from problems."

Sam spent two months at the Pontiac State Hospital. During that time, Sam participated in various recreational and occupational therapy sessions designed to offer some chance of rehabilitation, while at the same time provide the medical staff with an opportunity to observe him in a clinical setting.

In the summer of 1969 the world, and Sam from the television lounge inside the Pontiac State Hospital, watched as Apollo 11 landed men on the moon for the first time in history. That same year, thousands of young people attended a music festival in a place called Woodstock, New York, in part to show solidarity to their opposition to the war in Vietnam. That same year, the American Academy of Arts and Sciences finally honored John Wayne with the award for best actor for his performance in "True Grit" while the "Age of Aquarius" told us all to let the sunshine in and The Beatles hit, "Come Together" dominated the music scene. Richard Nixon was inaugurated as the 37th President of the United States and McDonald's introduced the country to the Big Mac.

On July 30, 1969 Sam was sent back to the Macomb County Jail after assaulting a staff nurse at the psychiatric hospital. Since he had been a patient in the hospital as a result of a court order, a technicality in the law prevented him from being charged with anything other than contempt of court. In jail, Sam resumed his duties as a trustee, washing police cars and performing other menial tasks assigned to those considered "trustworthy." "I was a good trustee. I could have walked away anytime I wanted to; I was free to go but I did my time," Sam said.

Five days after his release from the Pontiac State Hospital, Sam was described in a report written by staff physician Dr. Jerry Slobodow, as, "a patient who suffers from a personality disorder and an inability to control his aggressive impulses. It would be appropriate to place the patient in an institution where the sociopaths are treated, as hospitalization in a mental state hospital of our type, or placement in jail, does not seem to give significant hope for his improvement. The prognosis: has to be very guarded." As soon as Sam returned to the Macomb County Jail, his attorney, Don Ricard, negotiated a plea agreement with the prosecutor, whereby Sam would be allowed to plead guilty to a reduced charge of aggravated assault for having sexually assaulted Jane. This was a misdemeanor conviction, and dispensed with either party having to spend time preparing for a lengthy trial. Sam benefited by pleading to a lesser offense, while the prosecutor, received credit on his scorecard for a conviction. And, the court calendar was freed, something that pleases most judges because they can attend to other important matters. It was a situation where everyone but Jane could claim victory. After pleading guilty to aggravated assault, Sam was sentenced to one year in the county jail and fined $300. With seven months already served while awaiting trial, he had less than five months left before being set free. And, he was still not a convicted felon.

Chapter 3

Married With a Job

It was January 1970 before Sam was released from the Macomb County Jail. He had served the full year of his sentence for assaulting Jane. He had tried to get an early release in order to spend Christmas with his family, but the court refused his request.

Sam was just four months away from his 19th birthday. He had raped at least two women and physically attacked at least two others, but he was still not a convicted felon. His juvenile record was sealed and, because of legal constraints, could not be routinely accessed by law enforcement agencies. While the St. Clair Shores Police and the Macomb County Sheriff's Department knew of Sam's criminal record, other departments that inquired would only learn that he had two misdemeanor assault convictions.

When Sam returned home, his family, especially his father, greeted Sam with an almost hero's welcome. "My father never missed a chance to visit me that entire year," Sam said. "He came whenever there was an opportunity. I always knew that when visiting hours came, my dad would be there."

Sam spent little time relaxing. He needed money, but jobs were difficult to find for someone with his background and limited skills. He was forced to continue working as a common laborer and delivering pizzas, a job he had grown to like since he could eat all the pizza he wanted for free.

By now Sam had lost contact with many of his friends, especially those he had known in school. Most, like me, had put considerable distance between themselves and Sam because of his arrests. Still, Sam wanted desperately to meet new people and to be accepted by some group that he could call his friends. He had no girlfriend or real companion of any kind, and he began to sense the loneliness brought about by his newfound freedom. Jail had provided him with a regimented lifestyle. This lifestyle offered daily contact with members of both the criminal community, whom were his cellmates and with the professional staff, whom he grew to respect and admire. With the staff, he often shared his hopes of perhaps someday becoming a police officer himself. While his year in jail had restrained his freedom, Sam took pride in his work as a trustee, looking for acceptance from both the other inmates and his jailors.

Now Sam was forced to adjust to the accepted mores of society. He had seen his oldest brother, Joe, and his sister Grace, both get married. He had been conditioned to think marriage was what was expected of a person. To Sam, it was one more way to gain the respect of his father and other members of his family.

Sam met Cindy in May 1971 on a blind date arranged by his younger sister, Virginia, who was dating Cindy's cousin. "Cindy was only 19 years old," Sam said. "She wasn't allowed to date, she couldn't wear makeup, she couldn't wear nylons and had to wear socks. Her mother was very strict. Cindy was very thin, a bit homely looking with short black hair cut in bangs."

Cindy had finished high school the previous year and worked as a waitress at a diner in Detroit. She lived at home, under strict conditions imposed by her mother. When the date was arranged, Cindy had to sneak out of the house in the late afternoon and walk a block to meet Sam who was waiting in his car.

Sam was excited about meeting Cindy. He wanted to show her off to his family, so he brought her home to have dinner at his parent's house. The evening started on a happy note with Big Sam joking as he tried to make Cindy laugh, creating an atmosphere of enjoyment where she and Sam were the center of attention. Both parents enjoyed a temporary amnesty from the pain their son had inflicted upon them from his other contacts with women.

For the first time, Sam's parents experienced delight with their troubled son and prayed this new relationship might actually help Sam turn his life around. But any happiness the family and Sam were experiencing was short-lived. Somehow Cindy's mother learned of her daughter's absence and tracked her to the Consiglio home calling her there. When Cindy finished talking to her mother, she was in tears and asked that Sam take her home immediately.

"I'm driving down the street I live on and she's crying, she's scared," Sam said. "She keeps telling me her mother is going to beat her when she gets home. I'm taking her home to get beat. I really hated to do that, I felt bad. I tell her the only way we could avoid taking you home is to get married. I said this while I'm looking out the corner of my eye and she starts to smile. I looked over at her and asked her what she was smiling about. She says I'm game. I said, game for what? And she says, for what you just said. So I say, getting married? And she says, I wouldn't have to go home. So, I'm driving along and I'm thinking to myself, what the fuck, I get out of the house, she gets out of the house, I get all the sex I want. So, I said, let's do it."

Sam stopped at a local gas station at the end of the street and asked the attendant about places to get married quickly. The attendant told him to go to Covington, Kentucky. He even gave him directions.

Sam turned the car around and went home to tell his parents of their plans. "My mom and dad couldn't believe I was doing this," Sam said. "They just went into shock. I told them I was 19 and they couldn't stop me."

Big Sam was more than just angry; he was outraged. He took his son by the arm and walked him into the bedroom, hoping to convince Sam that getting married to Cindy now might not be the best thing he could do.

"You don't know this girl," Big Sam screamed.

"No, but I'll get to know her," Sam told his father.

"You're just doing this so you can get a steady piece of ass and so you don't have to bring her home where she'll get her ass whipped by her Mom, is that right," Big Sam asked.

"Yeah, that's about right," Sam said.

Big Sam was emotionally drained from his latest ordeal with his son. Hanging his head, Big Sam said, "I can't stop you."

Sam and Cindy drove straight through the night to Covington, Kentucky hoping to find a Justice of the Peace who would marry them. Along the way, they talked about their plans and how they would live when they returned to Michigan. Between the two of them, they had barely enough money for the trip to Covington and back, much less enough money to move into their own place. They agreed they would have to live with Sam's parents until they were able to afford a place of their own. But none of that seemed to matter to them. They had their own reasons for participating in this intimate union. For Cindy, it was a means to escape an authoritarian mother. For Sam, it was a way to demonstrate to his family that he was becoming a man. It was also his way of experiencing a woman in his life, someone who would be able to provide him with an opportunity to elude the negative impulses, which, had resulted in his physical attacks on unsuspecting women. As they continued their drive south to Kentucky talking about family and friends, hopes and dreams, Sam kept to himself, any of the information about his criminal past.

It was early in the morning when they arrived in Covington, both hungry and exhausted from the all night ride. The first thing Sam sought was a restaurant. He needed to eat, it was the one thing Sam enjoyed more than sex. At the same time, he hoped to find someplace where he and Cindy could get married.

"I found out this guy at the gas station lied to me," Sam said. "It takes three days to get married anywhere in Kentucky. So that shoots our plans. So I tell Cindy, let's go back home and tell everybody that we got married and hope they don't ask for proof. Meanwhile, we'll make arrangements to get married in Michigan. Cindy say's yeah, that's cool. Then we decide to go to a motel. Once we get to the motel, I find out she's a virgin, a fucking virgin. I couldn't get it in. I was sweating. I mean sweat was pouring off of me and shit. There was no air conditioning in the room, it was terrible and I remember it was like May, the middle of May. She was so small I couldn't penetrate her. I wasted money on the hotel. Luckily, it was only $5 for the room. So we drove back home and we told everybody that we were married. No one asked me for proof, at least right away. About a week later, Cindy's mother asked but we told her the marriage certificate was in the mail."

It was less than a week before Sam's father discovered that his son had not actually gotten married. By this time, Sam and Cindy had moved upstairs into the attic bedroom and were continuing to consummate their alleged union.

"It was terrible," Sam said. "My mom used to laugh at us. I'm trying to have sex with Cindy and I can't because she's so small. I'm getting frustrated because I never encountered anything like this before. Usually, I could drive a fucking truck through these women but this was the first virgin I'd ever been with. So finally, I go downstairs and I'm soaking wet. We had been making a lot of noise, her head smashing against the headboard and shit, I was embarrassed. But my mom told me to use Vaseline and it worked."

Sam kept telling everyone that he and Cindy were going to get married again in a few days so that everyone could be a part of the occasion. But Big Sam knew his son all too well. He suspected that Sam had never actually married and confronted his son on the subject.

"You ain't shitting me, you never got married in Kentucky," Big Sam told his son.

"Why do you say that?" Sam asked his father.

"Because you're cheap; you're not going to get married twice," he told his son.

Big Sam was able to use some of his limited political contacts to meet with a local judge on the Sunday before Memorial Day. After a short wedding ceremony witnessed only by Sam's father, Sam handed the judge an envelope. There was no card inside, just a Five-Dollar bill. "My dad had a fit," Sam said. "My dad said, 'five dollars, you gave the judge five dollars, you woke him out of bed at 7:00 o'clock in the morning, have him go down and open the courthouse and marry you and you gave the guy five dollars.'

"I told my dad, yeah, how many times am I going to get married. I'm not going to need him again," Sam said.

"I'm not talking about getting married," Big Sam yelled. "Don't ever get caught speeding before the son of a bitch or anything, he'll send you to fucking prison." It was Big Sam's slight attempt at humor. In truth, he would have seriously chastised his son had the envelope contained more than five dollars.

Sam and Cindy spent the next three weeks in the upstairs attic of his parent's home. Afterwards, they moved to a small apartment on the East Side of Detroit next to Art Van Furniture. Sam had gotten a job delivering furniture for Art Van, one of the largest furniture stores in the Detroit area.

Chapter 4

Kiss Me; You Need Me and I Need You

In May 1972, George Wallace, the Governor of Alabama, was shot in Laurel, Maryland, while campaigning for the Presidency of the United States. As a result of the bullet that entered his body, he would remain in a wheel chair until his death in 1998. In August of that year, five men were caught burglarizing the Democratic National Headquarters at the Watergate Hotel in Washington, D.C. In 1972, Harry S. Truman, the 33rd President of the United States, who had seen the country through the end of World War II and the beginning of the Korean War, executed the Marshall Plan designed to suppress the expansion of Communism in Europe and risked political suicide when he relieved General Douglas Macarthur of his command, died at the age of 88 in Kansas City, Missouri. Marlon Brando won the Oscar for Best Actor for his role as Don Corleone in "The Godfather," but refused to accept the award as an act of protest designed to evoke a sense of awareness to the plight of the American Indians. In September 1972, the summer Olympics was being held in Munich, West Germany. Mark Spitz took home seven gold medals in swimming while Frank Shorter became the first American to win the Olympic Marathon since 1908. Midway through the Olympics, Arab terrorists stormed the living quarters of the athletes and massacred eleven Israeli Olympians.

On September 12, 1972, Sandy was a twenty-six year old teacher. She was enjoying her newly discovered freedom and was especially excited about recently moving into a new apartment in Sterling Heights, Michigan. Earlier that morning, Sandy had given her apartment key to the manager of the complex. She had called him claiming that the mailbox was damaged and she could not get it open. The manager had been inside the apartment earlier to see about some other needed maintenance and claimed he would return later to finish making the necessary repairs. Sandy had given him the key in case she was not at home when he returned.

It was shortly before 5:00 p.m. Sandy had taken a few minutes after work to enjoy a short nap. But her slumber was interrupted by a knock at the door.

"Hi, Sandy," the man said, not identifying himself.

Still sleepy, Sandy thought that the man, who called her by her first name and walked into her apartment, worked for the apartment manager and was there to fix the bathtub. Sam started making small talk. He told Sandy that she looked tired and asked her how long she had lived at the complex. Sandy was fully awake now and asked the man in her apartment who he was. Like a seasoned politician, careful not to directly respond to a direct question, Sam answered by posing more questions of his own. As he asked his own questions, Sam sat down on the sofa in the living room and asked Sandy what particular color the walls were and how much rent she paid.

Sandy still believed that the man in her living room was there to fix the bathtub. She hoped he would, in fact, hurry up and make the necessary repairs and leave. She quickly excused herself and walked into her sparsely furnished bedroom to get a cigarette. When she turned to go back into the living room, she saw Sam standing in the doorway.

"Why don't you have any furniture?" Sam asked.

"Because I don't have any money," Sandy said.

"How much do you need?" Sam asked her, as he reached into his pocket, demonstrating that he had money to offer.

"I was bullshitting with her for a while," Sam said. "I'm thinking this girl has to be easy to fuck here; she'll be a piece of cake. After she lights her cigarette, she asks me if I'm going to get out of the way, and I say, no. She say's that if I don't, she's going to scream and I say go ahead."

Sandy became frightened and started to walk back into the living room. As she approached Sam, he blocked the doorway, looked directly into Sandy's eyes and said in a forceful, stern voice, "No."

Sandy realized that the man in her apartment was not there to fix anything. Her senses instantly told her that she was in danger. She turned quickly away from Sam, jumped on top of her bed, and began to scream. Sam ran to her, grabbed her from behind, and put his hand over her mouth. The force of his arms around her mouth was strong. But Sandy struggled and tried to scream. She bit her lip so hard it began to bleed. Sam yelled at her, demanding she stop screaming. But Sandy fought hard, twisting her body back and forth, struggling to free herself with each turn. With each twist of her head and shoulders, she tried to free her mouth of his huge hands so that she could continue to scream. But Sandy was no match for Sam who was bigger and far stronger. She grew tired from the struggle and quickly realized that she would not be able to overcome her attacker.

Sam threw Sandy onto the floor. She fell hard hurting herself even more. He positioned himself on top of her and demanded that she stop screaming. Sandy's heart was racing. She tried to maintain some composure, realizing that she needed to think her way out of this dangerous situation. Sandy thought that if she had any chance of surviving a beating or of being raped or killed, she would have to listen and follow the directions of her assailant. Sandy stopped screaming as her assailant demanded, hoping this would calm her attacker. Instead, Sam looked directly into her eyes and said, "Kiss me." Sam lay prone on top of her body. The force of his weight easily held her motionless as she felt the cold stiffness of the floor beneath her. Sam continued to stare directly into Sandy's eyes and again said, "Kiss me."

Sandy refused the order. Instead she turned her head away, not wanting to look into the face of the man attacking her.

"You need me, and I need you," Sam told her as he began to move his body in a hard rocking, rhythmic motion, simulating an act of sexual intercourse. His hands reached down between her legs, forcing them open as he slid the lower part of his body between her legs. Again, Sam told Sandy, "You need me, and I need you." But Sandy turned her head away as Sam pushed his face toward hers. Her fear mounted when she noticed blood coming from her mouth, blood that was now on her hands and clothes. Sandy continued to struggle, pleading with Sam to stop.

"If you stop screaming, I'll get off and leave, but you have to promise not to get me into trouble," Sam told her. "I knew I couldn't run out of there," Sam said. "That would be like the days before, so my instincts tell me to get her quiet and then leave. So I wrestled her to the ground. I had my hand over her mouth, and said I'm going to get off you. I haven't touched you. I haven't done anything wrong. I'm going to leave, I just can't leave with you screaming."

Sandy promised Sam that if he left, she wouldn't report the incident to anyone. With that assurance, Sam lifted himself up and started walking toward the front door. Still scared and shaken, Sandy followed close behind as Sam walked out of the apartment. As soon as Sam was outside, Sandy quickly locked the door and watched from her balcony as Sam approached the Art Van furniture delivery truck parked on the street. As Sandy stood on her balcony watching the man who just assaulted her walk away, Sam, smiling, pointed and said, "Remember, you let me in." Sandy felt a temporary sense of relief when she watched her attacker drive off in the furniture delivery truck. She paid little attention to the unknown black man sitting beside him.

Sandy sat alone in her apartment, afraid to call the police and report what had just happened. Sam had told her not to call the "cops" and get him into trouble. She was afraid he might come back and hurt her again if she did. Sandy was in a near state of hysteria when she called her boyfriend, Jack, and asked him to come over as quickly as he could. Once Jack learned of the assault, he instantly called the Sterling Heights Police Department.

It was Detective Frank Schoenrock who first met with the store managers of Art Van Furniture on Eight Mile Road in Detroit. Managers at Art Van told Schoenrock that they had received several telephone complaints from female customers about Sam Consiglio, but they had been unable to do anything about it because the alleged victims failed to file formal charges. Later that afternoon, Detective Schoenrock put together a series of black and white photographs, one of which depicted Sam Consiglio, and showed the photographs to Sandy. Sandy looked at each of the photos spread out in front of her and quickly identifyied the snapshot of Sam as the man who had assaulted her. Schoenrock was satisfied with his work and obtained a warrant for the arrest of Sam Consiglio.

On Thursday, September 21, 1972, nine days after entering Sandy's apartment, Sam, as he did most every other day, went to work as a delivery man for Art Van Furniture. He had worked for Art Van for less than two years. Within a year, Sam had been allowed to load his own truck for the day's deliveries. To Sam, that was the best part of the job since he always found room for an extra piece or two of furniture not scheduled for delivery that day.

"They weren't paying me enough, so I had to supplement my income," Sam said. "I took dressers, bedroom sets; I made a fortune. I sold a bunch of it to people and furnished my whole apartment. I never had a problem taking from a company like that because they're garbage. It would bother me to steal from you or it would bother me to steal from a homeless person. That would bother me. I couldn't do it. I even traded some (furniture) for sex. See I didn't have a problem with that. I felt good about doing that because when I left there, the people would always say, man, I got me a bedroom set and all I had to do was go to bed with this man. I mean really, I felt like I was serving a purpose for the public. That was easy, a quick screw with me could get you a new bedroom set. They never suspected me. I was their best driver."

At the end of the day's deliveries, Sam and his partner, a black male employee, were unloading their truck and completing paper work, when Detectives Schoenrock and John Gallagher arrived. Sam was placed under arrest for assault with intent to commit rape. In front of his boss and several other employees of Art Van, the two detectives handcuffed Sam and escorted him into the backseat of the waiting police car. As they drove to the police station, Sam told the detectives that he wanted to talk about the incident. Detective Gallagher immediately interrupted Sam and advised him of his constitutional right to remain silent and that any statement he made could be used against him in a court of law. After Gallagher explained to Sam the rest of his constitutional rights, Sam told him that he understood but that he still wanted to talk about the episode with Sandy.

"I went to Sandy's house to discuss the possible purchase of some furniture," Sam told the two police detectives. "As a result of my employment at Art Van's, I am able to buy furniture at cost and re-sell it for a profit. But the person buying it definitely makes a deal. I knocked at Sandy's door and when she opened it, she said, hi, I don't know who you are, but you can come in. I went in and we talked for about five minutes. I had talked to her about two weeks before about buying some furniture while making a delivery to another tenant in the building, but I don't think she remembered who I was. She told me she was still interested in buying some furniture, at which time we walked into the bedroom while we continued our discussion. I don't know why, but I just bent over and kissed her. When I did, she started to scream. I got scared and put my hand over her mouth. When I did, I fell on top of her."

"Did you spread her legs apart?" Gallagher asked.

"No," Sam said. "I just fell on top of her. She was screaming and I was scared. That's why I put my hand over her mouth. I had no intention of raping her. I would have had sex with her if she would have let me, but I never would have raped her. I've changed. Sam of old, when he had it in his mind to rape a woman would have raped her. But the Sam of new has changed. Once I quieted her down, I apologized to her. She then told me to leave and I did. I even called her again later that night to apologize and asked for her forgiveness. I did the same thing the following day. I was wrong in going there and wrong in kissing and tackling her. But I had no intention of raping her."

Sam told Schoenrock and Gallagher that the only reason he was being charged was because his boss had paid Sandy to make the charge so he could fire him. "Had I known you guys were going to arrest me today, I would have contemplated suicide," Sam said.

On September 21, 1972, Sam was arraigned in the 41st District Court in Shelby Township, Michigan, on the charge of assault with intent to commit rape. Sam, represented by Don Ricard, stood mute as the judge read the charges and asked how he pled. When Sam refused to answer, the court entered a plea of not guilty on his behalf. Sitting in the back of the courtroom, Big Sam watched as his son stood quietly as the judge read the charges against him. Big Sam was tired and hoped to take his son home as had so many times before. Sam's wife Cindy, looking pale and frightened as she held their new daughter Kimberly in her arms, sat quietly next to her father in-law.

The arraignment took only a few minutes. Sam was released when his father posted a $1,000 cash bond with the court. An examination hearing, designed to determine if enough evidence existed in the case to bind Sam over for trial, was scheduled for November 20, 1972. Art Van Furniture fired Sam that afternoon.

On November 20, 1972, while most of Sam's family prepared for the Thanksgiving holiday, Sandy took another day off from work to attend a court hearing. All parties were present, including Sam, his attorney Don Ricard, the prosecutor, Anthony Spada, and Detectives Gallagher and Schoenrock. Sitting in the courtroom, showing support for his son, Big Sam sat quietly, occasionally laughing with his troubled namesake, hoping to boost his spirits as they waited for the hearing to begin. Cindy sat next to her father-in-law holding her daughter, hoping to keep her quiet during the hearing. It was the type of family support Don Ricard wanted the court to see as he represented Sam on yet another charge of sexual misconduct. At the beginning of the hearing, Ricard made a motion asking that the court reassign the case to another judge, since judge Harvey had presided over a similar trial involving Sam in 1969. Not wanting to appear prejudicial, the judge granted the request. Since the case had just been reassigned, no date was set for the examination hearing. Sam remained free on bond and looked forward to eating his Thanksgiving turkey dinner with his family.

The New Year was almost three months old and still there was no date set for the examination hearing. Joe Consiglio, Sam's oldest brother who worked for a plumbing supply company, hired Sam as a deliveryman, allowing Sam to demonstrate to the court that he had obtained another job after being fired by Art Van. This was designed to portray him as a hard working and dedicated family man.

On the evening of March 20, 1973, Sandy was home alone thinking about the pending hearing and praying it would be over soon. She received a phone call from Sam's mother. "My son needs medical help, not jail," she told Sandy, as she pleaded for her to drop the charges against her son. "What exactly did he do to you anyway?" she asked.

Sandy was shaken by the call. "I told her that it was all a matter of court record and that if she had any questions, to contact the Police Department," Sandy said later when she called Detective Schoenrock to report the telephone call.

On April 12, Sam, appeared at the 41st District Court in Shelby Township to begin the examination hearing, which had been postponed three previous times. As always, his father and his wife Cindy, sat in the courtroom supporting him. Prior to the hearing, Ricard asked Assistant District Attorney Anthony Spada if he could speak to Sandy about postponing the hearing for another two months. Spada had no objection to Ricard speaking to Sandy. He couldn't stop him if he had wanted. Nor did he have a problem with postponing the hearing if Sandy agreed to it. Ricard told Sandy that he intended to ask the court for a two-month delay in the proceedings to allow Sam a chance to obtain some medical and psychiatric help. "My client needs help," Ricard told Sandy. "Jail is no place for him to get the help he needs right now."

Sandy's response was immediate and overwhelming, "No," she said. She insisted the hearing take place that day. "I have been forced to use personal and sick days to appear in court," she told both of the opposing attorneys. She had no personal days left and would be forced to start using her sick leave for any further court appearances. Sandy also told Ricard and Spada that if she agreed to the two-month postponement, the hearing would not take place until June, which meant that any trial in the Circuit Court would not take place until September 1973.

While Ricard appeared to listen sympathetically to Sandy's objections, it was his job to defend his client anyway that he could. When she finished, Ricard, who was actually indifferent to her concerns, asked, "What makes you think you'll get in the Circuit Court before September anyhow?" Ricard's responsibility was to his client, Sam. And if that meant getting futher postponements, that's exactly what he would do.

It was almost 5 p.m. before Don Ricard and assistant District Attorney Anthony Spada appeared before judge Burkharts to determine if and when the trial would begin. Sam sat next to Ricard while Sam's father and wife sat quietly behind them. Over the last several hours, the silence was broken only by intermittent verbal exchanges, all conducted in low whispers. Anthony Spada sat alone at a table a few feet away from the defendant, avoiding eye contact with his opponent as he made last minute notes to himself regarding the pending hearing. When judge Burkharts convened the court, Ricard stood and waived examination of the evidence to the Circuit Court. This allowed time to explore possible plea bargains, as well as delay the proceedings. Most importantly, it allowed Sam time to obtain medical assistance and to demonstrate further that he was not a threat to the community. No trial date was set and Sam was allowed to remain free on bond. He returned home with his wife and daughter and continued delivering plumbing supplies for his brother, Joe.

Just eleven days later, on April 23, Sam, in his continuous search for sexual pleasure, went to visit Tina.

"I met this very sexy girl while making a delivery," Sam said. "Her name was Tina. I made a lot of deliveries where she worked. She was short, about 5'4", maybe 110 pounds, and had light blond hair. She was real pretty, had a lot of sex appeal. She was a receptionist. As soon as I met her, I said to myself, I'd like to spend the night with her. She was very friendly, outgoing, and divorced."

Sam looked forward to making the deliveries that brought him into contact with Tina. Each time he talked to her, he smiled and made small talk, always showing an interest in her, doing whatever he could to make her laugh. "Eventually, I was able to get her address and phone number from her. One time, she told me to stop by sometime for a drink. Looking back, I'm not sure she meant it," Sam said.

Tina lived alone with her son in a modest working-class single family home in Troy, Michigan, not far from Sterling Heights. She had recently started dating again after her divorce and had found a new steady boyfriend. "I called home and spoke to my son in the afternoon, and he told me that Sam had been there," Tina later told the police.

"When I got home around 4:30, I saw Sam sitting in his delivery truck in front of my house. I spoke to him for a few minutes. He wanted to know if we could go out sometime and I told him no, that I was going with another guy. He seemed to be upset but I thought he understood. He then asked if he could come in for ten minutes and have a cup of coffee. I told him no and he got in his truck and left," Tina reported.

"She invited me in for a drink," Sam said. "We were having a drink, standing in the kitchen and she tells me, I have to leave. That fucking threw me off because I thought we were going to have a lot of time together. So, I remember putting my arm around her, pulling her to me, and kissing her and she didn't resist, so, I figured she is easier than I thought. We're not drunk; we hadn't even had one full drink yet. So after I kissed her, she say's, 'a little bit fast aren't you.' And I said you haven't seen anything yet. I remember picking her up. She didn't fight or anything but I remember her saying, 'what are you doing' and I said, just hold on a minute and I'll show you. I want to show you something. She say's 'that's an old one' and I tell her that I'm serious, just hold on. I remember lying her on the bed in her bedroom and I went to take her nylons and panties off. I remember I put my hands up to undress her and she says 'oh no' and she starts resisting me.

Tina denied ever, inviting Sam in for a drink. "It was about three minutes later when I heard the door open," Tina said later. "I walked down the hallway and found Sam standing there. As soon as he saw me, he grabbed me and shoved me back into the bedroom and pushed me on top of the bed. Then, he jumped on top of me. I tried pushing him away and asked what he thought he was doing. Sam kept telling me that he just wanted to kiss me over and over, and then he stopped. He didn't try anything else at that time. He got up and said, 'what am I doing? I almost raped you. I'm sorry, I didn't mean to do that.' He just wanted to kiss me."

Sam asked Tina, "Do you think I'm sick?" Tina didn't answer right away. Her first thoughts were to get Sam out of her bedroom and into the living room, as quickly as possible. When she finally got him into the living room, Tina asked Sam to leave, hoping to get him out of the house before her son returned home.

"Can I please have a glass of water," Sam asked, delaying his departure. Tina gave Sam a glass of water and asked him once again to please leave her home. As he drank the glass of water, Sam apologized for what he had done; telling Tina that he had never done anything like this before.

"I told him to seek medical help," Tina said.

"Why don't you just kiss me?" Sam asked.

"No," Tina told him, "I'm afraid of you." It was a mistake for any woman to tell Sam she was afraid of him. Being afraid is exactly what he wanted them to feel.

Sam quickly grabbed Tina again and started kissing her. She struggled to liberate herself from his hold but was unable to break free of Sam's tight grasp. Sam pulled Tina into the bedroom and threw her back onto the bed. Tina begged him to stop, but Sam refused. He lay on top of her, pinning her arms and hands down with his elbows as he kept trying to kiss her. Each time he tried to kiss her, Tina would move her head from side to side. "I am not going to rape you, I am not going to rape you," Sam yelled, trying to gain her confidence and reassure her that she would not be harmed and she should not be afraid.

"He lifted himself up momentarily and started to unbuckle his belt and undo his pants," Tina said later as she told her story to the police. "As he did, I got one arm free and reached for the phone. When I did, he reached down and covered my mouth with his hand. I saw that he had his penis out but he kept saying, 'Don't worry, I won't rape you.' He started pulling my pants and panty hose down but I kept my legs crossed. Sam kept pulling on my pants until he got them down below my knees. He then tried to remove my dress, pulling it over my head. When he couldn't get my clothes off, he quit. He just quit trying. There was anger in his face; anger was clearly visible in spite of the fact that he wore his sunglasses during the entire time. He then put his penis between my legs but never inside me. He started moving up and down until he ejaculated on me and the bed."

"She should have never invited me over for a drink. I got mixed signals," Sam said. "I really got carried away. I got stupid. I picked her up and carried her into the bedroom and took her nylons off. She kept asking me to stop, she was screaming, kept wriggling and saying, 'no, no.' She cried a lot, too. I don't know, I guess it was a combination of things, but I do remember all of a sudden stopping and saying, what the fuck am I doing here? I'm not going to do this. I remember stopping and she was very grateful. She gave me the impression that she wasn't going to call the police."

After he discharged his semen onto Tina's legs, Sam got up and sat on the floor alongside the bed. "I'm sorry," Sam told Tina as he sat, crying like a small child. "I didn't get in you, so you don't have to worry. Are you going to call the police?"

"No, but you need to get some medical help," Tina told Sam.

Sam told Tina that he had tried to get some medical help about a year prior but couldn't even get in to see a doctor. Sam asked her, again, if she was going to call the police. And again, Tina assured him that she wouldn't. She told Sam that her concern was for the safety of other young girls and urged him to seek medical help. "I told him to see a doctor and to bring me a letter within a week that he had done so. I told him I would not call the police if he did this and it seemed to calm him down," Tina told the police. "I then told Sam that I had to go and pick up my son. He and I left the house at the same time."

For about an hour, Tina drove around alone, afraid to return home. She was uncertain what to do about what had just happened to her. She was confused about how best to deal with what would remain a part of her for the rest of her life. Finally, Tina decided to report the assault to the Troy Police Department. While she sat recounting the episode to the police, Tina discovered a small red mark imbedded in her chin left over from her struggle with Sam.

It was around 6:00 p.m., when Tina telephoned home to speak to her son. She wanted to let him know that she would be late and not to worry. Her son told her that she had just one message; someone named Sam had just called.

The following day, detectives met with Tina at her home. Tina had saved the bed sheets, the panty hose and underwear that she had worn when Sam attacked her. She also saved the glass Sam drank water from and turned all of those items over to the police. On that same afternoon, police obtained a warrant for Sam's arrest, charging him with assault with intent to commit rape.

"I found out from my brother, Joe, that the police had called and had a warrant for my arrest," Sam said. "I didn't want them to arrest me at the shop and embarrass Joe, so I called the police and asked if they did have a warrant for me. When they said they did, I told them I would turn myself in. I wanted to turn myself in and, hopefully, get a good bond. So I called this lawyer in Oakland County, some old man. He was senile as shit, but I needed somebody to go in for me. He got a copy of the warrant and I turned myself in."

Sam was placed under arrest and advised of his constitutional rights. By now, he could recite those rights to himself. The police took the required number of photographs and fingerprints, and then escorted Sam directly to court for arraignment. Because he had a job and had surrendered himself to the police, the judge released him on a $1,000 personal bond.

Sam went home and told his wife, that he had no idea what this recent charge was all about. "I kept telling her that I wasn't guilty and I didn't know anything about this," Sam said. But his brother, Joe, knew otherwise, and so did Joe's boss. Sam was fired that afternoon from his job delivering plumbing supplies.

On August 13, Sam, accompanied by Cindy and Don Ricard, appeared in judge Burkhardt's court. The purpose of the hearing was to conduct an examination of the evidence on the charge of assault with intent to commit rape of Sandy. At the conclusion of the hearing, Sam was bound over for trial and allowed to remain free on the $1,000 bond posted eleven months prior.

On October 29, Sam agreed to a plea bargain offered by the prosecutor's office, and negotiated by the old attorney he had hired to represent him on this charge relating to the attack on Tina. Sam hoped that perhaps because this matter was in another court's district, Don Ricard might not immediately learn about it. Sam sensed that Ricard was tiring of him and did not want to anger his advocate more than he already had.

The agreement allowed Sam to plead guilty to a reduced misdemeanor charge of assault and battery for his attack on Tina. He received the maximum sentence allowed by law at the time, 90 days in the county jail. Sam was also fined $100.

"It was kind of hard for me to keep telling Cindy that I didn't know anything about this after I agreed to plead guilty," Sam said. "So, I explained the whole thing to her. I served 90 days in the Oakland County Jail, the best ninety days I ever served in my entire life. They sent me to a camp, the Oakland County Trustee Camp. You should see this place; it's unbelievable. You get up in the morning and you go to the dining room and this woman back there, like Aunt Jemima, asks you how you want your eggs, and would you like potatoes with it. I mean it's not like being in jail at all. It was no jail; you lived free. There was no fence; I could leave whenever I wanted to. They would take us to the city and we would pick up some trash as part of their recycling program. Sometimes they would have us cut trees. But I didn't like that. That's too heavy for me. I didn't fuck with that shit. But it was hard being married while Cindy was waiting for me. It was really hard on Cindy. Things were tough for her. With me, I mean, I had it made, I'm locked up, but I'm not really locked up. I had a place to sleep and plenty to eat."

On November 15, Sam was taken from the Oakland County Trustee Camp to the Circuit Court in Macomb County for his arraignment before judge Stair on the charge of assault with intent to commit rape in the case of Sandy. With Don Ricard at his side, Sam stood mute when the charge was read. The court entered a plea of not guilty on his behalf. Trial was set for December 5. Judge Stair allowed Sam to remain free on the $1,000 bond after he completed his 90-day sentence for the misdemeanor assault on Tina. The trial was delayed due to scheduling conflicts with the court and because of motions filed by Don Ricard on behalf of his client.

"I actually did about 75 days," Sam said. "I tried to get out for Christmas. I even wrote the judge, but he said, 'are you joking; are you nuts?' So, I didn't get out until sometime right after the first of the year, in 1974. But Cindy had stuck with me the whole time. I remember telling her to wear a dress when she picked me up, with nothing underneath. It had been awhile and I didn't plan on waiting until I got home. They let me out at 4 a.m. I remember it was still very dark outside. I had it all planned. I had my sister Grace drive and Cindy and I fucked in the back seat of the car while Grace drove us home. I couldn't wait. I didn't think I'd be able to do it with my sister driving, but I did."

"I don't remember them doing it in the back seat while I was driving," Grace said. "I might have pulled off the side of the road though. I really don't remember."

After his release from the Oakland County Work Camp, Sam went to work in Detroit driving a truck for the Koenig Coal Company.

Chapter 5

If I Had Known She Was a Cop's Wife...

In 1974, gasoline shortages caused by the Arab oil embargo, created gas lines up to six miles long at some New York gas stations. President Nixon was named by a federal grand jury as a co-conspirator in the Watergate break-in and cover-up. Later, he would become the first sitting president in American history to resign from office. Hank Aaron, a member of the Atlanta Braves, hit his 715th home run, passing Babe Ruth as the greatest slugger of all time. In 1974, Barbara Streisand sang "The Way We Were" while Eric Clapton recorded "I Shot the Sheriff."

On January 28, 1974, Don Ricard and Anthony Spada appeared before Circuit Court Judge Edward Gallagher to hear motions in the case involving Sandy. Ricard was seeking to suppress statements made by Sam to the police at the time of his arrest for the attack on Sandy, arguing that they violated his Fifth Amendment Right against self-incrimination. Ricard wanted three statements from Detective Schoenrock's report deleted from the evidence that the prosecution sought to introduce at trial against his client. First, Ricard wanted Sam's remark "with my past record, I couldn't just run out of there," deleted. Second, Ricard asked that the statement, "I am not the Sam of old" be eliminated. Finally, Ricard asked the court to remove any reference to the statement, "please do not be against me because of my past record."

Anthony Spada argued for the prosecution that Sam made the statements voluntarily, after being told of his constitutional rights. The statements, argued Spada, also went to show Sam's state of mind or his consciousness of guilt at the time of the alleged assault. Courts have held that both the prosecution and the defense can introduce testimony which reflects what a person was thinking or their emotional feelings at the time a crime was committed in an effort to prove guilt or establish innocence.

After listening to the two attorneys, Gallagher gave the prosecution two weeks to find any case law or previous court decision, which would allow for the prosecution to indirectly violate the defendant's right to Fifth Amendment protection against self-incrimination. Spada had not presented any such evidence during the motion hearing and was not confident he would find any to present in the two-week stay the judge had just given him. Ricard had, for all practical purposes, successfully kept the three incriminating statements out of the prosecution's limited arsenal of evidence. No jury would hear testimony of Sam's prior acts of violence committed toward women.

Just before the hearing was adjourned, Ricard requested that Sam be given a polygraph test in connection with the case pending before him. Detective Schoenrock made the necessary arrangements with the Michigan State Police to have the examination conducted.

On February 13, Sam was administered a polygraph examination at the Sterling Heights Police Department. The examination took almost three hours. Sam was asked a series of questions relating to the attack on Sandy, all designed to provide the examiner with an opinion as to his truthfulness about the events in question. At the conclusion of the test, the examiner offered his opinion to Spada that Sam was not being completely truthful to the questions asked him. Sam failed the polygraph examination. Sam left the police department and went back to work delivering coal while he remained free on $1,000 bond. The case was still pending with no date set for the trial to begin. The results of the polygraph would never be presented to a jury.

Later that week, just days after failing the polygraph examination, Sam was making a coal delivery in Detroit when his truck broke down. Lisa, a 16-year-old girl attending Osborn High School in Detroit, was on her way home when she saw Sam attending to his disabled truck. Sam introduced himself and asked if she could help him by calling his company and telling them of the breakdown since he was unable to leave the truck unattended. She agreed and telephoned the Koening Coal Company. When she returned, Sam had gotten the truck running. He then offered Lisa a ride home. She accepted.

"She had actually been hitchhiking when I met her," Sam said. "She told me she went to high school, but I was sure she was in her senior year. Afterwards, we became friends."

Six weeks later, Sam telephoned Lisa at her home and asked if she would go out with him. She said, "no". But Sam insisted, and told Lisa that he would pick her up from school later that week. Lisa really thought no more about Sam's call, certain that her refusing to go out with him would be the end of any further contact with the nice man who was eight years older than she was. Three days later, as school was letting out, Sam appeared in the parking lot of Osborne High School looking for Lisa. Lisa was insistent, telling Sam again that she could not go out with him, but that she would appreciate a ride home. Lisa got into Sam's car thinking that she was going to get a ride home.

But instead of driving Lisa home, Sam drove to a parking lot behind a church. He parked the car behind some school busses and asked Lisa if she had ever smoked any "grass." Lisa told him that she had not and that she wanted to go home. Sam then put his arm around Lisa and tried to kiss her. She pulled away from Sam and asked him to leave her alone. He became angry, Lisa later told the police, and said, "If you don't do what I want you to do, I will kill you."

Lisa told the police that she tried to get out of the car by opening the front passenger door. But Sam reached across the seat of the car, pulled her back inside, and pushed her into the backseat. "Relax," Sam told Lisa, "and you will like it."

Sam ripped Lisa's slacks and panties off one leg while he unzipped his pants, exposing himself to her. He grabbed her arms and pinned them tightly over her head. Lying on top of her, Sam raped a crying Lisa in the back of his car. After he satisfied his own sexual gratification, he asked Lisa if she was going to call the police and have him prosecuted. Lisa was too frightened to respond. She sat quietly, trying to regain her composure, not answering Sam's question. Getting no response, he drove Lisa within several blocks of her house and told her to get out of the car. She walked home and told her mother what had just happened to her.

"I think this happened on the second occasion I was with her," Sam said. "I told her to get into the back seat. I am sure the only reason she did it was because I told her to, not because she wanted to. I am sure she was intimidated; I know she was scared of me. I mean, I didn't say to myself, I'm going to intimidate this bitch and screw her. But looking back now, I think in the back of my mind, I knew I was intimidating. She didn't holler. She didn't scream. There was no force, no beating; but I knew she didn't want to do it. I think she got upset because afterwards, there was no talking and I just dropped her off near her house. Maybe I should've talked to her, even taken her out to dinner. So, she goes home, all upset and tells her mother that she just had sex with this guy, me, and that she didn't want to. So the mother calls the cops."

The Detroit police were able to identify Sam within hours of the complaint being lodged by Lisa and her mother. As soon as Sam learned of the outstanding warrant for his arrest, he surrendered himself to the Women's Division of the Detroit Police Department. He confessed he had been with Lisa but said he did not have sexual intercourse with her. Later that day in a line-up, Lisa positively identified Sam as the man who had raped her. After she made the identification, Sam was formally charged with carnal knowledge of a female over 16. He was held in jail after bail was set at $10,000.

On April 29, Sam was sent to the Certified Forensic Facility of Recorder's Court in Detroit for an evaluation to determine his competency to stand trial. Michael B. Ferrara, Ph.D., a clinical psychologist, and Albert J. Wallaert, M.D., chief psychiatrist at the Forensic Center, took just two weeks to conduct the necessary examinations and to render an opinion for the court regarding Sam's competency to stand trial. In their report, Ferrara and Dr. Wallaert wrote:

"During the evaluation, Mr. Consiglio presents as a short-obese young man who despite his need for a shave, is adequately groomed in other respects, even though he is dressed in jail clothes. His communications are consistent with his average intelligence. He is obviously lucid and coherent in his thinking and his verbal communications. He gets rather emotional as he attempts to discuss his past history of deviant sexual behavior and he certainly becomes quite emotional in discussing the present case. He tells us that he is very interested in having his bond reduced so that he might be able to go out and continue working as well as perhaps borrow some money from friends so that he might be able to pay his defense lawyer. He indicates that because of his past criminal cases, his finances have been drained and his resources for loans have been waning.

"Despite the tears and his claims that he has been very upset because of his current court involvement, he can become rather facetious and jocular at times. One most certainly gets the impression that this naturally disarming young man is subject to manipulative ploys. He most certainly is glib and evidence of a true depression does not seem to be indicated.

"In reference to the offense in question, he tells us, `at the beginning, I had a history of sex offenses dating back to 1965. My biggest problem was not being able to control my impulses. Married life has done wonders for me although I have a tendency to cheat on my wife. I paid this girl, who is a little tramp, twenty dollars, but afterwards, I took my money back. For a measly twenty dollars, I'm stuck in the vicious circle because of my past.'

"In reference to competency to stand trial, it is felt that he is capable of understanding the nature and object of the proceedings against him. The defendant is in fact so far free of mental defect, disease and derangement that he understands the nature of the charge pending against him and his relationship to it. Further, he is able to aid and assist counsel in his own defense.

"Considering his extremely poor judgment and lack of self- restraint over his sexual impulses, it is felt that he would be a poor risk in the community. We are thus inclined to suggest that release on bond be denied in view of his potential for repeating sexually assaultive behavior. A long-term prognosis for adjustment is felt to be quite poor. However, if there is any chance at rehabilitation, group or individual psychotherapy is suggested exclusively within a correctional setting."

Sam was returned to the Wayne County Jail and in spite of the medical recommendation that he posed a serious risk to others and that bail should be denied, Sam was released on $25,000 bond. Big Sam paid a bondsman the normal 10 percent fee to post the bail and pledged his home as surety. Sam went home to his wife and his daughter, hoping to return to his job delivering coal. Sam was now free on two separate bonds as he awaited trial on two felony charges related to sexual assaults, one in Clinton Township and one in Detroit.

On a Sunday, six weeks after being released from the Wayne County Jail, Sam went to St. Clair Shores to visit his parents who were preparing to celebrate their wedding anniversary. His visit was short, as was the celebration. It would have been unusual for his parents to go out to a restaurant since Sam's mother almost never left the house. She prepared her own anniversary dinner, as she did virtually every other meal in the Consiglio home. Sam stayed a few hours, ate dinner and paid his respects to both his parents. It was around 10:30 p.m. when he said good-bye to his mother and father. On his way home to his wife and daughter, Sam drove down Deziel, the street where he had grown up. He had only driven a block when he noticed a young woman riding a bicycle approach the intersection of Deziel and New York. Sam thought the woman appeared to have gotten her pant leg caught in the bicycle chain.

Darlene was the mother of three children. She lived in a modest middle class home about 10 blocks from Sam's parents. Almost every night for five years, Darlene rode past the Consiglio home as she went on her 30-minute bike ride. Darlene was conscientious about riding every evening regardless of weather conditions. She made a determined effort to keep as fit as possible and bicycling was her way of keeping her weight under as much control as possible. That night, the hem of Darlene's blue jeans got caught in the chain. As she was trying to free herself, she heard someone ask if she needed any help.

"I saw this man sitting in a car," Darlene said. "I told him that I didn't need any help. Before she could free herself from being caught in the bicycle chain, Sam grabbed the handlebars of the bicycle and held the front wheel between his legs.

"What is your name?" he asked.

"I don't know your name," Darlene answered. "I won't tell you my name."

But he persisted, demanding again she tell him her name. Darlene finally relented and told the man her first name. "Now let go of my bike," she demanded.

"Not until you kiss me," Sam demanded.

"I don't know you," Darlene cried.

"My name is David Oldani. Now kiss me," Sam said again.

When Darlene refused, Sam grabbed her and pulled her off the bicycle. He dragged her over the grass and pushed her to the ground. "I struggled with him," Darlene said. "He pushed me to the ground and laid on top of me. My legs were open a little bit and he was lying between my legs. He started to kiss me."

Darlene explained later how the man had her pinned by the shoulders. "I begged him to let me up and asked why he was doing this but he didn't answer. He just grabbed me by the breast and squeezed real hard. He was kissing me. I moved my head to one side but he kept getting my mouth. He was drooling all over me, over my mouth and it was making me sick." Darlene begged her assailant, "Please don't do this to me." But Sam didn't respond.

"He kept breathing real heavy, like a bear. I never heard anything like that before; like a rasping type of growl. Sounded like an animal. At that point, I panicked," Darlene, explained later.

Darlene continued struggling, turning her head away as her assailant continued his effort to put his lips against hers. Frustrated that his attempts were being thwarted, Sam grabbed Darlene as he rose to his feet. "Get up, you are getting in the car," he ordered in a loud, demanding voice as if giving an order to a military recruit.

"He had me by the arm and the back of the neck. He was pushing me toward the car. He was trying to shove me in headfirst and I wedged one foot on the car and one hand on the window and I started screaming as loud as I could. But he wouldn't stop. He got madder and squeezed tighter," Darlene said later.

As she continued to scream and fight her attacker, a car approached. The headlights momentarily reflected directly on Darlene and her assailant. For a moment, Sam froze like a deer temporarily blinded by the lights of an oncoming car as he took a moment to reassess his next course of action.

"He threw me on the ground real hard and said, real mean like, get out of here. I jumped on my bike and rode away."

Darlene peddled her bike as fast as she could up to the next corner and ran to a neighbor's front porch. She rang the doorbell and banged on the front door, screaming for someone to help her. As she did, Sam drove by in his car, laughing and yelled, "only kidding darling." Darlene contacted the St. Clair Shores Police Department where her husband worked as a police officer. She didn't speak to her husband when she telephoned; she was too afraid of how he would react. "I had told her not to ride alone late at night," Darlene's husband Tom said. Tom, who retired from the St. Clair Shores Police Department in January 1991 after 23 years on the force, continually pleaded with Darlene not to go out at night alone. He was concerned for her safety.

Instead of calling her husband, Darlene spoke to Sergeant Joe Henry Yoe, Jr., and reported what had just happened to her. Yoe told her she would need to obtain a license number of the car for him to be able to help her.

The following day, Darlene rode her bike around the area where she had been attacked. "I saw the car in the driveway," she said. "It was a Gremlin. He was standing in the driveway, painting a garage. He turned around and he just stared at me. He looked puzzled as I wrote down his license number. At the time, I knew it was him."

Sam watched as Darlene drove away. He went back to painting his parent's garage. Darlene took the information to Sergeant Yoe. Yoe got a black and white photograph of Sam from the police records division and placed it among four other snapshots of men bearing a similar resemblance. Darlene immediately selected the photograph of Sam as the man who had attacked her; the same man she had seen earlier that day painting a garage on Deziel. A short time later, six St. Clair Shores Police cars converged on the home of Big Sam and Lucy Consiglio. Sam's mother watched as her son was handcuffed and placed into the back seat of a police car. Sam was charged with assault with intent to commit rape. Bond was set at $25,000. It was a bond Sam and his father were unable to post.

"I was walking down the street," Sam said, "not driving. I heard a noise behind me and I turned around and when I did, this woman, a big woman, about 140 pounds, runs over my foot with her bike. She looks at me and says, 'move your fucking foot the next time,' and I called her a stupid bitch. I picked her off her bicycle and threw her over the bushes. She hollered out something like, 'you're going to regret you did that; my husband is a police officer.' If I had known she was a cop's wife, of course I wouldn't have done that, I don't think. I would have given it a little more thought. She angered me."

On the way to the St. Clair Shores Police Department, Sergeant Yoe informed Sam of the arrest charge.

"When did this happen?" Sam asked.

"Sunday evening, June 2," Yoe replied.

Sam told Sergeant Yoe that he had been at Harsons Island that evening with his mother and brother and that he had returned home about 10:30 that night. Sam of course, had no misgivings about lying to the police. He was conscious of everything he said whenever he spoke, especially to the detectives, knowing that what he said might come back to haunt him.

"I was painting the garage when I saw her pull up in the driveway," he said. "She had been looking for me. The police arrested me right away on a charge of assault with intent to commit rape. There was never any intent to commit rape, but they charged me with that because of my past. When they put me in jail, I just lost it. I had a breakdown in the county jail. My dad came right away to visit me. I asked him if Cindy was going to hang in there and he said, 'No, forget Cindy.' Then Cindy came and told me it was all over. I just fell apart. The only things I remember was my hands were all swelled up and my head was bruised and shit. My dad thought the police had beat me up, but I told him, no, the police haven't touched me."

Once again, the Consiglio family turned to Don Ricard. "I didn't want to take the case," Ricard said. "But Big Sam called pleading, actually crying, as he begged me to represent his son. I couldn't say no."

Sam had been held in the Macomb County Jail for less than a week when he began to complain to the sheriff's deputies about some medical problem he was experiencing, as well as other stress-related problems. He asked one deputy if life insurance companies paid off on suicide. Two psychologists on staff at the Macomb County Sheriff's Department who observed Sam, said he was "extremely suicidal and homicidal and should be watched closely." Concerned for Sam's welfare, Big Sam and Don Ricard obtained a court order transferring Sam, on an emergency basis, back to the Center For Forensic Psychiatry.

On June 14, Sam was admitted to the center for a 60-day diagnostic order to determine his competency to stand trial. Dr. Leon J. Quinn, a forensic psychiatrist on staff at the hospital, was assigned to examine Sam. Quinn was familiar with the patient, having examined Sam on two previous occasions while he was in the Wayne County Jail on charges relating to his assault on Lisa.

In his report submitted to the court regarding Sam's competency to stand trial, Dr. Quinn wrote, "At the time of his hospitalization, Mr. Consiglio presented as a heavy-set, Italian-looking, Caucasian male, who had a moustache and long sideburns. He talked in a usually child-like fashion with rather simple sentences, and an often rather histrionic overlay. He denied ever having had any contact with this examiner and denied ever being incarcerated in the Wayne County Jail. He was quite upset that one of the patients reported that they were cellmates apparently while he was in the Wayne County Jail and he immediately accused the other patient of lying about him. He similarly had very little knowledge as to why he was at this facility, other than to be checked out by doctors, because he had been bad. The self-imposed bad behavior had been, according to Mr. Consiglio, looking under the skirts of women and he knew this was wrong. Despite his lengthy history of problems with rape, he denied having any knowledge of such prior offenses. He talked instead about frequently visiting prostitutes and one prostitute in particular, named Margo whom he had heard about on a television news show. He seemed to indicate that his sort of behavior was consistent with what his father did. In reviewing the available records, the primary diagnostic impression seemed to be one of a personality disorder with resulting sexually deviant behavior. At no point is he depicted as being psychotic or demonstrating any symptoms of a neurotic or psychotic illness. The impression is gained that he seeks help only when under the gun of having charges pending. He expressed some fear that the other patients were going to hurt him and talked vaguely in terms of they're going to get me.

"The mental status examination revealed a helpless, dependent, rather child-like individual whose interview responses were rather peculiar. He talked of not liking it at this facility and wanted to die but did not actually talk about specific suicidal intentions.

"It is not quite clear what phenomenon is occurring in this case and it might either be explained in terms of some regressed psychotic condition or as a manipulation on the part of the patient to avoid prosecution. He certainly seems unable at this point to attend to the charges pending against him but it remains a mystery as to what sort of clinical condition is responsible for this inability. A period of observations seems indicated before a response to the question of competency can be given.

"From a diagnostic standpoint, Mr. Consiglio remains a puzzle. It is difficult to characterize his behavior as being representative of any clear-cut type of mental illness at this point. How to label his condition at this point remains unclear, except perhaps to attribute it to some sort of hysterical psychotic illness. Unfortunately, there does not appear to be a readily available diagnostic category under which to record this. One must keep in mind, the possibility that Mr. Consiglio is either malingering or exaggerating his symptoms, because it is advantageous to do so."

In June, while undergoing psychiatric evaluation, a staff member told Sam that he might be eligible for social security benefits due to his mental disability. It was only a short time after Sam made a formal application for disability that the Social Security Administration, based on the supporting medical documentation, approved his request for disability benefits. The Social Security Administration awarded Sam $380.20 in monthly assistance.

On July 19, Sam was found incompetent to stand trial. He was turned over to the Michigan Department of Mental Health where it was determined he should be committed for treatment at the Forensic Center in Ann Arbor. The cases pending against him for the assault on Sandy, Lisa and Darlene were all delayed indefinitely.

The following year, in April 1975, while Sam was undergoing treatment at the Forensic Center, the Social Security Administration terminated his monthly benefit claiming his mental impairment was not severe enough to warrant a disability claim

On June 30, 1975, having spent almost one year in a psychiatric hospital, Sam was found competent to stand trial and was returned to the custody of the Macomb County Sheriff's Department. Arthur W. Bahr, a forensic psychologist on staff at the Forensic Center, wrote judge Edward J. Gallagher of the Macomb County Circuit Court that, "when the patient was originally seen at the Forensic Center, he demonstrated a rather psychotic and regressed behavior. These early behaviors improved over the first few months at the Forensic Center and the patient progressively became more involved in ward activities. In addition to being actively involved in treatment programs, such as occupational therapy and recreational therapy, he was seen in intensive psychotherapy since January 1975. It is felt that Mr. Consiglio has improved to the point of being considered competent to stand trial."

"Questions may be raised concerning competency since the patient claims amnesia for the alleged offense. It is felt that the memory loss is genuine and that further treatment will not result in retrieval of lost memory. Furthermore, it is felt that the patient is fully capable of assisting counsel in a reasonable and rational manner with the partial memories that he does possess." Dr. Bahr told the court that Sam was competent to stand trial.

On August 22, 1975, 14 months after the alleged assault on Darlene, Sam appeared at a preliminary hearing in Municipal Court for the City of St. Clair Shores on the charges of assault with intent to commit rape. This time the only person present to show support for Sam was his father. Cindy had divorced him during his detention in the psychiatric hospital. His mother chose not to attend any legal proceeding involving her son, a promise she would keep to herself until the day she died.

On direct examination conducted by Beverly Grobbel, a young attorney from the Macomb County Prosecutors Office, Darlene described the events surrounding her attack. But by the time the hearing took place, Sam had gained a substantial amount of weight and had grown a beard.

But the change in his appearance did not alter Darlene's ability to identify him as the man that attacked her.

On cross-examination, Ricard's plan was to generate sufficient doubt in the court's mind to have the charges against Sam dismissed. Ricard knew this was going to be another exercise in futility. But it was an exercise that had to be performed. It would ultimately provide him with an idea of what Darlene's testimony would be like against his client at the time of trial. It would also provide him with the critical information he needed to determine if it would be in Sam's best interests to negotiate some sort of plea agreement.

Ricard questioned Darlene about Sam's size, and his appearance. He asked about any outstanding features such as scars and the color of his eyes. Darlene maintained her composure as much as possible, although her frustration was starting to show.

"I don't know the color of his eyes. I wasn't looking at the color of his eyes that night," Darlene answered in a stern, cocky manner.

"Did it ever occur to you that you might have the wrong person?" Ricard asked.

"No. Never. I would never come here and point to anybody if there was any doubt in my mind. I have two boys myself and I would never do that. If there were any doubt in my mind I would not be here. I wouldn't do that to anyone."

Darlene was infuriated. Ricard was attacking her integrity. She wasn't use to being treated like that. Ricard knew that her statement, that she would never lie about such a serious thing like being attacked, needed to be offset during cross-examination with testimony that would be beneficial to Sam.

"Now, taking you back to when this incident occurred, and the defendant was on top of you, and while all this is happening, he didn't ever remove any of your clothing did he?" Ricard asked.

"No." Darlene answered.

"And did you notice whether he removed or opened any of his clothing?"

"No, because he had one arm holding me down, and the other squeezing my breast. He couldn't have," Darlene said, snapping back at Ricard.

"At no time did he put either of his hands below your waist, I assume?" Ricard asked.

"No."

Ricard shifted his focus and began to concentrate on Darlene's description of the car used by her assailant.

"What color did you say Sam's car was that night?"

"I didn't say."

"Could you tell us?"

"It was goldish or yellowish."

"That is the same color car that was in the driveway when you saw it?"

"That was his car, and that was him in the driveway. If I said yellow and it was lime green that is neither here or there. I knew it was the car and it was, him."

Ricard interrupted Darlene before she could go on any further. Her voice was becoming louder and it was clear that Ricard had frustrated the state's chief witness.

"What kind of car is that again?" Ricard asked.

"A Gremlin."

Ricard knew that Sam didn't drive a Gremlin; he drove a Pinto. Ricard asked Darlene if she knew the difference between a Gremlin and a Pinto. She said that she did.

The prosecution concluded its presentation at the preliminary hearing with Darlene's testimony. Ricard then called Sergeant Yoe to the witness stand for the defense. He had sat in the courtroom during the testimony of Darlene. Yoe testified that he did not hear any errors in Darlene's testimony. Ricard then focused his questioning on the telephone call made by Darlene in which she reported the attack.

"Did you indeed talk to her on the morning of June 3rd as she described?" Ricard asked.

"As far as I can recall, yes, sir," Yoe replied.

"And did you suggest to her there wasn't much you could do without a license number?"

"I don't know if that was my exact conversation with her; however, I think I said a license number would be helpful."

"And did you suggest that she go up and down the streets and see if she could find a license number?"

"No, sir," Yoe responded.

"Did you suggest to her that the person who did this to her might live in the area?"

"No sir."

"Did you have her draw a picture of him?"

"I think I told her to go ahead and draw the picture."

"That was by telephone."

"I don't recall if it was by telephone. No, I believe I saw her personally."

Beverly Grobbel objected to Ricard's line of questioning. "I can't see the materiality here, to his line of questioning, with reference to whether it was either personal or telephone conversation. I wish the Court would ask counsel to indicate what he is attempting to draw attention to, if anything."

"I can assure the Court my questions are in good faith, and with a purpose," Ricard said. "Now if Beverly would be able…"

Judge Parris interjected. "I think the point she is trying to get to and I tend to agree is, this might all be relevant but its value isn't commensurate with the time. It may be relevant but are you trying to find conflicting statements? Give me a hint."

Ricard told Parris, "I think it is most unusual that a complaint of this nature is handled solely by telephone for the entire next day as the complainant said it was. She may be mistaken or she may be absolutely correct."

"We are here to show probable cause and not to pass on the techniques of investigating by the St. Clair Shores police department," Parris told Ricard.

Sergeant Yoe felt uncomfortable in the situation he was in, testifying for the defense against the wife of a fellow officer. Ricard then focused on the photo lineup.

"Is there any reason you did not get Sam to put him in a lineup rather than show her five photographs?" Ricard asked.

"I felt the photographs were sufficient."

"And neither you nor anyone you know suggested to her in any way that Sam Consiglio lived in a house on Jefferson or on Deziel or anything like that, is that right?"

"I had no knowledge it was the defendant here until I had the license number and the identification," Yoe answered.

Ricard, his voice now raised, looked directly at Sergeant Yoe and said, "I suggest to you that isn't so. And I suggest to you that you wrote your report on the 3rd of June, and on the 3rd of June you put Sam Consiglio's name and address on your report."

Beverly Grobbel sprang from her chair objecting to what she claimed was harassment of the witness. "The witness indicated when he wrote the report and he did not know the identification of the person involved in this incident until there was absolute identification from the first witness here, the complainant."

The objection was overruled. Ricard continued his questioning, showing Yoe a copy of the report he made relating to the assault on Darlene. The report reflected that it was prepared on June 3, 1974, the day following the assault.

"You show me on here where is the date of your report?" Ricard asked.

"It isn't on here."

"I ask you, are you not supposed to record the date you made the report?"

"That is the date of the incident, sir."

"Underneath that is another date: June 2, 1974, Sunday, 10:30 p.m. Would that be the date of the incident?"

"That would be the date of the incident that happened here. In other words, the date of June 3, 1974, is when the report was submitted to our statistic files at the police station."

"It indicates day, Monday, time, 3:00 p.m. How received; Headquarters received, by Sergeant Yoe," Ricard read to the witness. "But you are telling me now, that you didn't do this report on the third of June?" Ricard asked.

"I am saying the report doesn't have to coincide with the date of the incident that was reported to the statistics," Yoe said.

"And there are no other dates on this report other than the second and the third of June; is that true?"

"That is true. It isn't unusual for a report to be written maybe a week after it was originally reported."

"Wouldn't you put the date on?" Ricard asked.

"Not generally. Because during this time an investigation is being done."

As soon as Ricard concluded his presentation he recommended to the Court that the proper charge, if Sam were to be bound over for trial, should be assault. Beverly Grobbel moved to have Sam bound over to the Circuit Court on a charge of assault with intent to commit rape; a charge with which judge Parris agreed.

Ricard then made a motion to have Sam's bond reduced.

"There is a $25,000 bond that has been set on the defendant which I think under the circumstances, as has been disclosed by the testimony, is excessive bond at this time under those facts," Ricard told the judge.

Judge Parris was not persuaded by Ricard's plea. His response was short and direct. "I couldn't disagree with you more, Mr. Ricard. The defendant is bound over to the Circuit Court to stand trial. Bond is continued as previously set."

With that order, judge Parris adjourned the court. Unable to post a $25,000 bond Sam was returned to the Macomb County Jail.

While Ricard failed to have his client's bond reduced, he was successful in keeping the photo line-up out of evidence. Ricard aggressively attacked the photo line-up conducted by Sergeant Yoe.

"They showed Darlene Sam's picture in a photo spread after taking her to his parents' house where she identified him. The police tainted the photo line-up," Ricard said.

During the next four months, Sam sat in jail as Ricard explored every possible avenue to help his client. After a series of discussions between Sam and the prosecutor's office, an agreement was reached whereby Sam would plead *nolo contendere or no contest* to a charge of assault. *Nolo contendere*, meaning "I am willing to contend," or no contest simply meant that Sam did not dispute the charges against him. It was as close to entering a guilty plea without actually pleading guilty that Sam and Ricard would agree to. The *nolo* plea would also result in Sam facing a prison sentence of three to five years.

Part of Ricard's strategy in having Sam plead nolo to assault, was to have the charges pending against him in Sterling Heights for the assault on Sandy, dismissed. On September 25, 1975, Assistant District Attorney Anthony Spada telephoned Sergeant Frank Schoenrock. Spada suggested that it might be in the best interest of justice to dismiss the charge against Sam, with the stipulation that he pleads guilty or nolo to the charge of attempted rape against Darlene in St. Clair Shores. It had been three years since Sam had attacked Sandy, and she was no longer anxious to testify. Schoenrock agreed with Spada's recommendation. The charges against Sam for assaulting Sandy would be dismissed if he pled guilty or nolo in St. Clair Shores.

Ricard's next move was to negotiate a similar agreement with the Wayne County Prosecutor's Office in Detroit. Meeting with the young prosecutor in Detroit, Ricard argued that Sam was facing a prison sentence of at least three to five years for the case pending in St. Clair Shores. Knowing that, Wayne County could save itself the expense of a trial by dropping the charges against Sam for the alleged sexual assault on Lisa. But the prosecutor insisted that Sam either plead guilty to the charge of sexually assaulting Lisa or face trial. Ricard, feeling confident that he could win, especially since he almost always did with Sam, agreed to go to trial.

The trial involving Darlene had been assigned to Circuit Court Judge Edward Gallagher of the 16th Judicial Circuit in Mount Clemens. Since Gallagher was familiar with Sam's criminal history, he was not inclined to accept the *nolo* plea agreed to by the prosecutor and the defense. In a letter dated December 18, 1975, to both Don Ricard and the Macomb County Prosecutor's Office, Gallagher wrote:

"I have determined, after a great deal of deliberation, that I must refuse to honor the commitments made at the time of the taking of a plea of nolo contendere (sic) in this matter. I am aware that this is upsetting to a number of applecarts, including the defendant's. But, I believe if any concessions other than those ordinarily pursued in the process of a criminal case are to be extended to Mr. Consiglio, they will have to be extended to him by the medical profession rather than by the law. My conscience will not permit me to do anything in reference to the Defendant, which would put him back on the street. If he is put back on the street by either the medical profession or a jury, then the processes are satisfied.

I feel it necessary to point out to you that some of my attitude in this matter has been dictated by the lack of reliability of the Mental Health Department of the State of Michigan. As I previously indicated to you, once I have decided this matter, there will be no further discussion on it. I would suggest to you, therefore, that you meet with Mr. Spada (the prosecutor) relative to preparation for trial in this case."

Both Sam and Ricard were stung. The message from Gallagher was loud and clear; he didn't trust or like Sam. The trial began on January 6, 1976. It was a short trial. Only a few witnesses testified, with most of the testimony coming directly from Darlene and Sergeant Yoe. Ricard was basing his defense on a case of mistaken identity. He attacked Darlene's description of her assailant as well as her description of the car. It was revealed that Sam drove a Pinto, not a Gremlin. The discrepancy in the dates on the police reports caused the police and the prosecution further embarrassment. In his opening remarks to the jury, Ricard said that he would prove that, "the victim is mistaken" about the identity of the young boy who attacked her. Ricard did not dispute the fact that the victim, "a nice woman," was attacked. He disputed only that Sam had been the one to assault her.

During his opening remarks to the jury, Ricard sought sympathy for his client. He explained that Sam had had a nervous breakdown three days after being arrested on this charge. He said his client, "this nice young man," had to be hospitalized for over a year, undergoing therapy to "restore his mind." Ricard also set the stage for an insanity defense in the event the jury did not agree with the mistaken identity argument.

The defense never called any witnesses and Sam never took the witness stand on his own behalf. On January 8, two days after the trial began, the jury returned a verdict of not guilty on the charge of assault with intent to commit rape.

"If they would have just charged me with assault, they would have had me," Sam said. "But because of my past, they threw in, with intent to commit rape, in order to enhance the possible sentence. We wouldn't allow for the jury to convict on the lesser charge. It was all or nothing and it paid off."

Of course, the legal system, protecting the rights of the accused, prevented the jury from ever hearing any testimony about Sam's past or that he had tried to negotiate a guilty plea prior to trial.

On the advice of his fellow officers, Darlene's husband, Tom, never attended the trial, hoping to avoid doing anything that would harm the prosecution's case.

"I don't know how he got off," he said. "Darlene may have gotten mouthy, as she was inclined to do. I don't think the case was investigated as well as it could have been. It was just little things, like not trying to get prints off of her bike. Sam got to be a joke with everyone. Whenever he was arrested, no one congratulated the guy who got him. We knew he'd get out. It was just a question of how. It didn't hurt Sam that his father worked for Tom Welsh, the so-called Democratic political boss of Macomb County. Big Sam was able to use that political clout to his son's advantage."

The Monday following the verdict, Ricard accompanied Sam to Recorders Court in Detroit to defend him on charges that he sexually assaulted 16-year-old Lisa. It was Sam's contention that Lisa had freely engaged in sexual intercourse with him. And the only reason she was pressing charges was to protect herself from her mother's indignation. Ricard again attacked the victim's story. It was easier this time. Lisa was not the wife of a police officer; she was an 18-year-old girl who, over a year prior, had freely gotten into a car with a man who was much older. Lisa claimed that during the assault, Sam threw her over the front seat of the car and into the back seat. Ricard was able to demonstrate how difficult that would be in a Ford Pinto such as the one Sam drove. Once again, without taking the witness stand and without producing any other witnesses, Sam was found not guilty of the charges levied against him.

"As we left the courthouse, I told Sam that if he ever looked at another woman wrong, not to call me. I had my fill of him," Ricard said.

Ricard explained that the police were so anxious to convict Sam that they just got sloppy in their investigations.

"It's like they knew Sam had done whatever he was accused of, so they did things without thinking them through. I always hoped that he'd straighten up. When he wasn't involved in these episodes, he was a pretty decent guy. I concluded that Sam was guilty of most of these crimes, but my job is to afford my clients all the protections allowed by law. I was just doing my job," Ricard said.

Chapter 6

Beware of the Mask of Sanity

Big Sam feared the worst for his son. In spite of the two acquittals, Sam and his father expressed fears about possible reprisals against Sam from the St. Clair Shores Police. After all, Sam had just been acquitted of trying to rape the wife of one of its officers. On the advice and persuasion of his father, and the concurrence of the medical staff of the Forensic Hospital in Ann Arbor, Sam agreed to continue his psychotherapy on an outpatient basis. Dr. Arthur Bahr, who had previously provided counseling to Sam, agreed to continue treating him twice a week. On January 16, 1976, one week after being acquitted of assaulting Darlene, Sam spoke to Bahr about continuing his therapy and agreed that if he got into any trouble with the law he would explain the problem to the doctor. He also agreed to turn himself in to the police if he got into trouble, at which point, his outpatient therapy treatment would be terminated. The following day, Sam rented a small room at the YMCA in Ann Arbor, Michigan in order to be close to the Forensic Center.

Ann Arbor seemed to offer an opportunity to resolve several of Big Sam's concerns. His son would continue to receive medical treatment and he would be well out of the jurisdiction of the St. Clair Shores Police and the Macomb County Sheriff's Department, two law enforcement agencies Sam had eluded once too often.

"I wanted to get a fresh start and keep up with the therapy," Sam said. Sam needed money and so he signed up for food stamps and unemployment benefits at the local welfare office.

It was the middle of January 1976, when Ann and her young son moved to Ann Arbor from Massachusetts. Ann, known as Annie by her small circle of friends, had never been married and hoped to establish a better life for her and her son by moving to Ann Arbor. She had been to Ann Arbor three months earlier and had posted notices on bulletin boards around town that read, "Woman with child needs apartment." The search for an apartment in Ann Arbor can often be a difficult one, especially during the school year since the University of Michigan is in the middle of the city. One of the places Annie placed a notice was the Ozone House, part of the Community Student Housing Program, which assisted students in their search for housing.

On January 21, Annie, still spending her first few days in Ann Arbor with her sister Susan, received a telephone call from Sam. He told Annie that he worked for the Ozone House and offered to help her find an apartment. She told Sam she had found a place to live but she still needed furnishings. Later that afternoon, Sam went to Annie's new apartment located on West Liberty in Ann Arbor.

Sam and Annie talked about the things she needed for the apartment and her 16-month-old baby boy. Sam asked Ann to sit next to him. When she refused, he got up and sat next to her. He put his arms around her and kissed her, running his hands over her breasts, grabbing her as he felt her thin body. As Sam picked Annie up and attempted to carry her into the bedroom, she began kicking and struggling to free herself. Succeeding, she sat down. Momentarily shocked by the experience, she tried to regain her composure.

Sam apologized. Trying to inject his aberrant sense of humor, he told her, "I can understand how you feel. I respect my dick as much as you respect your cunt." Sensing that Sam may have misread her, Ann accepted the apology. She and Sam talked for another three hours before he said good-bye. They agreed to meet the next morning at her sister's apartment to go to the welfare office. Susan had agreed to baby-sit while Ann and Sam painted Ann's new apartment.

Ann's apartment was sparsely furnished. Several old mattresses stacked on top of one another served as the only bed. The apartment had no curtains and a few stacked boxes served as a table. A few folding chairs was all that was available to sit on. She had envisioned how she would decorate it. Stringed beads would cover the doorways leading from one room to another and the lighting would be dark, perhaps with a black light to highlight a particular area.

Sam and Ann painted late into the night. It was just past midnight when most of the apartment had been painted. They talked and laughed as they worked to get the apartment close to livable condition. It was now Ann's 21st birthday. Her birthday celebration involved eating a pepperoni pizza, Sam's favorite, followed by some cold soft drinks. About 1:30 in the morning, both Ann and Sam were too tired to paint anything else.

"Let's crash here for a couple of hours," Sam told Ann.

"No. My sister wouldn't like that," she told him as she went into the bedroom to get her coat.

Sam, who had been cleaning the paintbrushes, followed Annie into the bedroom. "I'm really angry," he told her.

"I can't help that. Besides, I don't want to stay here," she said.

Sam picked up Ann and laid her down on top of the three mattresses. Ann kicked and screamed as she tried to break free. He put his hand over her mouth and nose, trying to control her screaming. Ann was having difficulty breathing. Sam started kissing her as he removed his hand from her mouth.

"Why are you screaming?" he asked. "You don't have to scream," he told her as he began to undress her.

"I just want to go home," she begged.

"Do you want to have oral sex?" Sam asked. He didn't wait for a response. Instead, he ripped off her flannel shirt tearing it at the seams. He removed her T-shirt, then her blue jeans. It was easy for Sam since he was almost twice her size. Sam lay on top of her, the full weight of his body preventing her from escaping. Without changing his position, he removed his pants.

Ann said later that, "Sam appeared to have ejaculated inside her after only a few moments and after moving slightly." Afterward, Sam laid inside her for a about a minute. Ann, still shaken, and with tears running down her face, told Sam she was scared. But Sam wasn't concerned with her fear or anything else other than his own gratification. He was determined to dominate Ann and have her anyway that he pleased. He had beaten the police so often and with the help of his father, he was confident that he could beat anyone, anytime. He considered himself untouchable.

"Have you ever had anal sex?" Sam asked his victim.

"Yes," she responded. "And I don't like it."

Sam rolled Ann over onto her stomach, pinning her hands under her body. Sam tried to enter her, but she struggled, moving her body back and forth. Angry, Sam rolled her over again and started to penetrate her as he had before. As he did, Ann raised herself up far enough to position her knee against Sam's chest. With all her remaining strength, Ann somehow was able to kick him in the chest and again in the groin, knocking the wind out of him. Sam fell over backward. Still being held by Sam, Ann fell over with him. As they landed next to the mattresses, Ann grabbed Sam by the hair and bounced his head off the floor. Sam, who had just felt the force of a knee to his groin, was momentarily stunned and unable to strike back. It was all the time Ann needed. Now free, Ann jumped up and ran, naked, outside the apartment and down a flight of stairs to the apartment of a friend.

Her friend Kathy was an assistant librarian at the University of Michigan School of Law. She was asleep when she was awakened by the sound of a woman's voice screaming and banging on her door.

Ann waited in Kathy's apartment until they heard someone run down the stairs. Later, the two women went back upstairs to get some clothes before they returned to Kathy's apartment for the rest of the night.

The next morning, Ann went to her sister's apartment and told Susan about being raped by Sam. At Susan's urging, Ann called the Women's Crisis Center in Ann Arbor. Ann was told to go to the University of Michigan Hospital for an examination. However, it revealed no presence of sperm in her vagina and the vaginal area was normal according to the medical report. She had bruises on her left hip, left elbow and face, the report said.

It was the following day, January 24, when Ann contacted the police. "I was confused and wanted to make sure I had all my facts together," she told the patrolman who responded to the radio call alleging a rape complaint. The officer collected the clothes Ann had worn the night before and placed them in a brown paper bag. The clothes would be sent to the lab and examined for evidence of the assault.

Two days later, Detective Sergeant Canada spoke to Dennis Robinson, one of Ann's neighbors. Dennis told Canada that he had been awakened in the early morning by the sound of a woman screaming and banging on the doors. "I got out of bed and cracked the door long enough to see this heavy-set guy come out of Ann's apartment. It was the same guy I had seen earlier leaving the same apartment." Dennis had seen Sam earlier in the day when he had been out walking his dog. Dennis told Canada that he thought, "The guy had been afraid of the dog."

Later that afternoon, Canada assembled a series of black and white Polaroid photographs that included one of Sam. Ann, the first to view the photographic line-up, identified Sam as her assailant. Then, Susan identified Sam from the photos as the man who had accompanied her sister to her house earlier on the day of the alleged attack. Dennis Robinson also easily identified a photo of Sam as the heavy-set man he had seen run down the stairs in the early morning hours of January 23rd.

Sam's version of the incident differed from Ann's.

"I met this girl, Annie, at the welfare office. I was applying for food stamps. She was a hippie, very small, tiny girl. We struck up a conversation and she asked me to help her move some stuff in her apartment. Once I got there, I ended up staying a few days. She was nuts, but it was a piece of ass. The first two nights I stayed there, everything went fine. I had sex with her two nights in a row. But, she was fucking nuts, you know, weird. She was a vegetarian, didn't believe in television, and didn't listen to the radio. I just felt uncomfortable around her. So, I told her that I was planning on leaving. But, I figured I'd get one more piece of ass before I left. But she said, no, we weren't going to have sex. I got pissed. Now that I'm leaving, she doesn't want to have sex with me. I figured we had been living together, kind of like a marriage. So, I figured I had it coming. She really didn't fight me, but I knew she didn't want to have sex either. As soon as I got off her, she lost it. She started screaming and punching me. She grabbed a hanger and started beating me with it. I told her to lighten up, but she wouldn't. The next thing I know, she's running down the street screaming. It's three o'clock in the morning and there is snow on the ground."

"I knew this wasn't going to look good," Sam said demonstrating his unique ability to understate the obvious. "I just beat two cases and I knew nobody was going to believe me when I told them this girl was nuts."

The following day, Sam went to the welfare office to inquire about his food stamps. One of the service clerks told him the police were looking for him and that they had been by the office earlier that morning, showing his picture around.

"I called the police and asked if they had a warrant for me," Sam said. Detective Canada told Sam that he was being investigated for rape, and suggested that Sam come to the police station to discuss allegations that he sexually assaulted Ann.

"I knew I was in trouble and had to get out of town," Sam said. "So, I told him I'd be there in about 10 minutes, and to wait on me. I figured I had to get out of Ann Arbor fast." About an hour later, Sam telephoned Canada, who told him he was officially being charged with raping Ann.

Sam telephoned his father and told him about his latest problem. Big Sam and Lucy had enjoyed less than two weeks of tranquility since their son's last acquittal. They both wanted to believe Sam when he told them he hadn't done anything wrong, but they both knew he was lying. Still, Big Sam, unable to deny his namesake, helped his son once again. Big Sam helped Sam get fictitious identification and provided him with money to get out of Michigan.

The following day, Sam telephoned Dr. Bahr and told him that he was having some difficulties with the police in Ann Arbor. "I strongly recommend that you appear at the Ann Arbor Police and talk to them," Dr. Bahr told Sam. It had been ten days since Sam was acquitted of sexually assaulting Lisa and one week since he had moved into the Ann Arbor YMCA.

In January 1976, Greyhound was offering a special promotion for its customers: $250 a month for unlimited travel anywhere in the Continental United States. Sam took advantage of this special offer and with the money provided by his father, purchased a thirty-day bus pass.

On Sunday, January 25, Sam called Dr. Bahr again. "He told me he would not be able to make our preplanned and regular therapy hour on Tuesday due to difficulties with the Ann Arbor Police. I asked him if there was a warrant for his arrest and he said he didn't know. All he knew, was that they wanted to talk to him," Bahr recorded in his journal.

"I just went sight seeing," Sam said. "I went to every major city in the United States. You know every city listed in the newspaper showing the temperature for the major cities, I went to all of them. I had fun for several months, just traveling."

The following day, January 26, Sergeant Schoenrock of the Sterling Heights Police Department wrote a supplemental report to the file, relating to the investigation of the attack on Sandy. "With the findings from St. Clair Shores and Detroit, as well as the dismissal of all charges reference to our case, it should be noted that once again, the defendant, (Sam Consiglio) has ended up with no sex crime felony conviction on his record."

Since Sam had not pleaded guilty as agreed; Schoenrock sought to have the charges against him re-instated. Schoenrock's priority, like that of Canada's, was to locate Sam.

Sam was now living on Greyhound buses. He'd sleep on the bus, getting off in different cities to sometimes sight see or just long enough to eat. At the larger bus stations, he'd sometimes shower. At the smaller stations, those without a shower, he would simply splash water on his face and underarms, (a technique he employed in junior high school that contributed to his poor grooming and hygiene) before moving on to the next city. Sometimes he'd walk around a city for a day before getting on another bus, never really concerned about the direction it was headed. While touring the country, Sam posed as a free-lance writer.

"I would bullshit a lot on the bus," he said. Disguising himself as a writer offered Sam opportunities to initiate conversations with people, especially women who rode the bus alone. But in spite of his masquerade, he felt lonely and was constantly looking for someone with whom he could talk.

"I couldn't call home, that cost money," Sam explained. "So, I called this teen-age runaway hot-line. It didn't cost anything. Then, I just started calling all the hotlines and 800 numbers. I started talking to a lot of different people, all for free. But this one woman in Houston was especially friendly. I told her I might just come to Houston to see her and she said okay."

Sam was near Houston when he made that call. The following day, he telephoned the hotline and told the friendly woman that he was in town and wanted to meet her.

"She was a heavy-set, older woman," Sam said. "She was big, a 400 pound mamma. I didn't like that. But I had been on the road for a while and I went for her. She brought me to her apartment and gave me a bologna sandwich. I felt certain that if I didn't fuck this broad or at least try to penetrate the bitch, somehow, she was going to beat my ass. She was a trucker and had a Harley parked in her living room. I got myself a piece of ass and got out of there. When I finally escaped from her apartment, I vomited as soon as I got outside. This one cured me of calling anymore 800 numbers looking for pussy."

Sam was careful not to remain very long in any one place. Usually, he would walk around whatever city he was in (mostly during the day), eat, and then get back on the bus and sleep while he traveled at night. "I was just looking to survive," Sam said. "I figured the police didn't have a network on the buses. As long as I stayed on the bus, I figured I was okay."

In El Paso, Texas, Sam slightly altered his routine. "I met this girl at the bus station. She needed a place to stay. She didn't look that hot, kind of reminded me of a bag lady. But I said fine, and we rented this room by the hour. As soon as we get in the room, she starts to go to sleep. Then she says, 'You're trying to fuck me aren't you?' Then she tells me I can screw her but that afterward, I have to let her sleep. She took off this thing she was wearing and I couldn't believe it. Her body looked awful. I only fucked her that one time. The next morning, I got up and just took off."

Sam continued on his bus journey, never really concerned about where he was going or if he had already been to that city.

"I loved Birmingham," he said. "I mean, as far as the people are concerned, they are the best, no comparison. In Birmingham, everyone you say hello to says hi back. In New York, nobody would say hi. They would look at me like I was nuts."

In Washington, D.C., Sam visited many of the sights taken in by thousands of tourists every year. The National Monument, the Lincoln Memorial and the White House were some of his favorites. But the sight he enjoyed most was a tour of the J. Edgar Hoover Building, the headquarters of the Federal Bureau of Investigation. "I was a little nervous walking through the building," he said. "I saw this gorgeous blond there, who I thought was a female agent. But now, I think it could have been Hoover himself dressed in drag."

About the time he visited the nation's capital, Sam mailed Ann a card with a picture of a rose on the front. Inside, he wrote a short note telling her that he was sorry for what he had done and asked that she forgive him. Ann called the Ann Arbor Police and turned the card and envelope over to Detective Canada.

After several more weeks of traveling, Sam sought one particular destination. It was a city that revealed a world never experienced before by Sam. The neon lights, the thousands of people crowded into the streets in the early morning hours, and the scent of excitement lured Sam like an animal in heat. He had been traveling on the Greyhound circuit for six weeks when on March 8th he decided to spend the night in Las Vegas.

"I had come up with this plan to find the most gorgeous hooker I could," Sam said. "I mean, the most beautiful women in the world are in Vegas and I wanted to find the most beautiful blond, blue-eyed, call girl in town and bullshit her into thinking I'm a high roller so I could spend as much time as I could with her. And, that's exactly what I did."

It was almost midnight when Sam found a call girl sitting at the bar at the MGM Grand Hotel. "I knew right away that she was a hooker. I mean she is a natural blond, green-eyed, absolutely gorgeous. She told me her name was Dee."

Dee was not the woman's name; her real name was Tricia. She was a working girl trying to make a living and had heard every pick-up line before. Nothing Sam said was new to her. To her, he was just another potential customer. Tricia and Sam talked for a few minutes before settling on a price of $50 "for services to be performed."

"When I met her, my mouth just watered," Sam said. "I just started talking to her, pretending like I was a big shot. I asked her if she wanted to go out somewhere and she asked me how much money I had. I told her money wasn't a problem; that I would pay her whatever she wanted, when I was done of course. I really am good at it, or I was back then," Sam boasted. "But I was good, I really bull-shitted her."

Sam convinced his hired companion they had to leave the hotel, pretending that he was not there alone. They drove to the Minute Man Motel where the velvet pictures of Elvis Presley hanging on the walls remind the visitors that they are not at a resort casino. The hotel served several purposes. Most notably it was a haven for the down and out, a cheap room to sleep off a drunk or to take a hooker for a few hours.

"I had nonstop sex with this woman all night long. I mean my dick never got soft, never. She was the most beautiful woman I had ever been with," Sam said.

In a couple of hours, the sun would rise over the desert town and Sam would return to being just another passenger on a Greyhound Bus.

"It was early in the morning. We just laid there and I told her, honey, when you're ready to leave, you tell me and I'll pay you'," Sam said. Tricia thought she had finished entertaining a wealthy client and was ready to clean up and call it a night when she excused herself to go to the bathroom.

"While she was in the bathroom, I noticed her purse lying there. I had a little money, but not much. I was between checks. I could have gotten my dad to send me some from the bank, but I thought, this is easy. So, I decided to look in her purse to see if she had any money. I'd never done that before. I didn't think of her as a poor person; I thought of her as big business. She had some money in her purse and I took it. As she walked out of the bathroom, she caught me taking the money.

"Does this mean I'm not getting paid?" she asked.

"Yeah, that's what it means, I told her. I then pulled the car keys from her purse and said I'm taking your car, too. I'll call you later and you can pick it up."

Tricia yelled at Sam, "You fuck me all night long, you're not paying me, and, you take my money. Now, you're going to take my car. Why don't you just take my fucking life?"

"Look, I've got to get out of here. I've got to get a ride, I told her. I figured the girls in Vegas worked for the mob. Once this got out, I figured I'm a dead man. I just wanted to get out of there quick so I had to make my move." A sense of panic began to creep over Sam, but he fought it.

"I felt bad," Sam said. "I mean, I had fun with her, I didn't want to leave her like that. She was crying her heart out over my taking her car. I told her I didn't want to take her car but that I had no choice."

"Let me give you a ride. I'll take you wherever you want to go," Tricia begged. "She pleaded with me," Sam said. "So I agreed to let her drive me downtown."

He told Tricia she could drop him off near the bus station. His immediate thoughts were simply to get out of town. Tricia stopped crying as soon as Sam got into her car. As they started driving, she put her foot down on the gas pedal as far as she could and sped down the middle of the Las Vegas strip at speeds of over 80 m.p.h. Sam yelled for her to slow down but Tricia refused. Tricia was too street smart to let this "john" get away with robbing her.

"When the cops pulled us over, she jumped out screaming that I had robbed her," Sam said. "I told the cop, `she's a prostitute, don't believe her.' Then, the cop pulls his gun on me and said `we protect prostitutes in this town.' And then, he fucking arrested me."

Tricia's version of the incident, as she related it to the investigating officers, parallels Sam's but only to a point. Tricia told police that she met Sam, who identified himself as John Henderson, around midnight at the MGM Grand Hotel. She agreed to "perform certain services," including sexual intercourse with him, in return for $50. They went to the Minute Man Motel.

"After we had sex, he tied my arms and feet to the bed and had sexual intercourse with me at least four more times," Tricia told the Las Vegas Police. She told police that Sam had claimed to be a mental patient and he would do weird things like this because all women were against him and that he was going to get even with them. Tricia also told police that Sam threatened her with a knife while she was tied to the bed, as he demanded her money.

Sam was charged with armed robbery and held in the Las Vegas County Jail after he was unable to post a $30,000 bond. "They never found a weapon and I never used one," Sam said. "She manipulated me. She got me." Sam was booked in the Las Vegas County Jail under the name of John Matthew Henderson after he provided the police identification indicating that was his name. The money Sam had on him, $96, most of which he had stolen from Tricia, was placed into evidence and would be produced later in court.

Sergeant Don Simons, a detective with the Las Vegas Metropolitan Police Department, reported that torn sheets with knots were found inside the room at the Minute Man Motel. Just outside the front door, Simons found a knife.

"I asked John Matthew Henderson (Sam) if his rights had been explained to him and he said yes," Simons reported. "He said he had never before been arrested and that he was sorry that he had done this act and that he meant no harm. All he wanted, he said, was his money back. He said he had not threatened Tricia with bodily harm and told me again that he was sorry for what he had done."

Sam spent just over three weeks in the Las Vegas jail where he worked as a trustee. On several occasions, the jailers would call out the name "John Henderson," but Sam would fail to answer. "I just forgot that I was using that name," Sam said. "I think they started to get a little suspicious."

After three weeks, the local assistant district attorney was required to present the facts in the case before a judge to determine if sufficient evidence existed to hold Sam over for trial. When the hearing was set to begin, the prosecution's chief witness, Tricia, failed to appear in court. The prosecutor asked the judge for a postponement, hoping to parlay the delay into an opportunity to find his witness. But the judge refused the young district attorney's request, telling him that John Henderson had been in jail for almost 30 days. Since there was no victim, the judge dismissed the charges against Sam and ordered that he be released.

"I couldn't believe it," Sam said. "I robbed that fucking hooker and they never cross-checked my prints. If they had, they would have learned who I really was and the D.A. would have gotten his delay, especially if they could have shown that I lied about my identity. But they never checked, never learned that there was an outstanding warrant for me in

Ann Arbor. So, now, I've got to be a smart-ass. I go to see the D.A. and ask him for my $96."

"What are you doing here?" the prosecutor asked.

"You owe me some money," Sam said. "I want my money."

But the district attorney refused to give Sam any money and ordered him out of his office. Sam went straight to see the judge who, moments before, had dismissed the charges against him. "The judge called the D.A. over to his office and gave him 30 minutes to give me my money. After the prosecutor turned it over to me, I went to the Lucky Lady Casino and hit a jackpot for $500. I remember it was the first of April, April Fools Day. Right after that, I got on the fucking bus and headed toward L.A."

On April 12, Sam called Dr. Bahr from Los Angeles. "Sam said that he was on his way home to Michigan and would call me when he reached the area," Dr. Bahr recorded in his journal.

When he arrived in Los Angeles, Sam got off the bus and decided he'd been traveling long enough. He planned on staying in L.A. and decided to drop in on his cousin Gilbert. But Gilbert wasn't especially happy to see Sam. They had never been close and he had always been apprehensive of Sam. Gilbert grew more suspicious of his manipulative cousin after discovering that Sam was using the alias of John Henderson.

Gilbert quickly grew tired of his intimidating cousin and after learning of the outstanding warrants for his arrest, decided it was in his best interests to get rid of Sam. So, Gilbert arranged to throw a small party to celebrate Sam's 25th birthday on May 17.

"I was visiting my cousin Gilbert," Sam said. "It was supposed to be a surprise. I even waited outside for awhile before going in."

What Gilbert didn't tell Sam was that, after learning about the outstanding warrants in Michigan, he added the Los Angeles police to the guest list. While a few people yelled surprise, the Los Angeles Police yelled, "You're under arrest." On the night of his 25th birthday, as a gift from his cousin Gilbert, Sam, at gunpoint, was handcuffed, placed in the back of a police car and taken to the L.A. County Jail where he was held without bond.

Sam knew he'd have trouble earning "trustee" status in the L.A. Jail. Unlike the work camps he was accustomed to in Michigan where he could get fresh eggs made to order, the L.A. County Jail was a melting pot. He didn't intend to stay there long. "I called the Ann Arbor Police, collect," Sam said. "I agreed to waive extradition if the police would send someone for me right away." Three days later, Sam was escorted by Detective Canada and two other Ann Arbor police officers aboard an airplane and flown back to Michigan to stand trial for sexually assaulting Ann. This time, he was held in the Washtenaw County Jail on a $50,000 bond.

Four days later, on May 24, Lucy Consiglio called Dr. Bahr at the Center for Forensic Psychiatry. "My son is in the county jail and would like to see you," she said. Dr. Bahr told Sam's mother that he would see him within the week.

It was another four days before Dr. Bahr finally met with Sam. Their meeting lasted about an hour, with most of the time spent re-engaging in their "therapeutic alliance." Dr. Bahr agreed to meet with Sam on a weekly basis while Sam was awaiting trial.

On June 8, Sam appeared before judge Thomassen in the 15th District Court in Ann Arbor. Represented by an attorney appointed to him by the Washtenaw County Public Defender's Office, Sam listened as Ann related the events of the night of her 21st birthday. There was no testimony provided by any defense witnesses at the hearing. Leonard Kowalski, the prosecutor, moved to bind Sam over to the circuit court for arraignment and trial. The judge granted the request. The judge also granted the appointed public defender's motion to have Sam's bond reduced from $50,000 to $25,000. But even that was too much money. Big Sam was unable to help his son post this bond. He had over-extended himself the past year and had offered his home as surety far too often. This time, Sam would remain in jail as he awaited trial.

On October 13, while awaiting trial in Ann Arbor, Sam agreed to plead guilty to a reduced misdemeanor charge of assault and battery for having attacked Sandy. Sandy now refused to appear in court or testify against

Sam. It had been over four years since Sam assaulted her and she had experienced enough frustration and anxiety as a result of the judicial delays to pursue the matter further. She wanted desperately to forget the incident and she was equally disillusioned with both the prosecutor's office, and Sam's defense attorney, Don Ricard. No longer having a victim to testify for the prosecution, the Macomb County Prosecutor's Office accepted Sam's plea to a reduced misdemeanor charge of assault. Judge Edward Gallagher, who had refused to accept Sam's negotiated *nolo* plea that would have exposed him to a prison sentence of three to five years, sentenced Sam to 90 days in jail. Since Sam had already spent 90 days in jail in connection with this case, he was given credit for time served and released back into the custody of the Washtenaw County Sheriff's Department. The case involving Sandy was now closed. And Sam was still not a convicted felon.

On November 17, Sam, represented by his court-appointed public defender, appeared in the Circuit Court of Washtenaw County. "I had only one defense," Sam said. "I kept telling my attorney, she's a nut. The broad's a nut, just keep on her, she'll get mad and do something. He kept telling me that it was a risk, that if she didn't do something we would lose the case. I had to help this guy with the defense."

The young court-appointed attorney listened to his client's advice and continued an aggressive line of questioning during his cross-examination of Ann. Sam appeared to be enjoying his situation immensely, smiling most of the time, sometimes smirking, like he knew something everyone else in the courtroom didn't.

Ann considered herself a free spirit. She had lived as part of the 60's and 70's drug culture and had been part of the anti-war movement. She was not accustomed to the disciplined court environment that was part of the so-called "establishment", which was challenged by many young people her age at that time. It's not certain at what point Ann had had enough of the questioning by Sam's attorney to cause the outburst. But as Sam had predicted, Ann did something that turned the jury to Sam's favor.

"She flung a chair across the courtroom," Sam said. "She won it for me." The trial was a short one. Once again, Sam never took the witness stand and the defense never called any witnesses after Ann's outburst. They rested immediately after the prosecution did. And the jury again, never heard any testimony about Sam's previous arrests for sexual misconduct. After witnessing Ann's emotional display, the jury adjourned for less than thirty minutes before returning a verdict of "not guilty." Once again, Sam was acquitted of all the charges against him and once again, he got into a car driven by his father and went home to St. Clair Shores.

As he had for most of his life, Sam found himself living upstairs in his parent's house. He returned to the type of world that he knew best; delivering pizzas part time. At the same time, he started driving a taxi for the Carriage Cab Company in Mount Clemens. He'd been able to get the job since his application for a taxi cab driver's license had been approved without the standard police checks. At the time of his license application, Sam's police record included four assault convictions, one conviction for sexual misconduct and two convictions for obstruction of justice. The city of Detroit had previously denied Sam's application for a "cabbies license" after his criminal record was disclosed during customary police records checks.

"We denied it last July because we didn't want a person of his character molesting women in our city," Detroit Police Officer George Penick said. Carriage Cab, for reasons unknown, failed to conduct these same checks.

During the time since Sam's Social Security benefits were terminated, he had aggressively sought to have them reinstated.On November 1, 1977, Dr. Raymond G. Mercier wrote Social Security Administration officials that, "Mr. Consiglio does in fact have a serious emotional illness. I do believe that the most accurate diagnosis would be hysterical neurosis, dissociative type, but I wish to add, that frankly, Mr. Consiglio is functioning in a psychotic state most of the time." Dr. Mercier also wrote, "I do not believe that Mr. Consiglio has been qualified to compete on the open labor market during the time in question. I believe all the evidence in this case is consistent with the findings of a serious mental disorder from the alleged onset date of June 7, 1974, until present."

Eighteen days later, on November 18, in response to Sam's appeal for social security benefits, George L. Carpenter, an Administrative Law Judge, signed the necessary order authorizing benefits to Sam.

The order signed by Carpenter was retroactive to April 1975. Shortly after the decision, Sam received a check from the Social Security Administration for $9,600. He quit his part-time job delivering pizzas and purchased a new 1978 Oldsmobile. He also began receiving $492 a month in social security benefits.

"I never knew I was entitled to this money until this woman mentioned it when I was in the psychiatric hospital," Sam said. "I had gotten a few checks and then they stopped sending them. They told me that I wasn't sick enough to get paid. They wanted me to pay the money back and that's when I appealed. I had to fake it because I wasn't paying anything back. So, I faked mental illness. The Social Security Administration paid to have three psychiatrists interview me. I just had to prove that I was incompetent, which was easy. A lot of guys do it. Just tell the doctor you're hearing voices and then when they show you the inkblot test, get everything fucking distorted. You could make yourself psychotic; it's not that hard, I mean anybody that has a brain could do it. The system is fucked up. A lot of guys do it that don't want to go to trial. They fake their own illness. The doctors can't prove that you're not hearing voices. The doctors fucked with me. They gave me these puzzles, four blocks and told me to put them together. I couldn't do it; I got frustrated and threw them. I was good. I was mad and determined. When I had to put on an Academy Award performance, I did it and everybody was there to see it," Sam said.

Chapter 7

Lying is Usually the Utmost in Insincerity

Sam met Lila when he was delivering pizzas. Lila was certainly not attractive. She had two young children from a previous relationship. But she slept with Sam and that was all he really required from any woman at that point. The next day, Lila and her two children moved in with Sam in the attic apartment of his parent's house. They lived there only a few weeks before renting the downstairs flat of an old house in Mount Clemens.

Around the same time Californians voted in favor of a State Constitutional Amendment called Proposition 13, cutting property taxes generated from homeowners by over $7 billion. That same year, in Jonestown, Guyana, over 900 members of the People's Temple, led by religious zealot Jim Jones, died in a mass suicide after drinking Kool-Aid laced with cyanide. The first baby conceived outside the human body was born to a British couple. The technique, called the test tube baby technique, was developed by two British researchers who estimated that this method of artificial insemination could help one fifth to one half of infertile women achieve pregnancy. The Bee Gees recorded "Staying Alive" as disco enjoyed its prominence. Barbara Streisand and Neil Diamond sang, "You Don't Bring Me Flowers" and James Belushi starred in "Animal House", while Robert DeNiro was the "Deer Hunter". The year was 1978.

It was during the first week in April 1978, that Carol Lynn, a 15-year-old girl, telephoned the Carriage Cab Company. Carol, who lived in Sterling Heights with her mother and stepfather, needed a ride to meet some of her friends that afternoon at the local shopping mall. Carol's parents had divorced several years earlier. When she was younger, an uncle allegedly had sexually molested her. But Carol kept the incident to herself for over five years before telling her family. The stress and family turmoil that followed contributed to her mother and father divorcing.

Carol had been a troubled child. She had difficulty in school, which was a result of her inability to cope with its social atmosphere. She was subsequently placed on social probation from high school, which required her to do most of her schoolwork at home. The Oakland County Youth Authority had also placed Carol on probation after she was caught shoplifting. The probation followed a two-week stay in a youth home where Carol claimed to have witnessed an assault and attempted murder of one of the matrons. She testified in court about the attempt on the matron's life, causing her added fear and anxiety about possible retribution. Carol attended regular therapy and counseling sessions in hopes of relieving some of the tensions and pressures she was experiencing. She was afraid her stepfather didn't like her and she felt that her probation officer was not very understanding or sympathetic to her problems. One of the things Carol feared most was being sent back to the youth home. When the cab arrived to take her to meet her friends, she met Sam.

"He seemed almost nice, kind of brotherly," Carol said. "He told me how pretty I was and asked me my age. I told him I was 15."

Carol told Sam she was on probation for having been caught shoplifting the previous summer, and was afraid of being sent back to the youth home. "He told me that he knew a good lawyer who could make sure I was never sent back to the youth facility and that if my parents could not help me he would get his lawyer to help," Carol said later.

Sam continued making small talk with Carol as he drove her to meet her friends. "Have you ever used any marijuana or used any speed?" he asked.

"Sure," she answered.

Sam told Carol that his sister Grace sold marijuana and mescaline. He offered to take her to meet Grace right away in order to buy some drugs. He also asked her if she would like to go out with him. Carol declined both offers. When they arrived at the scheduled stop, Carol paid Sam for her fare and got out of the cab to meet her friends.

Over the next two weeks, Sam called Carol several times, hoping to convince her to go out with him. Carol had been successful in avoiding most of Sam's calls, opting instead to have her mother take messages. When her mother asked who Sam was, Carol lied, saying he was the older brother of a friend.

When the telephone rang at Carol's home on the morning of April 16, she answered it. It was Sam.

"He asked if I would go out with him that night," she said. "I thought he might be able to put me in touch with an attorney to help me with some of my probation problems, so, I told him I would go out with him. He asked if he should meet me somewhere or pick me up at home. I told him to pick me up at the house about 6:30 that night."

When Sam arrived, Carol's mother and stepfather watched from the living room window as Sam sat in the car waiting for Carol. Carol's mother told her that the man looked too old for her to go out with but Carol reassured her that everything was all right. It was Sunday evening, and her mother asked Carol not to be out to late. Carol told her that she would be home early.

"The first thing Sam did was stop at a convenience store in Utica, a neighboring city, to buy some beer. We then drove around for a while. He took a lot of turns and I really wasn't sure where I was. He was drinking the whole time and I probably drank a half a can of beer myself. He then offered me a black molly, a brown pill that acted like speed. I took one because I didn't want to make him mad. He seemed like such a nice guy, easy to talk to. He seemed very understanding. He told me that he wanted to go to his sister's house, I think to get more drugs, but then he pulled into the parking lot of the Twin Rock Motel. I still wasn't sure where I was, but I remember it was raining. I realized that I was probably in some danger. I started to get scared, but I didn't really know what to do. I didn't even know where I was."

Sam got out of the car and told Carol that he would be right back. He was gone for only a couple of minutes. When he returned, he told Carol he had gotten them a room. She told him she didn't want to go into the motel, but he told her they would just finish drinking the beer and watch some television.

"He started acting weird in a way difficult to explain, but I felt sure that if I didn't do as he said, that I would be harmed in some way," Carol said. "He never threatened me but I still felt threatened. I felt I would be beaten if I didn't do what he told me to, so I went into the room with him."

Sam turned on the television and began watching a rerun of the "I Love Lucy Show" as he sat on the edge of the bed. Carol sat in a chair next to a small table across from Sam.

"He asked me to come sit next to him, but I said no," Carol said. "He was asking in a nice way, but I was scared. I kept telling him I didn't want to and then he got mad and pulled me by my wrist onto the bed with him. He then unbuttoned my shirt and threw it off of me. I was scared and told him that I had to go to the bathroom and he said okay. I got up and went into the bathroom and shut the door. I was only in there for a few minutes, hoping he might calm down. I was really afraid that he might come in after me so I came out after a few minutes. When I did, he was standing in the room completely naked in front of the television. I saw my shirt on the floor and reached down to pick it up. When I did, he grabbed me and unsnapped my bra. He then started pulling my jeans off. I tried to keep them on, but he kept brushing my hands away as he climbed on top of me, almost sitting on me. He then started kissing me on the mouth and neck. After that, he rolled on top of me and pushed himself in me. He was very hard. He began bouncing up and down on me violently. His face became red and he started to sweat all over me. The sweat was pouring off him. I remember him having an awful body odor. He was moving up and down very hard and then he ejaculated. I could see semen dripping down my legs. Sam sighed heavily and rolled over onto his back and pulled me next to him."

Carol Lynn was scared, not knowing what to do as this man, twice her size and 12 years older, lay there exhausted from his attack.

"After a few minutes, he told me that he would eat me if I would suck him," Carol said. "I couldn't, the idea made me sick and I told him no. He then got angry and told me I better suck him. He wasn't asking me, he was telling me. I was afraid of what he would do if I didn't. He laid on his back and I took him in my mouth for about 15 seconds. It really made me sick and I couldn't do it anymore. He rolled me onto my side and shoved himself in me again. After he finished, I told him I had to be home by 9 p.m. because my probation officer would sometimes call, checking up on me. We got dressed and started driving home. On the way, he asked me if I wanted to get something to eat. I told him no. He then asked if I wanted to go out with him again and I told him I wasn't sure. I thought that if I told him no, he would get mad and not take me directly home. Once he got me home, he asked again if I would go out with him and this time I told him no, that I never wanted to see him again."

Carol jumped out of the car and raced into the house as Sam drove away. She went straight to her room, deciding not to tell her parents anything about the attack.

On April 15, about the same time Sam was calling Carol trying to get a date with her, Connie arrived at Selfridge Field Air Force Base in Mount Clemens. She was beginning a nine-day encampment, which was part of her obligation as a U.S. Air Force reservist. Connie was 21 and had been in the Air Force Reserve for less than two years. Performing her reserve duty at Selfridge Field was convenient since she lived in Bellsville, just an hour's drive from the base.

It was two days later, around 5 p.m. when Connie, having been at Selfridge Field only three days, decided to go to the base commissary to shop for a few personal items. The weather had been rainy since she arrived to begin her reserve duty. The light rain continued as she finished her shopping and walked, with her arms wrapped around a large brown shopping bag, toward her car. Her car was parked far enough away from the commissary entrance to allow the rain to dampen more than just her spirits. Her mood was dampened even more as she tried several times to start her car. With each turn of the key, the sound of nothing more than a grinding gear told to her that she was about to get even wetter as she was forced to walk to her quarters, a small apartment some distance from the commissary.

"I had just dropped off a fare at the base," Sam said. "I noticed this woman walking with a bag in the rain. I asked her if she needed some help and she says could you give me a ride back to my place?"

Sam drove Connie back to her apartment, then offered to help her get her car started.

"I almost gagged on the gas fumes," Sam said. "I knew she had flooded the car. I just held down the gas pedal all the way to the floor and turned the key. It started right up."

Connie was happy to have her car running again. But she allowed Sam to follow her home in case it broke down again.

"He asked if he could come by sometime to talk," Connie said. "I told him it would be okay and that we could visit in the lobby room."

The following evening, just three days after his attack on Carol, and one day after meeting Connie, Sam drove off to buy a puppy for his live-in girlfriend, Lila.

"I was going to surprise her, and that was the only thing on my mind at the time," Sam said. "It started raining harder and I found myself in the area of Selfridge Field. I decided not to get the puppy. Instead, I went over to see Connie."

Mieczyslow Swidwinski, a Department of Defense police officer, was assigned to security at the main gate of the base that night when Sam arrived. Sam told the guard he worked for Carriage Cab and wanted to enter the base to pick up a fare. "I asked him why the pick-up was being made in a privately owned automobile," Swidwinski said. "He told me that his cab was in the shop. He showed me his company's identification card, at which time I allowed him onto the base."

"It was sometime after 6 p.m. when he came to my door and asked if he could visit," Connie said.

She agreed and told Sam they could go into the lobby that served as a common area. They talked briefly, mostly about Sam's new Oldsmobile, which he had recently purchased with his Social Security money. He was proud to show off the new car, explaining that he had paid cash for it and suggested they go for a ride. Reluctantly, she agreed.

"We went for a short ride," she said. "I don't remember all the roads, except that we drove through New Baltimore. He told me he had worked for a trucking firm and talked about his visits to California, Las Vegas and New Mexico. He seemed very polite and courteous."

"I asked her if it was okay to park and just talk for awhile since it was raining and the roads were bad, some of which were flooding," Sam said.

Connie agreed but told him that she would be able to stay for just a short while since she had other plans for the evening.

"After we stopped, Sam tried to kiss me," Connie said. Sam told her to kiss him, to hug him. When she didn't, Sam grabbed her by the hair, trying to push her down in the seat.

"I put my arm around her, but she didn't pull away," Sam said. "I went to kiss her and she kissed me. Then she pulled away."

"He told me he wasn't going to rape me," Connie said. "He said what he was doing was not rape if he didn't take my pants off. I pleaded with him not to hurt me. I grabbed his beard hoping I could stop him but he placed both hands around my neck and started choking me. He was violent, and said he just wanted to dry rock me." She had never heard that phrase used before, and had no idea what Sam meant to do to her.

"He was on top of me and forced his hands between my legs. He grabbed at me and unzipped my pants. He kept trying to place his fingers inside me. He slapped me across the face and knocked my glasses off. I was afraid for my life," Connie said.

As she struggled, Sam's size and strength easily overpowered her ability to resist his assault. "I kept trying to resist and grabbed at his beard. I kept my legs closed as tight as I could," she said.

"He then moved his hands under my shirt and began fondling my breasts. I just kept crying," Connie said later, fighting back tears as she recalled the incident. After Sam ejaculated, Connie asked him to take her back to the base.

"He then became very apologetic. He told me the reason he did what he did was because he didn't think he stood a chance with me any other way. He even offered to take me to a doctor and pay the bill if he hurt me."

Sam even offered to take Connie to the police if she wanted. But she was still frightened. Her immediate concern was for her safety. She also wanted to get back to the base.

"As we approached the gate, Sam stopped the car and told me to get out, claiming if he went onto the base, the MPs (military police) would beat him up," she said. "I got out of the car and ran to the gate as fast as I could."

It was about 8 p.m. when Patrolman Robert Scott, a GS 5, Department of Defense security officer, working the main entrance, noticed a woman in what he described later as an hysterical condition, run up to the gate. "She claimed to have just been sexually attacked by a man off base," Scott reported.

Officer James Tokarski, on patrol when Connie arrived at the main gate, later heard a description of her alleged attacker. Tokarski remembered stopping a Carriage Cab driver a month earlier for speeding. He also remembered the driver's name being Sam. He checked the log entries and found the driver to have been Sam Consiglio, a white male with a date of birth of May 17, 1951. A description on the log claimed that Sam was 5'10" tall, weighed 185 pounds, had shoulder length hair, a moustache and a full beard. The security police referred the investigation to the Macomb County Sheriff's Department.

Detective Jerry Bomber had been with the Macomb County Sheriff's Department for 13 years. He had known Sam for almost eight of those years, having first met him in 1970 during a routine prisoner pick-up and transport. "I remember the first time I ever met him," Bomber recalled. "From the time he was placed in the back of the van in Oakland County until we arrived in Mount Clemens, he never shut up. He was quite the talker. Just listening to him during that drive, I knew this was someone who was dangerous."

Detective Bomber showed Connie a series of police photographs of possible suspects. One of the photographs was of Sam. But she was unable to make a positive identification. Bomber was convinced it was Sam who had attacked Connie, but he was unable to prove it because the victim was unable to identify him from the photographs.

"I asked her to get in the car with me and we drove around together," Detective Bomber reported. "I wanted to try and locate the place where the assault had occurred." In less than an hour, Connie was able to identify the place she had been attacked. She did so by remembering a newly constructed building in Clinton Township on the western edge of Macomb County.

As they drove back to the police station, Bomber and Connie passed a vacant lot across from the Carriage Cab Company. Parked in the lot was Sam's new Oldsmobile. Connie recognized the car. Connie recognized the car as the one driven by Sam when he tried to rape her. Bomber now had enough probable cause to get a warrant for Sam's arrest, charging him with assault with intent to commit criminal sexual conduct in the second degree.

Detective Bomber telephoned and left a message for Sam at the cab-company. The message was simple; he wanted to speak to him. Sam returned the call and said he would come to the sheriff's department around 6:00 p.m. Instead of waiting, Sam appeared at 3:45 that afternoon, more than two hours early. Bomber immediately placed Sam under arrest and advised him of his rights. Sam told Bomber he understood his rights, that he waived his right to counsel, and that he did indeed wish to talk to him.

In a tape-recorded interview, Sam told Detective Bomber that on April 18, he had dropped off a passenger at the Selfridge Air Force Base when he noticed a woman walking with a bag. Sam said it had been raining, so he offered her a ride and the woman said yes. Afterward, Sam said he helped her get her car started.

"She was very happy that I was able to get her car started," Sam said. "She told me she spends about one week a month at the base. And, if I had any time off between now and Sunday to come and see her. I said okay, will do. The next evening, I went to visit her at the base. I knocked on her door. She answers and says something about sitting in the lobby and talking. I said, instead of that, why don't we go out for a ride in my new car, and she says okay."

"We drove around for a while," Sam said. "It was raining and the roads were very wet, some were even flooding. I asked if we could just park for a while and she said yes. I put my arm around her and she didn't pull away. I went to kiss her and she kissed me. After she kisses me, she pulls away. I still had my arm around her and I pulled her toward me. She got frightened and says, 'You're not going to rape me are you?' I said, no, I'm not going to rape you. But she didn't believe me because she just grabbed hold of my beard and yanked it. She had a really good hold on it. My reflexes took over and I came around with my left hand and I hit her in the face and she let go. I didn't think I'd hit her that hard though. After that, I let go. She was scared. She thought I was going to rape her. She was acting flaky. On the way back to the base, I kept trying to convince her that I was not going to rape her, but I didn't think she believed me. I got a very uneasy feeling about her. I thought she might get some of her friends to jump me if I went back onto the base. So, I let her off outside the gate," Sam told Bomber.

During the question and answer session, Bomber asked Sam if he ever put his hands around her neck.

"No, Jerry, no." Sam said as he tried to personalize his relationship with his interrogator, acting as if they were old friends.

"But you state you slapped her," Bomber said.

"Yeah, with an open hand."

"Did you put your hand underneath her blouse?"

"I never touched her parts in anyway, Jerry, never", Sam told the detective.

"It was very apparent that Sam was comfortable around the police. And, it was very clear that Sam thought he could easily out-smart the police," Bomber said later. This was not a startling revelation. There was ample evidence found in the number of acquittals that Sam had obtained to substantiate Bomber's theory.

"Did you unzip her pants?" Bomber asked as he continued questioning Sam about the assault on Connie.

"No, that's why the charge is what it is, huh? Is that what she said?" Sam asked.

"Did you put your hands between her legs?"

"No," Sam snapped back.

"Did you offer to take her to the police station?"

"Yeah, I did."

"When would that have been?" Bomber asked, confused as to why Sam would make such an offer.

"Just before I got to the base," Sam said. "I shouldn't have hit a woman, even though she poured beer down me. Not supposed to hit a woman," Sam said as he began to cry. "If she wanted to file assault and battery against me, then cool," Sam said. The tears and emotional display were still very present. But they didn't fool Bomber.

"When you asked her if she wanted to go to the police station, what did she say?" Bomber asked.

"She said no, you didn't do nothing wrong," Sam claimed.

When the question and answer session ended, Sam was taken to a cell and held pending the posting of a $10,000 bond.

On April 21, after pleading not guilty to assault with intent to commit criminal sexual conduct in the second degree, Sam, with the help of a bail bondsmen and his parents, posted a $10,000 bond. He was also ordered to undergo an evaluation of his competency to stand trial. Sam went home to his common-law wife, Lila, and the two made plans to get married. Sam also went back to work driving a taxi for the Carriage Cab Company.

It was sometime during the first week of May 1978, when Barbara, who was 27 years old, watched a Carriage Cab approach her home. The driver got out of the cab and walked slowly to her front door to ask if she had called for a taxi. Barbara was surprised by the question.

"I told the driver that I did not call for a cab," Barbara said. "He introduced himself as Sam Consiglio and after a few minutes of conversation, he left."

A week later, another woman, Susan, did telephone the Carriage Cab Company. Her car had broken down and she needed a ride home.

"On the way home, the driver introduced himself as Sam," Susan said. "He was very friendly. He told me that he had worked for a furniture company in Fort Lauderdale and I told him that I had a residence in Florida before moving to Sterling Heights. When we got to my house, he asked if he could take me out sometime. I told him that I had a steady boyfriend and couldn't go out with him. He was very nice about it and drove away."

Sometime in mid-May, Sam returned to Barbara's house. "Sam told me he knew I had not called but that he merely wanted to get to know me better. He asked if he could come inside for a drink of water," Barbara said. "He came in for about 10 minutes and we talked about nothing in particular. He left, but a little while later he came back with some cold drinks and roses. This upset me; I didn't know what to do but I accepted the soda and the flowers but told him I had a busy schedule and he would have to leave. He agreed to go and as he did, he grabbed me and kissed me very quickly on the lips. I never expected him to do this. He left right away without anything else happening."

It was about 7 a.m. on May 31, when Susan heard someone knocking at her front door. "I looked through the viewing port to see who it was and saw it was Sam, the cab driver," she said. "He was knocking very loud. I didn't want any contact with him so I didn't answer the door. He left and walked toward his car, but then he came back and started knocking real loud again. I didn't answer the door but could see that he was turning the doorknob and pressing against the door. He couldn't open it because I had set the deadbolt, and after a few minutes, he left and never returned."

About 30 minutes later, Barbara answered a knock at her door. "It was Sam," Barbara told the police. "He asked if he could come in and I told him no. He said he had just been to the hospital for minor surgery and that he wasn't feeling well and asked if he could come in and lie down. I told him if he was in pain, he should not have been released from the hospital and if he felt weak, he should lie down in his own car. When I wouldn't let him in, he got into his car and left."

It was just 30 minutes after Sam had been to Barbara's home, when the ringing of her telephone awakened Debra, who worked as barmaid. Debra had been asleep in her apartment with her young son by her side. When she awoke to answer the phone, she could see a man standing at the foot of her bed, staring at her. Debra got up and walked quickly past the man and headed down the stairs to the first floor of her townhouse. The man followed her down the stairs. The phone was still ringing, but Debra walked to the front door and told the man to leave. "I thought at first, that the man may have been from the apartment complex maintenance crew with some sort of legitimate reason for coming in the apartment," Debra said. "I answered the phone and it was my friend Claudia. I told her to hold on, there was a man in my apartment. I had never seen him before and felt he had no reason whatsoever for coming in without my permission."

Debra put the phone down and asked her visitor his name and what he was doing in her apartment.

"I'm John. Don't you remember me?" the man asked.

"No," Debra said. "I think you should leave." "He insisted that he knew me and told me my name was Debra and told me that I had a little boy. He insisted that I should have remembered him. I kept telling him I didn't remember him and kept trying to usher him out of the door. He then said I had told him he could come back when he had some money. At this point, I started hollering at him, to get out of my house and he did."

Debra watched as the man got into a 1978 blue Oldsmobile and drove away. As he did, she wrote down the license plate number and told her friend Claudia she would call her back. Debra wanted to call the police and report the man she had found in her apartment.

"I remember calling Debra at exactly 8 a.m.," Claudia later told police. "I remember the phone rang for an awfully long time. In fact, I put the phone down, and went to the bathroom and rinsed my hands and face with water. When I got back, the phone was still ringing. When Deb finally answered, she said, 'Hold on, there's a man in my house.' I could only hear one side of the conversation. I heard Deb say, 'Honey, I don't know you, you've got the wrong person.' Then, I could hear a man's voice say 'Well, I know you.' Both Deb and the man appeared to be shouting, their voices were certainly raised, and I was getting nervous. When Deb got back on the phone, she told me she didn't know who he was but that he had left."

Officer A.K. May received the radio call to answer a complaint regarding an alleged unlawful entry at Debra's apartment in Sterling Heights. The police dispatcher gave a description of the suspect identified as "John" and the blue Oldsmobile that had just left the vicinity of the alleged break in. Before Patrolman May was able to arrive at the apartment to take what he thought would be just another routine report, he heard a report over his radio from Officer Morrison. Morrison had found the vehicle described moments earlier in the broadcast, in the area of Canal Road and Garfield, in Clinton Township. May raced to meet Morrison, who had pulled Sam over and was detaining him just long enough for May to arrive. May and Morrison asked Sam if he had been to Debra's apartment.

"He told us that he had been there to collect a taxi fare which she had owed him from a month ago," May reported. "He said he had knocked on her door and entered after hearing the phone ring. He claimed he walked upstairs and found her to be asleep. I asked Morrison to take him to the police station while I went to meet with Debra."

"I didn't notice anything missing," Debra told May as he completed the police report. She did say later, she was certain that her purse had been gone through and that a piece of white drapery cord, which had been hanging on a clothing valet in the bedroom, had been moved. She also said that a pair of freshly washed pantyhose, which had been inside her dresser drawer, had been removed and laid on top of the dresser.

Just under 45 minutes after Debra called the police, Sam was charged with breaking and entering. After being advised of his rights, Sam told May he had met Debra several weeks before when he had picked her up in his cab. "She had propositioned me," Sam told May. "I told her I didn't have any money and she told me to come back when I did. I went back today, because I had some money."

During the booking process, Sam was fingerprinted and photographed. Among Sam's personal affects, was a series of small slips of paper containing the first names and telephone numbers of six women including Carol, Susan and Barbara.

Less than an hour after Sam's arrest, he was questioned by Officer Gerard Griesbeck of the Crime Prevention Division. Griesbeck had grown up with Sam, and they had gone to school together. "I had just come in from my shift on patrol when I saw Sam sitting in the holding cell," he said.

It had been several years since Griesbeck had seen his childhood friend. "Sam was always a little different. He was always overweight, a bit sloppy. He could be a troublemaker, always looking for attention, but he was certainly friendly. When we were in the sixth grade, a number of us were selected to be safety boys. We would stand at certain corners in the mornings and afternoons and make sure no one jumped into oncoming traffic at the crosswalks. Sam had not been selected to be a safety boy, not for any particular reason, we just had enough people already. But Sam wanted to be in the safety patrol very badly. He was very big for his age and authoritative. The safety patrol offered a degree of authority by virtue of its position. Perhaps he saw this as a way of legitimizing his influence over people. I was on the student council and I made a pitch to get him in the safety patrol. Based on my recommendation, he got in. He was a nice guy."

Griesbeck and Sam drifted apart in junior high school. Griesbeck was athletic and Sam wasn't. Griesbeck concentrated on sports, ultimately playing football and baseball in high school before going on to Wayne State University to major in police administration. Sam went to work in a local neighborhood grocery and also into the criminal justice system, although from a different direction.

"I remember Sam playing one year of little league football with us on the Green Hornets," Griesbeck recalled. "He always had trouble making the weight requirement. The age limits for the league restricted how much a person could weigh. Sam didn't play much that season. The fact he was on the team at all after having not been picked when the final selections were made was because Big Sam had called the coaches and insisted his son be put back on the team."

Before talking to Sam, Griesbeck notified his superiors that he had known him for almost 20 years.

"Sam told me he had been operated on earlier that morning at a hospital to have a cyst removed from the lower part of his back. He then claimed to have gone to Barbara's home in order to comfort her child before an upcoming hospital visit. Sam also told me that he had also gone to Debra's. He claimed that the screen door was closed but that the stronger interior door was open. He claimed to have knocked several times but got no answer. After the phone started ringing, he stepped inside to see if it was going to be answered."

"I was surprised she didn't recognize me," Sam told Griesbeck. "I had met her several weeks prior when I gave her a ride in my cab. When we got to her house, she offered me a glass of water. After some casual conversation, she propositioned me. I refused, and told her that I could get it without paying for it," Sam said. "This is the truth, Jerry. Lying is the furthest thing on my mind," he told his childhood friend.

Griesbeck prepared his report, describing the events as Sam related them. At the conclusion, Griesbeck wrote: "It is this officer's opinion that Mr. Consiglio's statement is basically true. He probably did visit all the places he says but he isn't as innocent as he says. Sam appears to have two personalities. On one hand, he is innocently naive and will do anything for a friend. But on the other hand, he can become an untamed, violent monster when some small incident doesn't go his way. Sam is also very narrow-minded and this may explain why he acts as he does once he is caught."

"During the interview, Sam was very emotional and appeared to mean exactly what he said and claimed that lying was the furthest thing from his mind. Because of his strong mindedness, he probably tends to block out certain unpleasant things. I truly hope that Sam is sent to a mental institution and doesn't talk some foolish doctor into believing he's incapable of inflicting any harm on anyone," Griesbeck wrote. Griesbeck knew that his old friend had lied throughout the interview and that Sam was becoming increasingly disconnected from reality.

Just less than an hour after Griesbeck had questioned his childhood friend, Detective J. Paul Carey met with Sam. Carey, who joined the Sterling Heights Police Department the same day as Griesbeck in 1973, was assigned to the General Crimes section of the detective bureau. "I advised him of his rights," Carey said. "Sam told me that he had met Debra four to six weeks prior when he had given her a ride in his cab. Sam claimed that he told Debra about his new car in an attempt to impress her and that after a short conversation she offered to have sex with him for $20. Sam claimed he told her that he didn't have any money and that she told him to come back when he did."

Sam told Carey the same basic story he had told Griesbeck. "He emphatically denied he had gone upstairs," Carey reported.

"I never went beyond a few feet just inside the front door on the first floor," Sam told Carey. "You guys are going to persecute me because of my past criminal record," Sam yelled, the anger growing in his voice as he began to cry.

"I have been misjudged," Sam told Carey, as tears ran down his face. "My legal problems stem from my own poor judgment. When I am with a girl, I tend to make a pass at them. I don't know when to stop making sexual advances. But I am the only one who knows if I have really broken any laws."

"Sam vacillated during the interview," Carey, said. "His personality shifted quickly back and forth between that of a little boy, who was scared and needed protection, to one of being violent and domineering. It all depended on how he thought the person across from him would respond. He had an insatiable curiosity about the crime he was being charged with. He would ask pointed questions about certain bits of information as if he was already preparing for his defense."

Sam was arraigned before judge Andrew Dranchak in the 41st District Court in Sterling Heights on a charge of breaking and entering an occupied dwelling with intent to commit a larceny. Robert E. Hader was appointed by the court to represent Sam on the charge. When asked how he pled, Sam stood mute before the court, so the judge entered a plea of not guilty on Sam's behalf. Judge Dranchak then ordered Sam to undergo a 12-day examination to determine his competency to stand trial. Bond was set at $50,000. Unable to post this bond, Sam was remanded to the custody of the Macomb County Sheriff. He went to jail.

Armed with the phone numbers found in Sam's possession, Carey contacted each woman until he was able to reconstruct Sam's activity that morning. When he contacted Carol, she described her ordeal with Sam. Carey asked Carol's mother if she and her daughter would testify against Sam. At first, they agreed, but several days later, they changed their minds. Carol's mother did not want to subject her daughter to another courtroom experience. Carol had just recently appeared in court to testify about the attack of a matron at the youth home. With Carol's refusal to testify, Carey was unable to file additional charges against Sam.

Sam was eager to get out of jail and ordered Robert Hader, his court-appointed attorney, to do whatever he had to, to get him out. An attempt to have the bail lowered failed. Sam then wrote a letter to judge Deneweth, another circuit court judge, hoping to get his bond reduced.

"Dear Judge Deneweth:

"Please help me. I know you won't believe me but I'm not guilty. Just make them treat me fair until I get my trial and you will see I'm telling the truth. My wife is an epileptic and I can't stop worrying about her. If something happens to her, I will hate myself the rest of my life. Please help me your honor. I don't know where to turn to anymore. The pressure hurts so much I feel my head is going to explode. I can't sleep; I can't read or play cards. All I think about is my Lila and children. I can't crack up and won't but you are my only hope.

I went to judge Havey today and he left my bond at $50,000 for B & E. Mr. Hader, my lawyer said I was going in front of you next. I thought he was a good lawyer but he must not be because he didn't make them lower my bond. My mom and dad said they would put up their house as bond. That's $30,000. Isn't that enough? I promise you, I won't even be late for any court dates. Just let me wait for trial and be with my kids and take care of my wife. Don't punish me now before you find out the whole truth. Please help me, I beg you. You won't be sorry if you do. Just help me please."

Sam signed the letter, "Sam Consiglio, Macomb County Jail-W23, Mount Clemens, Michigan." He added a post-script after his signature, which read, "I live in Mount Clemens and have three children ages six, one and a half and two months and have a steady job driving a cab." There were only two children. And, they were all Lila's from previous liaisons.

Sam wanted desperately to hire Don Ricard again to represent him. But Ricard didn't come cheap. And Sam didn't have the money that Ricard wanted to defend him yet again.

"Frankly, I didn't want to represent him. I've had enough of him," Ricard told Gordon Wilczynski, a reporter for the Macomb Daily who had followed Sam's criminal career since 1976. "I've handled a lot of his cases and told him the last time he had gotten into trouble that I had enough."

Sam realized he couldn't afford to retain Ricard, but that didn't stop him from trying to have him represent him. Sam petitioned the Public Defenders Office to have Ricard named as his court-appointed defense counsel, but his request was denied. The legal aide department would not allow a defendant to pick their own attorney.

On July 17, for the third time in his life, Sam was referred to the Center for Forensic Psychiatry for evaluation and a determination of competency to stand trial and criminal responsibility. During the evaluation process, Sam told Paul B. Revland, Ph.D., and Certified Forensic Examiner, that he supplemented his income as a taxi driver by soliciting business for various prostitutes in his community. According to Sam, he would receive a kickback for each customer he would bring them. Sam claimed that Debra was one of the prostitutes with whom he had such an arrangement and that he had brought her several customers but had not collected his fee. "On the morning they arrested me, I was in the area and just stopped to get my money," Sam told Dr. Revland. "I didn't tell the police the truth when they arrested me because I thought they would have charged me with soliciting a prostitute."

Sam begged Revland to keep him at the Forensic Center and not allow him to go back to the Macomb County Jail. "Doctor, could you keep me here, please. I'm afraid. I'll be good, I promise you," Sam pleaded as he tried to elicit a tear.

"I told him that hospitalization occurred only in response to genuine illness," Dr. Revland said. Sam then launched into a discourse about committing suicide, stating that he was thinking of hanging himself. Sam then showed Dr. Revland a superficial mark on his wrist, which he apparently inflicted by stabbing himself with a pencil.

In his final report to Circuit Court Judge Raymond R. Cashen, Dr. Revland wrote, "I seriously question the genuineness of the defendant's emotionality as the components of the emotional response that are essentially involuntary were absent while those under voluntary control were magnificently displayed. The mental status examination was clear and revealed absolutely no evidence of cognitive impairment. The defendant is clearly in contact with reality and capable of clear, coherent, goal-directed thought and communication. The defendant is a basically unsocialized and impulsive individual who calmly leads an anti-social life-style until he is apprehended by authorities. Where upon, he assumes a panicky, sick role. He is remarkably disarming and manipulative and skillfully employs his emotional self-dramatization in an effort to avoid punishing experiences. His deeply ingrained anti-social personality and his criminal record certainly suggest that he is dangerous. Nevertheless, he has not suffered mental illness as defined in the Michigan Statutes."

"As the defendant understands the nature and object of the proceedings against him and is capable of rationally assisting counsel, it is therefore recommended that he be adjudicated competent to stand trial. It is also my opinion, that the defendant was not legally insane at the time of the alleged crime and that he should be considered criminally responsible for his actions at that time."

Revland concluded his report by diagnosing Sam as anti-social personality with pronounced hysterical features.

On August 13, while Sam sat in the Macomb County Jail awaiting trial, a sheriff's deputy walked up to his cell and, in a jovial manner said, "Hey Consiglio, your old man just kicked the bucket." At first, Sam was stunned. He couldn't believe it. "I was devastated," Sam said. "I just wanted to go and see him. I begged but they said no." After continued pleading, no doubt in part to shut him up, the Sheriff's Department relented. After the funeral home had closed that evening, two sheriff's deputies escorted Sam to pay his final respects to his father. Standing in front of his father's casket, Sam wept as he said good-bye. His father, too, would have cried had seen his son standing next to him with his hands and feet bound together and locked in chains. Sam loved and respected his father. But he also hated him. Mostly, what Sam felt for his father, was just disturbing and confusing for him. Sam's final visit with his father was a short one, lasting a few brief minutes. Afterwards, he was returned under close guard to his solitary life inside a jail cell.

Sam sat alone in his cell fighting to hold back the tears that he hoped the other prisoners wouldn't see. Who would protect him now, he wondered to himself? Who was going to bail him out whenever he got into trouble again? What Sam feared most, was that for the first time in his life, he'd be facing a trial without the support and presence of his father.

Chapter 8

Father Knew Best; Now What

One day after his father died, Sam again asked the court to reduce his bond. And again, the court refused his request. Two weeks later, after a series of disputes related to his defense strategy, Sam dismissed his court-appointed attorney and retained Ellen C. Wallaert to represent him.

The same week Sam's father died, Tom Gettner, a police officer from St. Clair Shores woke up and found a note left by his wife Darlene. The message was a short one; "I'm gone" was all it said. Darlene had left. She had packed her cloths and run off with her boyfriend to Tennessee. "I had no idea she had been seeing someone," Tom said. "She left me and the three kids." Tom raised his children alone before remarrying four years later. Darlene finally settled in New Orleans. Several years later, her second husband committed suicide.

On October 11, 1978, a jury was impaneled in the Macomb County Circuit Court to hear Sam's case on the charge of breaking and entering with intent to commit the rape of Debra. Prior to hearing testimony in that case, Ellen Wallaert filed a motion to dismiss the charges due to a lack of evidence; a motion Raymond Cashen quickly denied. Two days later, the jury returned a verdict of not guilty.

"The girl lied," Sam said. "In court, she was asked if she was ever convicted of a felony and she said no. But while we were on trial, my attorney learned she was on probation for a charge in Florida, some drug or soliciting charge. So she had to admit she had lied. But it's the police that screwed up. If they had just charged me with burglary, they would have gotten a conviction. But they added that intent to rape which, had I been convicted, would have enhanced the sentence another five years. But there was no intent to rape, no evidence, and I beat it."

During the trial, Debra, while not lying, had certainly misled the jury during her testimony by trying to hide the fact that she had ever been arrested. Ellen Wallaert brought out on cross-examination that Debra had been arrested in Florida. "That discredited her testimony," Carey said after the trial. "The fact that she appeared to have lied and had a child that was the result of an interracial union no doubt swayed the jury enough to establish reasonable doubt. I blame myself for not having checked Debra's background prior to trial. I've thought about this many times over the last 15 years," Carey admits. "Since then, I've run a criminal history check on every complainant and alleged victim I've come in contact with, regardless of who they are."

"I wasn't sure why I broke into the place," Sam said later. "I really wasn't sure. I didn't know that anybody was there first of all. I was just looking for some money. I was walking through the apartment house checking doors and I ran into one that was open and I went in. I saw this girl sleeping and when I seen her, I tried to get out of there as soon as I could. I tried to get out of there quick but I tripped. I almost fell down the fucking steps and then I thought, I got down the landing okay and then I hollered up and said, is anybody home? I tried to fake her out but she knew I had been in the room. I never intended on raping her, I just wanted some money."

After the trial, Sam was taken back to the Macomb County Jail. He still had another hurdle to get over, the charge that he had sexually assaulted Connie.

Twelve days after successfully defending Sam on charges of breaking and entering Debra's townhouse, Ellen Wallaert filed a motion with the Circuit Court of Macomb County seeking another bond reduction for Sam. In her motion, Wallaert wrote, "The defendant Consiglio is a pre-trial detainee. His criminal record is limited to several misdemeanor convictions only. He has neither missed a courtroom appearance, nor has he had a bond forfeited or canceled." The bond was reduced to $10,000. With his mother putting up her home as collateral, Sam was set free.

On November 20, Connie, who had since gotten married, was sitting home alone when she received a telephone call at about 7 p.m. A man's voice identified himself as Doug Morris. "Your husband ordered a car part from me, are you going to be home so I can deliver it? Did I wake you up? We've met before. Your name is Connie. I have brown hair, beard and a mustache. You don't have brown hair; you're a red head. I've been watching you." Connie hung up the phone and called the Redford Township Police. She said she recognized the caller as the man who tried to rape her back in April. Connie asked the police to conduct checks of her house and neighborhood. Unfortunately, under the circumstances, that was all the police were able to do.

On December 7, Wallaert, who less than six weeks before had sought a bond reduction for her client, was now filing a petition for diagnostic commitment before the Circuit Court of Macomb County. In her motion, Wallaert wrote that she had personally known and observed Sam in the Macomb County Jail, at court, and in her office, and found him to act in an irrational, unpredictable, unreliable manner. As a result, he is unable to assist her at times with her representation. Wallaert wanted Sam committed to the custody of the Center for Forensic Psychiatry in order to have him evaluated as to his competency to stand trial.

On December 8, for the fourth time in his life, Sam was referred to the Center for Forensic Psychiatry. One of the first staff members to examine Sam, upon his arrival as an outpatient, was Dr. Philip M. Margolis, consultant psychiatrist for the Center.

During a series of examinations, Sam denied unzipping Connie's pants and putting his hands between her legs. He denied touching her breasts or reaching inside her underpants. He also denied having an orgasm but claimed that he may have grabbed her wrists briefly.

Margolis wrote in his evaluation that, "Sam presents as an articulate, reasonable and logical person. There is no gross evidence of organic brain damage. His stream of thought is orderly and to the point; his affect is appropriate. He comes across as an appealing young man who projects some responsibility onto others; in this instance, he suggests he committed simple assault but that's all. He says that he currently feels good about himself and the future, insists that he will plead guilty only to assault and battery, and says he is opposed to plea bargaining and making a deal."

"In reference to competency to stand trial, it appears the defendant does have recognition of the fact that he must face trial for the charge of criminal sexual conduct, second degree. He is aware of the consequences if convicted. He says that he has `the best lawyer in the world' that they can communicate well about his defense and other matters. He referred to the cops as a bunch of nice guys."

Sam told Dr. Margolis, "My father used to take care of me. I miss him now. I have to take care of myself. I thought I was doing a good job." After the short period of evaluation, Sam returned to Mount Clemens to live with his girlfriend, Lila.

On December 13, Sam went to work as a truck driver, delivering paper goods for Clark Products, Inc., a restaurant and supply company in Sterling Heights. He was earning just over $300 a week and still collecting about $540 a month in Social Security payments. Careful not to do anything that would interfere with his government subsidies, Sam, when filling out the Michigan Withholding Exemption Certificate and the Employee's Withholding Certificate for Federal Income Taxes, used his ex-wife Cindy's Social Security number.

Dr. Margolis wrote in a letter dated March 7, 1979 to George Parris, a prosecutor for Macomb County, "Mr. Consiglio presents as an articulate, reasonable and logical person, a bit flippant, but with some evidence of real feelings. He appears mildly depressed and mildly anxious; he exhibits no paranoid ideation, and there is no evidence of psychotic mentation. There is no evidence of any mental illness existing now or at the time of the alleged crime. The defendant freely admits that he was not crazy, then or now. He suggests that the only reason the victim is pushing this is that her father became angry and that he is (the one) really doing this. He says that it is impossible to have happened. In my opinion, he had the capacity to appreciate the wrongfulness of his conduct and to conform his conduct to the requirements of the law if he had chosen to do so. While somewhat impulsive, he would clearly seem to be deterrable. In my opinion, he was responsible for his actions." In a separate letter to judge Raymond R. Cashen of the Circuit Court of Macomb County, Margolis recommended that Sam be found competent to stand trial.

In the summer of 1979, Sam and Lila were married in a brief religious ceremony. There were four people present to witness the vows including Sam's sister, Virginia. Afterward, everyone went out for hamburgers.

On August 30, judge Cashen signed a court order requiring that Sam be given an evaluation of competency to stand trial. For the fifth time, Sam was referred to the Forensic Psychiatry Center. This time, Dr. Charles R. Clark, a certified forensic examiner on the staff of the Forensic Psychiatry Center, was assigned to evaluate Sam's competency to stand trial.

On September 11, Dr. Clark reported that, "the defendant's version of the incident as told to him, is in substantial agreement with his statements made to police at the time of his arrest. The defendant did state at the time that she (the victim) did seem like a real…easy chick. She didn't know who the hell I was and she got in my car. The way things are nowadays, a person should be more careful. A decent woman would have said no. The fantasy in my mind was if I was to say, let's go to a motel room, she would have said okay."

Dr. Clark stated in his report that Sam, "was very well spoken and artic-ulate and did not demonstrate any difficulty with attention or concentra-tion. Emotional reactions were well modulated, normal in range and appropriate to situation. Mood was even and consistent. While openly cooperative, it was apparent that Sam was exerting great effort to control his presentation in order to appear in the best possible light. Nonetheless, the shallowness of his emotional relations with other people, as well as a good deal of manipulativeness showed through. He stated, for example, that his only interest in a competency evaluation was to delay the trial proceedings. As regards to his sexual activity, the defendant stated he has not experienced any of his old impulses to attack women in the past year. He claimed that he has achieved great insight into his behavior, understanding that his attacks on women have resulted from negative experiences with his own mother."

"In summary, Mr. Consiglio presented a clinical picture of an antisocial personality with sexual deviation and probable drug and alcohol abuse. He is recommended as competent to stand trial."

In November 1979, Sam finally stood trial for the assault on Connie, the young air reservist. Having married and divorced during the time when she first encountered Sam and the trial, Connie exhibited the characteristics of an emotionally distraught person.

"I had to pick her up and take her home every day during the trial," Detective Jerry Bomber said. "I knew she was very emotional as we rode together. I also knew that if that same sincerity was projected during her testimony, the jury would find her to be a credible witness." While she appeared calm, trying to mask her fears, Connie's testimony did indeed come across as "sincere" as she related to the jurors her story of being attacked by Sam.

During the trial, Sam's attorney, Ellen Wallaert, asked Bomber to read the transcripts of the initial interrogation of Sam after his arrest for assaulting Connie into the court record. "I think this was a mistake on the defense's part," Barber said later. "The jury never got to hear Sam's emotional performance that had been captured on tape. I think that may have hurt Sam because he had relied so often on his ability to convince people that he was not harmful."

In November 1979, 19 months after he sexually assaulted Connie, a jury, much to the surprise and satisfaction of the police community in Macomb County, convicted Sam of criminal sexual conduct in the second degree. After the verdict, Sam was allowed to remain free on bond while he awaited sentencing.

On January 15, 1980, Dr. Terence W. Campbell, with the Psychodiagnostic Clinic in Macomb County, in response to an order by judge Cashen regarding sentencing, wrote:

"The defendant is well oriented to time, place and person. His thinking is appropriately organized. His expressions of affect are within normal limits. There can be no doubt that the defendant has recovered rather dramatically from his acute psychotic disturbance of 1974. Nevertheless, there is still a great deal about this defendants behavior that is very disturbing.

"The defendant is highly motivated to portray himself in a socially desirable manner in order to solicit the allegiance and loyalty of other people. In doing this, the defendant seeks to define his former assaultive offenses as atypical aberrations in his behavior that are in no way consistent with what he is `really' like as an individual at the present time. The defendant continues to feel that females are to be used for the immediate gratification of his needs. This attitude was acquired by the defendant, early in the course of his formative development and learned via imitation of paternal attitudes to which the defendant was exposed.

"The defendant is still very intent on establishing a father-like relationship with some male authority figure that will substitute for the void created by his own natural father's death. One must remember, however, that the defendant's father often covertly condoned the defendant's assaultive actions. As a result, this defendant could be expected to test the allegiance and loyalty of any male authority figure by getting into trouble and then determining whether that male authority figure will seek to rescue him as his own father did."

Dr. Campbell recommended that Sam be incarcerated for the longest period possible.

On January 30, Sam appeared before judge Raymond R. Cashen for sentencing. Before being sentenced, Sam asked to address the court. "All right. Mr. Consiglio, you have the right to speak. Is there anything you would like to say at this point?" judge Cashen asked.

"I would like to ask this court to take into consideration, number one, I am not guilty of this charge," Sam said. "I understand that I was found guilty by that jury. That verdict is not a true verdict. I am not guilty of this charge. I don't feel that I got a fair and just trial through no fault of the court. I do put blame on the prosecutor and the police involved and I think there is things that did not come out even to this day, that should have come out. This was held back and there is no doubt in my mind that it was held back because if it were brought out it would be in my favor. First and foremost, your honor, I am not guilty. No way am I guilty. I will do whatever you want, give me a lie detector test. I have offered to do that and nobody seems to want to do it."

After listening to Sam deny any guilt associated with the matter before the court, judge Cashen stared down from the bench at Sam who was standing next to Ellen Wallaert and said, "You have a history of assaults on women. In my opinion, you constitute a danger to society. There is no way you can refute your past. It is absolutely replete with assaults on women and convictions, not just charges, but convictions that I am talking about. The doctors think you are dangerous from a medical point of view and I can only accept that as being factual. Your demeanor, your articulation, belies all this. It just does. I just feel that you have to be put away, Mr. Consiglio. I am the judge and I am to protect society. You do not belong on the street and it is that simple. It is the judgment of this court that you be turned over to the Michigan Corrections Department at Jackson. You will serve a minimum of seven and half years from and after this date with a maximum of fifteen years. I am going to recommend that you avail yourself to all the facilities at the Corrections complex and that psychiatric treatment be accorded to you."

Ellen Wallaert made a motion to allow Sam to remain free on bond pending an appeal. Cashen quickly denied the request.

In 1980, Mount Saint Helen, a volcano in southeastern Washington State exploded sending volcanic ash as far away as 100 miles. The volcano's eruption killed eight people. That same year, an attempt to rescue American Hostages being held in Iran met with disaster when a helicopter collided with a transport plane in the Iranian desert leaving eight American servicemen dead. Ronald Regan was elected President of the United States and Honda announced that it would start building passenger cars in the U.S. At the age of 52, Gordie Howe retired from professional hockey and John Lennon was shot and killed by Mark David Chapman as he entered his Manhattan apartment building. In 1980, at 29, Sam, for the first time in his life, became a convicted felon. He would begin serving a sentence of seven and one half to fifteen years in prison for the assault and attempted rape of Connie.

"I should have gone with Don Ricard," Sam said later. "He would have won that case. But I tried to save some money and went with this woman. Had to give her my car, which was paid for, to represent me."

Chapter 9

Still Not Learning From My Mistakes

Sam was sent to the Muskegon Correctional Facility, a minimum-security prison in Western Michigan. "I thought I had died and gone to heaven," Sam said. "It looked just like a college campus with a fence around it. I had a private room with my own key to the door. The only time we had to stay in our rooms was between midnight and six a.m. The rest of the time we could do anything we wanted except have sex with one another, but there were some that even did that."

"We were allowed televisions, stereos, microwaves, and once a month, we could order out from Domino's, McDonald's or Burger King. We had basketball courts, baseball fields, and tennis courts, weight pits and a cushioned quarter-mile running track. Wouldn't you like to see the look on the faces of Bob Dole and Newt Gingrich if they ever were to get a tour of that place?"

In spite of the collegiate atmosphere of the Muskegon Correctional Facility, Sam had difficulty adjusting to his new environment. He complained to prison officials about everything imaginable, fought with other prisoners, and argued constantly with the guards. His weight ballooned to close to 300 pounds as his anger increased over his imprisonment.

Even while serving his sentence, Sam continued receiving the customary cost-of-living increases and was now collecting just over $600 a month from the Social Security Administration. Charles Reagan, an Operations Supervisor with the Social Security Administration in Muskegon, Michigan, learned that Sam was not participating in a court-ordered rehabilitation program in order to maintain disability benefits. He also learned that Sam had worked at Clark Products during 1978 and 1979, while collecting benefits. Reagan sent a letter to Sam in April 1981, giving him 10 days to furnish a statement, outlining evidence to the contrary. Failure to do so, Reagan told Sam, would result in a suspension of benefits beginning June 1, 1981.

At the same time Reagan was informing Sam that his benefits were about to be terminated, Lila initiated divorce proceedings. "I called Lila to talk about it," Sam said. "When I did, a man answered and told me Lila was still in bed and that she couldn't come to the phone." Sam did not contest the divorce.

Sam was outraged. Not so much with Lila. He never really loved her anyway. Instead, his anger was directed at the Social Security Administration. Sam had no intention of allowing the government bureaucrats to terminate his benefits. He was making too much money to give it up without a fight. So, Sam began his assault with a massive letter-writing campaign. His first letter, handwritten, was to Charles Reagan.

"Dear Sir:
I just got your letter…Please don't hurt me anymore. I am trying real hard to make myself better but now I feel like killing myself. Please don't take my money again. The last time you did, the judge gave it back to me and promised me he won't let you do it again. Please don't hurt me.

Another judge sent me here to get better. I am going to school and I have my own doctor but I have to pay him a lot of money. If I don't have money, I can't pay my doctor. Please help me and don't hurt me. Okay."

Sam never revealed who his doctor was or what type of treatment he was receiving. Another letter was sent to Sam from the Social Security Administration looking for the answers to these and other questions.

On May 14, Lucy Consiglio wrote a letter to Charles Reagan on behalf of her son.

"My son called me and he was pretty upset because someone is lying about him and he asked me to write to you. If anyone has told you that he has worked in the last seven years, they are liars. The last job he held was in 1974 and he hasn't worked since because he isn't mentally capable to work. He used to always stay here and help me around the house. So, whoever is telling you this should be investigated because they are up to no good. If you need anymore you can call me."

Three days later, Sam sent another letter to Reagan.

"I'm in dire need of psychiatric treatment and because it is almost non-existent in prison, my mother has been sending a private psychologist to see me which I have to pay about $50 an hour for. His name is Dr. Paul Fuller and he's from Grand Rapids.

I am involved in vocational rehabilitation. My goal is (to receive) a degree in business management in the field of auto repair. I am now in the first phase of that goal. I have a lot of very nice people who have been trying to help me for a long time and I will always love them for that. Thank you Mr. Reagan for being so patient and courteous with me.

Two weeks later, on May 31 the Social Security Administration cancelled Sam's monthly disability check of $619.20.

On June 23, Reagan sent another letter to Sam to inform him the Social Security Administration had obtained sufficient information to establish that he had worked for Clark Products for almost a year during 1979. Reagan explained the rules relating to an individual's receipt of disability payments while employed. Sam had violated the rules by demonstrating ability to sustain gainful employment activity. As a result, the last disability check he was entitled to was for October 1979. While the government terminated Sam's disability checks, they continued to send his daughter Kimberly, $309.60 under the Social Securities disability entitlement program.

Three days after receiving Reagan's notice, Sam, forged a letter in the name of his brother, Joseph, and sent it to the Social Security Administration.

"I have been made aware of the fact that you are accusing my brother, Sam, of working in 1978...I am very upset at the way you are treating my brother. I don't know where you are getting your information but it is false. I strongly feel that what you are doing is nothing but continued harassment. I don't think I have ever been this angry. My brother has never worked for any Clark Products Company.

I am requesting additional time before you make a formal determination, so that I can assist him in preparing a defense to your allegations. I am requesting thirty to sixty days. I am retaining an attorney and hiring a private investigator. I will get to the bottom of this once and for all. Once we do prove to you that you made a mistake we will expect a formal apology."

The following day, Sam sent Reagan another letter. This time, it bore his signature along with that of a Notary Public.

"I have received your letter dated June 23, 1981, in which you made some serious and ridiculous accusations. I can only say that your information is totally false. I have never worked for any company called Clark Products.

It is my understanding that my brother has written you and so has my mother. They have verified that I have not worked. I am very upset that you don't believe them and that you are in fact calling them liars.

I am requesting additional time before you make your formal determination to allow me to defend myself against these allegations. I am retaining an attorney and a private investigator. I am requesting an additional thirty to sixty days. Hopefully, within that time I will be able to present a statement to show just how ridiculous your allegations are.

I ask that you send me copies of whatever information you claim you have. With your assistance, I'm confident that I will be able to expedite this matter. It would be very unfair if you continued to ignore me."

On August 5, Sam received another letter from the Social Security Administration, informing him evidence in his case had been thoroughly evaluated and the evidence did not reveal that he had been participating in a rehabilitation program specifically approved by a court of law. It also explained that Sam had the right to appeal the decision.

On August 6, Sam responded to the latest letter from the Social Security.

"Because you have stopped my money, I am unable to retain an attorney. My brother has investigated your allegations and he has told me that you are out to get me and that I don't stand a chance.

I have never worked at Clark Products. I have never used any one else's Social Security Card. If you would do your job you would find out that I am telling the truth. My brother has found out that someone by the name of Sam Consiglio or at least he used that name, worked at Clark Products and used Cindy Consiglio's Social Security number.

I don't know who is responsible for all this harassment nor do I care. I am asking that it stop now. I will not allow it to continue any further. If you allow this harassment to continue, you will be solely responsible for whatever happens to me. I will never let you get away with these lies. You have already caused me a lot of undo pain and I will never forgive you for that. I await your reply."

It was during Sam's massive letter writing campaign with the Social Security Administration, that he first went to a De Colores religious retreat. Sam had learned about the De Colores from his English teacher at

Muskegon Community College, where he was taking classes through the prison educational system. "She was always smiling," Sam said. "Always at peace. I wondered what her secret was." It was at this retreat, that Sam met Tom and Loretta Sieffert.

"De Colores in Spanish, means the Colors in Christ," said Tom Sieffert, a radiological technologist who had been active in the De Colores with his wife, Loretta, since 1978. De Colores was started on the island of Majorca, off the coast of Spain, around 1940 by the Catholic Church. At the time the Catholic Church sensed it was losing its religious connection with many of its men. In order to reverse this trend, the church organized cursillos or weekend retreats, which were initially for men. This met with tremendous success. In the early 1960s, cursillos were being held by the Catholic churches in the U.S. In Muskegon, Michigan, Catholic leaders allowed Protestants to join in the weekend retreat.

Normally, the De Colores weekend begins on Thursday evening and continues until mid-day on Sunday. There are a series of lectures that each person is required to attend. Leaving is not permitted except under the most exigent of conditions. Two days into the De Colores, Sam was begging to leave. But the people running the retreat, including Tom Sieffert, convinced him to stay.

"On the third day, a peacefulness came over me," Sam later told Susan Harrison, a reporter for the *Chronicle* in Muskegon.

After completing his De Colores weekend, Sam returned to the prison determined to make changes in his life. The first thing he did was telephone his mother. He told her how much he loved her. Sam felt like he had an emotional and spiritual base from which to build. He maintained close contact with Tom and Loretta Sieffert, writing them and calling whenever he could. Sam began to set goals for himself. After getting a full-time job in the prison athletic department, he began running, working his way up to distances of 10-12 miles a day. In less than a year, he'd lost 80 pounds and was in the best shape of his life. His long black hair was now neatly trimmed. His beard was cut short and groomed. "He could have passed for a Viennese banker," Susan Harrison reported to her readers in an article about De Colores and Sam.

After the De Colores weekend, Sam began to attend weekly meetings through the prison ministry. These meetings included lectures, prayers and song. Muskegon residents often befriend the prisoners who attend a De Colores weekend. Many communicate on a regular basis while others assist prisoners in bringing family members to visit. Others even promise employment to an inmate upon his release.

"He always called me ma," Loretta said, even though she was only six years older than Sam. Her dark eyes, thinly cropped hair and slight figure helped her maintain a youthful appearance, certainly nothing like someone who could have been mistaken for being old enough to be Sam's mother. Loretta married Tom in 1965. For over 20 years, she had worked as a volunteer for the church and community organizations. "I never once feared him," Loretta said. "He never tried anything with me or any of my daughters. I don't know if it's out of respect or fear, but I think Tom and I may be the only stable thing in his life."

On February 26, 1982, the Social Security Administration terminated Sam's disability insurance benefits being paid to support his daughter, Kimberly.

On March 29, a hearing was held to determine the Social Security's initial finding that Sam was no longer entitled to disability insurance benefits. Accompanied by prison guards to Lansing, Sam took his place in the small, nondescript room, as Edward M. Yampolsky, administrative law judge with the Social Security Administration, conducted the hearing.

Sam testified that he could not remember where he had been employed before being sent to Muskegon. Sam told the judge that he was not participating in any rehabilitation program at the Muskegon Correctional Facility.

"The prison would not let me take vocational training because of the charges for which I was convicted," Sam told the judge. When judge Yampolsky asked Sam if he had ever worked at Clark Products during

1978 and 1979, Sam told him he could not remember. It was Sam's testimony that he could not remember anything in 1979.

Leonard Speckin, a Detective Lieutenant with the Michigan State Police and a documents examiner, testified as an expert witness. During his 18 years with the state police, he had examined over 3,000 questioned documents. Speckin testified that Sam had authored the state and federal income tax certificates being presented as evidence.

Jeff Page, the assistant division manager at Clark Products identified Sam as the man he hired as a truck driver on December 13, 1978. As the warehouse manager in 1978 and 1979, Page was Sam's immediate supervisor. He testified that he saw Sam every workday morning when Sam left in his truck to complete his assigned route.

Page offered even more damaging testimony when he told the judge that part of Sam's duties required physically unloading items weighing between 20 and 30 pounds at each stop. There were between 10 and 20 stops each day.

There was no testimony provided by any member of Sam's family, nor was there any testimony from a "Dr. Fuller," indicating that Sam had been receiving psychiatric therapy. Before issuing a final ruling, the judge gave Sam 30 days to provide evidence that he was receiving psychological counseling. Sam never provided any such evidence.

Shortly after that hearing, Sam attended his second De Colores retreat. He worked as a "cha-cha" or servant. While motivational speeches were given, and prayers were conducted, Sam mopped floors and waited on tables. "What affected me most," Sam told Susan Harrison, "is the community (Muskegon) and the love they felt for us. The only way I can describe it is to say that I felt like I just got out of prison. I always thought that it was this prison that had bars, but it was inside of me. My whole life has changed. The worst part for me is going back to the hateful society within the prison. If you want to find out about love, go on a (De Colores) weekend."

In spite of Sam's newfound love for Christianity and his fellow man, he continued trying to prevent the Social Security from terminating his monthly allotment.

On June 15, Yampolsky ruled that Sam had committed an "intentional wrong" against the Social Security Administration in receiving disability insurance benefits under the Social Security number of another person. The judge also found that Sam was not entitled to any payments after October 1, 1979. Through February 26, 1982, Sam had been overpaid disability benefits totaling $20,745.10. The judge ordered Sam to repay the money.

Sam returned to his private cell at the Muskegon Correctional Facility. He wasn't upset about loosing the decision to keep his Social Security benefits. And, he really didn't concern himself with the debt he had just incurred. He had no intention of ever paying it. He was pleased that no criminal charges were being filed against him for the fraud he had committed. It is not clear why federal charges were never filed against Sam in this case. Whether a criminal case was ever presented to the local U.S. Attorney's Office is unknown. If indeed the facts of this case had been presented, it would not have been unusual to have such a case declined for prosecution in the federal system because of the small amount of money involved. Federal prosecutors traditionally look for cases with a much higher dollar impact than the amount Sam had defrauded the government out of. While technically Sam's actions fit the parameters of a federal crime, there are far too few prosecutors to devote time to such a "small" case.

On October 12, 1983, Sam was given an early release from his sentence. "I was actually kind of pissed," Sam said. "I was going to have to leave, go home and get a job."

Sam moved back into the attic bedroom of his mother's house in St. Clair Shores. By this time, the only people living in the house were Sam's mother and his younger brother, Jimmy. It was shortly after moving back to his mother's home that Sam met Garylyn.

Garylyn had been dating Sam's brother, Louie, for almost two years when they broke up. Seeing an opportunity, Sam wasted no time and asked Garylyn out. She said yes and within a few days, she moved upstairs with him. Garylyn was 12 years younger than Sam. She was short with dark hair and fair skin. And, she was very attractive. Garylyn provided Sam with a sense of having achieved what he alleged to others he had always been looking for, an attractive woman who would support him. Not financially, but emotionally.

On June 23, 1984, just six months after they first met, Sam and Garylyn, who was now 20, were married in a short religious ceremony at Tom and Loretta's home in Muskegon.

"There were over 50 people at this wedding," Tom Sieffert said. "Mostly people from Muskegon who knew Sam from De Colores. People in Muskegon loved and accepted him."

"My dad once told me that the best way for a man to show a woman how much he appreciates her, is to be willing to marry her," Sam said.

Once again, Sam just couldn't seem to stop showing women the full extent of his appreciation. At the same time, Sam was still trying to please his father.

By the fall of 1984, less than five months after he married Garylyn, Sam became restless. Feeling the need to be with other women again, he started to associate with prostitutes. When this proved to be insufficient to satisfy his needs, Sam tracked down Carol, the teen-age girl he had taken to the Twin Rocks Motel for sex six years before. Since no charges had ever been filed against him, Sam thought he might be able to realize a repeat performance of that night.

"I went to see her, hoping to get an easy piece of ass," Sam said. "I also wanted to tell her there were no hard feelings. I should've known that girl was going to be afraid of me. She thought I was going to kill her; she freaked out."

Carol, now 21, never allowed Sam inside the house. Scared, but no longer easily intimidated like she had been as a teenager, she immediately telephoned the police. When Carol "freaked", as Sam described it, he simply sat on the back steps waiting for the police to arrive. It was almost as if he wanted to be caught.

It was easy enough this time for the police to deal with Sam. At a parole hearing in Plymouth, Sam tried to present evidence that he was a changed man with a new life by showing pictures of his wedding. The Seiffert's sat in the small room listening to evidence that Sam had violated his parole. "The parole officer was hard on Sam," Tom said. "He told Sam that he fooled all of us and that he was nothing but a liar."

Sam's parole was revoked for "threatening and intimidating" behavior. He was sent to the minimum-security section of the State Prison at Jackson to serve the remaining four years of his sentence for assaulting Connie.

"I gave them 90 days," Sam said. "That's what I felt I should do." Sam thought 90 days was enough for having gone to see Carol. Any more than that, he considered cruel and unusual punishment, which is why Sam planned his escape.

While in minimum security, Sam again earned himself a position as a trustee. As a trustee, Sam, like several other trustees, was allowed to wear civilian clothing as he worked in the hospital area. For several days, he wandered the hallways of the minimum-security area making "dry" runs, walking past the guard at the highly congested front desk of a general administration area. "I had this little manila folder I would carry," Sam said. The folder helped Sam look official, as if he were some member of the staff. After several successful attempts at getting through the front door and into the main parking lot, Sam was ready to make his escape.

"I called Garylyn and gave her the time and place to meet me," Sam said.

It was the first week of February 1985. It was winter in Michigan, a time when the sky is dark for months and the days are short. On this day, the temperature was below freezing and there was snow on the ground. Sam, as he had several times before, walked past the guard and into the parking lot. His heart was racing. This was not a dry run but a commitment on his part to leave prison and not look back. He lingered in the parking lot as the cold winter air cut deep into his lungs. Holding a manila folder in his hand and trying not to appear impatient while he was freezing, Sam waited for his wife Garylyn. She was late.

"I'm in the parking lot looking like a jerk," Sam said. "It's freezing and this guy blows his horn at me. It's a cop." Sam's heart was racing even faster. But he was determined to remain calm and maintain a cool and confident outward composure. While he was certainly frightened, he would never reveal his inner fears to anyone unless it served a specific purpose. Fooling people was something Sam was good at; he knew it was not the time to panic.

When the police officer asked Sam what he was doing out in the cold, Sam responded, "waiting on a client."

No doubt thinking he was talking to one of the staff doctors, the unsuspecting cop said, "Get in and get out of the cold. You can wait in my car."

Sam sat patiently for what seemed like an eternity engaging in small talk with the cop who had stopped to write a report in the warmth of his police car. When Garylyn arrived a few minutes later Sam told his host, "there goes my client." The cop glanced at Garylyn then looked back at Sam. "The cop thought I was going out for a nooner," Sam said as he smiled. "I didn't try to change the officer's mind." Sam got into the driver's side of the car telling his wife that he would drive. "I told her to just move over, not to say anything and to just relax," Sam said. Garylyn did exactly as Sam instructed. As they drove away, they waved at the police officer, still sitting in his car, with his engine and heater running. The cop waved back and continued writing his report as Sam and Garylyn fled south.

Before he left the prison, Sam left a note for the prison guards saying he was leaving because he was under a great deal of stress due to continued threats of physical harm by fellow inmates. However, Sam had not experienced any threats. "I was just mad because they prosecuted me for nothing," he said.

Sam and Garylyn spent their first night on the run at a motel in Fort Wayne, Indiana. The following morning, they drove to Daytona Beach, Florida. Then, they headed for California.

Sam and Garylyn had less than $2,000 and a couple of credit cards between them. In preparation for Sam's escape, Garylyn had liquidated all of their possessions. Everything they had, besides each other, was in the back seat and trunk of their car. The minimum-security prison that Sam had been sent to had more than lived up to its title of "minimum-security."

Chapter 10

Cheat, Look for Escape, or Infidelity

It's unfortunate that most people are brought up to be honest and trusting and lack the experience or direct relational experience to identify the Sociopath after a brief meeting.
Damian

Driving to California, Sam and Garylyn interrupted their journey long enough to enjoy a couple of nights of entertainment in Las Vegas. Sam had always enjoyed the excitement of the Las Vegas nightlife and decided to take advantage of his newfound freedom to show his wife the "city of lights." It was an attempt to ignore, even if only briefly, the stress they both were feeling now that Sam was a fugitive. Las Vegas had previously known Sam only as John Henderson. Sam, now posing as his brother, Lou Consiglio, and Garylyn spent two nights in Las Vegas. With one of their fraudulently obtained credit cards, Sam bought two front-row seats to a Diana Ross Show. It's unknown if Sam ever used his real name on any occasion while in Las Vegas.

Their next stop was Canoga Park, California, where Sam found work managing a small 40-unit apartment building. The position only paid $150 a month, but it offered a small apartment, which along with the utilities, was rent-free. The job also paid cash, so Sam felt certain the police would be unable to track him. Garylyn found a job with Kelly Services as a word processor. This led to a job with a major defense contractor. Not suspecting that law enforcement authorities would attempt to track him through his wife, Sam didn't concern himself when Garylyn used her real name and Social Security number at her new job. At her new job, Garylyn needed a security clearance. It was nothing more than a simple background check to ensure the government and the defense contractor that she was not a security risk. But the authorities in Michigan had set up a tracking system using personal information not only about Sam, but Garylyn as well. When the Defense Investigative Service (now called the Defense Security Service), which is the federal agency tasked with awarding such clearances initiated its background check, law enforcement authorities learned about Sam and Garylyn's whereabouts.

They had been in California just over 90 days when the police knocked on the door of the manager's office early one June morning. Sam knew it was the police and not some insurance agent by the loud and forceful knock at the door. He peered through a small peephole and froze like a deer blinded by the headlights of an approaching car, not wanting to give himself away. Sam stood silent, as the police waited for someone inside the apartment to respond. Several minutes passed before the police left. Sam remained inside, almost frozen. He didn't move. He didn't answer the phone. He did nothing that might reveal his presence to anyone outside. To Sam, the time seemed like an eternity. Thirty minutes later, he fled his apartment and went to one of his tenants', Craig and Kathy Showers.

Craig and Kathy had been married less than a year when they first met Sam and Garylyn. They had moved into the apartment complex in Canoga Park a few months before Sam took over as the apartment manager. "When I first met him, he introduced himself as Lou Consiglio," Kathy said. "He was always a gentleman. I spent hours on end with him and he never pulled anything on me. But I didn't know that he had escaped from prison." Kathy was in her early 30's when she met Sam.

Craig, a quasi-professional student, studied computer design, while Kathy worked as an office manager in a sheet metal shop. "They appeared to be a great couple," Kathy said. "We socialized with them some during the week, always seeing them around the apartment complex. Sometimes we would go to dinner. They seemed like very nice people."

Sam called Garylyn at work and ordered her to leave immediately. She was to go to Craig and Kathy's apartment and not talk to anyone. "Garylyn ran into the house crying," Kathy said. "She was hysterical. She told me that the police were after Sam but she never said he had been wanted for rape. She just sat on the couch the whole time crying."

Sam and Garylyn spent the night in a motel, far from the Canoga Apartments he had managed for less than three months. With the help of Craig and Kathy, Sam arranged to have his possessions, of which there were few, loaded into a small U-Haul trailer. Sam had accumulated about $2,000 since his escape from Michigan, enough to hold them for a short while. Once again, Sam found himself in Las Vegas.

Sam and Garylyn rented a small house and spent most of their time inside, seldom venturing out. "It was just a fun vacation," Sam said. "We played Atari and ate a lot of cheap meals." But eating junk food and playing games ultimately got boring. Sam and Garylyn got homesick for Los Angeles. In August, after hiding in Las Vegas for two months, they went back to California. Sam found another job managing a larger apartment complex in Thousand Oaks, a suburb outside of Los Angeles.

For the next couple of months, things appeared to be going well for Sam and Garylyn. Sam leased the vacant apartments, made sure the pool was kept clean, collected the rent and attended to small repairs. Careful not to expose herself to the authorities with her Social Security number again, Garylyn assisted Sam by answering the phone in the office and helping with the books, keeping track of rent payments, and occasionally showing vacant apartments to prospective tenants. With another free apartment at their disposal and a monthly salary, again paid in cash, Sam was confident he would be able to maintain his mask of deception long enough that Michigan might eventually forget about him. While trying to project an image of respectability, Sam began an affiliation with the Christ Community Church in Canoga Park. He attended worship services almost every Sunday and established a friendly personal relationship with the church pastor, Eric Thomas.

In his youth, Eric Thomas had been restless. Like many kids, he was rebellious, unsure of what he wanted to do with his life. He left home at an early age, drifting around the country with a friend, neither of them having any particular destination in mind. When they got hungry, they stole if they didn't have money. At 16, Eric had committed a series of burglaries in Louisiana. Before the police were able to catch him, he and his accomplice fled the state, finally ending up in Ohio. It was there, for the first time, that Eric got a real taste of the judicial system. "I had broken into a Frosty Freeze ice cream store for money," he said. The police caught me and I was sent to prison for a term of 1-15 years." The prison authorities didn't know that Eric was only 16. He had convinced everyone on his cross-country journey that he was older. Eric quickly learned that an adult maximum prison is not the best place for a skinny, 16-year-old.

"When I told them my age, hoping to get out of the place, they told me that they would have to make that information public while they checked out my story. If I kept my mouth shut, I could be out in a year," Eric said. The state of Ohio didn't want to be embarrassed over sending a 16-year-old to an adult maximum prison, and Eric didn't want the other prisoners to know that a 16-year-old was living among them. So, Eric kept his mouth shut and his back to the wall.

"I got out after one year, just as they told me," Eric said. I don't know how I did it but I was unharmed the whole time. I had to make sure that everyone around me knew that if they touched me, I would kill them. It's the only way to avoid the violence and degradation inside a prison. There is a tremendous amount of unfairness in our criminal justice system. It may be the best system in the world but it's still a brutal system."

After his release, Eric was extradited to Louisiana to face charges on the burglaries he had committed there. But once the authorities learned he was only 17 and had been a juvenile when he committed the break-ins, they dropped the charges. Eric was later arrested in Texas for vagrancy. "I'm not sure why, except that I think it's illegal to be in Texas if you're from California," Eric said, half-joking but half-serious. Eric continued to drift for a couple of years, finding odd jobs when he could while taking temporary lodging with friends. When he was 23, Eric had a spiritual awakening. He began studying theology at the Life Bible College in Los Angeles and worked as a youth pastor. In 1976, Eric became the pastor of Christ Community Church, an independent evangelical church in Canoga Park, California. It was in 1985 that Sam became one of the 125 parishioners of the church.

"I knew him as Lou Consiglio," Eric said. "He was a member of the church for about a year or so. I remember that he was very excited about his faith. He was anxious to serve in the church. I knew that he had been in prison and, of course, I had told him that I, too, had served time in jail. I think that may be why he felt close to me. Sam was the perfect parishioner. He would do anything the church asked him to do. He was especially good at helping at a boy's camp that housed juveniles who had committed some type of violent offense. He would share his experiences and attempt to relate to the kids, hoping to help them in some way. He told them that crime didn't pay and tried to convince them to get an education. I had no idea that he was an escapee."

As his life appeared to be moving in a worthwhile direction, Sam was nonetheless, a fugitive. As a prison escapee, he and Garylyn maintained a constant vigil over their environment.

It was early October 1985, just two months after returning to California, when the battery in Sam's car died, stranding him along the highway. After jumpstarting the car, Sam drove to a local car dealer to have a new battery installed. "I had forgotten my wallet with all my charge cards," he said. "So, I had to leave the car and hitchhike home."

It was during this time that Los Angeles police were searching intensively for the night stalker believed to be responsible for the violent deaths of a number of people. As part of their search, the police were looking for "legal" ways to question hundreds of people who they might not otherwise be able to query. One such way was to question hitchhikers who did not have both feet on the curb.

"Because I didn't have two feet on the curb, a cop pulled me over and asked me my name," Sam said. "I panicked and made one up. I said something stupid to the cop like I couldn't remember too much since I had amnesia. The cop knew I was lying and when he asked for identification, I didn't have any."

Sam was taken to the Los Angeles Police Department where he was fingerprinted and photographed in connection with his hitchhiking ticket. Garylyn raced to the police station and told them Sam's name was Lou Consiglio. He had told her to use that name, confident the name would come back "clean". Garylyn posted a small bond for Sam, and they returned to their apartment in Thousand Oaks.

Sam was free once again, but he knew it was only a matter of time before the prints were checked and the police would know his real identity. "I knew they would be coming," Sam said. "I could have split before they got me, but I was getting tired."

In late October, Sam, was arrested at his apartment by the FBI and the Los Angeles Police. "I think it was the day after Halloween," Sam said. "I remember them coming to my apartment pointing a gun at my head and saying, trick or treat Sam, you're under arrest. At first I thought they just wanted a piece of candy, but looking down the barrel of the gun, I realized quickly that they wanted a piece of my ass. I think I may have wet my pants. I know I damn near shit them."

Sam held Garylyn in his arms, tears falling down both their faces, as the police allowed them a few brief moments to say good-bye. On the way to the Los Angeles County jail, Sam smiled and acted cheerful as he sat handcuffed in the back seat of an FBI car.

"The FBI agent asked why I was in such a good mood," Sam said. "I told him that the police in Michigan had failed to get me and the L.A. Police had failed. So they had to call in the big guns of the FBI. I told him it was very rewarding to know that I was beaten by the best, but I never should have made it so easy for them."

The following day, Sam wept as he appeared before Robert Stone, a federal magistrate in downtown Los Angeles. When judge Stone asked him why he was taking this so hard, Sam told the grandfatherly Magistrate that he had been trying to get Garylyn pregnant so that she would have his child to keep her company during his absence. Now he would not have a chance to fulfill that dream.

Judge Stone told Sam that he was allowing the state of Michigan 19 days to arrange for this transfer. After that, he would consider allowing Sam to have a bond. In the meantime, Sam was housed in solitary confinement at the Terminal Island Federal Prison.

"I remember getting down on my knees and crying out to God," Sam said. "I was hurting very badly. For the next 19 days, I prayed with my whole heart and soul for the Lord to show me a miracle." On the evening of the 18th day, with still no word from anyone in Michigan, Sam was positive that a miracle was in the making.

At 5 a.m. the next morning, a prison guard awakened Sam. He was told to get his things together, that he was being released. "I was ecstatic," Sam said. "It was one of the happiest moments of my entire life. I couldn't get my heart to stop pounding." Sam actually believed he was being released until two hours later, when he and several other prisoners were loaded onto a bus and driven to the Federal Building in downtown Los Angeles.

"I asked the marshal who was driving us if I was indeed getting out," Sam said. "The guy laughed and said 'are you kidding? You're going back to Michigan.' I just couldn't believe it. How could God do this to me?"

As he waited in a small holding cell inside the federal building, Sam continued to pray. "Mostly, I was talking to "God," Sam said. "I asked him, Lord, why did you do this to me? I asked for a miracle and believed in my heart you were going to show me one." Later that morning, Sam was taken to Ventura County to appear before the same magistrate that had given Michigan 19 days to pick him up. Garylyn, Craig Showers, and Eric Thomas, the Pastor of the Christ Community Church, were in the courtroom to offer Sam their support. When the authorities from Michigan failed to arrive within the 19 days, judge Stone, after Craig and Eric agreed to guarantee a personal bond, allowed Sam to be released in the custody of his friends and Christ Community Church.

That night Sam, along with his friends, Craig and Kathy Showers, celebrated his freedom. Sam knew it was only a matter of time before authorities would come to California and take him back to Michigan. At the urging of his friends, Sam agreed to go back to Michigan and surrender. Driving to Michigan with Garylyn, Sam hoped to work out some sort of deal with the States Department of Corrections that might reduce the amount of time he would have to serve. He also hoped to be housed in a safe prison environment, perhaps Muskegon once again, as opposed to the violence-prone Jackson State where sex offenders faced their own type of torment from the other prisoners.

But the Department of Corrections wouldn't make any such deals. He was a fugitive and they were not about to offer any deals to anyone under those conditions. Sitting with Garylyn in a motel room in East Detroit, Sam still considered turning himself in, but changed his mind after learning that Garylyn was pregnant.

In November, with the news that he was going to be a father for the second time in his life, Sam and Garylyn drove back to California. He knew the FBI would be looking for him again, especially now that he had left Thousand Oaks and violated his "personal bond" requirements. His first concern was to dispose of his car.

"I went to Phoenix to get rid of the car and get a truck and instantly fell in love with the place," he said. Sam wanted to remain in Phoenix but Garylyn was hesitant. She told him she would give him 48 hours to find a job. If he didn't, she insisted they return to California.

Sam, now using his cousin's name, Social Security number, and date of birth, went to the AAA Cab Company looking for work as John Trupiano. "All they asked was did I speak English? When I told them yes, they said, 'you've got the job.' They never checked my background. It's really stupid. There were no regulations."

While Sam was starting his next job as a Phoenix cab driver, Eric Thomas was becoming suspicious. He had not heard from Sam for several days. Two weeks after being released on a personal bond guaranteed by Eric and Craig, Sam was due back in court to face extradition to Michigan. But Sam never appeared. "I was very upset about his not showing up," Eric said. "I believed with all my heart that he would have shown up. I had no idea he was fleeing. I never would have believed that Sam would have lied to me about this. Now, I had to deal with a very irate judge who was not shy in making me the target of a significant amount of verbal abuse. The whole event turned out to be a very valuable experience for me. Sam has called a number of times and often writes. He has apologized many times for what he did. I still believe that Sam is a victim of a very brutal system. But I also think he is redeemable."

While Sam continues to communicate with Eric, the pastor of Christ Community Church has not seen him since the day he testified on his behalf

For just under two years, Sam lived and drove a taxicab in Phoenix. While living there, he met Stephen and Lauren Skye, both cab drivers.

"Lauren and I were driving for the Mercedes Cab Company," Steve said. "We were a rival cab company only in the sense that our company had the licensing contract for the airport runs. Other cab companies were not allowed to charge the same rate if they went to the airport. So, most drivers would tell the passengers that the meter was broken and charge the customer the going rate anyway. None of the drivers really cared; we all got along pretty well. But the airport commission hired a private investigative agency to look into the problem. They hired a bunch of people posing as travelers to see how much the other cab companies were charging. When the drivers got caught charging more than they were allowed, they would have to appear before a licensing board hearing. Sam would always go with whoever had to appear and provide them moral support and give them legal advice as to how to answer the questions. Everyone liked Sam, or John Trupiano. That's the name Sam gave us. We had no idea that he had escaped from prison or had ever been to jail."

During the time he drove a taxi in Phoenix, Sam successfully avoided contact with any law enforcement agency. This was remarkable since he had established a referral business to a number of call girls in the area. "When people came into town, they would look for women," Sam said. "They would always ask the cab drivers. I had several girls I would get customers for and the girls would give me money and freebies. I bet I cheated on my old lady a couple hundred times. That wasn't right though, I shouldn't have done that." During a normal 12-hour shift, Sam could easily earn $100. If he were successful introducing a customer to one of the call girls he had an agreement with, he could easily expect another $10 or $20 from that transaction, that is, if he didn't receive payment in some other way.

"I've driven cabs in Minnesota, Phoenix and San Diego," Steve said. "Knowing where the hookers are, the titty bars, its all part of the business. Businessmen come into town and they want to know where to find those types of things. It's like we're expected to know and Sam certainly knew as well as anyone. Some drivers even know where the drug activity is, not necessarily who is dealing drugs, but certainly what parts of town someone can score in if they want to."

Garylyn was not oblivious to Sam's sexual encounters with call girls, nor was she surprised. She often confronted him about his infidelity, crying and begging him to stop. But women, especially prostitutes, were like used cars to Sam, to be bargained for at the best price possible. It's not clear why Garylyn put up with Sam's cheating for as long as she did. She certainly knew that Sam had perversity in his heart. He was hardly a solicitous lover. Sam admitted that he sought only his own satisfaction and that he would lose all interest in her or any other woman once he had satisfied himself.

But he was not devoid of all feelings for his wife. While he freely admitted each of his marriages were for his own personal convenience, Garylyn was carrying his child. For that, and for her loyalty to him, Sam felt some remorse for his conduct. Other times, Sam felt he had a right to do as he pleased with whomever pleased him. He had learned from his father that a man could be with another women if and whenever it suited him.

"One time, Garylyn called, asking some medical advice, claiming that she had gotten hurt fooling around," Tom Sieffert, Sam's friend from the prison ministry said. "Other times, Sam would call me, collect of course, and ask questions about female problems that Garylyn was having. It was pretty clear to me that the symptoms he was describing were associated with syphilis and gonorrhea. On a couple of occasions, I told Sam that he should get Garylyn to the hospital right away."

Finally convinced herself she had enough information to prove Sam had been unfaithful to her, Garylyn called Kathy Showers to help her move back to California. "I drove to Phoenix in a truck and helped Garylyn pack her things and then drove the truck back to Canoga Park," Kathy said. "She stayed with us for about a month before Sam came and begged her to take him back." He made a very emotional plea and Garylyn forgave him, agreeing to go back to Phoenix.

But Phoenix can be brutally hot in the summer. Being pregnant was difficult enough for Garylyn. Hoping to get away from the oppressive heat, she pleaded with Sam to take her back to California, at least long enough to have the baby. Sam, wanting to make his pregnant wife happy, especially after she forgave him for his unfaithfulness, agreed to move to San Diego. He had saved enough money from driving his taxi to take three months off while Garylyn prepared to have her child.

"I hadn't seen Sam for well over a year," Steve Skye said. "It was always our intention to move to San Diego. Phoenix was just a short stop for us, a chance to make some money. I actually lost all contact with Sam until one afternoon when I was walking my dog, I saw Sam walking his dog. I couldn't believe it.

"It was only then that we actually began to socialize. But Sam lived in one of the worst apartment complexes in the Ocean Beach area. It was a dump. The rent was cheap enough but the place was rundown, one of the worst in San Diego. It seemed like everyone who lived there was poor and were always trying to get money from Sam. He would never give them any but he would always make sure that whomever needed milk or food, especially the kids, got it. He would buy the milk and food himself instead of giving the money away to the parents so they wouldn't spend it on booze or drugs."

"They lived in a small ten by ten room," Kathy Showers said. "It was a dump. I asked Sam how he could live there with Garylyn being pregnant but she defended him and the place. It's near the beach she would say, and that's all that mattered."

On August 8, 1986, Garylyn gave birth to Sam Robert Consiglio, named after Sam's father and the judge who nine months earlier allowed him to go free on a personal bond. It was the happiest day of Sam's life; he had a son. A few weeks after the baby was born, they moved back to Phoenix. Sam returned to driving his cab. But Garylyn was restless; she never liked Phoenix. After a few months of listening to Garylyn's complaints, Sam agreed to move back to San Diego where they found a job managing a small apartment complex in El Cajon, just outside San Diego.

Craig and Kathy Showers drove down to El Cajon on an occasional weekend to spend the day with Sam, Garylyn and the baby. But Craig was starting to feel uncomfortable with Sam. The relationship began to sour over the next several months as the Showers saw less of the Consiglio's. On July 1, 1987, while visiting Craig and Kathy in Canoga Park, Sam and Craig got into a violent argument over Craig's dog. When the dog got too close to Sam Jr. and frightened the child, Sam's temper rose and he threatened to shoot the dog. Two days later, on July 3, it appeared that the relationship between the Consiglio's and the Showers was finally at an end. As Sam was leaving his apartment, he noticed a large gathering of police officers down the street. "It looked like they were having a goddamn convention down there," Sam said. "I knew they were after me and I didn't want them to arrest me in front of Garylyn again. So, I drove about three blocks away and they pulled me over. I knew I didn't have any chance to get away."

After Sam's arrest, he was taken to the San Diego County Jail to face not only his extradition to Michigan for escape, but new federal charges related to his flight after being released on bond. However, shortly after his arrest, the federal charges were dropped leaving authorities free to extradite him back to Michigan. "There's no doubt in my mind that Craig Showers turned me in over that dog incident," Sam said.

"That accusation is totally false," said Kathy Showers, who has since divorced Craig. "Craig never called the police."

While Sam sat in the San Diego County jail playing cards with the other inmates, he heard a call over the cellblock loudspeaker, "Consiglio, rollup, you're getting released." Sam's heart was racing. It was just after 6 p.m. He thought that he was being released and had convinced many of the other inmates that he would indeed be leaving. Some of the prisoners even asked Sam to leave them his last few remaining cigarettes; but Sam refused. There had been no word from the prison officials in Michigan and since the federal charges had been dismissed, Sam was confident another miracle was about to be bequeathed upon him. Sam took a moment to call his mother in St. Clair Shores. He told her he would call her within the hour if he were released. If she didn't hear from him, that meant he would be flying to Michigan. As Sam was escorted downstairs from his cellblock, he saw a deputy standing beside the release desk. The deputy was holding handcuffs along with leg and belly chains. Sam knew that he wasn't being released and was glad that he had not given his cigarettes away.

As Sam was being restrained in chains, he asked the officer what time the flight to Michigan was. The deputy told Sam that their flight was leaving in five minutes. Sam was escorted outside the jail and placed in the back of a large van with six other prisoners.

"The place smelled like a locker room," Sam said. "I noticed we were going in the opposite direction of the airport but I didn't say anything. As soon as the van started heading eastbound, I asked the driver where we were headed. He said `Michigan.' I was stunned. We were driving to Michigan. I couldn't believe it." Sam was concerned about his mother and Garylyn. Both would have suspected that he would have flown back to Michigan; neither of them would know his whereabouts. All Sam could think about was getting to a telephone. He wanted to call his mother.

Just outside of Los Angeles, the driver of the van stopped for gasoline at a Texaco station across the street from the apartments Sam had managed before being arrested. He prayed that he would see someone he knew so he could ask them too call his mother for him. But after almost 20 minutes, no one he knew came to the station. The officers refused to allow Sam to make a phone call.

While Sam was beginning his trek across the country, Garylyn was rushing to get to Michigan. "Right after Sam was arrested, Garylyn called me and asked me to help her pack her things to go to Michigan," Steve Skye said. "I helped her load a U-Haul. We packed everything she had into the truck. She put the baby and the dog in the front seat with her and drove to Michigan. I've never heard from her since."

Sam and the other prisoners drove until almost 10 p.m. The van stopped at McDonald's in El Centro, where the prisoners were given two cheeseburgers and a coke. "That sure tasted great," Sam said. "It just wasn't filling enough. It was also a new experience; trying to eat with your hands chained to your waist."

As the van continued its trip east, traveling through the night, Sam tried to sleep, but couldn't. He was too excited. The van was approaching Phoenix, a city that Sam enjoyed and felt a bond with more than almost any other. He wanted to see the city again, even if it was from the inside of a hot, stuffy van as he sat chained to another prisoner. He had only been gone two months, but to Sam, it almost seemed like a lifetime. As the temperature inside the van rose, causing Sam and his fellow travelers to perspire, Sam escaped into a private reverie, his thoughts centering on hot summer nights in Phoenix and long walks he had taken with Garylyn. Sam promised himself that he would return to that world someday; someday very soon, with his wife and son, Sam Jr.

As the van headed east, leaving Phoenix behind, Sam closed his eyes and went to sleep. He was awakened for breakfast just inside New Mexico. Another McDonald's served as the restaurant of choice for the gang of seven. This time, each prisoner received an Egg McMuffin, hash browns and a cup of coffee. Inside the van, the temperature continued to rise.

"I was having a little bit of trouble with this guy next to me," Sam said. "His breath stunk something fierce. His body stunk, too. He was a stupid Texan and all he did was complain. I couldn't wait to get rid of him. We all spent the whole second day working to achieve that goal. We were really putting on the miles. Going through Texas is boring. I could tell this wasn't going to be a good day. The only highlight was getting a double cheeseburger, fries and a shake for both lunch and supper."

In Amarillo, Sam received some good news and some bad news. The good news was he was now rid of the stupid smelly Texan. The bad news; Sam and his traveling companions had to spend the night in the county jail. "The place was the pits. We weren't allowed to smoke; there was no water to drink or shower with, and no mattress. There was a toilet but no toilet paper. And, the toilet was right in front of a clear window and right across the street was this office complex. I figured I would just hold it until I got to Michigan," Sam said.

As soon as Sam was booked into the jail for the night, he started pleading with the local deputies to let him call his mother. It took almost an hour of pleading before one of the guards, sympathetic to Sam's begging, allowed him to make a very short telephone call.

Sam learned that Garylyn had arrived at his mother's home several hours earlier, and that she and Sam Jr. were fine. Sam explained that he was traveling by van and would be in Michigan in a couple of days. "It was a load off my mind," Sam said.

The drivers of the van had told Sam and the other prisoners that they would be leaving the following morning. But it was almost 5:00 the next afternoon before everyone was loaded back into the van for the journey north. The next stop was in Tulsa, Oklahoma, to drop off another passenger and drive through another McDonald's. "Right after that, I went to sleep," Sam said. He woke up in St. Louis, just in time to see the big Golden Arch. After a quick stop and another Egg McMuffin and coffee, Sam was on the road again.

"I was really getting to hate this trip," Sam said. "Not because I was getting closer to Jackson (State Prison) but because I was in Chicago. And Chicago sucks like Detroit and I never thought I would ever have to leave San Diego or Phoenix and return to this garbage."

A few hours later, Sam and the other prisoners arrived at Jackson State Prison. "All through the whole trip, I was kind of the life of the party," Sam said. "I kept telling them all my little stories and they all listened attentively, like little kids listening to a bedtime story. I know they all liked me because when we got to Jackson they all got out of the van to give me a hug. I learned something on that trip; people like me for what I am and not for what I at times pretend to be."

Sam was back in the State Prison in Jackson. It had been two and half years since he had left the minimum-security part of the prison. When he arrived, Sam thanked God he had made it back. He felt like he was home. Sam imagined that he would do a year in prison; then, he'd be free again. He'd return to Phoenix or San Diego with Garylyn and Sam Jr. They would manage another apartment complex and everything would be better than before. They would be a family, not having to worry about the police knocking on the door. No more lying and deceiving their friends. Garylyn, Sam thought, would live with his mother until he was free again.

But the prison officials in Michigan had no intention of letting Sam out in a year. His escape severed any chance he had of being released early, a chance he had two and a half years earlier. For almost a year, Garylyn lived with Lucy Consiglio. She'd travel with Sam Jr. to the State Prison in Jackson to visit Sam as often as possible. But the visits got to be demanding. The pressure of being apart began to wear on both Sam and Garylyn. They would argue during the visits and Sam's moods would become violent. He accused Garylyn of being unfaithful to him, which she adamantly denied. Sam had no proof of Garylyn's unfaithfulness. Perhaps it was the stories told by the other inmates about their own unfaithful wives or perhaps it was Sam feeling guilty about his own unfaithfulness that bothered him most. Whatever it was, Sam was in no position to do much about it from inside a maximum-security prison.

While serving his sentence in the Jackson State Prison, Sam continued his affiliation with the DeColores through the church ministry. That's when he met Wava Howley.

For 30 years she was an independent woman doing what she always wanted to do. For her there was no more noble a profession than teaching. From 1958, after graduating from Arkansas State University, until her retirement in 1988, Wava Howley taught school in the small town of Cassopolis, Michigan. Located about 45 miles south of Kalamazoo, Cassopolis is home to about 2,500 people. During her 30 years as a teacher, Wava taught everything to almost everyone who lived there. She taught kindergarten, junior high and senior high school. At the end of her career, she was the director of adult education. When she wasn't teaching, Wava enjoyed singing gospel at the Methodist Church of Cassopolis.

In the fall of 1987, Wava learned about a religious weekend retreat for women, being hosted by another church. Anxious to learn more about Christianity, a subject that occupied her mind as much if not more than teaching, she decided to attend.

Wava arrived on Thursday evening, as did the other participants. Once there, they were expected to stay. Leaving before the retreat adjourned on Sunday was not allowed.

The women slept on cots and had their meals prepared for them by volunteers hosting the retreat. There was singing, group meetings and motivational speakers. It was all designed to provide an uplifting, loving weekend, learning about the Bible and how to be better Christians.

One of the speakers was from a local prison ministry. He talked about having helped people in prison find faith in Jesus Christ, how becoming Christians helped these people cope with their environment while in prison, and how it helped many make a positive transition to private life, once they were released. The speaker used Sam as an example. However, he failed to say Sam was serving time for trying to rape a young woman.

"They told us that Sam was a Christian now," Wava said. "They mentioned that he did escape, with the aid of his wife, and that he lived a crime-free life for two and half years. He was truly a changed person, they told us."

Wava had heard how people who served time in prison had a high rate of recidivism because people on the "outside" didn't give convicts the friendship and support they needed to make it on their own.

"When I heard these people from DeColores speaking about this, I said, well, here's my chance to make a difference," Wava said.

Wava wrote to Sam, introducing herself as a fellow Christian, offering spiritual support. She also wrote the warden of Jackson State Prison, where Sam was serving his sentence for sexually assaulting Connie. She told Sam that she felt he deserved a chance to go free and make a new life for himself. She had never met Sam, nor was she aware of why he was in prison. Nonetheless, after hearing the positive things about Sam at the DeColores retreat, she felt writing the warden was the "Christian thing to do".

Sam was thrilled when he received Howley's letter offering her support to both his spiritual needs and his efforts to gain an early release. Wasting no time cementing this newfound friendship, Sam wrote a letter to Wava, his new supporter.

"He told me a little about himself," Wava said. "Sam said he was in prison for sexual misconduct; claimed that a girl he was dating wanted him to marry her. He didn't want to, so she got mad and pulled his beard and he slapped her. That's why he was in prison. He wrote friendly letters. After a while, he wanted me to come and visit him."

Wava visited Sam at the prison. They met in an outside courtyard where prisoners congregated. For about half an hour, they talked, mostly about Sam, his dreams, finding God and his hopes to be reunited with Garylyn and Sam Jr.

"He was very articulate," Wava said. He seemed sincere, very docile. I couldn't imagine him ever being violent. He was very polite. He said he needed a friend, somebody to confide in."

She visited Sam two other times in early 1988. By the time summer arrived, Wava prepared to move to Arkansas to enjoy her retirement. By the time she left Michigan, Wava still believed Sam was in prison for slapping a woman who pulled on his beard when he refused to marry her.

For the next two years, Sam wrote Wava, often weekly, continuing to tell her of his faith in God and how things were going to be better as soon as he got out of prison. He also called her collect, as often as the prison system would allow.

"He was getting to be a nuisance," she said. "I was getting an uneasy feeling about him, but I didn't have anything substantive to pin it on."

Wava continued to correspond with Sam and accepted his collect phone calls, always trying to reassure him that if he kept his faith in God, that God would provide for him.

Realizing that Sam was going to be in prison longer than a just a year, Garylyn moved out of Lucy's home and started divorce proceedings. On May 25, 1989, Garylyn was granted her divorce. She moved away from the area and later remarried. The divorce decree provided Sam limited visitation rights to see his son whenever he is released from prison.

During his time in the Jackson State Prison, Sam became the model prisoner. He attended worship services and worked regularly in various jobs offered by the prison. He worked hard to get along with other prisoners, in part, to demonstrate to prison officials that he was a worthy candidate for early release and, to keep from being harmed by any of the more violent inmates.

In December 1990, it appeared that Sam would be released during the early part of the following year. After a massive letter writing campaign initiated by Sam's mother, Lucy, Tom and Loretta Seifert and his friends (most of whom he had met through the DeColores), prison officials notified Sam that he would be released on April 9, 1991.

Just one month before his scheduled release, Sam was notified that his mother had suffered a severe heart attack. He wanted desperately to visit her and asked the warden for a compassionate furlough. "He said I'd have to be escorted in shackles," Sam said. "I was told that my mother was going to be okay, so I decided to stay in prison and avoid the embarrassment of being seen in shackles."

On March 18, 1990 Lucy Consiglio died. Sam never had a chance to see or say good-by to his mother. He was never able to tell her how sorry he was for all that he had done to hurt her. If there was ever anything or anyone that Sam may have actually loved more than himself, it might just have been the woman who brought him into this world. But, as when his father died, Sam was in jail. This time, he didn't even get a chance to pay his respects at the funeral home.

Three weeks later, on April 9, Sam was released from prison. He was just six weeks away from his 40th birthday. Once again, he went to the house he grew up in, the one place that had become his sanctuary. Now, he was the only one living there. His parents were dead and his brothers and sisters had long since moved away. Sam was alone.

Sam certainly didn't intend to remain in his parent's old home very long. He knew that his future in Michigan, especially St. Clair Shores, wasn't a good one. Instead, he planned to head for San Diego. But first, he had some personal business to attend to, such as buying a new car, obtaining some credit cards, seeing old friends, and helping his brothers and sister, Virginia, get his parents home ready for sale. From the time he got out of prison until the time he left for California, Sam spent most of his free time painting and making minor repairs to house. On Memorial Day weekend, 1991, Sam left his parent's home for the last time. He had taken out a lease on a 1991 Pontiac Grand Am and headed south. His destination was California, with a short stop over in Florida. He left his sister, Virginia, with power of attorney. As soon as the house was sold, Sam expected to receive about $6,000 as his share of his mother's estate.

Chapter 11

Fooling Them Can't Be This Easy

Sociopath: Those who instinctively prey on the lives of others, through manipulation, for their own personal gain and agendas without regard to the consequences of their victims.
Damien

It was 2 in the morning when Sam drove his black 1991 Pontiac Grand Am onto Interstate 4 just outside Winter Haven, Florida. Sam had been driving for hours since leaving Michigan and hoped to get some sleep before continuing on his journey. He was headed to Tampa where he hoped to find Marie, an acquaintance from Muskegon. He had met Marie while in prison on a DeColores religious retreat. They had become friends and now, Marie was divorced, living in Florida. Sam hoped to expand his relationship with Marie, if only he could find her. It was Memorial Day weekend and Sam had been out of jail for about seven weeks. In Sam's mind, Florida was just a short stop on the way to California, but a stop worth making if he could find Marie.

Tired from driving straight through to Florida, Sam pulled off at a local truck stop to try and get a few moments of sleep. "I had nodded off for a short time when I opened my eyes to see the blue lights of the police car," he said. "I thought they were going to come after me."

But the police were interested in someone else. They had been continuing their efforts to crack down on prostitution at the rest stops along Interstate 4.

Jamiss was only 19 when the police questioned her at the rest stop. Jamiss was not exactly anyone's idea of petite. But, at 5'6", and 150 pounds, she carried herself well enough to earn extra money working as a prostitute in the Orlando area. She had moved to Orlando from Rochester, N.Y. to be with her boyfriend, Michael, who was assigned to the Naval Training School in Orlando. Michael had met Jamiss in October 1990 in Rochester, N.Y., where she was working as a manager at a local McDonald's. They began dating and shortly thereafter, became engaged. Michael joined the Navy in January 1991. Jamiss joined Michael in April of that year and the two of them moved into an apartment in Altamonte Springs.

The police asked Jamiss what she was doing at the rest stop that hour of the morning. Although they knew, they decided to give her a break. The sheriff's deputies took her snapshot to have her photograph on record, then, let her go with a warning.

"I was in need of money and decided that I would prostitute myself in Orlando to raise money," Jamiss claimed. "While I was at this rest area, I noticed a man watching everything that was going on."

"I could see the police talking to her," Sam said, "I knew what she was up to, I thought they were going to arrest her."

"I got into my car to leave right after the deputies left," Jamiss later told investigators of the Naval Criminal Investigative Service. "After I got down the road a ways, this guy from the rest stop started flashing his lights at me. I thought I had something wrong with my car so I pulled over. The guy came up and said what happened to me back at the rest area wasn't right and the police shouldn't have treated me the way they did. He told me he could possibly help me out and asked me to meet him for a cup of coffee. We went to the Denny's restaurant in Altamonte Springs. He told me his name was Sam Consiglio."

"She told me she had been working as a prostitute trying to earn extra money," Sam said. "I asked her what she was doing and how much she was charging. Jamiss told me that she was giving blowjobs for $10 and would hope to earn $40 a night. I told her that was crazy, she should be getting $40 a trick."

Jamiss listened patiently to Sam. He was very convincing, she thought.

"He told me he was from Michigan and was in Florida looking to buy apartments for a friend. He also told me that he used to pimp girls in Las Vegas, Michigan, and out in California."

Sam smiled as he told Jamiss he was on his way to Tampa and offered to set her up with some business people where she could earn some extra money as a prostitute.

Jamiss was in dire need of money, so she agreed and told Sam to follow her back to her apartment where she picked up some clothes. Sam and Jamiss then drove, in separate cars, to Tampa. Tired from the long drive, Sam rented a room at a Best Western Motel so they could get some rest.

"I soon realized, that Sam didn't have any business people that were going to come over," Jamiss said. "He told me that unless I had sex with him, he would not let me leave. He also threatened to tell Michael how I was making money and how we met. I gave in and had sex with him, both regular sex and oral sex. Afterward, I told Sam that what he had just done to me was rape."

"I know, I'm sick and I need help," Sam told Jamiss.

"I told him that what he just did was not new to him and that he had done it before," Jamiss said.

"You're right," he admitted.

"Sam told me that he had threatened other girls similar to the way he threatened me. He also told me that he once blackmailed a girl to the point she committed suicide. I didn't know who this girl was, but Sam showed me a picture of some girl he carries on a key chain," Jamiss said. "Afterward, Sam let me go under the condition that I return later in the day. He threatened to tell Michael if I didn't. I went back and forth from

Orlando to Tampa almost every day for two weeks. I would pick Michael up at the Navy base around 5 p.m. and we would go back to my apartment and stay until about 10 p.m. I would drive Michael back to the base and then drive over to Tampa and be with Sam until one or two in the morning," Jamiss said.

"It had been a couple of weeks of great sex and she was wearing me out," Sam said. "I needed to get some rest and get to California. She was terrific, 19 years old and a nice tight body. The girl wore my ass out," Sam declared, smiling as he boasted of his latest conquest. "After two weeks, I knew it was time to leave and head toward California."

During those two weeks, Jamiss's car was involved in a minor accident. Sam knew he could help her get it fixed by telling his insurance company he had hit her. Sam accompanied Jamiss to the Car-O-Van paint and body works in Orlando. An employee of Car-O-Van told Navy investigators that a woman named Jamiss and a man named "Sam" had told her they were brother and sister and asked that repair work be done to Jamiss's car. "I told the garage my insurance company would pay for it," Sam said.

Sam also contacted an auto insurance adjuster for Sewell, Todd and Broxton Adjustment Company, and reported that he had backed into Jamiss's car while in Tampa. The adjuster later told Navy investigators that Jamiss claimed to have retained legal counsel and was filing a suit against Consiglio for personal injuries suffered during the alleged accident. "I couldn't believe it when the bill came, it was $4,000," Sam said, smiling, knowing that he had just falsely reported this claim to his insurance company. "I had just helped her get her car fixed, spent $4,000 on the broad, she owed me something."

During the time Jamiss's car was being repaired, Sam went back to Orlando and rented a motel room at a Best Western Inn. For almost another two weeks, Sam continued to threaten Jamiss with telling Michael about her involvement with prostitution. To keep Michael from learning about her secret life, Jamiss continued her previous arrangement of meeting Sam at night after she had driven Michael back to the base.

"Sometimes, during the afternoon, I would go meet Sam and he would take me shopping," Jamiss said. "He had taken me to Lerners Department Store where he bought me some clothes. Each time we went to Lerners, he used a Lerner's charge card to make the purchases. Sometimes, he would use his American Express Card."

"Getting the credit cards was easy," Sam said. "All I had to do when I got out of prison in Michigan was to apply. I used my mother's home address and indicated that I was self-employed in property management. If you list a long-distance telephone number on the application, they seldom call to check up because the banks are cheap."

After spending two weeks in Orlando, Sam was ready to continue his journey to California. But he was broke. Not having enough money to travel west, Sam called his friend, Wava Howley.

"He needed money," Wava said. "He called and appeared to be upset. He said he made this girl have sex with him because he threatened to tell her boyfriend about her if she didn't. He said it was the best he ever had but that it was psychological rape because he was making her do it against her will."

Sam pleaded with Wava. He needed more money to get to California. "I thought, what a foolish man," she said. Still, Wava wired him $200. "I felt sorry for him," she said. "He promised he would pay me back."

With $200 of Howley's money, Sam left Orlando and drove to San Diego. When he arrived, he embarked on a campaign to have Jamiss come to California. Part of his strategy was to call her almost every day and threaten her.

"I told Sam that Michael was being transferred to South Carolina. Sam told me he was going to set me up with an apartment and a job in South Carolina so that he would be able to keep tabs on me," Jamiss said. "About that same time, I got an eviction notice from my apartment owner and I told Sam about it. He called my landlord, and told her I was his employee and that if I couldn't make my rent payment, he would make it for me."

The landlord later told investigators of the Naval Criminal Investigative Service that Sam Consiglio had contacted her. Sam claimed that Jamiss worked for him for the past five years and that he would personally take care of the late rent payments.

"Not even a week had gone by since Sam had left Orlando and arrived in San Diego before he called and told me he wanted me to come out," Jamiss said. "He told me that he wanted me, that he was obsessed with me and had to see me." At first she refused, but Sam persisted.

"He told me, don't try and fuck me over or else you'll see what will happen to your life," Jamiss said. She was afraid Sam would tell Michael about their relationship, something she hoped to avoid at virtually any cost. Jamiss realized later that she hadn't tried hard enough to avoid seeing Sam again.

"Eventually, I agreed to go out to San Diego. Sam mailed me a ticket; it was a roundtrip ticket, leaving Orlando on Thursday, June 27, and returning on Sunday, June 30. I was afraid that if I didn't go, Sam would tell Michael about my past," Jamiss said.

"As always," she said, "Sam threatened me with ruining my life if I did not agree to have sex with him. During the weekend, he took me to Mexico where he bought me some clothes. He also took me to the Rosanne Barr Comedy Show at Charlie's nightclub. On the night that we were going to see Rosanne Barr, we had approximately an hour before the show started and Sam drove me to a homeless shelter in downtown San Diego. He told me he had gone into the homeless shelter and told people there he was looking for apartment managers. I thought this was a legitimate business that Sam was in as far as hiring people to manage apartment complexes."

On the day Jamiss was to fly back to Orlando, Sam cancelled the flight. "I was at the Denny's across from the Best Western Hotel and I was crying because Sam had cancelled my flight and would not let me go," Jamiss said. "He told me that if I didn't stay and have sex with him, he would not let me go at all. So, we went back to the hotel and I had sex with Sam."

The following day, Sam drove Jamiss to the San Diego airport and bought her a ticket for her return flight to Orlando.

"Once I got back to Orlando, Sam continually called me and threatened that if I left and didn't tell him where I was going, or didn't do exactly what he would say, he would find me and ruin my life," Jamiss said. "Because of this, I called Sam every night like he instructed me to. He had given me his AT&T calling card number so I could call him. I eventually told Sam to leave me alone, that I wanted nothing more to do with him. He then threatened to call the Navy and make up stories about Michael and try to get him in trouble."

While Jamiss was in San Diego, Sam gave her a phony California birth certificate in the name of Shannon Hyatt. He also gave her a phony Social Security card and he showed her how to get a charge card using false information. Sam told Jamiss that the best credit card to get was Citibank MasterCard.

On July 16, 1991, Sam telephoned the office of the Judge Advocate General at the Naval Training Center in Orlando. He said he wanted to report allegations of criminal misconduct by Jamiss and Michael. Special Agent David G. Early of the Naval Criminal Investigative Service returned Sam's call.

"Sam claimed he had met Jamiss in Orlando and learned that Michael was forcing her to work as a prostitute," Early reported. "Sam also told me that he was in the property-management business in San Diego. He claimed to have pledged to assist Jamiss in obtaining legitimate employment. According to Consiglio, Jamiss and Michael were involved in selling marijuana, and were also using his personal credit cards to make purchases and conduct unauthorized long-distance telephone calls."

According to Early, Sam claimed he had been driving from Michigan to Tampa when he pulled off at a rest stop in Altamonte Springs to rest. "I saw the Seminole County Deputies arrive and arrest a young white female prostitute who was in a car parked nearby," Sam told Early. "I interceded on her behalf and convinced the police officers not to arrest the girl.

Afterward, the girl told me her name was Jamiss. She claimed to be living in Altamonte Springs with Michael who was in the Navy. She also told me that Michael had forced her to work as a prostitute," Early reported. According to Early, Sam claimed he told Jamiss he had contacts in the property-management business and could help her find a job.

Early also reported that Sam told him that Jamiss flew to San Diego to meet with him and to work on her resume. It was Sam's contention that Michael had purchased Jamiss's airline ticket, not him.

"I paid for her hotel room, meals and bought her clothing while she was here," Sam said. "I also showed her various apartments and educated her on the apartment management business."

"I had sex with her, but I felt uncomfortable about it because of our age difference," Sam told Early.

According to the investigator, Sam reported finding $200 in cash missing after Jamiss flew back to Florida. "I also noticed that my Amoco and Lerners credit cards were missing from my wallet." "There was an additional $800 on my Amoco card and the Lerners card was over the $300 limit," Sam said.

"Consiglio told me that he telephoned Jamiss and she admitted using the cards," Early reported. "Consiglio also claimed that Jamiss admitted to giving Michael his AT&T long-distance calling card number and that he had been placing calls on his account."

Early reported that, "Consiglio wanted to pursue criminal charges against Michael for the unauthorized use of his telephone calling card. Consiglio claimed to be working as the property manager of the Valley House Apartments in El Cajon." Sam also told Early that he was part owner of several apartment duplexes in Michigan, L.A., and San Diego."

On July 19, Jamiss allowed the Naval Criminal Investigative Service to search her apartment in Altamonte Springs. The search produced an airline travel itinerary in Jamiss's name describing travel from Orlando to San Diego, and an Illinois birth certificate in the name of Shannon Ann Hyatt.

The following day, Jamiss and Michael were married in a brief civil ceremony in Orange County, Florida.

On August 13, Special Agent Early prepared his final report of investigation relating to the allegations made by Sam and the information subsequently provided by Jamiss and Michael. Early concluded in his report that, "this investigation has determined that Sam Consiglio made false allegations implicating Jamiss and Michael in criminal activity. Due to the State of Florida's unwillingness to pursue investigative jurisdiction of Sam Consiglio for extortion…this investigation is closed."

Chapter 12

It Just Gets Easier and Easier

It was early in the evening in late May 1991. Darkness had descended on San Diego. Traffic that had choked the roads earlier as city employees, storeowners, attorneys, bankers and doctors made their way home on another typical refreshing cool night in the city had cleared. Carolyn, known on the streets as Sue Edwards, was just starting work. That's when she met "John" as she was hitchhiking in the vicinity of El Cajon Boulevard and College Avenue. He picked her up in his new black car with bucket seats. There was nothing special about this man, Carol thought. He was just another potential client who drove a nice new car.

Carol was 38-years-old. Her police arrest reports listed her height as 5'4" and her weight at 124 pounds. Her long brown hair and blue eyes compensated for a small scar over her left eye. She was attractive enough at least for her to earn a meager living as a prostitute. She had been arrested on several occasions for prostitution and petty theft. Once, after being detained by a security guard after shoplifting a pack of cigarettes, she offered to have sex with the guard if he would let her go.

Carol wasn't sure how long she'd been working as a prostitute because of a head injury she'd suffered years earlier. She had been hit over the head with a crescent wrench, the result of an abusive one-night stand. Carol experienced some long-term memory loss and had some difficulty remembering many of the things she did on any given day. Because of the injury she suffered during this attack, she received a monthly check from Social Security. But it was never enough to pay her bills. So, she supplemented her income by renting her body to most anyone with a few dollars and a car. Rooms cost money and she certainly was in no position to charge as much as an upscale call girl whose clients had plenty of cash for nice rooms and drinks beforehand. Her clientele were less likely to pay more than the absolute minimum for her services.

But she remembered "John." "He was about 5'10", 200 pounds and had dark brown wavy hair," she recalled. Carol got into the car with him and made small talk as she would with many of her customers before exchanging in some sort of sexual act. Carol couldn't recall exactly what type of sex she offered or the man sought, nor could she remember the amount of money they had discussed. She remembered that John didn't want to have sex with her; he only wanted her phone number so he could schedule a date with her for some other time. Carol gave him her phone number and got out of the car. Thinking little about this meeting, Carol went back to selling herself for money as the cool evening continued late into the night. She wondered anxiously if there would be enough opportunities for her to perform this night. Her mission each evening was a simple one; do what the customer asked, collect her money, (preferably in advance) and hope that she was not robbed or assaulted.

A few days passed before "John" called. When he did, he told Carol he was a policeman and that he was going to arrest her. "He also told me we could work out a deal for sex in exchange for my not going to jail," Carol said later.

She had been to jail before for various misdemeanor offenses and certainly didn't want to go back. So, Carol agreed to the deal, convinced she didn't have much of a choice. She gave John her home address and waited for him to pick her up.

"He was driving the same black car I first met him in," she said. "He picked me up and we drove to the area of 54th Street and Trojan Avenue in San Diego where he parked the car. He wanted me to put my mouth on him, all he wanted was oral sex." Carol performed as she had been instructed and as she had done for so many other clients. Only this time, she wasn't being paid for her services. Instead, she convinced that this was her way of staying out of jail.

Afterwards, Sam, posing as "John the police officer," called every week, often several times a day, always demanding sex, usually oral sex. Carol was always quick to comply, fearful that if she didn't, she'd be arrested and sent too jail.

"I even asked once to see his badge," Carol said later. "He told me that if he did show me his badge he would have to put me in jail. On one occasion, John took me to a motel for sex. This was because he had been unable to position himself in his car to have regular sex. I remembered it being the 4th of July. I remembered the fireworks. He demanded anal sex, but I refused. John got very angry and threatened to beat me. I told him that I had herpes but he told me he didn't care. He just wanted sex. I was afraid he'd beat me. So I did what he asked." Sam stopped calling for sex after that night. Carol didn't know why until later.

Chapter 13

Lie And Blame Everyone Else

She had been down on her luck before. But this time was different. Being homeless was a new experience. The strain of not having a job or a place to live was weighing on her far more than anything she'd experienced. She had reached a new personal low. Karen was two weeks shy of her 30th birthday when, on May 13, 1991, she made an emergency application to stay at the Saint Vincent de Paul Joan Krock Center on Imperial Avenue in San Diego.

Karen told the intake counselor at the shelter that she had arrived in San Diego from South Carolina just three days before. She said her ex-husband had physically abused her to the point of breaking her jaw and wrist, which put her in the hospital. Moving to San Diego offered her a chance to get away from this hostile environment to one where she would feel safe from any further assaults. As Karen said later, all she wanted was, "to relax my mind so that I could put my life back together and find a good job."

She tried to present herself as independent, motivated, someone of integrity, and someone who was willing to take on new challenges. Although she had been a drug abuser, she said she'd been clean for three years. The drugs, physical abuse and street life had certainly contributed to her rough appearance. She was tall, almost 5' 10", very thin, and had light-colored hair. Her wire-rim glasses gave her the appearance of looking older than her 29 years. It also suggested a style more familiar with a generation that sought free love and sex, than the generation that not only engaged in sex with latex barriers but also invested in the rubber companies that made the protective shields.

It was about a month later when Sam contacted Robert Knott, a case manager at the shelter who helped the shelter's homeless clients obtain training, in order to find a job. Knott and the shelter were always eager to find employers who were willing to hire one of their homeless residents, and had a successful record of doing so through their "Help Program" which was funded by the U.S. Department of Labor.

It was early in the afternoon when Sam met Knott at St. Vincent's. He introduced himself as the manager of several pieces of rental property, and said that he was looking for potential property managers. "I took him on a tour of the facility," Knott said. "I told him how we help the homeless at the center."

During the tour, Sam told Knott that he had one immediate vacancy for a property manager but he expected to have more in the near future. "He specifically requested a female between the ages of 18 and 35. He said he wanted the person to do minimal accounting for the property, and, in return, they would receive an income and be provided with a place to live."

Knott knew of one particular person at the shelter who was not only looking for a job, but who fit the profile Sam had requested. He gave Karen, who had been at the shelter about six weeks, Sam's number and suggested she call him.

Sam and Karen met on Monday, July 1, 1991, at the shelter. It was within hours of Sam having dropped Jamiss off at the San Diego Airport. The meeting had been arranged after Karen's telephone call to Sam. He picked her up for what Karen believed was to be a job interview. They drove in Sam's car, to an apartment complex in Carlsbad, just outside San Diego. Since arriving in San Diego, Sam had been looking for work. He filled out applications and passed out resumes that contained false names and addresses as references to prospective employers. Like so many other things, Sam simply lied about the personal details.

On the way, Sam stopped at the Jack in the Box, famous for having made several people sick a years prior after serving meat that had been undercooked. Sam had a hamburger and something to drink. Karen just had a coke. Neither of them became ill after their brief encounter at Jack in the Box.

They weren't at the apartment complex very long. Sam spoke to a woman Karen remembered only as "Bobbie", and thought he was talking to her about setting up a meeting with someone else for another time.

"He told me he wanted me to see the complex, to see if I liked it. I was going to be the bookkeeper for that complex and that if I wanted it, he would train me into management," Karen said.

After the short meeting in Carlsbad, Sam drove Karen back to St. Vincent's. He told her he wanted to meet with her and return to Carlsbad the following morning at 11. Karen was excited about the prospect of getting a job and moving out of the homeless shelter. Sam had asked her to dress nice because they were going to have lunch with Bobbie. It was important, he told her, that she look "good" for the interview.

Not having anything particularly suitable to wear, Karen borrowed a black and white jumpsuit from her friend, Jackie, who lived in the room next to her at the shelter.

Sam was late picking Karen up. She had gotten worried and called his apartment. When there was no answer, she left a short message on his answering machine. A little over 30 minutes after he was scheduled to pick her up, Sam arrived at Saint Vincent's. As the two of them drove toward Carlsbad, Sam counseled Karen as to how she should act and what she should say should Bobbie ask any questions. Sam told Karen to say they had known each other for about five years.

"Once we got to Carlsbad, we met with this lady. She started to ask me some questions, but Sam cut me off," Karen said. "Anytime I tried to say anything or answer one of her questions, he would interrupt. She started to ask me directly how long we had known each other, and when I started to say anything, he said, well, I've known her about five years."

The meeting in Carlsbad was a brief one. Sam drove Karen back to Saint Vincent's early in the afternoon. He asked if she would like to have dinner with him that evening, claiming he had cooked up some spaghetti. But Karen declined. Sam insisted that they meet again later that day, claiming he wanted to show her another apartment in El Cajon. It would be a smaller one-bedroom apartment but it would still allow her a chance to get out of the shelter, something she desperately wanted to do. Karen agreed to meet Sam later that afternoon and even agreed to meet him somewhere so he wouldn't have to drive all the way back downtown. Sam told her he appreciated the offer and to meet him at the Trolley stop located at 32nd Street and Imperial in San Diego.

It was about 4 p.m. when Sam and Karen drove to an apartment complex in El Cajon. But they never actually met with anyone to discuss Karen's working or living there. Sam made small talk, telling Karen the place needed a lot of work. She really didn't care; she saw the place as a means to get her life back on track.

Sam told her he needed to make some phone calls and drove back to the apartment he was sharing with Steve and Lauren Skye, whom he had met several years before in Phoenix.

"He went in to use the phone," Karen said. "He asked me to come in and I told him I didn't want to, that I would just sit in the car."

When he returned about an hour later, he appeared hurried and told Karen he had forgotten something in El Cajon. On the way to El Cajon, he told her he needed to make another phone call and pulled off the freeway, into Wells Park.

Sam told Karen he was going to look for a telephone. As Sam walked around a building he disappeared briefly from Karen's sight. Karen, having sat in the car for over an hour, got out and leaned against the hood of the car. When he returned, he reached up and grabbed Karen by the throat, squeezing, as he pushed her against the hood of the car. Karen struggled, trying to push him back, but she was no match for Sam who was stronger and outweighed her by over 100 pounds.

"He told me not to scream and not to fight him," she said. He said he didn't want to hurt me. He told me to take off my jumpsuit. I was scared; he still had his hands on my throat so I did what he told me to do. After I pulled down my jumpsuit, he pushed me back across the hood of the car. I was still scared, frightened. He spread my legs open with his legs and pushed himself inside me. I was praying to God not to let this be happening to me," Karen recalled, as she wiped the tears from her eyes.

"He became more violent each time he took himself out and shoved himself back in me. I couldn't scream because he had me by the throat. I knew I didn't have any chance to get away; he was much bigger than I was. I was just scared and in a lot of pain," Karen said.

Karen claims that when Sam was finished sexually assaulting her, he drove her to the El Cajon Trolley Station and gave her a dollar for the fare because she didn't have any money to get back to the shelter. "He told me not to tell anyone and said that if I did, he knew who my friends were and how to find me," Karen said.

In shock, Karen got on a trolley traveling in the opposite direction of shelter before she realized her mistake. She took off her shoes and stood barefoot on the trolley platform for what seemed like an eternity before getting on another trolley, one that would take her back to the safe haven of Saint Vincent de Paul's.

After arriving at the shelter around 10 p.m., one of the women at the intake desk stopped Karen to tell her that her boss had called twice. According to the message, Sam had been very insistent on talking to her, wanting to know exactly why she wasn't at the shelter.

"I'm not sure why, but I called him," Karen said. He wanted to know why it took me so long to get home. He asked if I talked to anyone and I told him no. Sam then told me that if I took the job at the apartment complex in El Cajon, I could live with him and that I would be better off than what I had." Karen did not agree and hung up the phone.

She didn't tell anyone that night that she had been raped. She was still terrified and felt filthy, saying she took three showers just to get the "feeling of him off of her." After the first shower, she ran into her friend, Jackie, and told her she would wash the jumpsuit before she gave it back to her. It was early the next morning when Karen told Jackie she had been raped.

Officer Ricky Powell had been with the San Diego Police Department for less than three years when he received a radio call at about 11 a.m. to go to the Saint Vincent de Paul Center to investigate a rape.

"When I first met Karen she was very upset and would not even talk to me," Powell reported. "I think I spent about seven hours with her that day. Later, she opened up a bit, telling me what happened."

But Powell knew he didn't have all the facts required for his preliminary report, especially the exact location of the alleged rape. That would have to be determined later by the investigators who followed up on rape cases. His job was not over, however. He was still gathering information and evidence related to Karen's accusations. Part of his responsibility required that he take Karen to the hospital for a rape examination.

Several days later, Karen, at Jackie's suggestion, sat down and composed a letter describing the attack and her feelings:

"I tried to laugh and smile, but I guess it's a cover-up for the pain and anger that I really feel inside. I want so much to just be me again but I don't know if I could. No matter how much I pray, his devil eyes keep looking at me and the sound of his voice keeps playing over and over in my ears (don't scream or fight with me or I'll hurt you and I don't want to mess up a pretty lady like you.) I can feel his cold hand on my neck as he holds me back across the hood of his car and his other hand holds my left hip firmly against the side of the car. All I could do was close my eyes, cry, and pray that it would all soon be over. He kept telling me that I was a beautiful woman and I liked what he was doing and if I would relax, he wouldn't hurt me and it would be okay. I wanted to scream but he would hurt me more or even kill me (I wasn't sure) so I just laid there praying and crying. I tried to push him off but the way he had me on the hood of the car. I had no strength to get up. I felt so helpless. I wish all of this madness would go away. I can't take it much longer. If I could end my life right now, I would (just to get away from this torment he is putting me through.) But I know I would never find the nerve to do it. I'm praying that somehow, God will give me the strength to make it through all of this and what's ahead. If I could only have one wish come true right now, (it) would be to wake up and it all be just a dream."

One week later, on July 10, 1990, Detective Harry Hicks of the El Cajon Police Department received orders to investigate the alleged rape of Karen. Hicks, after more than 15 years with the El Cajon Police Department, took pride in keeping himself in good shape. He stood just over 6 feet, wore glasses, and sported a neatly trimmed moustache. His youthful appearance did not suggest he was only a few years away from retirement, bringing with it the possibility of leaving the San Diego area and sailing the blue waters of far off distant islands. But such reverie, engaged in by most everyone in Hicks profession, had its time and place. Hicks would escape to those thoughts again some other time.

Hicks picked up Karen and her counselor, Belkis Bottfield, and drove around El Cajon, trying to find the park where the alleged rape occurred. Karen could recall little about the park except that it had a children's jungle gym near the parking lot and that the man who attacked her had been wearing a white shirt, black pants and a tie with a Chicago Bulls tiepin. As they drove into Wells Park, Karen began to cry, shaking her head, she told Hicks, "This was the place."

On July 12, Hicks learned that Sam Consiglio was residing at the Buena Vista Apartments in El Cajon. The assistant manager of the complex had given him a description of a man fitting Sam's description who had been house sitting for the tenants in apartment #3. Hicks drove by the apartment complex early that afternoon but there was no sign of Sam or his car.

At 7:50 that evening, Sam contacted the El Cajon Police Department to report a break-in at a neighbor's apartment.

"When I arrived at the apartment, I knocked on the door. A voice from inside told me to come in," Hicks said. "I recognized Sam Consiglio from the description given to me by Karen and from a booking photo I had obtained earlier. I told Consiglio I was placing him under arrest for the rape of Karen. He told me he had no idea what I was talking about, but he did know a Karen from Saint Vincent de Paul's but he never had sex with her."

Hicks continued to listen to Sam, who appeared irritated at the accusation, telling Hicks the only reason he was there to arrest him was because of his past criminal record. Hicks told Sam that he didn't know anything about his past record.

"Consiglio told me that he had been in prison for fondling a girl's breasts," Hicks said. "I asked him how long he had been in prison and he told me '8 years.' I told him that that seemed to be quite a harsh penalty for fondling a girls breasts." Hicks then advised him of his rights, the ones that afforded him the opportunity to keep his mouth shut, which was something Sam was not accustomed to doing.

Sam told Hicks that he understood his rights and that he was more than prepared to discuss the allegations. He gave Hicks consent to search his bedroom and closet for clothing. During the search, Hicks found a black pair of pants and a white shirt and tiepin with a Chicago Bulls "World Champions, 1991, NBA" logo on it. When Hicks and Sam arrived at the El Cajon Police Department, Sam provided the investigators with a urine sample. Afterward, Sam was taken to the Valley Medical Center in San Diego, where medical personnel took vials of blood samples from him.

Later that evening, Hicks questioned Sam about his relationship with Karen. "I asked Consiglio why he was seeking another job in Carlsbad when he had just become an apartment manager in El Cajon," Hicks said. "He told me that he was trying to get into a bigger complex and to do this, he needed someone else to accompany him and thought this (having a woman along) would be a good business arrangement. I also asked him if he had any sexual contact with her, whether it was kissing, fondling or sexual intercourse and he said very emphatically, never. He told me he couldn't think of any reason why Karen would make these allegations against him."

Before Hicks finished questioning Sam, he asked Robert Aptman, an evidence technician with the El Cajon Police Department, to obtain physical evidence from Sam. In addition to taking a variety of photographs of Sam, Altman collected a saliva sample, hair from Sam's head, mustache, and chest, samples of pubic hair, and two swabs taken from his penis glands and urethra penile.

On July 13, 1990, Sam was told his bond on the charge of rape was $25,000. Sitting in the San Diego County jail with no money or means to post his bond, Sam telephoned American Express. He had been a cardholder less than three months. On his application, completed shortly after his release from the Michigan State Prison, he had provided fictitious information about his employment and financial status. But based on the information Sam had provided, American Express agreed to guarantee payment for the bond. Later that afternoon, Sam posted bail through a local bail bondsman and was released. He paid the standard 10 percent fee to the unsuspecting bondsman using his American Express card. Sam later said that, "American Express certainly gave new meaning to the words in the commercial, don't ever leave home without it."

Mike Przytulski could never be accused of being a slave to fashion, or getting caught up in the fitness craze. But, as a deputy district attorney for the County of San Diego, Przytulski's reputation as a prosecutor who demonstrated a bulldog's tenacity made him a favorite of many cops who hoped to gain convictions of those they arrested. Przytulski had been assigned to Hicks' case involving Karen's allegation, that Sam had raped her.

P. J. Harn was more conscious about his appearance. After 17 years as an investigator with the San Diego County District Attorneys office, Harn still kept himself relatively trim. Like Hicks, Harn wore glasses and kept a neatly trimmed moustache. His appearance exhibited every bit the image of a professional investigator. On July 16, Harn and Przytulski went to see Sam at his apartment in El Cajon to discuss the allegations that he raped Karen. But Sam wasn't home and they both had other matters to deal with, so Przytulski left Sam a message to call him.

"When I called him, he asked if I would come in and talk so we could hopefully clear up the case," Sam said. "I know you should never talk to the D.A. but in this case, I felt that because I was completely innocent and had nothing to hide, it would be in my best interests to cooperate as much as I could. Besides that, he did sound sincere about clearing everything up."

The following day, Sam drove to the San Diego District Attorney's office to meet with Przytulski and Harn.

Harn started the question-and-answer session by reading Sam his constitutional rights. Sam, as he had indicated to Hicks four days prior, told Harn that he understood his rights. Harn asked Sam if he still wanted to talk to him and Sam said, "most certainly." After asking a series of simple background questions including information such as where do you live, phone number, date of birth, all of which Sam offered cooperatively and without hesitation, Harn began to focus on the more significant questions. These questions dealt with Karen's accusation that Sam had raped her.

Sam told Harn that he came up with the idea of using a homeless person to help him get a job. "I thought it was ingenious at the time, I really did," Sam told Harn.

"Do you remember the first day you spoke with Karen?" Harn asked.

"The first day I spoke with Karen was July the first. Bob Knott called me, I believe on Friday morning because I had requested a female between 25-35 and that the only requirement be that she looked presentable," Sam said.

"Once you met Karen, did you tell her at that time what her specific duties were going to be?"

"I started to explain the job completely, I left nothing out," Sam answered.

"Did you indicate to her that you were just going for a job interview and that there was nothing in concrete?" Harn continued.

"Of course," Sam responded. "I explained everything to her. I mean, before we got there, she knew exactly what we were up against. She was very excited; she was looking forward to it. I can tell that she was very happy about it."

Sam told Harn that he and Karen drove to the Coast Apartment complex in Carlsbad where they met with a woman named Bobbie. Sam had already sent Bobbie a resume indicating that he had been in the property management business since 1980. The resume didn't indicate that Sam had also been in a Michigan prison for a large part of that time. But the decision of who to hire as the apartment manager was not up to Bobbie. Her boss, Elizabeth, maintained that responsibility and Elizabeth was not available.

Sam continued telling Harn that he and Karen drove back to San Diego where he placed a telephone call to Elizabeth and told her that he would take the apartment. Elizabeth was stunned. She told Sam that was not the way it worked and offered to meet him the following day at noon for a formal interview. Sam told Harn that he drove Karen back to Saint Vincent's and told her he'd pick her up the following morning.

"Did you pick her up at 11 the next day, July 2nd" Harn asked?

"No," Sam responded. "I did not. I think it was 11:30. It was about 11:15 a.m., I was leaving the apartment when Karen called. I didn't pick up the answering machine because I was afraid to get tied up. Karen sounded very, very impatient, I can't remember her exact words, something to the effect, it's 11:15, you told me you'd be here at 11. I don't know what's going on. Hearing that, I figured I'd better get going before she really got upset. I didn't want her to get upset and change her mind."

"So you picked her up at approximately 11:30 on July 2nd, where did you go from there?" Harn asked.

"We went directly to Carlsbad," Sam claimed.

Sam told Harn that he and Karen met Elizabeth to discuss their managing the apartment complex. Sam complained that he was a little uncomfortable since the discussion involved salary. Sam said he was forced into discussing salary with Elizabeth in front of Karen who he had hoped would not be made aware of any information involving compensation. Sam never really intended to pay Karen, or if he did pay her anything, it certainly would not have been much. Sam's plan was to provide Karen a room to live in at no charge and little to nothing else. Sam told Harn that Elizabeth asked Karen if she had any experience doing bookkeeping.

"Karen really caught me off guard when she says yes," Sam said. "I didn't really expect her to say that at all. I knew that was a bad move on her part."

When Elizabeth asked Karen for references, Karen claimed she had worked for a restaurant in Seattle, which had gone out of business. "Elizabeth knows that's a lie," Sam told Harn. "That's common for people to say something like that. So, I kind of blame myself, because I wanted to make sure we got the job. That was the bottom line."

After a short break in the interview process, Harn and Mike Przytulski continued questioning Sam. Before resuming, however, Harn reminded Sam of his constitutional rights and his right to remain silent. Sam challenged his interrogators. He told Harn, "not only do I understand my rights very clearly, but I urge you to continue the interview."

"On the way back from Carlsbad to Clairemont, I made it very clear to Karen that I was not optimistic about our chances of getting the job," Sam told Harn. "Karen was very upset and became a little argumentative saying I don't care what you say, I think we got it."

Sam told Harn and Przytulski that he drove Karen back to Saint Vincent's sometime around 3:40 p.m. and dropped her off. "I asked Karen if she would be interested in a spaghetti dinner. She agreed, so, I made plans to meet her later that evening."

"Where did you go from there?" Harn asked.

"I went back to Clairemont Drive. I was there the rest of the evening."

"What did you do after that?" Harn continued.

"I don't have any solid evidence but I do know that I never left that evening. I made many phone calls and when I make phone calls, they are long distance and they are through my AT&T calling cards."

"Did you call Karen at any time?"

"No," Sam responded.

"When was the next time you talked to her?" Harn asked.

Sam started laughing, looking directly at Harn and said "You're doing it to me again buddy, there's something that's important here."

Harn was feeling frustrated. But he was a seasoned cop and knew it wasn't time to reveal his anger at his opponent. He'd seen this type of behavior before in suspects charged with every type of crime. Maintaining his composure, Harn asked Sam to tell him about the last time he spoke to Karen and then, Sam could explain whatever it was he considered important.

"Okay, that's fine, I can go with that," Sam said. Sam was feeling even more confident now that he had negotiated himself an opportunity to tell his story.

"The next and last time I ever had any contact with Karen was on July the 3rd and that was between the hours of 11 p.m. and midnight," Sam said.

"Now it's your turn," Harn told Sam.

"Thank you," Sam said, making sure he demonstrated the proper courtesy and respect he felt Harn wanted. "She called me, okay. You cannot call into Saint Vincent's after 9 p.m. Prior to 9, I did leave a message and it took her that long to get back to me."

"What was the purpose of that call?" Harn asked.

"To tell her I found out I didn't get the job."

"Okay, go ahead," Harn told Sam.

"I have a very good friend in Florida. I talked to her that night at 10. I remember that very clearly. I watched television until midnight and then I went to sleep. The thing that I wanted to point out is that I honestly forgot about the spaghetti dinner. I don't know if that bothered her or what, I can't figure it out. But I forgot. I was just too busy talking on the phone."

"That was the second," Harn said. "I want to know about the third."

"The third is when I got up and said I was cleaning the apartment. I spent most of the day cleaning (the apartment) in Clairemont and talking on the phone. I called Karen several times and left messages. She finally returned my call between 11 and midnight. She was unhappy. I offered her an apartment in El Cajon but there was no job involved for her. I could tell she was unhappy. I went to sleep around one in the morning. That was the last time I ever spoke to her."

"When did you move into El Cajon?"

"I went to El Cajon on the morning of the 4th. I can be very, very specific for you because I have receipts to back everything."

Sam told Harn that on June 28th, he had already signed a contract to manage a smaller apartment complex in El Cajon. The complex came with a two-bedroom apartment and a salary of $400 a month.

Harn, confused about Sam's actions on the second and the third, asked Sam why, if he had a job before the 28th of June, he took Karen to look at an apartment complex in Carlsbad.

"The job in El Cajon had been the first real offer I'd received since arriving in California," Sam explained to Harn. "When the possibility of managing a larger complex came up, I was excited. I thought, I'm gonna double my income here. I'm not stupid, I figured I got nothing to lose."

"How can you double your income if you split your money with Karen?" Harn asked.

Sam laughed, telling Harn, "I didn't plan to give her half of what I made."

Harn was still trying to sort through Sam's evasive answers. He certainly believed that Sam had danced around the questions as well as anyone he'd seen in years. Still, Harn had to establish or at least clarify, where Sam claimed he was on July 2nd and especially the 3rd. Sam was adamant he had not been to El Cajon on July 3rd. But Harn wanted proof. Sam said he was still living with his friends, Steve and Lauren Skye, on that day.

"No doubt in your mind?" Harn asked, losing patience, but not allowing Sam to see his frustrations.

"No doubt," Sam said. "Believe me, I'm a phoneaholic. I have to have a telephone. There was no phone for me. There was no furniture, nothing, not even a bed." Sam was starting to reveal his anger while Harn pressed for specific answers.

"The only way I can verify this is through AT&T charges, okay. If we get those, it will help," Sam said.

"Okay," Harn said. "We are going back to when Karen called you. Did she say how could you call me after what you've done to me? Did she make that statement to you?"

"Never," Sam said. "Never made any statement like that whatsoever."

"Okay, what did she say when you told her we're out of the job?"

"She reminded me of a little kid. I felt kind of bad for her, you know. She was disappointed so I made her an offer. I said, I don't have to do this but I don't want to let you down. I got this two-bedroom apartment, if you want to, you don't have to live in the shelter anymore, you can have the other bedroom. I was going to rent it out anyway. We can work it out later, but you're gonna have to pay rent and utilities," Sam told Harn.

"Did you know that Karen had roommates at Saint Vincent's? That she had a roommate who loaned her a jump suit specifically for the ride to El Cajon? She was to get a job interview with you," Harn told Consiglio.

The anger in Sam's face was clearly visible now. He looked at Harn with demonic intensity in his eyes, and screamed, "No, that's not true, that's not true, that is not true, I'm telling you. These fucking women, they got you buffed. You're wrong, she has never been with me in El Cajon in her life, in my life she would never be with me in El Cajon. Never happened, never will and there's no way you are going to sit there and try to convince me or anyone else because you're wrong and you let her pull the wool over your eyes. She's never been there, so help me God."

Harn had certainly heard the introduction of God during interviews with subjects before. The importance of introducing the Almighty usually meant the person opposite him was looking for some way out of the corner they were boxing themselves into. Harn began to press Sam, knowing he was growing irritated at the questions. Harn knew this was no time to let up.

"Tell me about the Trolley ticket," Harn asked. "It's just, you know, she's not familiar with the town. She's never been to El Cajon. She says she's been there once, that was with you. And, that you dropped her at the Trolley stand and gave her a buck for a one-way ticket and the ticket shows that."

Sam moved in his seat, his face tensed. He looked at Harn and in a loud, angry voice said, "What are you talking about? I don't know what the hell you are talking about."

"I'm talking about rape, Sam," Harn shouted back. "I'm talking about you dropping the broad off at the Trolley station in El Cajon. Giving her a buck to get back, that's what I'm talking about, Sam."

"She's lying, she's lying," Sam screamed. His agitation was turning to anger.

"Is that ticket lying?" Harn yelled back at Sam. "The ticket can't lie."

"I can't say she's lying about that, but I can tell you where she is lying. She's never been with me in El Cajon and I've never touched her. The tests will tell the story," Sam said, his voice calmer now as he tried to gain more control of emotions. "I want the results now," he demanded, "that's why I came in today. I don't want this to hang over my head. I want to resolve it now."

Przytulski sat patiently as Harn and Sam exchanged verbal blows, each trying to remain on the offensive as the two played off each other in a game of cat and mouse. Przytulski had waited long enough for his turn to enter the challenge. Calmly, he looked at Sam sitting across the desk and asked, "Sam, a personal question, do you have herpes?"

"No," Sam said.

"Have you ever had herpes?" Przytulski asked.

Again, Sam simply said "No."

Przytulski changed the direction of the questions asking Sam if he knew where Wells Park was.

"I don't know Wells Park, period," Sam replied.

Przytulski was surprised by Sam's answer. Wells Park was well known to the residents of El Cajon; it was the biggest park in the city.

Sam was adamant, telling Przytulski, "I don't know where it is at as we speak."

Harn listened for several moments as the deputy district attorney asked Sam several more questions, all of which had been asked and answered in one form or another earlier in the interview. Now it was Harn's turn to interrupt. He looked directly into Sam's eyes and said, "I think you did it, I think you screwed her. But you know, my only question is, was it consensual or was it forceful, that's what it comes down to in all rape cases. Was it either consensual or was it forced?"

"You apparently have no faith in your own testing system," Sam told Harn. "Cause if you had faith, won't…"

Harn interrupted Sam, stopping him from further delusion. "I have no faith in you Sam," he said. "I don't deal with tests, I deal with people."

Sam shot back at Harn, "Wait for the tests. The test will exonerate me. I never touched her, period. I repeat no part of my body has ever touched any part of her body at anytime. Those tests, if you have faith in them, will prove it. All I can say, is you'll see."

Outwardly, Przytulski maintained a calm appearance, while inside he felt the same anxiety as Harn. Neither man believed Sam. But Przytulski wasn't about to let Sam know how he felt, not yet.

"Did you ejaculate inside of her?" Przytulski asked Sam.

"I never touched Karen, never," Sam said.

Harn fired back a series of questions as Sam turned in his chair, answering the questions as fast as they were delivered. "At any time, did you insert your penis in Karen's vagina?" Harn asked.

"No, never," Sam fired back.

"Did you ever insert your penis in her anus?" Harn continued.

"No, never," Sam said, not altering his composure, as he sat confident of each of his responses. Sam had seen this look before. It was a look of frustration in Harn's face and Sam loved it.

"Did you ever take your clothes off? Did you ever just unzip your pants?" Harn asked.

"Never made any sexual confrontations whatsoever. Never, not even close," Sam continued as he maintained his innocence. But it was apparent to Sam that he had, no doubt, misunderstood Harn's fascination for trying to get at the truth.

Przytulski slowed the rate of verbal exchange and re-directed the focus of the examination. "Sam, I've seen a copy of your resume, you lied deliberately?"

"I needed to get a job," Sam said, beginning to show signs of anger and distress. "Let's point out what you're talking about. It's not fair to put that on tape if you're not gonna clarify what the lie is."

"You're absolutely right," Przytulski said. "You put on your resume that from 1980 to present, you've been employed in property management, right?"

"That was false," Sam said.

"That was false because you had actually been incarcerated for all but eight years of that time," Przytulski followed.

"And you think it's fair to do this?" Sam asked, knowing Przytulski and Harn had been able to capture him in a lie, a lie he was unable to explain away. "You don't have to say anything about that. That's not fair. I can't believe you guys did that and I trusted you," Sam said, angry that Przytulski and Harn had asked these questions while the tape recorder was still running.

Przytulski directed the questioning back to the incident involving Karen. "Did you lie to the people at Saint Vincent's when you went down there to tell them what you wanted Karen for?"

"I never told them the…"

"The truth," Przytulski interrupted as he answered the question for Sam.

"The whole picture," Sam said, preferring his answer to the one provided by the deputy district attorney. "You guys aren't interested in the truth at all."

"I think we are," replied Przytulski.

"We've been here for almost two hours talking to you," Harn interjected.

During two hours of questioning, Harn had noticed that Sam failed to react the way most innocent people do when confronted by the police. He exhibited no signs of shock or fear. His anger was focused and controlled. There was no threat to sue the police or the victim for harassment. Harn was convinced that Sam had lied.

"That was a trick and you know it was a trick," Sam said. "But that's okay because it doesn't matter to me. I have nothing to fear. You can do all the tricks you want. The bottom line is the only thing that is important to me is that I never touched that woman, ever."

At the conclusion of the recorded interview, Sam felt confident that he had presented his case to Przytulski and Harn. He was certain he had convinced them that he was innocent of Karen's charges, or at the least, they would never be able to prove otherwise.

As he stood preparing to leave, Sam told Harn and Przytulski that since arriving in San Diego in late May, he had not committed any crimes whatsoever.

"None?" Przytulski asked.

Sam took a deep breath, smiled and said, "None. Nothing other than getting a free blow job from that hooker."

Sam's demeanor turned more jovial as he tried to put a humorous slant on his response, actually trying to impress Harn and Przytulski. "I felt I had nothing to hide," Sam recalled. Sam told Harn and Przytulski that, "the worst thing I've done, even though it wasn't illegal, was having sex with this ugly hooker who wasn't charging me anything because she thought I was a cop and I never did anything to correct her thinking."

Sam was playing his typical self-serving, self-amusing game with his patronizing smile and smirks. They had nothing on him; he was convinced of it. Trying to impress his interrogators, Sam volunteered Carol's name, address and phone number to them.

After a few minutes, Harn placed Sam under arrest for the rape of Karen. This was the second time Sam had been arrested for allegedly raping Karen.

"At the time I made those comments, I had no idea the D.A. would try and build a case on that (Carol) too," Sam said.

Based on new evidence of yet another similar crime, Przytulski was able to convince municipal court judge Lawrence Sterling, to raise Sam's bond to $1 million. This time, Sam was unable to use his American Express card. The million dollars required for bond was just over his credit limit.

Chapter 14

"All Warfare is Based on Deception"
The Art of War, Sun Tzu

Sam sat alone inside a small cell in the San Diego County Jail. His thoughts centered on the new charges related to his sexual encounter with Carol. It would have been his mother's 68th birthday. Four days later, Karen noticed an outbreak of blisters in the area of her vagina. She went to Mercy Hospital in San Diego where the doctor who examined her diagnosed the blisters as herpes. About the same time Karen was learning that she was going to have to live with this new disease, Sam was contacted by a public defender.

"My spirits really picked up when this guy told me the date the D.A. was alleging I raped Karen was that of July 2, 1991," Sam said. "I knew I could prove that I was home in my apartment all that day. I was on the telephone all day and would be able to prove it using my phone bills as evidence."

But the public defender had other ideas. He recommended Sam seek a postponement in the proceedings, hoping to use the time to negotiate a plea bargain, or, to give Karen the opportunity to leave San Diego, as many "homeless and transient" people often did. Sam protested, insisting that this case move forward without delay. He insisted that he was innocent of the charges and wanted out of jail as quickly as possible. The attorney objected to Sam's strategy and stressed the importance of seeking a delay, emphasizing that time could be their greatest ally. But, again, Sam refused the advice of his counsel. "There was no way I could allow him to represent me," Sam said. "So I went out and hired my own attorney."

Several days later, Harn and Przytulski contacted Carolyn at her small apartment in San Diego, where she lived with her boyfriend, Ronald. Carolyn told Harn she had been working as a prostitute and she didn't know anyone by the name of Sam Consiglio. However, she told Harn about a policeman on the vice-squad named "John" who was blackmailing her for sex. Carolyn described John as being about 5'10", 200 pounds, with dark wavy hair. She remembered that John drove a new black car with bucket seats.

"The last time I had sex with him was on July 4," Carolyn told Harn. "He took me to a motel in the Clairemont area of San Diego and made me perform oral, vaginal, and anal sex with him. I tried not to have anal sex, but he got real mad and threatened to beat me. I told him I had herpes but he said that he didn't care. He would usually come around once or twice a week, but around the middle of July, he stopped coming. Sometimes he would call, but I haven't seen him since," she told Harn.

While Carolyn was relating her story of how John made her pose for nude photographs in the motel room, her phone rang. Ronald rushed into the room where Harn and Przytulski sat questioning his girlfriend. "It's him", he said. "He's on the phone." Harn walked into the back room and listened as Carolyn spoke to John. "I recognized the voice to be Sam's," Harn, said later. "I don't want to have sex with you," Carolyn told the caller.

"That's okay. I'll see you in a few days and we'll just have coffee together and talk," Sam said.

"Are you a cop?" Carol asked.

"I told you I wouldn't talk about that on the phone. I just want you to not say anything, you watch my back and I'll watch yours. I'll see you in a couple of days."

Carol said good-bye and hung up the phone. Harn told her that the blackmailer was not a police officer, his name was Sam Consiglio, and that he was in jail on another rape-related charge. Carol breathed a sigh of relief and told Harn that she was happy to know that.

"I was pretty sure I was going to get this case dismissed but I didn't want to give the D.A. anything he could use against me," Sam said. "I thought I'd call Carol and make sure the D.A. wasn't planning any surprises for me. We only talked for about five minutes. I didn't think anyone had contacted her yet, so before hanging up, I told her that in case she was ever contacted, she shouldn't talk to anyone about everything we had done. It was more out of embarrassment than anything else. How the hell was I supposed to know that when I called her, the D.A. was sitting there listening to my every word?"

From inside the San Diego jail, Sam continued making phone calls to anyone who would accept the charges or to anyone that he thought might be able to help him. Some of those people, he thought, were local news reporters. The DA's office had Sam placed in segregation after witnessing the call to Carol. While there, Sam lost all his telephone privileges.

On July 31, Sam represented himself at his preliminary hearing on the charge of sexually assaulting Karen. The hearing was held before municipal court judge Jane Kintner in the San Diego District Court. It was a relatively short process. Karen provided testimony describing the date, time, and place of the attack committed against her by Sam Consiglio. Deputy District Attorney Przytulski asked Karen how many times Sam entered her during the alleged assault.

"Three times," she replied. After Karen concluded her testimony, Sam approached the judge and presented her with a copy of his telephone bill covering the early part of July.

"I knew the phone bill would show that I was on the phone at the time Karen claimed I raped her," Sam said. He thought the phone bill, which revealed a long series of phone calls on the night of July 2nd, would get the case dismissed and he would be on his way home. But judge Kintner told Sam he was going to have to find a way to present his evidence properly.

"Mr. Consiglio, let me tell you, the truth is very important," the judge said. "But the law, the legislators, and the courts have devised ways to make sure the truth comes out, and not something that is not the truth.

That is called the evidence code. That determines what can come in evidence and, therefore, somebody cannot just pick up a piece of paper and have the court consider it. If it were obvious to me that there was a way to get it in, I would tell you. I cannot see a way because you seem to have a document that is from some agency that is not represented here."

Sam had no idea how he was going to do that. He figured he'd take the stand and get the phone bill admitted through his own testimony. He had obviously not done his homework. What Sam didn't realize was that he was going to be cross-examined by the D.A.

Przytulski asked Sam about his relationship with Carol and told Sam he was at her apartment when Sam called her. "That really caught me off guard," Sam said. "Instead of trying to protect myself, I just made myself look guilty."

"You indicated, Mr. Consiglio, that you were cooperative, right?" Przytulski asked Sam.

"Yes," Sam said.

"You were truthful to the district attorney's office?"

"I think the term I used was cooperative."

"Well, I am asking you, were you truthful?"

"Yes."

"In everything?"

"Yes."

"Did you impersonate yourself to a prostitute as a police officer for the purpose of forcing her to have sex with you?"

"No," Sam said.

"Did you ever tell anybody in the district attorney's office, myself and P.J. Harn, in particular, that there was a prostitute that you had sex with on July 4th in which she thought you were a police officer, and that you let her believe that?"

Sam drew a long breath. "I don't recall ever saying that to you or Harn."

"Do you remember the name Carol?"

"No."

"Do you remember providing us with a name and phone number of this prostitute?"

"I don't recall, no."

"Yesterday, at approximately 2 in the afternoon, did you call this prostitute and tell her that she wasn't to say anything to the district attorney or anybody when they came to talk to her?"

"I talked to a prostitute named Sue yesterday."

"Did you tell her not to cooperate with the district attorney?"

"No, I did not say that."

"What did you tell her?"

"I just told her to keep quiet."

"Keep quiet about what?" Przytulski asked.

"About our relationship."

"What was that relationship?"

"I was a customer and she was a prostitute."

"Did you represent yourself as being a police officer?"

"No. She always thought I was a police officer, but I never told her I was one."

"Do you recall her asking you yesterday on the phone, are you really a cop? Do you recall that question?"

"I told her I didn't want to talk about that right now," Sam said.

"Why didn't you want to talk about it with her?"

Sam was incensed at the district attorney's questions. He was more aggravated with himself because the questions dealt with another case, not with Karen's allegations. Not knowing how to stop the district attorney's line of questioning, Sam turned to judge Kintner and asked, "Your honor, I don't understand the relevance of this at all."

"Well, you told us you were cooperative and truthful, right? Przytulski asked.

"I was," Sam answered. "I don't see what bearing this has on anything."

"Well, she just overruled the objection."

"I overruled it in view of your testimony where you insisted on talking about being cooperative with the district attorney" judge Kintner told Sam.

"The fact is, at some point in time when you met her you told her you were a vice cop, didn't you?" Przytulski asked.

"Never," Sam yelled.

"And you told her that if she didn't have sex with you she was going to jail?"

"Never, never, never, never said that," Sam fired back.

"In fact, you took her to your apartment up in Clairemont on the 4th of July and you had sex with her then, right?"

"Not on the 4th. No."

"You didn't have oral, vaginal, and anal sex with her?" Przytulski asked quickly, his voice raised, almost shouting.

"No," Sam yelled again.

"You didn't threaten to beat her up if she didn't have anal sex?"

"No," Sam shouted.

Judge Kintner interrupted the heated exchange between Sam and the district attorney and instructed them they were going to have to get back to the case involving Karen.

Przytulski questioned Sam for over an hour about his previous convictions, his escape from a Michigan prison, and other allegations of sexual misconduct. Sam was careful to listen to each question and, when convenient, would not recall the correct answer or would avoid the question by providing some justification for his actions. Frustrated with his performance as a trial attorney, Sam turned to the judge and said, "I am very disillusioned, your honor. I mean, I am an innocent person here. I have evidence that proves without a doubt that I am innocent. And you won't let me get it in. I understand you have rules and regulations. Maybe I should have had an attorney with me, but the attorney I had was not going to allow me to represent this evidence at trial and I thought that was stupid because it proves without a doubt that I am innocent and they can't cover it up. The truth should be first and foremost." Sam was never able to get his phone bill entered into evidence.

Judge Kintner told Sam that the judicial system aims to uncover the whole truth and that is the reason for the rules of evidence, rules, which prohibit people from introducing anything they want without the proper legal foundation. At the conclusion of the hearing, judge Kintner bound Sam over on three counts of rape and one count of great bodily injury because of his alleged transmission of herpes to Karen. He made a motion to have his bond reduced but the judge denied his request and instructed him to raise that issue in Superior Court. Sam was returned to his cell in the San Diego County Jail where he remained confined under a $1 million bond.

During the first week of September 1991, Sam represented himself at a second preliminary hearing, this one dealing with the charge that he raped Carol. "I did better this time," Sam said. "I was still bound over, but going pro per, that is defending myself, forced the court to release me from segregation. I got a private cell, equipped with a free telephone. I also asked the judge to appoint me a public defender on this case to help me."

Sam was still representing himself on the upcoming trial on charges that he attacked Karen. But he realized that by not agreeing to a postponement, as his first court-appointed attorney had recommended, his trial was quickly approaching and he was unprepared. With almost unlimited free use of a telephone, courtesy of the taxpayers of the State of California, Sam began calling various attorney's in the San Diego area, looking for one who would not only assist him, but also accept his Visa card as payment. Sam had to use his fraudulently obtained Visa card since he had no money to pay for legal fees.

"I got lucky right away, or so I thought, when I found this guy, Neal Gibbons," Sam said. Gibbons agreed to take Sam's Visa card as a retainer. "I should have been a little suspicious, when after hearing all the facts, he said his fee would only be $3,000. I was sure it would have been closer to ten or twenty thousand." Gibbons told Sam that the low fee would only cover the actual hours he spent in court and that Sam would have to take care of all the other expenses related to any investigation in preparation of trial.

But Sam was desperate and time was short, so he agreed to the terms. "Hell, I figured this case was simple, the evidence in my favor was irrefutable. I could hire Donald Duck for this case and win it. Little did I know, it was Donald Duck that I hired."

On October 10, 1991, trial began in the Superior Court of the State of California in the County of San Diego. The honorable Frank A. Brown presided and would hear evidence in the case of Sam Consiglio, now charged with three counts of raping Karen. The courtroom was just one of many in the courthouse; most all confined inside the seven-story building, allowing the room to be completely enclosed. The room's temperature and lighting were artificially controlled. There was no natural sunlight or windows to see outside. There were no plants or paintings in view to offer distractions. The purpose for the room was for the jurors to see and listen, without distraction, to what the witnesses had to say.

Sam sat at a small brown table next to his attorney, Neal Gibbons. To Sam's left, sitting at a separate table turned facing the defendant, was a uniformed bailiff whose purpose it was to keep order, especially in the event Sam became violent or tried to run. But that wasn't Sam's style. In a courtroom setting, Sam was on stage and he'd never leave before the final act. At a matching table, immediately to Sam's right, sat Sam's co-star and antagonist, prosecutor Mike Przytulski.

Judge Brown was the first to speak after the jury was seated. He told them they had been selected to act as jurors in this case and that they would be the judges of the facts. He would be the judge of the law, and at the conclusion of this case he would instruct them how to apply the law in this case. He told them they were to presume a witness spoke the truth. The presumption, however, could be overcome by the manner in which that witness testified. "The character of his or her testimony, his interest in the case, if any, his bias or prejudice, if any, any inconsistent statements that he or she may have made, or any contradictory testimony that may be given," Brown said.

"Sometimes, there will be a question asked and there will be an objection. I'll sustain the objection but you'll hear the answer. I may sustain or when I sustain an objection, that means that you shouldn't have heard the answer, so I'll ask you to strike that answer. Do not speculate, if I sustain an objection, what the answer might have been. During times in the trial, there may be hearings out of the presence of the jury. Those conversations that I have with counsel will usually take place in the other room. They will concern issues of law. When we do that, don't worry about it or speculate what it was all about."

The judge had just told the jury that they would be instructed to disregard certain answers given by witnesses. Whether they were true or not, didn't matter. When the lawyers were speaking privately to him, they were to not let their curiosity get the better of them.

In Przytulski's opening statement, he said, "Karen is the victim in this case. Karen will tell you how old she is, that she was one of the residents at Saint Vincent De Paul's, that she had roommates there, Rosalind Bell and Jackie Thomas."

"Sam Consiglio came to California about a month or so before the July time frame. When he got here, he was living at the Buena Vista Apartments off Clairemont Drive in Clairemont. When he got here, he had a resume and the resume indicated that from 1980 to the present time, 1991, he was involved in property management."

"Mr. Consiglio went to Saint Vincent De Paul and asked them if they had a girl that he could hire, a woman, as a bookkeeper. The people at Saint Vincent's, were very happy because one of the things they try to do is place their residents in employment."

Przytulski described how Sam was introduced to Karen and how he made arrangements to pick her up from Saint Vincent's and take her on what was to be a job interview in Carlsbad.

"On the way up to Carlsbad, Sam's pointing out buildings; saying 'I own this building; I manage this building.' It's all lies; the big con; this is all a con," Przytulski continued. "On the way up to Carlsbad, Karen suspects that something is wrong, because all of a sudden, he's telling her, 'you can't tell them where you're from. You're going to have to act like we're together, business partners, because we'll have a better chance of getting this job if there's two people.' And so they have their interview at the Carlsbad Apartments. Sam didn't think the interview went too good, and thought that Karen didn't do too good of a job. But on the way back to Saint Vincent's, Sam suggested to Karen (they have) a spaghetti dinner that night. Later, Sam drives her to Wells Park in El Cajon. When they get to Wells Park, Sam rapes her. It's around dusk, sometime between 7:30 and 8:30 p.m. After he rapes her, Sam then gives her a dollar and drops her off at a trolley station."

"Sam is going to deny doing this, but he is going to tell us that everything Karen will tell you about their contacts up to about 3 on the afternoon on the date of the rape is true, that Karen tells the truth about everything up until then. You'll see some inconsistencies in his statements. You'll see some outright lies. And, it's going to be your job to judge the credibility of these people and return a verdict."

Mike Przytulski thanked the jury for their attentiveness and sat down, alone at the prosecutor's table. Judge Brown then offered Neal Gibbons an opportunity to make his opening remarks to the jury. But Gibbons declined telling the judge he would reserve his opening statement after the people rested their case.

Karen's friend, Jackie Thomas was the first witness called by the prosecution. "How are you today?" judge Brown asked.

"I'm fine. A little bit nervous," Jackie said.

"A little bit nervous," the judge replied. "Good, it's healthy."

Jackie testified she was living at Saint Vincent De Paul's on July 2, 1991 and that she had lived in the room next to Karen during that time.

"Now, on July 2nd, were you aware of Karen seeking some employment with a Sam Consiglio?" Przytulski asked.

"Yes, I was," Jackie, said.

"Did you have some clothes that she borrowed?"

"Yes, I had a jumpsuit. Karen, at that time didn't really have a lot of clothes to go out looking for a prospective job."

"Did she in fact take that jumpsuit and wear it?"

"Yes she did."

Jackie testified that as far as she knew, Karen met with Sam that day but Jackie was worried about her when she didn't return to the shelter until just moments before 10 that night.

"Tell the jury what Karen's demeanor was like. How was she acting?" Przytulski asked.

"I could tell that something was wrong, although I didn't know what at that particular time. She went down to her room, and I went into my room. Shortly thereafter, she did come into my room and appeared to be very shaky. Her eyes were, just very big and very scared looking. A few tears started to form, but she did not actually cry. I asked her what was wrong, what happened, and she still didn't say anything had happened."

Jackie testified that Karen left for a short period, returning about 30 minutes later after taking a shower.

"What was her demeanor like then?" Przytulski asked.

"About the same. She was just very nervous. She sat for a while. I did try to question her, ask her what was wrong. She had a couple of cigarettes and then she started to cry and said Jackie, I've been raped."

"Objection," yelled Neal Gibbons.

"Judge, fresh complaint," argued the district attorney.

"I'm going to overrule. The answer will stand," Brown said.

"When she told you she had been raped, what happened next?" Przytulski asked as he continued questioning his witness.

"She started crying. I put my arms around her, and she just couldn't stop crying. At that point, I said Karen, don't you know that we need to go and tell someone what has happened? She said no."

"What happened next?"

"Well, Rosalind and I, without Karen's permission, went and told the duty intake counselor what had transpired. After the police arrived, they said that they couldn't do much unless Karen gave them a name. I told the police to let me try and get a name from Karen, that she seemed to trust me. I went over to Karen who was in the library with Belkis Bottfeld, her counselor, and another police officer and I knelt down in front of her. She had her head down and I just put my hands on her and I said, Karen, if you don't feel like talking, if you don't feel like mentioning any names or a name, I'll state the name and then you just can answer if you want to. Shake your head yes or no. At that point, I said, Karen, was it Sam Consiglio? With her head still hanging, she started nodding her head up and down."

"Did she still appear to you to be traumatized at that point?"

"Yes, scared, very much. She didn't know how to talk about it."

"When Karen came home, did she put something in writing for you?"

"Yes she did. It wasn't that particular evening, and here again, I'm guessing. It might have been two or three days later. It was very hard for Karen to talk about it openly, and I told her, Karen, sometimes, you just have to get it out of your system. It's good to write something down on paper, just to release it out from your system, which she did."

"She wrote it out for you?"

"Yes, she wrote down what happened."

Przytulski produced a three-page hand-written letter and asked the court to mark the document as people's exhibit one, for identification. He presented the letter to Jackie and instructed her to read it out loud.

"I try to laugh and smile, but I guess it's a cover up for the pain and anger that I really feel. I want so much to just be me again but I don't know if I could. No matter how much I pray, his devil eyes keep looking at me and the sound of his voice keeps playing over and over in my ears, don't scream or fight with me or I'll hurt you, and I don't want to mess up a pretty lady like you."

As Jackie read the letter composed by Karen, Sam sat at the defense table, furious. He told his attorney that he objected to this testimony and ordered him to object immediately and stop the reading of the letter. But Gibbons refused and allowed Jackie to continue.

"I can feel his cold hand on my neck as he holds me back across the hood of his car as his other hand holds my left hip firmly against the side of the car. All I could do was close my eyes, cry and pray that it would all soon be over," Jackie continued.

Sam squirmed in his chair as he looked away from his attorney. He demanded that Gibbons object, but again, the lawyer refused his client's instructions.

"I wish all this madness would go away, I can't take it much longer. If I could end my life right now, I would, just to get away from the torment he is putting me through. If I could only have one wish come true right now, it would be to wake up and it all be just a dream."

When Jackie finished reading the letter, Przytulski sat down. It was Gibbons' turn to question the witness.

"Did you actually see Karen write that statement?" he asked.

"Yes, I did. She was on her bed. I did see her write it."

"And did you read the contents of the letter at that time?"

"Yes, I did."

With that answer, Gibbons told the court that he had no further questions for Jackie.

Przytulski then called Karen to the witness stand.

"Karen, I want to show you exhibit one. It's a copy of some stuff you wrote. Do you recognize that handwriting?" Przytulski asked.

"Yes," Karen, said, her head hung low as she tried not to look at anyone.

Judge Brown interrupted the district attorney's questioning and told Karen, "Now look here, this is a boxful of tissues. I keep it here because it's a good investment. You're going to have to call upon whatever inner strength you have at this time and I know that the subject matter we're going to talk about in front of 14 people and more (in the courtroom) that you don't know will be embarrassing to you. I know that. I can't take away that concern. But I can tell you there is no need for you to be embarrassed or reserved in your testimony, but rather answer the questions as best you can for both lawyers, okay."

Karen testified that she was 30 years old and that she had lived at Saint Vincent's for approximately six weeks. She said she had called Sam Consiglio after Bob Knott had given her his name and phone number indicating that he was looking for a bookkeeper at an apartment complex.

"What happened next?" Przytulski asked.

"We set up a time to meet. He said he wanted to take me to see an apartment complex and talk to me."

"Did he tell you what kind of business he was in?"

"He said that he was in property management."

"What happened next?"

"It was Friday and we set up a time to meet on Monday morning."

"That would be July the 1st."

"Yes."

"What happened on Monday morning?"

"We drove to Carlsbad to look at an apartment complex."

"What happened when you got up to Carlsbad?"

"We walked around. Then on our way out, we stopped at the office and, I guess, the assistant manager of the complex, her name was Bobbie, was there and he talked to her and wanted to set up a time to meet with someone."

"Okay, what was the purpose of going up there?"

"To see if I liked the complex."

"Is that what he told you?"

"Yes. He said I would be the bookkeeper for that complex and that if I wanted it, he would train me into management."

"What else happened? You meet Bobbie, and what, if anything else is decided?"

"He made a phone call to the woman we were supposed to meet and set up a time for the next day to meet with her."

"After he made this phone call, what did you do?"

"We went back to Saint Vincent's. He dropped me off and before I got out of the car, he said he wanted to meet with me around 11 the next day to go back up there. I said okay and got out of the car and went inside."

"Then what happened?"

"He called me later that night and asked me if I was interested because he had other women who had applied for it but they weren't interested or he wasn't interested in them."

"What happened next?"

"He just verified that we were going to meet the next morning at 11."

"Now, roughly about 11 the morning of the 2nd, are you expecting to go with him somewhere?"

"Yes, we were supposed to go back to Carlsbad to the apartment complex."

"Did you make any special preparations for getting dressed for that event?"

"Yes. He had asked me to wear something nice because we were having a luncheon because we were to meet the woman at 12:30."

"So what did you wear?"

"I borrowed a jumpsuit from Jackie who lived in the room next to me. I had a white and black jumpsuit on."

"What happened next?"

"He showed up around 11:35. We got on the freeway on I-5 going north and started back up toward Carlsbad."

"Did Sam start preparing you on what to do and how to act?"

"Yes. He told me to say if the lady asks anything, to tell her that we've known each other for approximately five years. Then he got upset and said that if she says anything, to let him do the talking. He told me not to say anything."

"Did you ever know that he was just applying for an apartment manager's job?"

"No."

"What happened next?"

"We got to the apartment complex, and we met with this lady. We talked to her and she started to ask me some questions and he cut me off. Any time I tried to say anything or answer one of her questions, he would interrupt. She started to ask me directly how long we had known each other and when I started to say anything, he said, well, I've known her about five years."

"How long did this meeting take place?"

"About 30 minutes. We weren't there long. Then we drove back to Saint Vincent's."

"Then what happened?"

"On the way back, he was talking about a tour of Saint Vincent's. I told him I would check to see if anyone was around to give the tour. So we got back to Saint Vincent's and I tried to get Bob Knott to give him a tour."

"And do you know if he gave Mr. Consiglio a tour?"

"I think so."

"Was there any talk about dinner that night?"

"While we were waiting for Bob to come down, he asked me if I liked spaghetti. I said yeah. Then he said that he had made some spaghetti and asked me if I wanted to come over and have dinner. I told him no and he said, well, I wanted to take you out to the apartment complex in El Cajon and let you look at it."

"What was the deal with the El Cajon apartment complex?"

"He said it didn't offer a two-bedroom apartment like the Carlsbad Apartment job did but it was still a one-bedroom apartment and it would get me out of Saint Vincent's and get me back on my feet. I said okay and he said he wanted to meet with me about 3:30."

"What happened next?"

"He said he had some errands he needed to run and that he would be in the area later. I told him if he wanted, I would meet him somewhere so he wouldn't have to come all the way downtown and he said that would be fine."

"Where did you agree to meet him?"

"At 32nd and Imperial just off the 32nd Street trolley stop."

"And what was the purpose in doing that?"

"To look at the apartment complex."

"Have you ever been to El Cajon before?"

"No."

"Do you have any idea where Sam lives in El Cajon?"

"No."

"But he did take you to an apartment complex?"

"Yes."

"Okay, what happened when you got there?"

"We parked on the side of the building and we got out and we walked around. He said this was smaller than the other apartment complex and that it needed a lot more work."

"When you got back into the car, where did you go to?"

"He said he needed to go back to his apartment and make some phone calls. So, we went to his apartment on Clairemont Boulevard."

"So you went into the apartment complex?"

"Yes."

"Okay. Now when you went there, what happened?"

"He went in to use the phone. He asked me to come in and I told him I didn't want to, that I would just sit in the car."

"How long was he inside?"

"I have no idea."

"Was it a long time?"

"Yes."

"Could it have been as long as an hour?"

"Yes."

"Okay. At some point, did he return?"

"Yes he did. He said that he needed to run back out to El Cajon because he had forgotten something. He asked me if I had time and I said yeah. I told him I wasn't in a hurry to get back. So we drove back to El Cajon."

"Then what happened?"

"We got off the freeway and he took a side street. It was a wide one. He said he needed to use the phone again. So, we pulled into the park and there was a building there."

Przytulski introduced photographs of the building Karen had referred to in her testimony and established the location to be inside Wells Park in El Cajon.

"Karen, when you got to Wells Park, what happened?" Przytulski asked.

"Sam got out of the car to go look for a telephone around the building."

"Did he actually walk around the building?"

"Yes he did. He walked around the building and then came back around the same way he had walked and he started toward the car. I had gotten out of the car and was leaning up against the hood of the car. He walked up toward me and he just grabbed me by my throat with his hands."

"What happened next?"

"I pushed him back and he grabbed tighter. He told me not to scream and not to fight him. He said that he didn't want to hurt me. He told me to take my jumpsuit off."

"Did you?"

"Yes."

"Why?"

"Because I was scared," Karen said, in a low voice, as tears began to slip from her eyes.

"Did he still have his hands on your throat?"

"Yes."

"What happened next?"

"I pulled my jumpsuit down. He pushed me back across the hood of the car.

"What happened next?"

"He raped me." Karen's answer was brief and unequivocal. Przytulski could only hope that the jury had heard it as deeply and profoundly as he had heard it himself.

"Karen," Przytulski said, in a soft, clear, voice, trying to be as gentle as possible with his witness, "we all know what rape is, but there are legal terms here. Can you tell us what he actually did?"

"He spread my legs with his leg and he pushed his penis inside of me."

"Karen, how many times did he actually do that where he was inside of you and then was out of you and then went back in?"

"Three times."

"Was that the total?"

"Yes."

"Then what happened?"

"He stopped."

"Do you know if he ejaculated?"

"No, I don't know."

"What were you feeling at that point?"

"I was just praying to God not to let it be happening."

"When he came out of you and stopped, I use the term he came out of you but what I mean, when he finished and he stopped, what happened next?"

"He would do it again more violently."

"When you indicate more violently, can you describe what you mean by more violently, please?"

The tears spilled from Karen's eyes, dampening her face as she tried to look away from everyone in the courtroom. Before she could answer the next question, judge Brown offered her the box of tissues. "You can use more of those if you want, you don't have to scrimp," he said.

"He would push very hard," Karen said, trying to answer the question as clearly as she could.

"What happened next?"

"He told me to pull my jumpsuit up. So I did and he said he was just going to take me to the trolley station and leave me there."

"Karen, how come you didn't scream and fight? How come you didn't do that?"

"Because I was hurt. He had me by my throat."

"Did you think that you were in some severe danger?"

"I was scared."

"Did you think you had any chance to get away?"

"No."

"Did you think he could hurt you?"

"Yes."

"Did he take you to the trolley station?"

"Yes he did."

"How were you going to get back to the house? Were you going to pay for the trolley?"

"He gave me a dollar to get on the trolley."

"Sam gave you a buck?"

Karen didn't answer. She just nodded her head up and down, indicating that the answer was "yes."

"Do you know what time you arrived at the trolley station?"

"No."

"After Sam dropped you off, did he just leave right away?"

"Yes, he left."

"What did you do?"

"I took my shoes off to go up the stairs and I got a ticket."

"Do you recall what time it was?"

"The time on the ticket said 11 something. So I figured it was around 9 because they're good for two hours. I knew that if I wasn't back at Saint Vincent's by 10 that evening, I wouldn't have a bed."

"What are you feeling like? At that time Karen, what's going on inside of you?"

"I was confused and scared. I felt filthy."

"Do you remember what time you got there, at Saint Vincent's?"

"Right at 10."

"What happened next?"

"I went upstairs."

"Did you go to your room?"

"No."

"Where did you go first?"

"I went to take a shower."

"How many showers did you take when you got home?"

"Three by midnight."

"How come?"

Gibbons rose from his chair and shouted, "Objection, irrelevant."

Judge Brown shot back with one word, "overruled."

"Because I felt dirty and I wanted to wash him off of me," Karen said.

"Did you see Jackie that night?"

"Yes, after I got out of the shower and had taken her jumpsuit off. I told her that I would wash it before I gave it back to her."

"Did you tell her anything, tell her you were raped?"

"No."

"Do you remember talking to some policemen?"

"Yeah, the next morning."

"Did you tell Jackie who did it to you?"

"Yes."

"I know this is embarrassing, but I have to ask. Did you have herpes before this rape?"

"No."

"After the police talked to you, you were examined for a rape, weren't you?"

"Yes sir."

"About 10 or 12 days later were you examined for herpes?"

"Yes. I had an outbreak of blisters in my vagina area."

"Was that diagnosed as herpes?"

"Yes."

"You hadn't had any outbreaks at any time prior to that?"

"No."

"And in between the time you had sex with Sam Consiglio, the time he raped you, and the time you were examined for herpes, have you had sex with anybody?"

"No."

"Karen, when you got back at around 10 on the 2nd, the night Sam raped you, were there any phone calls or phone messages for you?"

"Yes. Lindsey, one of the girls that works the intake desk on the second floor, grabbed me as soon as I got off of the elevator and said I had a message from my boss and that he wanted me to call him right away."

"Did she indicate that she had more than one message?

"Yes. She said he had called twice that night. The first time he had talked to Rosalind, and he had insisted on talking to me. Then he called back 15 minutes later and wanted to know why I wasn't there."

"When he left you off at the trolley station after being raped, did he tell you not to tell anybody?"

"Yes."

"Did he ever tell you that he knew who you were and who your friends were?"

"Yes. He said if I said anything to anyone, that he knew where I lived and he knew how to find me."

"Did you return a phone call to him on the second?"

"Yes, I did."

"Why?" Przytulski asked.

"Because Lindsey was upset and she told me that I'd better call him."

"When you called him, what was said?"

"He wanted to know why it took me so long to get home. He asked me if I talked to anyone and I told him no. Then he said that if I took the apartment complex in El Cajon, it would still be better than staying at Saint Vincent's. He said I didn't belong in a place like that."

"Karen, I know you don't want to, but I have to ask this because I need you to identify the guy who raped you. Do you see him in court?"

"Yes."

"I want you to point to him and tell us where he's sitting and tell us that's the man that raped you."

Karen pointed to Sam. Przytulski then asked Karen if Sam was the man who raped her. When she answered yes, he thanked her and told judge Brown that he didn't have anything further to ask.

Gibbons, with a yellow legal pad in his hands, walked over and stood behind the same podium used by Mike Przytulski. He stood for a brief moment and looked directly at Karen and asked, "In your testimony, you were asked if Sam threatened you. Did you also say that at some point he knew where you lived and knew how to find you and knew your friends?"

"He didn't say that he knew my friends."

"Okay. When you left El Cajon on the trolley after the alleged rape, do you remember what time it was?" asked Gibbons.

"No, I do not."

"Do you remember approximately what time it was?"

"I went strictly by the trolley ticket, which was stamped at 11:02" Karen said.

"Is it true that you had to arrive at Saint Vincent's before 10?"

"Yes. If you're not in at 10, it's past curfew and you lose your bed," Karen said.

"So you definitely arrived before 10?"

"I arrived right at 10."

"Did you in fact take a trolley at 9:02 p.m. from El Cajon after the alleged rape?"

"I don't know what time it was I got on the trolley. I know I purchased my ticket at approximately 9:02 because I know they're good for two hours."

"Do you ride the trolley often?"

"Yes."

"Do you know exactly what time you left on the trolley?"

"No."

"How far of a walk is it from the trolley stop at Imperial and 12th to Saint Vincent's?

"About three minutes."

"Okay. I want to call your attention to Wells Park where the alleged incident occurred. Do you know at what time that occurred, approximately?"

"No, I do not know. I knew it was sometime around dusk when we were there. The lights were on in the parking lot of the park."

"You are pretty sure it was dusk?"

"Yeah, it was more dark than light."

"Was it a clear sunny day during the day, or was it foggy? What were the conditions?"

"It was clear."

"And the lights were on?"

"You couldn't see anything if the lights weren't on in the parking lot," Karen said.

"So the lights were definitely on, you're 100 percent sure?"

"Yes."

"Now, what were the conditions in the park at the time of the alleged rape? How many cars were in the lot?"

"There was one car in the lot."

"Isn't that a pretty dramatically public place?" Gibbons asked.

Przytulski objected to the question explaining to Brown that the question was certainly argumentative.

"She knows the scene personally. I'm just asking her to describe the scene," Gibbons told the judge. Brown overruled the district attorney and instructed Karen to answer the question.

"Yes," Karen said.

"You say there was just one other car parked in the lot at the time? There were no other cars around you?"

"No."

"Within 100 yards, was there another car parked?"

"There were cars parked across the street."

"But not actually in the lot?"

"Not in the lot."

"Were you aware of any public events there that night?"

"No."

"Was there a softball tournament there that night, to your knowledge?"

"Not to my knowledge."

"Okay, after the alleged rape, you decided to take a trolley back to Saint Vincent's, is that correct?"

"Sam told me he was going to take me to the trolley."

"Why didn't he just take you to Saint Vincent's?"

Again, Przytulski objected. "The question calls for speculation. How would she know why he didn't take her to Saint Vincent's?" Przytulski asked. Brown sustained the objection, forcing Gibbons to rephrase his question.

"Did you just desire to take the trolley?"

"I took it because that's where he took me."

"Okay, did you have money in your possession to pay for a ticket?"

"No."

"So you said you obtained a buck, one dollar from Sam to pay for the ticket is that correct?"

"Yes."

"And did you in fact buy a ticket with that one dollar?"

"Yes sir."

"And what was the cost of the ticket?"

"It was $1.25."

"How did you pay the twenty-five cents?"

"I just got a dollar ticket."

"You were able to buy that two-hour ticket with a dollar and a quarter?"

"All the tickets are good for two hours. It doesn't matter how much you pay for them," Karen explained.

"So maybe you couldn't go as far as you planned?"

"Right, that's how they rate it, I guess. I purchased what I could. I had a dollar and I got a dollar ticket."

"You just said, I want a dollar ticket, is that right? I don't mean to make a joke of this. I just have to understand the cost because it could become relevant. Okay?"

"The cost to go from El Cajon was $1.25. He gave me a dollar. That's it. I bought a ticket for a dollar and just decided to take my chances," Karen said, her voice starting to reveal anger as she looked at Gibbons.

"Actually, you're riding illegally because you didn't have a proper ticket; is that correct?" Gibbons asked.

"Correct," Karen replied.

"If we could go through some of the times to review it in chronology so we can understand the definition of dusk. Is it true that you left El Cajon to go to Clairemont around 4:30?"

"I don't know what time it was."

"In the preliminary hearing you said that you had a friend that walked you to the trolley station at around 3:30 and that you met Sam around 4. Would that be accurate?"

"Yes, that's what I said."

"And then he took you to El Cajon by car, is that correct?"

"Yes."

"Would you agree that it might be around a twenty minute drive?"

"Twenty minutes or more," Karen said.

"Okay, and then you sat outside in the car while Sam was at the apartment; is that correct?"

"Yes."

"And would you estimate that to be 40 minutes to an hour?"

"I'd say approximately 45 minutes or longer."

"But it could have been slightly longer than an hour?"

"It could have been a lot longer."

"So why are you estimating 45 minutes?"

"Because it wasn't any less than that."

"So what's the longest period it could have been?"

"Hour-and-a-half, two hours" Karen said.

Judge Brown interrupted Gibbons' questioning of Karen to verify that he had heard the answer correctly. "It would be from 45 minutes to an hour-and-a-half to two hours maximum."

"Yeah," Karen told the judge. "My legs and my butt were going to sleep from sitting in the car."

"You know, that's a good point," Brown said. "I think we'll break right now before all of our butts go to sleep here. I've been sitting all day. This is a good breaking point."

Judge Brown told the jury that he was going to Mexico for the long Columbus Day weekend and that he would be refreshed when trial resumed on Tuesday morning. Before he dismissed the jurors, he told them not to form any opinions about the case, and not to discuss what they heard so far with anyone.

"I knew right then that I had a problem," Sam said. He considered Gibbons to be incompetent, even though only two witnesses had testified on the first day of trial. Both Jackie Thomas and Karen had made convincing witnesses. "He (Gibbons) should have never let Jackie read that letter Karen supposedly wrote describing the alleged assault," Sam said. "Whoever heard of a woman writing a beautiful and emotional short story about their experiences of being raped within a few days of the incident? It was ridiculous and caused me irreparable harm."

Sam agonized all weekend about what he considered to be Neal Gibbons' lack of aggressiveness. He passed the time in his cell watching the confirmation hearings of Clarence Thomas who had just been nominated to the U.S. Supreme Court. "At least that provided some humor," Sam said. "It was a circus that could have been called 101 Ways to Disrespect Women and still become a Supreme Court Justice." Sam hoped that judge Thomas would lose the nomination, fearing that if he won, the women on his jury would retaliate against him. When he wasn't watching the Congressional hearings, Sam was preparing to ask the court, when trial reconvened, to dismiss Gibbons and allow him to represent himself. Once he came to this decision, Sam felt like celebrating and ordered a large Pepperoni pizza from Domino's. He gave his name and the address of the San Diego County Jail to the young man who took the order. When the pizza arrived, the jailers confronted Sam with his latest indiscretion. Sam insisted he be allowed to keep the pizza as he was representing himself in the pending rape case involving Carol, and this entitled him to certain special privileges not enjoyed by the other inmates. When the jailers asked how he intended to pay for the pizza, Sam said he didn't intend to pay for it at all since the "kid" didn't get it there in less than 30 minutes. The jailers refused to let Sam keep the pizza.

When court reconvened on Tuesday, October 15, Sam was prepared to make a Marsden Motion to have Neal Gibbons removed as his trial counsel. But before the jury was brought into the courtroom, Przytulski asked to make a statement for the record.

"I want it to be clear," the D.A. said, "that the peoples position prior to this trial was that more investigation needed to be done on this case and the defense was aware of that. Nevertheless, the defendant refused to waive time and wanted this trial now. As a result, the rape kit has not been or was not finished testing. However, this weekend, we did receive a report as part of that rape kit from the Sheriff's Lab. It indicated some pubic hair samples taken both from the defendant and Karen and one hair on Mr.

Consiglio was consistent with the hair from Karen. I have provided a copy of that report to defense counsel. As for Karen, her background is in a state of flux. We don't know what is true and what isn't true. We haven't been able to prove that what she's told us is incorrect, and sources of information that we have show inconsistencies as well."

"I just want the record to be clear that that's what the situation is when the defendant is knowingly and voluntarily making us go forward without the waiving of time. So, we have some problems along those lines. We wanted more time. The defendant didn't want more time. I know he has that right but so long as the record is clear that the defendant has done that."

Judge Brown said the court understood the position of the district attorney's office. Gibbons then told the judge he had explained the advantages and disadvantages of going forward and that he felt Sam understood the pros and cons fully. When Gibbons concluded his remarks, Sam rose and told judge Brown he had a motion and requested that the district attorney be excluded from the courtroom.

"I can't do that," Brown said.

"I have a Marsden Motion, your Honor," Sam said.

"It is?" Brown replied, looking surprised.

"He has the right," Przytulski said.

"He sure does," judge Brown acknowledged. "We'll just clear the courtroom." No judge or prosecutor relishes a case where the defendant is proper, which allows them to represent themselves. Making the Marsden Motion, Sam was once again overestimating his own ability. But then again, he would not have been on trial, facing the present charges, had that not been a life long habit of his.

Sam told the judge that he wanted to represent himself through the rest of the trial and that he considered Neal Gibbons to be incompetent. But judge Brown knew that Sam was not capable of defending himself on such a serious charge and explained to him the reasons he should reconsider his motion.

"If it please the court, I would like to just put off for the time being so I can choose at a later time to defend myself and fire Mr. Gibbons," Sam asked.

"But we're talking about it right now," the judge said.

"But I might choose later on to take that action," Sam claimed.

"That's why we're addressing it right now," Brown said.

"I want to see what happens in the testimony first," Sam mumbled.

"You have made a motion to this court and I'm going to grant it or deny it. What I need to know, is do you wish to represent yourself or do you wish to keep your counsel? That's all I need to know so I can rule on this motion."

"I'll withdraw my motion your honor."

"All right," judge Brown said. "This will be my ruling. You have made a considered opinion and decision in this matter after conferring with your counsel, and after discussing it with me. This is not the first time this has come to the attention of the courts. Apparently, you didn't do a good job at a preliminary hearing and the intelligent conclusion has been that you're better off with being represented by counsel and we'll proceed on that basis."

When trial resumed, Przytulski called Dr. Dwight Lemon to the stand.

Dr. Lemon, an independent contractor physician who worked at Sharp Hospital in San Diego, was allowed to testify out of turn because of his schedule. Dr. Lemon, who claimed to have had conducted over 50 rape examinations in his career, had examined Karen on July 3rd, 1991.

"With regard to your examination of Karen, did you notice any tender area?" Przytulski asked.

"She had slight tenderness in the outer part of the forearm. She had tenderness on the lower part of her neck at the back aspect and the extreme upper part of her upper back. There was no visible evidence of trauma, but there was subjective evidence of trauma, that being that the patient complained of pain when the areas were touched."

"I want to assume, doctor, that a woman is raped against the hood of a car. In other words, she is leaning against the hood area. Would the injuries be consistent with that?"

"They could be."

"Did you collect some pubic hair from her?"

"Yes."

"Would you tell the jury the difference between body hair and pubic hair?"

"Body hair is on the arms or on the trunk and it typically is thinner than pubic hair and not curled like pubic hair usually is. Also, it is shorter and usually not as darkly pigmented. Those would be the physical differences."

"Did she indicate to you, or in your medical records, was she asked if ejaculation occurred?"

"Yes. She was unsure, as are almost all alleged victims. She thought that perhaps the defendant had ejaculated in the vicinity of her legs."

"Okay. Now, when you take swabs, doctor, you're looking for sperm that would be inside the vagina; is that correct?"

"Certainly we would look for it inside the vagina, but if there are suspicious areas outside the vagina, we would swab that area also."

"If a male did not ejaculate into the vagina area, would you expect the swabs to be negative?"

"They should be negative if the female has not had sex in the last two to four days."

"Thank you, nothing further," Przytulski said.

Gibbons then questioned the doctor about his examination of Karen.

"Dr. Lemon, you stated that there was redness on Karen's neck. You didn't see if there were any bruises or anything?" Gibbons asked.

"I've indicated she had areas that indicate slight tenderness without visible trauma. That would translate to you guys as some slight amount of pain when the area was touched or palpated by my fingers, but without any redness, bruising or other visible evidence of trauma."

"Did you see any frontal tenderness or frontal bruises?"

"Well, I did not note that," Dr. Lemon said as he referred to his medical report.

"So there's no indication at all of any kind of frontal tenderness? There's no tenderness or redness or anything indicating a frontal neck attack; right?"

"There's none indicated in the record."

"Do you have any way of evaluating during the exam whether the victim is being truthful about expressing pain or tenderness?"

"The simple answer is no," Dr. Lemon said. "No more than you have a way of evaluating whether what I say is true."

"Okay. Did you have any evidence of Karen douching prior to the exam?"

"Yes. According to the patient's history, she douched after the assault."

"Okay. Does that douching process affect the results of your rape exam?"

"I suppose it certainly could. The real physical way it would affect the results of the exam is if there was semen inside the vagina containing mobile sperm. Douching would probably negate that evidence. It would wash out any evidence to be collected."

"Have you had very many rape victims douche prior to the exam?"

"I would estimate about half the victims have douched prior to the exam. They have no idea that it will negate any possible evidence and it's probably a very normal thing to want to do."

"Was there anything specific in your examination of Karen where you could actually conclude that she was in fact raped by someone?"

"No," Dr. Lemon said.

"Thank you, no further questions," Gibbons said.

Judge Brown then called Karen back to the stand. He reminded her that she was still under oath and that Gibbons would be continuing with his cross-examination of her.

"Now I'd like to go through a series of times with you and review some testimony so we can maybe make something clear. About what time did Sam pick you up on the afternoon of July 2nd?"

"I figure it was around 4 O'clock."

"Now, why wouldn't you know whether you sat in the car for forty-five minutes or two hours? Why wouldn't forty-five minutes vs. two hours make a big impression on you?"

"There's a lot of time I spend meditating."

"So, did you lay down in the car at all?"

"No."

"You sat up the whole time?"

"Yes."

"Did you exit the car?"

"No."

"Did you play the radio?"

"No."

"So you just sat there in the car and meditated?"

"Yes."

"What time did you arrive at Wells Park?"

"I don't know."

"So, did the rape occur immediately after you arrived or was there some passage of time?"

"There was a passage of time when he went around the building."

"How long was he gone?"

"I don't know. I would guess approximately 10 or 15 minutes."

"So how long after the rape was it that Sam took you to the trolley?"

"I don't know."

"Do you have any idea?"

"No I don't."

"Well, he drove you to the trolley station, right?"

"Yes."

"So, did he drive you immediately afterward?"

"It was about five or ten minutes while I got myself together."

"And you know for a fact that you arrived at Saint Vincent's right before 10?"

"I arrived right before 10 according to their clock."

"In your previous testimony, you stated there was one car in the parking lot at Wells Park during the rape; is that true?"

"Yes."

"Did you see a baseball tournament going on at Wells Park that night?"

"No. I noticed the lights were on in the park."

"But did you see any type of baseball game?"

"I wasn't paying attention."

"Do you have an ex-husband?"

Przytulski jumped from his chair and hollered, "Objection, relevance your honor." As soon as judge Brown sustained the objection, Gibbons started to explain his theory of relevance. Judge Brown interrupted Gibbons and ordered the jury be removed from the courtroom while the issue of Karen having an ex-husband was argued.

"What's the relevance as to her marriage?" Judge Brown asked.

"She made comments, your honor, to Sam Consiglio that she put an ex-husband in state prison and that she can control men and do anything she wants to them with the system," Gibbons said. "Apparently, there was discussion that he beat her up in Seattle and that she had him put away by lying on the witness stand. The prosecutor is fully aware of all this testimony."

"I'm not aware of what she told Sam and what she told Sam is hearsay," Przytulski told judge Brown.

"But I'm asking her about her involvement with her ex-husband," Gibbons said.

"But how is that relevant to these charges?" Przytulski asked Gibbons.

"Because she's bringing a false charge here and she's trying to put Sam away."

"Do you have any independent evidence or good-faith evidence there is an ex-husband in Washington who was put away on perjured testimony by this witness?" Przytulski asked.

"When were these statements allegedly made?" Brown asked.

"On July 1st or 2nd," Gibbons answered.

"That's what I'm asking," the judge said. "Was it after she was allegedly raped?"

"I don't know," Gibbons told him.

Gibbons turned his attention to Sam and asked him to answer judge Brown's question. "From the moment she got in the car, she had a cast on her leg and I asked her how she got the cast," Sam said. "She told me a guy beat her up. I felt he had it coming your honor."

"Maybe she did put him in prison because he beat her up," judge Brown told Sam.

"I don't know your honor," Sam said.

"Well, I'm not going to allow you to inquire into that based on what I've heard."

When the trial resumed, Gibbons asked Karen a few more questions about her alleged bruises and injuries before concluding his cross-examination.

Przytulski then called Belkis Bottfeld, a counselor and therapist at Saint Vincent's, to the witness stand.

Bottfeld testified that she learned about the alleged rape of Karen from one of the other case managers, on the morning of July 3, when she arrived for work, and that she first confronted Karen about 9:30 that morning.

"Will you tell the jury what her demeanor was like on the morning of the 3rd?" Przytulski asked.

"She was extremely distraught. Very upset. I basically just sat with her and let her talk if she wanted to, or could, but she was really very non-communicative at that point."

"Was there any doubt in your mind that something occurred, that something was affecting her?"

"Not at all. I mean it just showed completely."

"Did Karen ever say or do anything that indicated to you that she was not being truthful about her allegations?"

"No, not at all."

Przytulski thanked her and told judge Brown that he had no further questions for this witness.

"Did she ever discuss the name Sam Consiglio with you?" Gibbons asked on cross-examination.

"I don't recall her specifically discussing the name, no."

"Did she ever discuss the details of the incident with you?"

"She never discussed the details of the incident with me, no," Belkis answered.

The next witness was Rose Marie Neth, a criminalist employed at the Regional Crime Laboratory of San Diego County. Neth testified that she had been a criminalist for four years after having obtained a Bachelor of Science degree in molecular biology. Her area of specialization was in analyzing hairs and fibers.

Neth was asked what the hair samples taken from Sam and Karen revealed.

"I looked at the samples to see whether they had fine or unfrayed tips, whether they had roots, if they could be other hairs such as dog or cat hair and so forth. Once I established the parameters of the two standards, I was mainly interested in Karen's pubic hair combing. In Consiglio's pubic hair, there were a total of 10 pubic hairs. None of those I classified as being similar to his own; dark, uneven, coarse pigmentation, coarse diameter, and wiry, stiff texture. But one pubic hair was quite out of the ordinary. It was very light brown. It had a very fine tip, a very fine diameter; a root was attached to it. When comparing the standards, I determined that this one hair could have originated from Karen."

"Can you tell if that one hair was actually Karen's hair?" Gibbons asked on cross-examination.

"No. I cannot say that," she said.

"So, if Sam had sex with anyone else, it could have been a pubic hair from any woman correct?"

"Not any woman. I would say it was from an individual or there was contact with an individual, with light brown pubic hair."

"And no way to really date the hair, is there? Either it could have been five or 10 days, even before July 10th or it could have been five or 10 days after?"

"Depending on the individual's personal hygiene, yes."

"So if a person took a shower, would it definitely wash off, I mean, there's no way for you tell that, either?"

"There's no real way to date it."

Robert Knott then testified that he had worked as a case manager helping homeless clients find employment or get job training at Saint Vincent De Paul's for 18 months.

"Did you come in contact with a Sam Consiglio a few days prior to July 2nd, 1991?" Przytulski asked.

"Yes; first by phone. He said he had potential employment for a client. We arranged to meet later. He presented himself as a manager of several pieces of property and needed property managers at that time."

"Did he request a male or a female regarding this managers job?"

"He requested a female, and I believe the age bracket was between 18-35. He wanted this person to do minimal accounting for the property and to be a physical presence at that property, and they would have an apartment and an income in addition to that."

"And did you tell Karen about this?"

"Yes, I explained to her what Mr. Consiglio had said to me and the requirements he had for the property manager. She was interested in that position."

In Knott's testimony, Przytulski established that Sam had contacted Saint Vincent's masquerading as a property manager and that he had specifically asked for a woman to fill that job. Gibbons, during his brief cross-examination, did not try to contradict any of Knott's testimony.

When Knott finished testifying, judge Brown allowed Wava Howley to testify out of order so that she could return to Arkansas.

Wava took the stand and testified that she had a long telephone conversation with Sam Consiglio on the night of July 2nd.

"How do you know it was July 2nd?" Gibbons asked.

"Well, I went back and thought about the day and I remember that I had gone shopping at a flea market and Wal-Mart," Howley said. "And to make sure it was that day, I found a receipt and a canceled check from the stores I had been to that day. I know for sure, that it was that day."

"About what time of the day did he talk to you?"

"Well, I had dinner at Wal-Mart's and they close at 9. So it had to be after 9 when I got home. I remember I was going to watch the news and then Cheers after that. The news comes on at 10 which is 8 California time."

"Okay. How long a conversation did you have with Sam?"

"Oh it was about an hour. I don't know the minute but it was about an hour because I missed the news and Cheers."

"When did you meet Sam?" Przytulski asked on cross-examination.

"It was in the fall of 87," Howley said.

"Where?" Przytulski asked.

"I met him through a retreat. It was a weekend retreat. They told us about Sam. I didn't meet him at the retreat, I found out about him at the retreat."

"Were you in a prison ministry?"

"It was a prison ministry group and they told us about Sam, and they asked us to write him a letter of encouragement."

"When did you meet Sam?"

"Some months after I had been corresponding with him."

"Now at some point, you started to visit Sam in prison; is that correct?"

"I visited him three times during a four-year period."

"Did you know Sam before you met him in prison?"

"No. I just knew him by writing to him, that's all."

"When did you move to Arkansas?"

"In July, 1988."

"And how would you describe your relationship with Sam when you were in Michigan?"

"Well, more or less a spiritual adviser. He would tell me his troubles and ask for advice and I would tell him what I thought was the right thing to do as a Christian."

"When did you first come into contact with Sam regarding your testimony in this case?"

"I don't remember the date. I remember Sam and I had a conversation. He said some woman was accusing him of rape and he hadn't done it," Howley said.

"Did he phone you?"

"Yes he did."

"Do you have an answering machine?"

"Yes I do."

"If you're not home, the answering machine clicks in and keeps the line open; right?"

"That's right," Howley said.

"Until the other person terminates it; right?

"Right."

"Who paid your way out here?"

"Mr. Consiglio did."

"And who paid for your expenses?"

"Nobody."

"Were you shocked to find out he was being charged with rape in California?"

"I was very shocked, yes."

Przytulski ended his cross-examination of Howley, suspecting she'd been less than accurate about her recollection of her July 2nd conversation with Sam. He had wanted the jury to see Wava as a Christian woman who had been manipulated by Sam even if she herself hadn't. What puzzled Przytulski most was that he was still unsure exactly what Howley's relationship with Sam actually was.

Gibbons stood and asked Howley what her occupation was.

"I'm a teacher. I've been a teacher for 31 years."

"And what do you teach?"

"I teach kindergarten right now.

"And you're 100 percent positive you had that hour phone conversation on July 2nd?"

"I'm 100 percent positive. I have no doubts at all," Howley said adamantly.

"And you wouldn't lie to protect Sam?"

I wouldn't be here if I weren't sure," she said.

After Wava concluded her testimony, Przytulski called P. J. Harn, followed by detective Harry Hicks to the witness stand. Harn and Hicks provided testimony relating to their questioning of Sam and Karen during their investigations. When Hicks concluded his testimony, Przytulski told judge Brown that the prosecution rested its case.

It was now Gibbons turn to make his opening remarks to the jury. He rose from his seat and walked to the podium next to the jurors. He looked directly at them and said, "If we go through when the rape could have occurred according to Karen, you'll find that the rape could not have occurred. I'm going to offer you witnesses to provide testimony to show that on July 2nd, Sam could not have committed this rape. Now this case really bores me. In 15 years of law practice, I've never seen…" He was unable to complete the sentence before Przytulski jumped from his seat and yelled, "objection."

"Judge, that's inappropriate," Przytulski said.

"Sustained," Brown said.

Gibbons continued to stand, letting the expectant quiet linger for several moments before continuing his opening remarks. "We have a case here that's difficult for you. We have a case that's difficult because Karen, if you analyze her testimony, something has happened, some type of interaction between Sam and her, or her personally, that has caused her to get on the witness stand where she seems very credible. There's no question that she's saying the rape occurred on July 2nd. Sam Consiglio, therefore, if he is not guilty, has to construct what he did during that day. He has to provide you an alibi in order to prove that he didn't commit the rape."

"But if you take the time before the rape, Sam picks up Karen at 4 p.m. At 4:30 p.m. Karen leaves with Sam. 4:30, they arrive in Clairemont. 5:35 to 6:50, they sit in Clairemont. She doesn't know if it's 45 minutes or two hours. But that would put her in Wells Park, according to her own testimony, 7:25, or if Sam gets out of the car and makes a phone call, 7:40.

"She say's the rape occurred at dusk. The Union Tribune says that the sun set at 8 p.m. So, dusk can be within a range around that period. But you've heard testimony that between 8 and 9 p.m. Wava said she talked to Sam on the phone. So, all I'm going to do is provide you with the testimony; you can judge it for yourselves. But I think that you will see clearly that there's something wrong with this case, and I'm going to be asking you for a verdict of not guilty."

The defense then called its first witness, Ted Schroeder, the director of recreation for the city of El Cajon.

"I'm responsible for the recreation activities in several areas of the city including Wells Park," Schroeder said.

"Do you happen to know with certainty what time the lights were turned on in Wells Park on the night of July 2nd?"

Judge Brown interrupted the questioning wanting to know to which lights Gibbons was referring. He ordered the witness to answer the question about the lights in the parking lot.

"Are there lights all over Wells Park?" Gibbons asked.

"Yes. On the parking lot, in the park, and in the ball field."

"Do any of those sets of lights turn on at different times?"

"Yes, the lights in the park are on time-clocks and all lights in the ball field are turned on manually."

"So the lights in the parking lot (are turned on) by computer?"

"It's by a time clock, yes."

"Okay. Do you have knowledge as to any activities on the night of July 2nd?"

"Yes, there were softball games and there were people in the park plus people wandering through the park."

"How many parking lots are there in Wells Park?"

"There's one public parking lot and one staff parking lot."

"If there are softball games or other athletic activities, do people generally park in that parking lot?"

"Yes, they do."

"And there was definitely a softball game on July 2nd?"

"The schedule shows that there were three games, one at 6:30, a game scheduled at 7:30 and another game at 8:30."

"Would there be any reason that cars would not park in that parking lot during those times on July 2nd?"

"Not that I'm aware of."

"No further questions," Gibbons said as he thanked his witness.

Gibbons then called Gary Godsey, a San Diego district sales manager with AT&T, hoping to have him introduce records as evidence of Sam's marathon telephoning the night of July 2nd. But Przytulski objected on the grounds of foundation. "He's a sales rep, your honor, not a custodian of records. Przytulski turned away from judge Brown and looked directly at Godsey as he apologized. "It's not derogatory, sir, it's a legal term."

"The subpoena I sent out, your honor was to AT&T, not to any one particular person, because we didn't have a person's name," Gibbons told judge Brown.

"Well, it needs to be a custodian of records," Przytulski said.

"They're the telephone records of AT&T, no question about it," Gibbons said.

Judge Brown asked Godsey where he obtained the records.

"Our subpoena management center through AT&T Corporate Security was requested that they send them to me, and what it is, is an actual record of calls made, or generated through our computer billing system."

"There's no foundation for the evidence," Przytulski told the court. "Again, judge, those records need to be sent from the business of the person being subpoenaed to the court pursuant to the code section, or a person has to come in and lay a business record foundation as the custodian of records. And this individual cannot do that."

Judge Brown told the lawyers he would postpone his ruling as to the admissibility of the phone records and asked that Godsey return to his office and try to obtain original billings of the phone records as well as a custodian of records.

Gibbons then called Katherine Showers to the witness stand.

"Do you know Sam Consiglio seated here at the defense table?" Gibbons asked.

"Yes, I do," Showers, said.

"How long have you known him?"

"Since 1985."

"Do you recognize his voice?"

"I should after six years."

"Can you remember talking to him in any phone conversation on July 2nd?"

"Yes, I do."

"Do you know approximately what time of day that phone conversation took place?"

"There were a few of them that day. I remember one in the afternoon. He was all excited because he was going on a job interview to be an apartment manager."

"What about later in the evening? Were there any phone calls later in the evening?"

"Yes, there was one. It was right around 7 and I remember yelling at him for calling me because that is always dinnertime for us and I was right in the middle of making dinner. I asked him where he was at and he said he was at Steve and Lauren's. I told him I would call him back after dinner."

"How long do you think the phone conversation took place?"

"I don't know. I'd say maybe a few minutes."

"Did you have any other phone calls with him after that time?"

"I forgot to call him back because he called me back around 10 that night. I remember yelling at him again because we have a curfew at our house, which is 10."

"No further questions," Gibbons said.

Przytulski began his cross-examination by handing Showers a copy of a resume used by Sam, in his attempts to obtain employment as a property manager. He instructed her to look at it. "Do you see here where it says, Saticoy Apartments - Canoga Park, California. Owner: Craig Showers, 1980-1991, as part of Mr. Consiglio's professional experience?"

"I see it, yes."

"Did your husband own the property at Saticoy Apartments?"

"No. Sam asked him if he could use him as a reference."

"You mean Sam wanted your husband to lie for him?"

"Basically, yeah," Showers said as she hung her head and stared at the floor.

"And your husband was willing to do that?"

"Of course."

"It was okay with you?"

"I don't see why not."

"You don't see why it's wrong to lie for Sam; right?"

"Well, other people do, when somebody fills out an application."

"Thank you, I don't have anything further," Przytulski said.

Neal Gibbons then called Lauren Skye to the witness stand.

Lauren testified that she had met Sam six years before in Phoenix, when they were driving a cab together.

"Where do you live?" Gibbons asked.

"I live in Clairemont at 3133 Clairemont drive."

"Has Sam Consiglio ever lived at that address?"

"He house-sat for us when we went on vacation in July."

"Did you authorize Sam to use your phone in that house?"

"Yes, we did."

"When you went on vacation, did you go with your husband?"

"Yes, I did."

"So the only person who would have access to your apartment, using that phone, would be Sam Consiglio, isn't that true?"

"This is correct, sir."

"No further questions," Gibbons said.

Gibbons then called Steve Skye, Lauren's husband to the stand.

"Do you know Sam Consiglio?" Gibbons asked.

"I do. I met him through driving a cab in Arizona."

"Did he ever have an occasion to house-sit your house?"

"Yeah, in July of this year when I went on vacation."

Gibbons concluded his questioning of Skye and walked over to the defense table to speak to his client. After a brief conversation, Gibbons called Sam to the witness stand.

"Would you please state your name for the court."

"Sam Consiglio, Jr."

"Were you ever known by the name of John?"

"Yes, John Trupiano."

"Why were you known by that name?"

"I was on escape status from Michigan. I just used my cousin's identification."

Wasting no time, Gibbons asked the direct question before the court. Already knowing the answer that would be given, he needed the jury to hear it instantly from Sam.

"Okay. Did you ever rape Karen?"

Sam's answer could not have been shorter or more definite. "No sir."

"Did you ever have sex with Karen?"

"Never."

"Did you ever go to El Cajon with Karen?"

"Never."

"Do you have any explanation for her demeanor on the witness stand?"

"I think it's a little bit unfair for people to expect me to come up with an explanation for Karen. I can't explain it. All I can tell you is she's lying."

"How long did you know Karen?"

"I met her physically on July 1st and the last time I saw here was at 3:30 on the 2nd."

"Did you at any time in your involvement with Karen do anything which would cause her to allege rape?"

"I never did a thing to her. I never even raised my voice to Karen. I was always very polite to her."

"Did you have any involvement with her the afternoon of July 2nd? Did you see her? Did you see her physically after 3:30 on July 2nd?"

"No, No. 3:30; that was the last time I saw her, at the shelter."

"Okay. Where did you go after 3:30 in the afternoon?"

"I got a tour of the shelter from Bob Knott, and, just guessing, I think it took till about 4 to complete the tour."

"Then where did you go?"

"I went to El Cajon to a meeting. I had to sign a contract."

"Where did you go from there?"

"I drove back to Clairemont where I was living."

"What did you do on the evening of July 2nd?"

"I was on the phone all night."

"Why were you on the phone?"

"I just got a little hung up. I use the phone a lot."

"But why did you make phone calls that evening?"

"Well, that particular day, I was excited about my new job, so I was calling. There is a certain group of people I call all the time if something good happens and that's what I was doing that night."

"Did you happen to call Kathy Showers?"

"Yes."

"Did you call Wava Howley?"

"Yes."

"How many phone calls did you make that evening?"

"I can't say the number. I'm not sure."

"When did you arrive in San Diego?"

"The exact date was Sunday, around 11:30 p.m., June the 9th."

"Why did you come to San Diego?"

"Well, my mom died in March and I came out here to make a new life for myself."

"Have you ever been convicted of a felony?"

"Yes, sir."

"And what was that charge?"

"The correct charge was criminal sexual conduct, second- degree."

"Can you please explain to the jury the circumstances regarding it?"

"I was on a date with a girlfriend and I put my hand on her breast. She pushed it away and I put it back on again and she got a little upset and she prosecuted me for it."

Sam was describing his version of the attack on Connie in 1978.

"Did you ever have sexual intercourse with her? Did you force yourself on her?"

"No. I mean I put my hand back the second time. That was the force."

"Do you believe you're guilty of that charge?"

"Not second-degree; no."

"How long were you in prison?"

"I was arrested in 1978. I was convicted on November 9th, 1979. I went to prison in January 1980. I was paroled on October 12, 1983. A year later, I violated parole and was told that I had to go back for four years and that's when I walked away from the minimum security. I was gone for two years from the state. Then I went back to do the four years."

"Okay. You heard testimony about those pubic hairs. There was a discussion of 10 pubic hairs, none of which were claimed to have been yours, and one other remaining pubic hair of unknown origin. Do you have any explanation for that particular pubic hair?"

"Of course not."

"Did that pubic hair come from Karen?"

"No way."

"Have you had sex with anyone around July 2nd where that pubic hair could have come from another person?"

"The last time I had sex was at 4 or 4:30 in the morning on July 1st. That was the last time."

"Why did you call Wava Howley and talk to her for about an hour on July 2nd?"

"She's probably one of my best friends, and I was pretty excited. I always talk to her for a long time."

"Why is she one of your best friends?"

"She came to visit me in prison. I thought that was pretty nice."

"Do you have genital herpes?"

"No."

"How do you know?"

"I don't really know that. I know I have herpes, but not genital herpes."

"Well, what's the difference?"

"Herpes simplex-1, 80 percent of the people in the country have that."

"Did you ever admit having herpes to the district attorney's office?"

"No I didn't."

"Did you ever have an outbreak of any type of herpes in early July?"

"I've never had an outbreak of herpes."

"When you made these phone calls on the evening of July 2nd, did you call collect, or did you just dial out?"

"I used my non-subscriber calling card with AT&T."

"Explain how that credit card works."

"It's called a non-subscriber telephone credit card, and it's not hooked into any local phone. It's whatever phone that I use it on will register as where the call is being made from and then it would also show where the call is being made to."

"So you get a separate bill for that; correct?"

"Yes."

"Did you have sex with anyone on July 1st?"

"Yes sir."

"And what was that person's name?"

"Jamiss."

"What color is her pubic hair?"

"I'd say between medium and light brown."

"Did you ever lie on your resume?"

"No."

"Is your resume fully accurate?"

"No, it's not. It's exaggerated a little bit."

"But were you trying to be basically truthful as to your overall experience?"

"I was very truthful as to my overall experience."

"Did you try to be fully truthful with the district attorney's office in their interview with you?"

"Yes I did."

"No further questions at this time," Gibbons told Brown.

To Sam, his testimony was not really a conscious bit of deceit, but rather a far more subliminal misrepresentation of the facts.

Przytulski stood and approached the witness stand to begin his cross-examination. He had plenty of questions for Sam. He didn't believe Sam's testimony at the preliminary hearing and now, he was going to make sure the jury didn't believe it either.

"Sam, you got seven and a half years to 15 years for that shindig in Michigan, didn't you?"

"Yes sir."

"And you had a parole violation; right?"

"Yeah."

"What did you do?"

"I raised my voice."

"Pardon me?" Przytulski asked, looking confused.

"Raised my voice," Sam said.

"To whom?"

"Parole officer."

"You raised your voice to a parole officer?"

"That's correct."

"According to the Michigan Department of Corrections, you went to the home of a woman you'd raped six years earlier and tried to gain entry by using a false name and referred to yourself as the one who had made love to her approximately six years prior. This incident frightened and intimidated the victim. All that's false?" Przytulski asked.

"All that's false," Sam said.

"Sam, you've had a sex problem for a long time, haven't you?"

"No sir."

Sam answered before Gibbons could object. Gibbons did however, try to get the answer stricken, but Brown let the answer stand.

"When you left Michigan, did you go to Tampa, Florida?" Przytulski asked.

"Yes, that's correct."

"Did you meet Jamiss there?"

"Not in Tampa, no sir."

"Where did you meet her?"

"I can't think of the name of the city, it's a suburb of Orlando."

"Do you know if Jamiss was a hooker?"

"That's not a fair question."

"Well, I'm asking the questions," Przytulski fired back. "Did you strike up a sexual relationship with Jamiss?"

"I sure did," Sam said proudly.

"Did Jamiss have a fiancé?

"Yes sir."

"Was he in the Navy?"

"That's correct."

"Okay. You and Jamiss get along pretty good?"

"We did."

"You filed a complaint with the Naval Investigative Service against Jamiss, didn't you?"

"That's correct."

"Why did you do that? Jamiss wasn't in the Navy, was she?"

"Her boyfriend was in the Navy. Jamiss was not in the Navy."

"If you had a complaint with Jamiss, why did you file a complaint with the Navy?"

"Because that is the best place to file it."

"Isn't it true that you were blackmailing Jamiss for sex because she had sex with you, and you threatened to tell her fiancé if she didn't continue that?"

"That's totally false."

"No truth in that at all?"

"No sir. I didn't want to cause them any trouble."

"Who?"

"Neither one of them. I just wanted them to stop using my credit cards."

"How did they get your credit cards?"

"At the time, I thought she stole my credit cards."

"Wait a minute. You said she was using your credit cards."

"I assumed that and I was wrong."

"You thought she took your credit cards on July 1st, right?"

"And some money, too."

"Does that mean you didn't have them on July 2nd?"

"I don't know."

"How did Jamiss get out?"

"She flew."

"Why?"

"She came out here to spend the weekend with me."

"Was that voluntary on her part?"

"I made her get on the plane and come here."

"Tell this jury how you made her do that, Sam."

"Come on, Mr. Przytulski," Sam said, revealing his frustration and anger at the question.

"No, Sam, tell them," Przytulski demanded, as his voice grew louder.

"She came out here voluntarily."

"Do you understand the question?" judge Brown asked.

"He's being very unfair, judge," Sam pleaded.

"Well, your lawyer is going to clear it up. I don't want a dialogue. Judge Brown ordered Sam to answer the question.

"How did you force her to come out here, Sam?" Przytulski asked again.

"I did not force her to come out. I was being facetious."

"Did you make some drug charges against Jamiss's fiancé when you did that?"

"That was one of the allegations, yes."

"How did that relate to the credit cards?"

"I just told the guy everything."

"In fact, Sam, you have a pattern when you meet people that you threaten them afterwards that you'll get them, don't you?"

"That's not correct."

"Did you tell us you had sex with two individuals since you came to California and that was with Jamiss and Carolyn on the 4th of July? Did you tell us that?"

"I think that's a fair statement."

"Okay. Now, you remember the preliminary hearing when I asked you, if you told Carolyn not to cooperate with the district attorney's office? And you said, 'I just told her to keep quiet.' Do you remember that?"

"That's correct."

"Why did you call Carolyn?"

"I was concerned about her."

"Why did you call her and tell her to be quiet?"

"I was protecting her."

"Did you feel that she was in some sort of difficulty with us?"

"I think there was a possibility."

"Why?"

"She made certain comments to me."

"How did you meet her?"

"She was hitchhiking."

"Was she a prostitute?"

"I believe so, yes."

"Did you have sex with her?"

"No."

"Ever?"

"One time."

"When?"

"I'm not sure of the date, sometime in mid-June."

"You were under oath at the preliminary hearing; right?"

"That's correct."

"And you were asked, 'In fact you took her to your apartment up in Clairemont on the 4th of July; right.' And your answer: 'Yes, we watched the fireworks.'" Przytulski was reading directly from the transcript from the preliminary hearing.

"That was my misstatement. It was not on the 4th of July."

"Well, Sam, why did you say that to us?"

"I was a little bit nervous, upset at the time."

"When?"

"When you were questioning me."

"About the same way you are now?"

"No. I think I was pretty upset then."

"Do you lie when you get nervous, Sam?"

"No sir."

"What kind of sex did you have with her?"

Gibbons quickly objected stating the question war irrelevant. Brown agreed and sustained the objection.

"What color was Carolyn's pubic hair?"

"I can't answer that question, sir."

Again, Gibbons objected citing relevance.

"Your honor, I would believe it would be relevant to eliminate the possibility of the pubic hair," Przytulski argued.

This time, Brown agreed and overruled the objection.

"What kind of sex did you have with Carolyn?" Przytulski asked.

"Oral sex."

"Where did that take place?"

"In my car."

"How old are you Sam?"

"I'm 40, sir," Sam said sarcastically.

"Did you tell Bob Knott you were looking to place other people in employment?"

"I told Bob Knott that I had a lot of connections in property management. I'm sorry. I have to answer that way. You're being unfair, Mr. Przytulski."

"I'm just asking what you told him, Sam. If I don't look at you when you're answering, that's just because I'm looking somewhere else. If it makes you nervous, I'll look at you all the time."

Judge Brown had been patient during the district attorney's questioning and wanted to keep the trial moving. He didn't want Przytulski and Sam turning this session into their own private war. "Next question," Brown told Przytulski. The DA knew it was the courts way of politely telling him to get on with the questioning. Przytulski had used up his nominal supply of outrage. He wouldn't be antagonized again. He smiled at Sam and continued his cross-examination.

"What kind of car do you have?" Przytulski asked.

"1991 Black Grand Am."

"And does it have the term Single, on a blue-type plate on the back?"

"That's correct."

The questioning continued for the rest of the morning. Przytulski continued to ask Sam about his whereabouts on July 2nd and 3rd. Sam maintained he had not seen Karen after 3:30 p.m. on July 3rd when he dropped her off at Saint Vincent's.

When trial resumed that afternoon, Brown, outside the presence of the jury, met with Sam, Gibbons and Przytulski.

"I've been thinking about the course of the defense's case. I want the record to reflect that I have witnessed what appears to be willingness on the part of the defense to be totally open and forthright and frank about their position. I know that earlier on, there was some desire on the part of Mr. Consiglio to represent himself. And, Mr. Gibbons, I couldn't help but notice that while you are trying the case on behalf of your client, you have conferred with him a lot. Is that correct?"

"Yes. I confer with him constantly."

"And the decision for him to take the stand?" Brown asked.

"Yes your honor. I didn't want any mention of prison in there. Wava Howley spilled the beans and made a comment about it, so it kind of came out. But it was still my feeling all throughout this trial that Sam should not take the witness stand." Gibbons didn't want to give Przytulski an opportunity to cross-examine Sam. But Sam insisted, telling his lawyer that he wanted to get his story told.

"I would like to be heard your honor," Sam said, interrupting the exchange between Gibbons and the judge. But Brown raised his hand and motioned Sam to wait while he continued addressing Gibbons.

"Everything concerning your client taking the stand and the questioning of him in that regard has been a part of the defense's strategy; that is, he is opening himself up to this jury; he wants to state his position. I thought I heard him say earlier that he wants to tell his story."

"That's right your honor, he wants to tell his story. Last night he says you can trust me, because I can handle Mr. Przytulski easily. He says, 'I didn't do the rape. I'm going to make that clear. I can handle his cross-examination. I want to testify; trust me Neal.'" This was one of Sam's problems, one of the holes in what he considered to be his impenetrable wall of dictoric intelligence. He thought he was smarter than most people were.

"All right. Now you don't have to make any statement at all," Brown told Sam.

"Oh, yes, I do, your honor," Sam said. "It was a really tough decision for me to make. I did not sleep last night. I stayed up all night. I put myself on the jury and the jury is going to hear overwhelming evidence showing that I could not have committed this crime and they're going to be sitting here wondering, why are we here."

Judge Brown interrupted Sam telling him that he didn't want him to disclose anything to the prosecution.

"You're an intelligent man. You're articulate. You've represented yourself four times before, and the procedures that you've embraced here in this courtroom and the demeanor of your lawyer is consistent with what you both discussed and settled on; is that right?" judge Brown asked.

"That's correct, your honor," Sam replied.

"The lack of objections when objections could have been made, you've weighed and considered the two-edged sword aspect of it in making or not making objections to questions by the D.A.; right?" judge Brown asked, directing his question to Neal Gibbons.

"Yes your honor. That is consistent with the philosophy of my client. And I've decided, since there are many questions where I could have objected (but didn't) because I decided to let it go out."

"Of course, you recognized those legal objections. But that wasn't consistent with your strategy, with Mr. Consiglio's strategy?" Brown asked.

"Mr. Consiglio and I have a difference of opinion about the strategy," Gibbons said.

"Is that true Mr. Consiglio?" judge Brown asked.

"You think I messed up, don't you?" Sam asked, answering Brown's question with a question of his own.

"No, I just want to know."

"That's right your honor." Sam said.

Before the jury was brought back into the courtroom, judge Brown called Gary Godsey from AT&T back onto the witness stand to testify about the phone records, which would allegedly prove that Sam had been on the telephone during the time Karen claimed to have been raped.

"The phone calls have not appeared on a bill. It turns out no bill has been registered yet because of internal screw-ups. That's the best way to describe that," Godsey told judge Brown.

"How do I get over the custodian-of-records hurdle?" Brown asked Gibbons.

"AT&T has informed me that he is designated the custodian of records, that he is custodian of records as far as AT&T is concerned," Gibbons said.

"It's inherent reliability that governs our rules of evidence. Obviously, Mr. Godsey doesn't know how the records are kept or who has access to them or how they can be tampered with or not tampered with," judge Brown said.

"By his own admission, he said yesterday, I'm not the custodian," Przytulski added.

"I don't know," Brown said. "I'm going to just have to consider it. But right now, my inclination is to not let these records in because they don't comply with the rules of evidence. That's my inclination, and I might change it."

"Your honor, I think this case could turn on this information. I mean, it doesn't look like it would be doctored in any way," Gibbons argued.

"I agree with you. That's what's bothering me. I mean, it's a valid objection, but do I have something within me that would cause basic unfairness in a trial that would require that I overrule that legal objection? You've already had witnesses come in and testify. Wava Howley came in and testified that from 8 to 9 p.m. our time, she was on the phone with the defendant."

"That's good evidence, but the phone bill substantiates and corroborates the testimony," Gibbons said.

"But there's no phone bill as to that long distance call," Brown shot back.

"Yes there is," Gibbons replied.

"No, no. There's a record, but for your own client, it's not just the defense's effort to secure those. The district attorney's office has tried by a search warrant to obtain those documents and have been denied and your client wanted a right to a speedy trial. Those records were not available. He knew it when we started this trial. And so, if he pushes his right to a speedy trial, he does so at his own peril. But just because something is probative doesn't mean it's admissible. We have guys that confess all the time. Yeah, I raped her, murdered her, chopped her up and threw her to the fish, and because he didn't get mirandized, the people (prosecution) don't get it in."

"In this case, it's different, you have inherently reliable phone itemization" Gibbons contended.

"All I'm saying is the rules of evidence have harsh results. Sometimes guilty people are let free because of rules of evidence. Of course, I'm subject to review," judge Brown said.

When the trial resumed, Sam took his place back on the witness stand as Gibbons began his redirect examination.

"In addition to the phone calls you made to Wava Howley and Kathy Showers in the evening of July 2nd, did you make any other calls that evening?"

"Several," Sam said.

"Who else did you call?"

"I called my sister Virginia. I called Tom Seifert and a girl I met on the East Coast, her name is Regina."

"When you called all these people, during what time period are we talking about?"

"Between 6 p.m. and 10:38 p.m."

"No further questions," Gibbons said.

Przytulski continued his cross-examination of Sam asking him about some photographs he allegedly tried to have hidden. When Gibbons objected, Przytulski told judge Brown that he had no further questions.

Satisfied that the defense had done its best to present its case, Gibbons told judge Brown that he did not intend to call any more witnesses. The judge then asked Przytulski if he wanted to offer rebuttal witnesses. Przytulski did and called Leslie Collins to the stand.

Collins testified that she met Sam after he responded to a personal ad she placed in the San Diego Union.

"When you met him, did Sam tell you some things about what he was?" Przytulski asked.

"Yes he did. We had several telephone conversations before we actually met. He said he was a property manager and that he owned quite a few buildings both downtown and in other states and other cities."

"Did he name the other states or cities?"

"Well, he talked about Los Angeles, Riverside, I believe, Michigan, Florida. I'm not sure, maybe Texas."

"Did he come on like he was a megabucks person with all this property?"

"Yes. I got the impression he was trying to impress me because I was in real estate."

"Thank you. No further questions."

Gibbons had no questions for Leslie Collins.

Przytulski then stunned the court and especially Gibbons when he called Sam back to the stand.

"Now, Sam, when we interviewed you on July 17th, on the tape you indicated that you were going to take Karen to dinner at Tep's, or it's also known as Villa Roma?"

"I would say that's a fair response, yes."

"But in the preliminary hearing Sam, you were asked, were you not, if you asked Karen to dinner, and you said, yes. And you were asked were you going to have spaghetti at your house and you responded that's correct. Do you recall that?"

"Yes, sir."

"Well, which is true?"

"They both are."

"How can both be true?"

"I intended to take her to Tep's."

"Why did you testify at the preliminary hearing that you were going to take her to your house?"

"I was very upset at the preliminary hearing, Mr. Przytulski and you know it."

"Were you upset enough to lie?"

"I didn't lie."

"You're upset now, aren't you?"

"No."

"You're not?"

"No."

"Are you saying basically we can disregard whatever you said at the preliminary hearing because you were upset?"

"No, I wouldn't say that."

"Well, what would you say? Are you saying that every time we catch you in an error or a mistake or a lie that it's because you were upset?"

"No, I don't think that's correct."

"Well, how would you characterize it?"

"I don't see where I've told any lies."

"Okay. Now, you managed an apartment in El Cajon in 1987 after you had escaped from prison; right?"

"That was one of my buildings, yes."

"How long did you manage an apartment there?"

"I'm guessing. Say three months."

"So you became familiar with the El Cajon area during those three months, didn't you?"

"No sir."

"Now, you indicated that when you were coming back, that Karen started to make you feel uncomfortable with the way she was looking at you. What did you mean by that?"

"She was staring at me, smiling. I could see her out of the corner of my eye."

"Why did you feel uncomfortable?"

"Because I wanted to keep it a professional relationship."

"Is that why you asked her to dinner?"

"I was just being nice."

"And you were just being nice when you asked her on the 3rd if she wanted to live with you free until she could get a job; right?"

"That's it sir."

The verbal exchange between Sam and Przytulski continued for several more minutes until judge Brown began to exhibit signs that he had heard enough. Przytulski was quick to see that he had done about all he could to demonstrate to the jury how evil Sam really was. When Przytulski said that he had no further questions, Brown, who for days had suffered from a severe headache acquired during the course of the trial, knew that he still had to deal with the issue of the phone records. Opting to treat his headache instead of the evidentiary issue, he adjourned court for the day.

Przytulski returned to his office and sat quietly behind his desk before beginning his preparation for the next day's testimony. His private thoughts reminded him that Sam was more intelligent than most defendants. He was also more deviant and immoral.

When trial resumed on the morning of October 18, Brown told the lawyers that he decided to allow testimony about the phone records. With that ruling, Gibbons called Gary Godsey back to the witness stand.

"Did AT&T designate you as custodian of records?" Gibbons asked.

"They claim they have, yes."

Gibbons handed Godsey a printout of telephone calls made on July 2nd. Godsey testified that the printout related to telephone calls charged to a calling card in the name of Sam Consiglio. The record reflected a call made to Arkansas at 7:54 p.m. that lasted 53 minutes.

"I also call your attention to a call made at 6:56 p.m. California time. How long was that call?"

"One minute and fifty-five seconds."

"Now, this phone itemization is it really a phone bill?"

"No, these are the call details that are generated by the computer network that eventually end up as the call details on the actual bill rendered to the client."

"And can you quickly count how many phone calls there are there?"

"Okay, the first one is 4:35. Then 5:30, 5:54, 5:58, 5:59, 6:48, 6:56, 6:57, 6:59, 7:19, 7:52, 7:54, 8:49, 9:17, 9:33, 10:10…"

"That's fine, thank you. No further questions."

Przytulski rose from the prosecutor's table.

"Mr. Godsey, are you the custodian of these records?"

"Again, the company claims I am."

"But you're really not are you?"

"These are not my records."

"Now, all it takes to make one of these calls is the number, right, the card calling number?"

"Yes. All you need is a calling card number that's a valid calling card number."

"So, if you give the calling card number to anybody, they can place a call; is that correct?"

"That is correct."

"I don't have anything further."

Gibbons rose from the defense table.

"Do you have any reason to believe that this phone itemization is not fully accurate and legitimate?"

"I do not. In fact, I was told that it's true and accurate."

Gibbons thanked Godsey and told Brown that he had no more witnesses. The defense was resting.

After a short recess, judge Brown lectured the jury about their duties to determine the facts from the evidence presented during the trial, and to apply the law to the facts as they determine them, to arrive at a verdict. Judge Brown ordered the jury not to be influenced by pity for Sam or by prejudice against him because he had been arrested for this offense and brought to trial.

"A defendant in a criminal action is presumed to be innocent until the contrary is proved, and in case of a reasonable doubt whether his guilt is satisfactorily shown, he is entitled to a verdict of not guilty, Brown told the jury.

"This presumption places upon the people the burden of proving him guilty beyond a reasonable doubt. Reasonable doubt is defined as follows:

"It's not a mere possible doubt, because everything relating to human affairs, and depending on moral evidence, is open to some possible or imaginary doubt. It's that state of the case which, after the entire comparison and consideration of all the evidence, leaves the minds of the jurors in that condition that they cannot say they feel an abiding conviction to a moral certainty of the truth of the charge."

After judge Brown finished his instructions to the jury, Przytulski rose again from the prosecutor's table and began his closing argument.

"The law is real clear in the case. This is not one of the legal trick cases that you got to look at. It comes down to just credibility. If you believe Karen that he (Consiglio) raped her, the elements of rape are all there. They're not manufactured. You have the threats; you have him grabbing her; you have him forcibly doing it."

Przytulski continued his closing argument summarizing the sequence of events, reiterating for the jury the time Sam met Karen, the time she claimed he raped her in the park on July 2; and the observations and testimony of Karen's roommate and Belkis Bottfeld.

"Its a very interesting thing, Sam is about as hard up as you can get for dates; Okay? He's out with Carolyn, the girl that came in here and stood. If you can't tell that Sam is having some difficulty here connecting, you're ignoring what the facts are here. He's involved in these dating services writing letters to the paper, anything he can do to get a date. I mean that's the defendant. Connect me with some girl, somewhere, somehow. He flies Jamiss out from Florida. We're talking about a man who's desperate."

"And, Karen is not an unattractive girl. She may be homeless; she may have had bad breaks in her life or whatever the case may be that comes out to why she's at the shelter. She's not unattractive and she's a girl that says I'll have dinner with you. And Sam says, I just forgot about it."

"And yet he says, I'm home calling the 900 number to find a date. Well, wait a minute. When Karen says, 'he's taking me out to supper,' the defendant would not miss a chance. He would not miss a chance because that's Sam Consiglio."

"And I use the term Sam, it almost humanizes him. But there's something about Sam that his level of conduct doesn't really come up in the things that he's said and done that really deserves that humanization. Maybe, you know, some sympathy, maybe some help. He's a sick man. There's no doubt he's a sick, sick man. And he's a danger to all women everywhere, any time, any place. And maybe it's wrong for me to dehumanize him, but there's something dehumanizing about the way he acts."

"But, you know; once you understand that (you realize) Sam is a manipulator and swindler, a threatener, a con man. Sam can do almost anything for an alibi. Sam can have anybody back him or do anything for him. Sam can manipulate, particularly if he intended to rape Karen."

"You've got this resume. What about Wava? Keep in mind Wava met Sam in prison. And Wava says, 'I was shocked to hear Sam was arrested for rape.' Well Wava, what was he in prison for? For sexual assault, she says. You see it just goes to that bias because you can't know all about Wava. But what you can glean is that everybody that Sam comes into contact with is manipulated, lies for him, covers up, is threatened, blackmailed, and cajoled, that's Sam. And Wava says I got an answering machine. If Sam calls and it's an open line, it stays open until Sam covers it up."

"Let's talk about the herpes a little bit. Again, out of nowhere, Karen says 'I never had herpes before.' On July 11, she goes to Sharp Hospital and she's found to have genital herpes. And she says, 'Sam gave it to me. He's the only person that could have given it to me.' Lo and behold, Sam is positive for the herpes virus. Nice guess, Karen. Good guess."

"Bob Knott was saying it was a fraud on Saint Vincent De Paul. Sam asked for a woman, between 18 and 35. This was a menu, and Karen was a nice part of that menu. He wouldn't let her go. He wasn't getting her a job, and he wasn't giving a job and he wasn't giving anybody at Saint Vincent's a job. This was a fraud. This was a fraud from a con man. And,

I'm going to ask you to convict Sam of rape with great bodily injury. That man had to know he had herpes when he raped her."

Przytulski thanked the jury and sat down at the prosecutor's table. He had done an excellent job summarizing the case. Like most prosecutors, he harbored a few personal doubts about his performance, wondering if he had addressed each of the major issues of the case before the court.

When the trial resumed after lunch it was Gibbons' turn to address the jury.

Gibbons told the jurors that Przytulski's efforts to dehumanize Sam, was nothing more than an attempt to compensate for the lack of evidence in this case. "He talks about him having sex problems or he's a liar. That's because he doesn't want to deal with the evidence because it hurts him," Gibbons said.

Gibbons pleaded with the jury to take special note of the phone records introduced by Godsey.

"If you look at the phone itemizations, you're going to find that the calls occurred all throughout the 6, 7, 8, 9 o'clock time period. On the phone bill, he has phone calls here occurring at 7:13 p.m. and 9:12 p.m. Those are the 900 numbers that Sam called. You've got calls occurring at 4:35, 5:50, 5:54, 5:58, 5:59, 6:48, 6:56, 6:57, 6:59, 7:52, 7:54, 8:49 and 9; 17, all made from the residence where he was house-sitting. Phone bills don't lie. Computer statements of phone bills don't lie."

"Wava Howley, a school teacher who's taught kindergarten for some 31 years, came out here from Arkansas because she felt it was her duty to explain that she was on the phone with Sam during that time. The phone records back it up. It's corroborated."

"Now, why would a woman who's been raped, lie? Why would she lie about the parking lot where she was raped? She says there were no cars. In the prosecutor's own photograph, we have cars, cars all over this parking lot where she circled where the rape occurred. There were three softball games going on that night. So at the time, there were cars in that lot. She's lying."

"Now, as you know, the rape test came back negative. Sam knew it would. He kept telling Mike Przytulski, 'the test will prove me negative.' But the district attorney says, 'well, she douched, that's why it came back negative.' But why douche? Everybody knows from watching television programs or movies that if you're raped, you've got to preserve the evidence and you don't just immediately douche, I don't care how dirty you feel. She's lying. She's hiding the evidence."

"Why would she write down facts about the rape the night it occurred? If she were raped, she'd be traumatized. She's not going to write down all the facts. She did that in order to preserve her testimony because she was confused about what she might have to say. She wanted it down in writing so she could think it out clearly. And I still don't understand why."

"Now, just a point that popped through my mind that I wanted to challenge that Mr. Przytulski made in his closing arguments. He mentioned that Wava Howley has an answering machine and therefore, Sam called the answering machine and that it was on for as long as he wanted. I don't know of an answering machine that lasts fifty-three minutes."

"I submit that there's no evidence offered by the district attorney to show guilt beyond a reasonable doubt. The one pubic hair can't do it because it's not conclusive. The rape test can't do it; the herpes test can't do it. Inconsistent statements can't do it and his previous sexual assault can't do it. He's failed to meet his burden."

"You're going to see that it's impossible to have committed this crime. And, even if you feel something happened from looking at Karen's demeanor, you still have a duty to find him not guilty based on his burden of proof. So, regardless of your gut feelings, I want you to come back here with a unanimous verdict of not guilty, and I really urge it."

Gibbons thanked the jury and sat down next to Sam. The prosecution, unlike the defense who is allowed only one opportunity to speak on behalf of their clients, is allowed to split its time and usually ends its closing arguments leaving some time to rebut anything said by the defense. Przytulski left enough of his allocated time to speak to the jury once again.

"You know, counsel (Gibbons) sort of finished up by saying even though you feel it in your gut, don't find him guilty. That's what this case is all about, the feeling in your gut. Counsel put emphasis on the fact that Mr. Consiglio indicated that he was so willing to take these tests, you know, the blood, so that they could test for the semen in the vagina. But, you know if you didn't ejaculate… because that's the only thing that will show up. The other part of that rape kit was positive, the hair samples; the pubic hair samples."

"He knows he didn't ejaculate into her, and that's so consistent with Mr. Consiglio, because with Consiglio, it's not the crime for sexual gratification. It doesn't have anything to do with some orgasmic pleasure, none at all. See Sam's pleasure is derived from the attack. The overcoming of the woman, the taking of her, that's Sam's pleasure. It's not ejaculation.

"He's a violent man. Karen say's, 'he put his arms around my neck.' And when Sam talked about his sexual assault in Michigan, he attempted to minimize it. 'I just touched her on the breast,' (Sam said) when he was asked to describe the charges."

Przytulski pleaded with the jury to convict Sam on each and every count of the information.

It was about 3 p.m. when the jury retired to the small room next to the courtroom to consider Sam's fate. About 90 minutes later, judge Brown adjourned the jury for the weekend.

As a Deputy District Attorney, Mike Przytulski had seen and prosecuted his share of sex offenders. But it seemed that Sam's mind and character were worlds away from the sex offenders he'd prosecuted. He had seen Sam's eyes and listened to his voice as he lied, ever so convincingly. Przytulski knew that no woman could expect to cross Sam's path and walk away unharmed.

The jurors resumed deliberations on Monday, October 21. Shortly after 2:30 p.m., Richard J. Scaglione, the foreman of the jury, notified judge

Brown that they had reached a verdict. Scaglione gave a sheet of paper used to record their verdicts to the judge. Brown took only a moment to read the verdict sheet before handing it to the clerk of the court. Mike Przytulski remained in his seat while Sam and Neal Gibbons rose from their chairs and stood quietly waiting for the clerk to read the verdict.

"We the jury in the above-entitled cause, find the defendant, Sam Consiglio, guilty of the crime of forcible rape, as charged in count one of the information, first penetration," the clerk of the court read. The jury spoke loud and clear, it found Sam guilty of inflicting great bodily harm on Karen.

Sam lowered his head. He didn't want to face the jury or anyone else at that moment. The clerk continued to read the jury's verdicts of counts two and three.

"We the jury find the defendant, Sam Consiglio, guilty of the crime of forcible rape as charged in count one of the information, second penetration." The clerk continued to read, "We the jury, find the defendant, Sam Consiglio, guilty of the crime of forcible rape, as charged in count one of the information, third penetration, dated October 21, 1991, signed Richard J. Scaglione, foreman."

Judge Brown thanked the jury for their patience and public service. He told them he hoped they found the experience of having sat on a jury, although grave in nature, to have been a rewarding one. Brown then ordered that Sam be remanded into custody without bail. Sentencing was set for December 6.

That night, sitting in his cell inside the San Diego jail, Sam became enraged. His anger grew as each minute passed, while he paced back and forth in his small cell. Sam had been convinced that he was going to be acquitted. He looked for someone to blame and that person was Neal Gibbons.

"I remember calling Neal that night and screaming my lungs out at him for screwing things up so bad," Sam said. "He said it was all my fault for not paying him enough money. He really made a big mistake saying something like that to me at that moment. I paid the idiot exactly what he asked me for." Sam became so upset with Gibbons' comment that before sentencing, he lodged a formal complaint with the California Bar Association. The following morning, after his verbal altercation with Gibbons, Sam telephoned the bank that issued him his VISA card and cancelled payment for Gibbons' services.

Afterward, Sam reviewed the trial in his mind. To him, he had been convicted on a small amount of circumstantial evidence. There were no witnesses to the crime itself. There were no traces of semen or other physical evidence that pointed to him. The prosecutions case was one based on the credibility of Karen as opposed to Sam's.

Sam kept detailed notes during the trial. Over the next several months, he dissected the transcripts of the trial with the precision of a seasoned medical examiner seeking a cause of death during an autopsy. Sam had a lot to do and not much time to do it. His goal was singular; to have this conviction overturned and obtain a new trial.

Chapter 15

We Don't See Things as They Are, We See Them as We Are

Anais Nin

The night of his conviction, Sam sat anxiously in his jail cell angry with Gibbons, and realizing he still faced charges relating to his sexual encounters with Carolyn. His thoughts were not only on those pending charges, but the appeal he was preparing in his attempt to have his most recent conviction for raping Karen overturned. Sam was confident he would be free again before the end of the year. Never losing his sense of humor, Sam recorded his thoughts in a letter about the pending trial involving Carolyn, the street prostitute.

"This ugly hooker is hitchhiking when I stop and give her a ride. And, I do mean ugly. In fact, if you look in the dictionary under the word ugly, you will see her picture. There was no way I would ever think this girl was a hooker. So, you can understand my shock when she asks, 'do you want a date?' She misunderstood the expression on my face and because of that she exclaimed, 'oh, my lord, your a cop.' I never said a word. I didn't have to. She then said, 'pull over and I'll suck your dick instead of going to jail.' I aim to please and I did just as she requested. To this day, I can't believe I let that thing touch my dick. Then, to top it off, after she's done, she say's she has several open sores in her mouth.

The girl never calls the police or complains to anyone. I told the D.A. about it and he turns around and forces her to prosecute me for Impersonating an Officer and Oral Copulation by Trickery and they aren't referring to Halloween. Don't worry, it is not a statute that's used very often. In fact, the last time it was used, was 1884.

Now, you can tell a woman, if you suck my dick, I promise I won't cum in your mouth. If you make such a statement and don't keep your promise, you will be the second person to be charged with that in the twentieth century.

There's one more thing. If you ask a woman; if I wash my dick will you suck it and she say's yes, you can't go to the john and just pretend you washed it. If you lie in California and she puts a dirty dick in her mouth, adios amigo.

Women can also be charged with this crime and I can think of many in my life that should be put away for many years for the shit that they pulled on me. 'I'm real clean honey,' yeah, right."

During the first week of December 1991, Sam wrote a letter to Carolyn Chapman, an attorney in San Diego pleading for her to represent him at his December 6 sentencing before judge Brown. That morning, two San Diego County Sheriff Deputies escorted Sam from his jail cell to the courtroom of judge Frank Brown. Dressed in standard jail issue clothing consisting of a white shirt, white pants and tennis shoes, Sam sat at the defense table next to Neal Gibbons and Carolyn Chapman. Mike Przytulski sat opposite Sam, as he had six weeks prior when he prosecuted him for raping Karen. When the judge opened the proceedings, Gibbons rose and made a motion to the court requesting he be allowed to withdraw as Sam's attorney. Gibbons told Brown that Carolyn Chapman would be substituting during the sentencing. As judge Brown was preparing to respond to Gibbons' motion, Chapman rose and addressed the court.

"Your honor, Mr. Consiglio has contacted me and requested that I sub- stitute in at the sentencing stage. But, it has come to my attention that there was perjured testimony that was given at trial. And, I cannot enter the case at this time."

Gibbons told the judge that Wava Howley had allegedly perjured herself during her testimony. The judge was outraged. Looking down from his bench, his eyes fixed directly on Sam, Judge Brown said, "Mr. Consiglio, you are a con artist. You are such a con artist that you even believe your own con. You believe what you're saying is the truth. That's how good you are. You don't know truth from reality. Your whole history is replete with sexual assaults and preying upon women. This is just another one. You don't think you're a pervert and you are." Brown ordered the district attorney to look into Chapman and Gibbons' allegations. Brown also postponed the sentencing for two weeks.

Four days later, Sam filed a Marsden Motion in the Superior Court of California to have Mike Dealy, his court-appointed attorney in the case involving Carolyn removed as his attorney of record. "He did nothing to prepare for trial," Sam said. "Whenever I talked to him on the phone, he'd say 'we'll just go to trial and see what happens.' I mean, I had just been convicted and sentenced for a crime I was completely innocent of and I was scared to death of going to trial on a case where I did not have some involvement. I had to be certain I had a competent attorney if I had any chance of winning."

San Diego Superior Court Judge Freddie Link denied Sam's motion. Sam appealed the decision to the California Court of Appeals.

That night, in his private cell inside the San Diego County Jail Sam considered ending his life. "I was angry, totally devastated and very despondent. I lost my will to fight," he said. "I cried so long I thought it would take forever to stop the tears. When I did, I decided I'd better get some help to make sure I never got that close to taking my life again. So I called the crisis hot line and they advised me to call one of the colleges that had a training school for people who were studying to become psychologists." Sam called the San Diego State University and asked for a female Psychologist to provide therapy. They were only too happy to accommodate him. Sandra Delehanty, a doctoral candidate majoring in clinical psychology was assigned to counsel Sam.

"I wanted a woman because it was a woman who had caused me to feel the way I was feeling and I planned to use her as a sort of punching bag to vent my anger," Sam explained.

But instead of using Sandra as a punching bag, Sam soon found himself falling in love.

The following week, Wava Howley wrote judge Brown the following letter:

"I, Wava Howley, declare as follows: Having been subpoenaed to testify in court in California during the rape trial of Sam Consiglio, I did tell the truth to the best of my ability and according to my best recollection of the facts concerning whether or not I was talking on the phone to Mr. Consiglio on July 2, 1991 between 10 and 11 p.m. Arkansas time.

Patrick Harn and Mike Przytulski harassed me through phone calls on December 5, 1991 accusing me of perjury. They intimated that I had called someone and confessed. They wouldn't give any basis for their accusations nor would they say what they believed to be false about my testimony. They urged me to change my testimony while I had the chance to do so.

Now I have been informed that Neal Gibbons said that I called him and admitted to perjury after the trial was over. This is absurd. The only contact I have had with Mr. Gibbons after I testified in court was on October 17, 1991, at 8:53 p.m. when I called him at his home to ask about the status of Mr. Consiglio's trial. The trial had not ended yet. That call lasted 15 minutes. On November 19, at 4:25 p.m., I called Mr. Gibbons' office, having been advised to do so by Susie Esqueda, judge Brown's senior deputy, regarding witness fees. I spoke only to Mr. Gibbons' secretary concerning this matter. This call lasted five minutes.

I declare under penalty of perjury that the foregoing is true and correct. Executed this 12th day of December 1991. signed, Wava Howley."

The following morning, Sam met with Sandra Delehanty. At the end of the day, his mood turned euphoric.

On Thursday, December 19, Sam, for the second time in as many weeks, stood before judge Brown waiting to be sentenced for raping Karen. Sam stood quietly as judge Brown prepared to render his sentence to a man he considered charming and intelligent but who used those traits as an effective facade to assault women. "At heart, you're a con man and a pervert and I'm going to warehouse you for as long as I can to keep you from preying on females any longer," the judge said. "You preyed upon this helpless person and you hurt her. You left her with a disease she'll have the rest of her life. The damage that you've done is not just to a particular orifice but to the psyche of the person you violated. You are an infection on society who must be excised. In other words, Mr. Consiglio, society doesn't like rapists. I think that the district attorney's position that I should run these consecutive in light of your criminal history; in light of the fact that you choked this vulnerable victim; in light of the fact that you planned this with such sophistication, setting up an alibi by the alleged phone call; that you looked this jury in the eye and lied to them during the trial, all show how dangerous you are to society."

Judge Brown sentenced Sam to eight years on each of the penetrations; three in all as charged in count one of the information relating to the rape of Karen. He added an additional six years to the sentence for inflicting great bodily harm after infecting Karen with herpes. Each sentence was to run consecutive with the other, meaning Sam was sentenced to 30 years in the California State Prison, the maximum sentence allowed by law. Before being returned to jail, Przytulski offered Sam a plea bargain on the charges related to Carolyn. If Sam would agree to plead guilty to raping Carolyn, the district attorney's office would recommend a sentence of 12 years incarceration to run concurrent with the 30 year sentence just imposed by Brown. With good behavior and a solid prison work record, Sam could be free again in 15 years.

But Sam refused Przytulski's offer, maintaining his belief that he would get this conviction overturned and that he would never be convicted of raping Carolyn.

Sam told Bill Callahan, a reporter for the San Diego Tribune, that afternoon that he was innocent. "I was convicted because of prejudicial behavior and legal rulings by judge Brown," Sam said. "I am not guilty of this crime. I never touched the victim. Mr. Przytulski continually offered me a plea bargain of eight years if I would plead guilty. Had I been guilty, I would have accepted that. I'm not a pervert. I never touched this person."

Later that same day, Sam filed a Petition for a Writ of Habeas Corpus alleging that he had been denied effective counsel during the Karen trial and that judge Brown had been prejudicial. While Sam certainly expected this petition to be denied, he nonetheless, hastily drafted the writ in order to begin the long process of getting a new trial. At the same time he filed a Notice of Appeal and Motion for Appointment of Counsel on Appeal with the Court of Appeal, Fourth Appellate District in California. Sam was asking the court to appoint him an attorney to handle his appeal, still confident that he would get his conviction of raping Karen overturned. In the meantime he would concentrate on preparing for his next visit to the San Diego Superior Court.

While he continued to maintain his innocence, Sam knew he was only a few weeks away from facing yet another trial; a trial he hoped to have postponed in order to gain time to have the conviction of raping Karen overturned. With all the cunning of a chess champion, Sam plotted his next strategic move. But with Christmas approaching, he began to feel the pain of loneliness. He had begun receiving weekly counseling from Delehanty and, while Sam looked forward to these counseling sessions, he knew they would terminate the moment he was transferred from the county jail to a state prison. And while Delehanty's weekly visits were a source of great comfort to Sam, they were not enough to deal with the solitary life he was experiencing. In an effort to compensate for this loneliness, Sam took out an ad in the Lovelorn Column of the San Diego Tribune.

"White male, 40, seeks white female for possible marriage. Should love travel, music and dining out. Send photo and phone number to…" Sam used the mailing address of his friends Steve and Lauren Skye so that women could respond to his ad.

On Christmas Eve, 1991, Sam sat quietly in his cell feeling despondent. He had met with Delehanty earlier in the day and was beginning to feel even more attracted to her. He wanted to tell her that she was the kind of woman he would be interested in if he ever got out of jail but decided not to, fearing that it would make her uncomfortable. He was afraid that his weekly therapy sessions with Sandra would be taken away from him anytime now.

"Christmas really sucks when you're alone," Sam recorded in a letter. "If it wasn't for God's help, I wouldn't be able to survive this. Whenever I pray, I ask him to please make Karen tell the truth. It's going to happen. I just have to believe that. In spite of all the bad I still must admit, I have a lot to be thankful for. I wish I had a woman to put my arms around and she would say she loves me. How long is God going to allow this to continue?"

That evening, Sam telephoned his brother, Louie, and his sister, Virginia, to wish them a Merry Christmas. Louie told Sam that the local newspaper had run a major story on his recent conviction and that the rest of the family was feeling depressed over having the Consiglio name spread across the papers once again. Sam told his brother he was sorry for causing his family this added pain.

But the depression was short-lived once he received a letter from Dana, who responded to his ad in the Lovelorn Column.

On Christmas morning, Sam, with his unlimited telephone privileges, called Dana. They talked for over an hour. Before hanging up, Dana agreed to visit Sam in two weeks.

On December 29, Sam telephoned Dana again. They spoke for about 15 minutes and Dana confirmed she would be visiting Sam soon.

The next day, after third session with Sam, Delehanty prepared an Intake Summary and Psychodiagnostic Impressions report relating to

Sam. In her report, she noted that during her sessions with Sam, he was over concerned with physical beauty and attractiveness. She also wrote that Sam had inappropriately flirted with her until, "the limits of the psychotherapeutic relationship were clearly defined."

Delehanty administered several psychodiagnostic tests to Sam, all designed to provide her with the type of information she would need in order to guide her through the therapy sessions. These tests included the Wechsler Adult Intelligence Scale-Revised (WAIS-R), which included the verbal subtests Vocabulary and Information and the nonverbal subtest Block Design tests. These tests include measuring what a subject knows based on their education. The block design tests problem solving. Sam's IQ, was estimated to be 104, considered within the average range of intelligence. She also tested Sam's ability to differentiate normals from mental illness. She concluded that the test results, "suggested an inability to form the type of close relationship required to build a therapeutic alliance. Persons with this configuration are often distrustful, deceptive, and employ passive aggression as a means of dealing with negative emotions. Persons with this profile are not generally capable of accepting a therapists services because they regard others, including the therapist, as objects of manipulation."

The results of the Rotter Sentence Completion Test, Delehanty concluded, revealed evidence of anger, helplessness, need for affection and poor judgment. Most answers beg sympathy, such as "people just don't understand me; my greatest fear is going to prison for a crime I didn't commit; I can't believe what is happening to me right now; and other people are treating me unfairly."

Sandra Delehanty concluded in her report that, Sam's ability to act without guilt or remorse, to rationalize his aggressive behavior and to deny his violent wrongdoings, contributes to an overall portrait of a psychopathic individual.

"Sam Consiglio, Jr. is not likely to benefit from long-term psychotherapy for many reasons. His behavior and personality are those of a man who is very self-centered and emotionally shallow. His narcissistic grandiosity compromises his judgment and clouds his self-awareness, hampering his ability to have meaningful insights. His ongoing goal is to manipulate and control others. He demonstrates no remorse for past manipulations that ended in hostile or aggressive behavior on his part. His has been a chronically antisocial lifestyle peppered with unstable relationships and sexually deviant behavior; he expresses no interest in modifying this way of life but instead seeks psychotherapeutic intervention for stress reduction. He wishes to be heard without judgment." She agreed to provide six sessions of psychotherapy after completing the report.

On New Years Eve, Sam, with great anticipation, looked forward to his weekly counseling session with Delehanty. He kept telling himself that 1992 was going to be a much better year. "No matter where I'm at, if I only have someone to love then everything else will be okay. I look forward to therapy more now than at any other time in my life," Sam said.

New Year's Day certainly didn't begin as Sam had hoped. Arguments with cellmates and deputies took place over television privileges and there were several fights among the inmates. "Every little thing is starting to bother me," Sam said. "Maybe I am going to spend the rest of my life here. If that was true, I wish God would take me now."

Over the next several days, Sam's thoughts focused on his upcoming visit with Dana. He began to feel self-conscious about his weight, which had ballooned to over 250 pounds. He spent much of his time watching football games on television and playing cards. His spirits were high as he anticipated his visit with Dana and he was pleased that he was getting along so well with the other prisoners. Later in the day, his mood was dampened when he telephoned his brother, Jimmy, collect, in Michigan. "He disappointed me by complaining about the cost of the call." Sam swore he would never call him again.

On January 8, 1992, Sam's trial on charges he raped Carolyn while posing as a police officer, was scheduled to begin in San Diego Superior Court. Sam arrived in the courtroom, dressed in his jail-issued white shirt and pants; prepared to defend himself. Seated next to him, was Przytulski, his nemesis, who was once again prepared to rid society of guiltless predators. Just before trial was to begin, Sam learned that the California Court of Appeals had issued a stay in the case pending a ruling that his court appointed attorney, Mike Dealy, be removed as his attorney of record. Sam was returned to his cell pleased that something positive had finally happened to him.

Four days later, Sam waited quietly in his cell, counting the hours and then minutes as they passed all too slowly. It was the day he would finally meet Dana. "I hadn't been that excited since waiting for Jamiss to get off the plane back in June," Sam said. "I had this feeling that she might not come or, if she did, she would walk out when she seen what I looked like."

But Dana did keep her promise and came to the jail and visited with Sam. She spoke to Sam by telephone as they looked at each other through the thick glass designed to separate prisoners from their visitors. "She was one of the nicest people I had met in long time. It was like we'd know each other for years. I didn't want to be impulsive but I thought we were compatible, at least non-sexually. I tried to do exactly what Sandra had recommended, that was to look at her as a friend, not just sexually. I thought I might actually end up marrying Dana." Sam felt better than he had in weeks. "I felt like I was dreaming, but I tried not to dwell on it fearing that something would go wrong."

The following day, Sam was notified that his Petition for Habeas Corpus was denied.

On Friday, January 17, 1992, Sam's thoughts were on the oppressive heat inside the jail and the fact that he had not heard from Dana since her initial visit. He called Dana's mother from his cell where he continued to enjoy telephone privileges afforded those prisoners defending themselves or acting as co-counsel on their own behalf. But Dana's mother was not encouraging. She told Sam that Dana had been very busy. Two days later, Dana visited Sam on Sunday afternoon. She asked Sam when he thought he might be getting out of jail. "In my opinion, I told her I should get out sometime this year but it could turn out to be much longer," Sam said. He asked Dana if she would be coming back next Sunday. She told him that she had other plans. "How about the following Sunday?" Sam asked.

"We'll see," she said. Sam knew another visit from Dana didn't appear encouraging. He was certain he would never see her again. Sam was finally right about something.

Over the next several weeks, Sam occupied himself with preparing for his upcoming trial on the charges related to his alleged rape of Carolyn. His primary concern was to delay the proceedings for as long as possible. He wanted to ensure in his mind that he had a competent attorney who would not make the same mistakes Neal Gibbons made during the trial involving Karen. He also wanted to delay being transferred to a state prison, which would result in the termination of his counseling sessions with Delehanty.

On February 14, 1992, the California Court of Appeals refused to overturn the denial of Sam's motion seeking to have Mike Dealy removed as his court appointed attorney. The following week, while in the San Diego City jail, Sam witnessed an altercation between two inmates inside the jail. Dealy was representing one of the inmates for whom Sam was now prepared to testify. Because Sam, Dealy's defendant in one case, was now a potential witness for a client of his in another pending action, Dealy declared a conflict situation with the court, and was removed as Sam's attorney.

On March 10, Logan McKechnie was appointed to represent Sam on charges that he raped Carolyn. On that same day, Jan Stiglitz, a professor of law at California Western School of Law in San Diego, was appointed to represent Sam in the appeal of his conviction of the rape of Karen.

Sam was confident his new attorney would be given ample time to prepare for trial, certainly at least several months, which would allow time for a possible reversal of his conviction for raping Karen.

Toward the end of March, Sam learned that the court was determined to conduct the trial involving the alleged rape of Carolyn in April. Yet, he searched for new ways to delay the trial. He thought again about filing yet another Marsden Motion seeking to have McKechnie removed as his attorney of record. Sam read an article in the Legal News detailing how a defendant physically attacked his attorney, forcing the judge to appoint him new counsel.

"I seriously considered that option," Sam said. "But I couldn't go through with it because McKechnie was too nice. I had to come up with another way that wasn't so violent. That's when I read about a guy who filed a formal complaint with the bar association. This created an irrefutable conflict. Even though I felt McKechnie was the best attorney I'd had so far, I didn't have any other options to ensure I'd receive a fair trial." Sam figured that once he filed the complaint, judge Link would be forced to appoint him a new attorney. Sam actually liked Logan McKechnie. Under different circumstances, he would have been happy to have him remain as his attorney of record. "The truth of the matter is that all of Mr. McKechnie's shortcomings were actually caused by the court not giving him the time needed to properly defend me," Sam said.

On Tuesday, April 14, 1992, at 11 a.m., in the Superior Court of San Diego County, judge John M. Thompson announced that he was ready to hear the case of the matter of the people of the State of California vs. Sam Consiglio.

Chapter 16

Oral Copulation by Trickery; Give Me a Break

Judge Thompson glanced down at the two attorneys who waited patiently for their chance to speak. Mike Przytulski was first. He stood and introduced himself, then introduced P. J. Harn, the investigator from the district attorney's office, who was sitting directly behind him. Dressed in a jail issued white shirt and white pants bearing the phrase, "San Diego Jail," Sam sat anxiously, at the table next to Przytulski. His attorney, Logan McKechnie, five foot-ten inches tall, heavy set with a moustache, who looked almost like he could pass as Sam's twin brother, stood and introduced himself as the attorney for the defense. McKechnie then told judge Thompson that Sam had a Marsden Motion he would like the court to hear.

Przytulski, still standing, told judge Thompson that he too, had several things he wanted to put on the record. Przytulski told the court that he had attempted to enter into a plea bargain with Sam. If Sam were to plead guilty to sexually assaulting Carol, the prosecutor's office would agree to a sentence of 12 years, which Sam could serve concurrently with the sentence recently imposed from his conviction for raping Karen.

"Your honor, he (Sam) would be more than willing to plead to the 12 years provided that Mr. Consiglio could withdraw his plea in the other case if overturned on appeal," McKechnie told the judge.

Sam wasn't sure which he detested more, the plea offer or his adversary, Mike Przytulski. As soon as McKechnie finished telling judge Thompson that Sam was refusing any offer to plead in this case, Przytulski and Harn were asked to leave the courtroom while Sam made his Marsden Motion hoping to have his attorney removed from the case.

"What is the basis of your motion?" judge Thompson asked sternly.

Sam never seemed to believe anyone was on his side, and this day was no different as he began his oral presentation of his Marsden Motion. "It's a very lengthy motion, your honor. If I can indulge the court's time, the D.A. has given you kind of a little overview. I would like to give you an overview."

"On September 5th, 1991, I was pro per on this case. On October 2nd, judge Link talked me into having Mike Dealy appointed too get rid of my pro per status. He didn't think I was qualified. On December 10th, I filed a Marsden Motion against Mr. Dealy because he failed to do anything in my case. Judge Link denied my motion and I immediately appealed to the court of appeals. On January 6, they issued a stay."

"On February 14th, the Court of Appeals refused to overturn judge Link's denial of my Marsden. In early March, Mr. Dealy declared a conflict. I'm a witness in a case that his office is handling."

"On March 10, Mr. Logan McKechnie was appointed to represent me. At that time, I was very optimistic. I guess you could say, overly optimistic. I spoke to him and an investigator. It's my understanding that the procedure in a criminal matter is that you have a lawyer. He investigates, he files pertinent motions, and based on those motions, is when the defendant can make a decision on what to do."

"I went over all this with Mr. McKechnie. The major issue in my case is I have two witnesses who will exonerate me. And I told Mr. McKechnie that both witnesses would be available in mid August. I don't see what the problem would be with that anyway. I'm doing thirty years so I'm not going anywhere."

"I just want to hear what you have to say; why I should remove Mr. McKechnie as your attorney," judge Thompson said.

"He's not been honest with me. I don't believe he's been honest with me all the way through this. I can't be much more specific. You want me to tell you the dishonesty involved?"

"I think you have to because you have to give me some reason and so far you haven't," judge Thompson said.

Sam told judge Thompson that McKechnie had assured him getting a delay until his witnesses were ready would not be a problem. That is what Sam perceived as dishonesty on the part of McKechnie. It was another example of Sam creating his own reality and expecting other people to not only believe it but to live with it.

"I asked him point blank, did the investigator go and speak to the complainant and he told me yes, but she refused to talk to him. I knew that he was being dishonest because the day before that, I talked to the investigator and he didn't even know where the girl lived. I talked to him after that and found out that he had never been there and he was supposed to go there this weekend, but I don't know if he did or not.

"A motion should have been filed to disqualify Mr. Przytulski because I filed a $5 million lawsuit against him in Federal Court. Plus, I filed with the state bar regarding malicious prosecution in the first matter. I feel that those are motions, your honor. I feel that Mr. McKechnie has violated his attorney-client privilege and has damaged the attorney-client relationship irreparably," Sam said.

"How has he violated your attorney-client privilege?" Thompson asked.

"There was certain things that he told the investigator about my past that I thought by telling him, was between him and I. If I had known that he would tell somebody, I would have never told him."

"I have one more point to raise, but before I raise it, I just want to tell the court that I don't want to prolong this case, your honor. I want the trial and I won't take time served. I don't care what the D.A. offers, if he offered me time served on a thirty-year case."

"Finally, I want to bring to the court's attention that the end of March, I filed a formal complaint with the California Bar Association against Mr. McKechnie. I'm just very, very unhappy with things. The investigation is just now getting underway by the Bar Association on that matter. Mr. McKechnie has failed to confer with me concerning the preparation of the defense. He has refused to communicate with me. He has failed, refused to perform investigations critical, necessary to the defense. He has failed and refused to prepare and file motions critical to the defense. Based on everything I've stated here today, I would ask this court to change attorneys. I believe that I'm only asking for effective representation, your honor, and I expect that the court will ensure that I get that."

Judge Thompson asked Logan McKechnie if he wished to respond to Sam's Marsden Motion.

"This is the first time I've heard there was a complaint with the state bar and that I was being investigated," McKechnie said. "Regardless of whether a client is maneuvering or whether a client is for real, it is very difficult for me to respond when I am now under investigation by the state bar. I don't know how to respond to the court."

McKechnie explained that most of Sam's complaints were problems associated with communications; in reality, Sam was not listening. He argued that he could not see how he could represent a defendant when faced with the possibility of answering to agencies that have the power to take his livelihood away. "I have to tell the court in all honesty, it definitely affects me," McKechnie told judge Thompson hoping to actually be removed as counsel.

Confident that Sam was attempting to stall the trial process, judge Thompson denied the Marsden Motion telling Sam that he did not think removing someone of McKechnie's experience would be in the interests of justice.

Sam, standing as he heard judge Thompson explain his decision, asked, "Your honor, could I have a couple of days to file an appeal with the Court of Appeals?"

"No," judge Thompson said sternly. "You can writ me up on the issue, but we're going to proceed with the trial."

That afternoon, judge John M. Thompson, Mike Przytulski, and Logan McKechnie selected a jury to hear the case of the State of California vs. Sam Consiglio in the rape trial of Carolyn.

The following morning at 9:00 a.m., Wednesday, April 15, 1992, Sam, as he had for almost 20 years, missed the deadline for filing his federal tax returns. Before trial began, McKechnie told judge Thompson that Sam wished to renew his Marsden Motion. Once again, Mike Przytulski and P. J. Harn were asked to leave the courtroom.

"Good Morning, your honor," Sam said. "I was in contact with the Court of Appeals yesterday afternoon and there are just a couple of things I want to clarify. When there is a complaint against an attorney with the bar association, it is an irrefutable conflict. And I believe that the Court of Appeals concurs with that because it was part of their decision in People versus Perez. So, based on that, I feel the court erred yesterday. I have filed, and they received it at 9:00 this morning, an emergency Writ of Mandate requesting emergency stay in this proceeding, but on a new area. I want to restate my Marsden Motion based on what's happened since my last Marsden Motion against Mr. McKechnie, that I feel he committed some errors yesterday. I brought to his attention, my mistreatment by the Marshals, which, I'm sure the court is aware of, and that Mr. McKechnie didn't want to (discuss) although today, everything is fine."

"Clothing is another issue. I feel that I got San Diego Jail written all over my clothing and I don't think that's fair. I don't have any money to buy clothes and I think when you are a court-appointed attorney, in past cases they have provided clothes somehow."

"Finally, I asked Mr. McKechnie yesterday to file a motion. I brought to his attention, a Supreme Court decision that came out April the 6th,

Joe Mario Revion versus Texas. I wanted him to file a motion to prohibit the state from using peremptory challenge to strike members of a certain ethnic group, in this case, blacks. For my experience, Mr. Przytulski has a very bad habit of getting rid of all blacks. And, I wanted blacks on my jury. We only had one on this panel. I know Mr. Przytulski, and I would have bet my life he was going to get rid of him and he did. So, the fact that my attorney did not make that motion yesterday could prevent me from bringing this issue up on appeal. I feel that what Mr. Przytulski has a habit of doing, is a violation of the 6th and 14th Amendment. One is for equal protection. The other one is due process. For those reasons, I would resubmit my Marsden at this time."

Sam's masquerade as an attorney was designed to impress everyone in the courtroom. Sam liked himself more than anyone in the world. Whether it was renting apartments or driving a cab, Sam's purpose was always singular, to prove to people that he was more than he was.

But judge Thompson had witnessed jailhouse lawyers before as they tried to impress him with their oral and written arguments. This only resulted in long costly delays to an already overburdened court. Still convinced that Sam was using this tactic to achieve another delay in his trial, judge Thompson denied his renewed request to have Logan McKechnie removed as his attorney.

Judge Thompson told Sam that the mere filing of a complaint did not automatically trigger the disqualification of an attorney from participating in a trial. If that were the case, a defendant, whose sole desire was to impede the progress of a case, could continually, with the appointment of each new attorney, file a complaint with the state bar. It was Thompson's position that Sam's complaint had no merit. Sam then began to address the issue of his treatment by the marshals.

"It wasn't a matter of mistreatment, your honor, I want to make that clear. They weren't mistreating me, but they were hanging on to me escorting me through the hallway. If a juror were to see that, it would make them believe that someone is dangerous. There's no (history) of escapes on my record anywhere. I'm not a threat. I've never attempted escape. So that the way I was treated in that respect was wrong."

"The marshals did not deny that they escorted you and that they placed their hands on your arms. It's my understanding that is the marshal's procedures any time (they are) escorting someone who is in custody, specifically when you're in the public areas. I would not order them to do otherwise once they are out in the public sector. It would be nice if they never had to confront a situation where you, meaning someone who is in custody, is put out in the public hallway. But this court, among other things, was not designed properly to accommodate that."

The next issue, which had to be addressed prior to the jury hearing any evidence, was a motion filed by the defense to exclude the transcript of the recorded question and answering session between Przytulski, Harn and Sam on July 17, 1991. To counter this motion, Przytulski called P. J. Harn to the witness stand.

"Now, on or about July 17th of 1991, actually just prior to that, were you assigned to assist me in the prosecution of a case which ultimately involved the defendant Sam Consiglio and a separate victim other than this case, Karen?" Przytulski asked.

"Yes I was," answered Harn.

"Now, as part of that investigation, did you come into contact with Mr. Consiglio on July 17th of 1991?"

"Yes I did."

"Was Mr. Consiglio in custody when you came into contact with him?"

"No, he was not."

"How did that contact come about?"

"I was looking for him. He returned my phone calls. I left a card at his house n El Cajon. He called me. We arranged for an interview at the district attorney's office.

"Did he express any reluctance to talk to you?"

"No."

"Was he eager to talk to you?"

"Very eager."

"Did he indicate to you that he wanted to tell you his story?"

"Yes."

"Did he indicate to you that he wanted you to get the facts clear?"

"Yes."

"Did Mr. Consiglio come to the district attorney's office on his own?"

"Yes."

"And did you bring him back and conduct an interview with him in which I was present?"

"Yes, I did."

"Was that interview tape recorded?"

"Yes it was."

"In its entirety?"

"Yes."

"After the interview ended, did Mr. Consiglio and yourself still continue to have some conversation about some things?

"Yes."

"Now, regarding the interview with him, did you review a transcript that had been prepared from that interview?"

"Yes, I did."

"Is that transcript a fair and accurate representation of what's on the tape?"

"Yes it is."

"Do you have an independent recollection of everything that was on that tape?"

"No I do not."

"And did you indicate to Mr. Consiglio that this conversation was being taped?"

"That's correct."

"Now, at that point in time did you mirandize Mr. Consiglio?"

"Yes, I did."

Harn, a seasoned investigator who had questioned hundreds of suspects during his career, like a veteran stage actor, knew his lines to perfection and quoted the Miranda Rights from memory. Afterward, McKechnie stood and asked judge Thompson if he could question the witness on Voir Dire. The purpose of a Voir Dire examination is to determine the competency of a person to be a witness, to see if that person is speaking the truth. In this case, McKechnie was not so much concerned with the competency of Harn but with the competency and potential admissibility of the transcript of the tape-recorded question and answering session between Sam, Harn and the district attorney.

"Mr. Harn, was there anything discussed during the time that the tape recording was on, dealing with this case, the case in which Carolyn is the victim?" McKechnie asked.

"Without reviewing the transcript, my best memory is no."

"There was absolutely nothing to do with this case contained in that transcript, is there?

"No."

McKechnie turned and addressed his next statement to judge Thompson, arguing that the transcript was not relevant and that it had no bearing on the case. Judge Thompson appeared to agree and asked the prosecutor, "What's your offer of proof as to relevance?"

Przytulski didn't hesitate. He was prepared to answer the question. "In this transcript, the defendant is mirandized not once but three or four times when we took breaks," Przytulski said. "We took two or three breaks. Each time the break was done, the defendant was re-mirandized. At all times, the defendant maintained he wanted to talk and that basically he was eager to talk. At the conclusion of the interview, the defendant was taken into custody pursuant to a revocation of bail status."

"The defendant at that point in time, indicated that he was asked questions which overlapped with Karen's case about how many people he had sex with since he'd been in California. He indicated two. One was Jamiss and the other one was this prostitute named Carol or Sue."

"Now, Sam told us it was Carol or Sue. And, he gave us (her) the phone number. In addition to that, Mr. Harn found in papers that were seized at the time when he was taken into custody, in a book that he had, the name Carol or Sue, and a phone number written in it. The phone number was (for) Carolyn, the victim in our case.

"So, the relevance of this transcript is an accurate reflection of the Miranda Warnings and the waiver to accurately portray those warnings and his waiver. He came in voluntarily. He was admonished. He waived, he understood, he answered the questions. That's all that Miranda requires."

McKechnie and Przytulski continued to argue the relevancy of the transcript and statements made by Sam relating to his sexual encounter with a prostitute named Carol or Sue, after the tape recorder was turned off.

McKechnie told judge Thompson, "Your honor, you can't use it to lull somebody into a false understanding. In this case, it was used as a weapon. It was used to lull. If that was the intent, maybe it was by accident. In any event, what the habit was and what they did in their over abundance of caution was to create an atmosphere and create a scene in which the defendant had an absolute right to rely on receiving that warning and understanding. And whatever he said was going to be used against him and when he continued to do that, then you stop, you're creating a different atmosphere. And if they choose to proceed in that manner, then they got to follow through all the way."

Judge Thompson had heard enough. Looking down at both attorneys from behind his bench, he said, "The issue is really one; what Miranda is intended for is to provide a defendant or a prospective defendant, someone who's subject to custodial interrogation, with an understanding of what their rights are. And, what the ramifications of them speaking with the police are. It's simplistic in that it is a timing issue."

"If Mr. Harn had gone through the numerous instances of mirandizing Mr. Consiglio and the interview continued on in the office as it did, then there was a break in the interview. Then, the defendant was arrested, taken into custody and five hours later or a day later Mr. Harn had gone to the county jail and brought the defendant into an interview room, I think we would all agree that his Miranda waiver of the day before would be inappropriate in that, quote, second, unquote, interview. I think we would all agree he would have to be re-mirandized. However, in the facts of our case, we have a continuous interview that took a substantial period of time. The defendant was arrested and as he was either being arrested or being escorted by Mr. Harn, when these statements took place. The question then becomes whether or not I can subjectively find that Mr. Consiglio, at the time he made those statements, was aware of his Miranda rights, had or was willing to waive them and agreed to talk with the prosecution. There's nothing to indicate that a sufficient amount of time had passed wherein the Miranda rights would not have been fresh in the defendant's mind as evidenced by his numerous statements to the court."

"I am not dealing with someone who is not intelligent here. And there's no doubt in my mind, based upon his willingness at the outset to discuss the matter with the prosecutor's office, that he was mirandized on several occasions at or near the time that he made this particular statement. He was well aware of his rights at the time. He made the statements to Mr. Harn and was not operating under any misconception that he was being lulled or something of that nature into the sense of false security or giving these statements. Or, that he continually thought at the time that he's making the statements to Mr. Harn that there's no way in the world these statements could ever be used against me because he either turned off the tape or when he turned it off he didn't mirandize me again. That, I'm unwilling to accept." Judge Thompson denied the motion to exclude the statement.

Shortly after 11:00 a.m. the jury was brought back into the courtroom. They had been forced to sit outside in the hallway while Sam resubmitted his Marsden Motion, and while McKechnie and Przytulski argued about the admissibility of evidence. The jurors would not know any of this as they took their seats in the jury box.

Judge Thompson apologized to the jurors for having to wait so long. He explained that the issues addressed outside their presence would help to move the case along more quickly than normal. Thompson then explained to the jurors what their responsibilities, as the judges of the facts would be in this case. It was the standard, canned presentation made by most judges and almost identical to the opening remarks made by judge Brown to the jurors in Sam's previous rape trial. When he finished instructing the jurors of their role in this case, Mike Przytulski, with Harn sitting directly behind him, stood and addressed the jury.

"The facts in this case are fairly simple. What happened in this case is somewhere in May or June of 1991, Carolyn was working as a prostitute up on El Cajon Boulevard. She was hitchhiking. She was picked up by the defendant in this case and given a ride. He told her he was a cop, a police officer. He gave her a ride, took her to where she wanted to go and there was some talk about sex, but nothing happened on that date. He did obtain her phone number and address from her. A few days later, as much as a week, week and a half later, the time frame will vary but it was later, he calls her up and he says, 'I'm a cop. You're a prostitute. I'm going to arrest you. I'm going to bust you.' He uses the term bust. I'm going to bust you. And, he wanted to meet with her. So, he came over to the house, picked her up. He says, 'you know, if you have sex with me you're not going to jail.' They drove to an area and she gave him oral sex. She referred to it as 'head' in the car. He always maintained he was a police officer and always maintained that 'if you don't, you're going to jail.' She asked to see a badge and his response was 'do you want to go to jail.'"

"Now, Carolyn has a memory problem. It's not a memory problem that's to be founded in credibility, but an injury. She was struck in the head and she will describe that to you, and suffered severe brain damage several years ago. She will testify and you'll judge her credibility, and you'll look at her credibility and you'll make an opinion based on it, but she'll describe that injury to you."

"She will also very candidly admit she is not good with times and she's not good with dates, but she's good with identifying Mr. Consiglio and saying 'he told me he was a cop. If I didn't do these things I was going to jail.'"

"Now, over the next few weeks, Mr. Consiglio contacted her once or twice a week and arranged to get this oral sex. On July 4th, 1991, he picked her up and he took her to his apartment up in Clairemont. He had regular sex with her and oral sex with her in that apartment. When she protested about the sodomy, he said basically 'I'll beat you up.' And she did submit. After it was over he took her home."

"You make a judgment and tell us if Carolyn is telling the truth and if the defendant did, in fact, force her to have sex with him, not in the force that you take, you know, by beating somebody, but (by saying) you're going to jail if you don't."

Logan McKechnie reserved his right to an opening statement, opting to wait until the prosecution had offered its case. Carolyn was the first witness called to the stand by the prosecution.

"Now, do you know the defendant in this case, Mr. Consiglio?" Przytulski asked.

"I don't think so," Carolyn responded. Przytulski was momentarily stunned by the answer. "Have you ever met him?" the district attorney asked.

"Yes."

"When did you meet him?"

"In May or June, 1991."

"Do you see him here in court?"

"I don't remember what he looks like," Carolyn said. Sam's appearance had changed dramatically since his arrest. The beard was gone and he had gained a considerable amount of weight.

"Did you ever identify somebody as Mr. Consiglio before."

"I don't know."

Przytulski, patiently guiding his witness asked, "Have you suffered an injury?"

"Yeah. I got my head caved in with a rusted crescent wrench. I have 62 percent of my brain robbed."

"When did that happen?"

"September 12, 1979."

"You indicated you knew Sam Consiglio, that you met him. What name did you know him by then?"

Carolyn testified that she met a man named "John" when she was working as a prostitute. This "John" didn't ask for sex on that first meeting but did ask for her phone number, which she readily provided.

"Now, when was the next time you heard from this fellow called John?"

"A few days later. He called me."

"What did he say when he called?"

"He said he was a cop and he was going to put me in jail if I didn't give him what he wanted."

"What happened next?"

"He came and picked me up and made me have oral sex with him."

"Do you use a different term when you use oral sex?"

"Yes. Giving head."

"What we need to do, is have you describe exactly what giving head is, okay. We have to do that" Przytulski told his witness, trying to be as tactful as he could under the circumstances.

In a gentle, nearly inaudible voice, Carol testified, "You put a man's penis in your mouth and suck on it."

Sam looked over at Carol, but she did not return his glance.

"You in fact did that; is that correct?" Przytulski asked.

"Yes."

"Why did you do that?"

"Because he said he was a cop and he was going to take me to jail if I didn't."

"Did you ask to see a badge?"

"Yes. He said, do you want to go to jail?"

"Did you believe that he was a cop?"

"Yes."

"Did he ever tell you he wasn't a cop?"

"No."

"But he told you in fact that he was a cop, didn't he?"

"Yes."

Carolyn continued her testimony telling the jury that Sam would telephone her once or twice a week saying that he was coming by to pick her up. When he did, she would go with him and he would make her "give him head."

When Przytulski asked her to recall the events of July 4th, 1991, Carolyn testified that Sam picked her up and drove her to an apartment in Clairemont. "He sodomized me and made me give him head," she said. "He said he was going to beat me up if I didn't. Then, he took some pictures of me naked."

"Did he talk about selling those pictures at all?" Przytulski asked."

"Yes. I think he said *Hustler*."

"When you talk about being sodomized, what do you mean?"

"He put his penis in my butt."

Carolyn explained how this hurt her and how she complained to Sam about the pain, but that he wouldn't stop. Afterwards, Sam immediately made her give him head again. Later that night, Sam drove her home.

"You never went to the police in this case, did you?" Przytulski asked.

"No."

"But Mr. Harn contacted you in reference to this John or Sam Consiglio; right?"

"Yes."

"And did you have any idea what Mr. Harn was contacting you about?"

"I was afraid I was going to be arrested, but he said that they had arrested him for doing this to other girls."

McKechnie shot up from behind his desk, "Your honor, I move for a mistrial."

"You better state your grounds," demanded judge Thompson.

"There is no way to unring the bell that has just been rung by the witness in the statement by Mr. Harn that Mr. Consiglio has been arrested for doing this to other girls. No admonishment, any framed admonishment is going to unring that statement. It would be impossible for me to present any evidence or to present any language to this court that is going to unring that. I'm prepared to start selecting another jury immediately, but this jury can't hear the rest of this trial."

Przytulski, still standing and feeling the weight of the unexpected response from his witness responded to McKechnie's motion for a mistrial arguing that he did not invite the witness's response.

Judge Thompson agreed that Przytulski did not intentionally invite that particular response from Carolyn. What he did want to know, is how he was supposed to address the fact that the jury had heard information to the effect that Sam had been arrested for doing the same thing to other girls.

Przytulski agreed, to a point, with McKechnie's argument. Trying to avoid a mistrial, Przytulski offered to put P. J. Harn on the stand. Harn could testify that he did not tell Carolyn that Sam had been arrested for doing the same thing to other girls and that Sam did not have any prior criminal history of "impersonating a police officer in order to obtain sex."

Judge Thompson agreed, confident this would remedy the potential harm that had been done. Harn took the witness stand and testified that he had never told Carolyn that Sam had been arrested for doing the same thing to other girls or that Sam had any prior criminal history of impersonating a police officer in order to obtain sex. McKechnie did not ask any questions on cross-examination.

Satisfied that this "unrung" the bell, judge Thompson denied the motion for mistrial. Carolyn was recalled to the witness stand and continued her testimony.

"Sam called me and said he was a member of the mob and I was going to die if I testified against him," she said.

"And do you recall, at one point in time when Mr. Harn first came to your house to talk to you, do you recall while he was there that this fellow John, this guy that was impersonating the police officer called you while P. J. was there?" Przytulski asked.

"Yes."

"And do you recall P.J. going to a second phone in the apartment so that he could listen?"

"No, I don't remember" Carolyn said.

"Okay. At some point, did Mr. Consiglio ask you not to talk to the police or the district attorney?"

"Yes."

"Did he tell you why?"

"He said he was going to have me murdered if I did, by the mob."

"Did he tell you he was a member of the Mafia?"

"Yes."

Carolyn explained that she had previously used the name of Sue while working as a prostitute. She had difficulty remembering how many times she had spoken to Harn or Przytulski over that past nine months. She did, however, remember Sam Consiglio as the man who identified himself as John, a police officer.

"Now, I want you, again, to take a look at the fellow here in the white shirt to my immediate right," Przytulski told the witness.

"Yes. That's him." Carolyn said.

"How do you know that?"

Carolyn, not hesitating, pointed her finger at Sam and in a low but audible voice, said, "He's gained a lot of weight and grew a mustache. His hair is longer, but that's him."

Przytulski had more questions. He was confident that the last answer given by Carolyn had stuck in the jury's mind.

McKechnie stood and wished Carolyn a good afternoon. He asked her how she was doing and she told him she was scared. He told her there was nothing to be afraid of.

Carolyn continued her testimony telling McKechnie and the jury that she met Sam while soliciting sex for money. She remembered Sam picking her up, but they did not engage in any sexual activity the first time they met. Before Sam left, he asked for and was given her telephone number.

"Why did you give him the telephone number?" McKechnie asked.

"Hoping to make some money."

"In other words, they would come to you and give you money for sex?"

"Yes."

"Did you have a rate that you charged?"

"Yes. Fifty bucks."

"And for fifty bucks, what was the person supposed to get?"

"Objection, relevance," shouted Przytulski.

Judge Thompson quickly overruled the objection and allowed Carolyn to answer the question.

"Head and sex," she said.

Carolyn testified that Sam, who she knew only as John, told her that he was a police officer. She was afraid he would have her arrested if she didn't have sex with him. Later, Carolyn testified that Sam called her from jail and told her he was a member of the mob that if she testified against him, he would have her murdered.

After Carolyn completed her testimony, P. J. Harn returned to the witness stand. Harn testified that he interviewed Sam for several hours on July 17th, 1991. (This was in connection with the alleged rape of Karen. However, this fact was not brought out during direct examination). As a result of this lengthy interview, Harn had become familiar with Sam's voice.

"During the interview of Mr. Consiglio on July 17th, 1991, did you ask him how many women he had sex with since he had been in California?" Przytulski asked.

Harn testified that Sam had told him that he had sex with two women; Jamiss and a prostitute named either Sue or Carol. Harn added that Sam had indicated to him that the last time he had sex was with this prostitute on July 4th at his apartment in Clairemont. Sam had remembered watching the fireworks, Harn told the court. Harn also testified that he had gone to Carolyn's apartment on July 26th to interview her. During the interview, the phone rang and Harn was told that it was "John."

"Did you listen to that conversation?" Przytulski asked.

"Yes," Harn answered.

"Did you hear a voice on the line that you recognized?"

"Yes. It was Sam Consiglio. I heard Carolyn ask Mr. Consiglio if he was really a cop. He said he wouldn't talk about it on the phone. Just wanted her to keep quiet. `You watch my back and I'll watch yours. I will see you in a couple of days.'"

McKechnie asked Harn very little during cross-examination. When he was through, Przytulski informed the court that the prosecution had no further witness. The State was resting its case on the testimony of Carolyn and Harn. McKechnie immediately made a motion to judge Thompson asking for a directed verdict of not guilty on the pending charges.

"People charged Mr. Consiglio with rape under the color of authority," McKechnie said. "To allow their case to go to the jury at this time, based on the evidence presented by the people is to allow the jury to totally speculate as to what occurred.

"The victim in this case, alleged victim, in this case, has testified that Mr. Consiglio identified himself as a police officer, a snitch, a member of the mob. The testimony even though she may have lost sixty-eight percent of her brain, is testimony that does not lend itself to a conviction.

"It's incredible testimony. It doesn't have dates, doesn't have times. Only thing she's specific about is he identified himself as a cop. She testified that she remembered the incident because he threatened to beat her up, but she couldn't remember any of the other instances.

"While I understand there are issues for jurors, there are times when the court has to exercise its discretion to take away something which calls for pure speculation. If I were to cross over the bar and argue for the people, I could say this is an issue the jury is going to have to understand. As for credibility, I can argue that she's got mental problems. She's got to take that into consideration. It still does not boil down to anything more than suspicion, and suspicion doesn't result in a conviction. It's not an issue for the jury. It's something that the court should exercise its judgment on and take it away from the jury."

Judge Thompson allowed McKechnie to conclude his argument. He then, quickly and without hesitation, denied the motion.

"Do you anticipate calling witnesses?" the court asked.

"I am going to rest," answered McKechnie. The jury was excused for the day at 3:35 p.m. The following morning, July 16, 1992, when the trial resumed, closing arguments were made to the jury. After being charged by judge Thompson as to their duties and responsibilities, and what charges they were to consider the jury retired to consider their verdict. That afternoon, Sam was found guilty on three charges of rape under Color of Authority for having posed as a police officer. The verdict by the jury allowed Thompson to impose the maximum sentence allowed by law; eight years in prison on each of the three counts. Sam was sentenced to twenty-four years of incarceration in the state prison. Sam considered that sentence to be more than just unfair for what he considered nothing more than engaging in what he termed "oral copulation by trickery." "I wanted to tell the judge, Your Honor, who among us hasn't used trickery at one time or another to get a blow job," Sam said after the trial. His humor was short lived, however, when judge Thompson imposed the sentence to run consecutive to the thirty years he had been sentenced to serve for raping Karen. Sam was taken back to his cell inside the San Diego County jail where he sat, facing a total of fifty four years of incarceration in the California State Prison. He was not having a good day.

Chapter 17

The Verdict Is Not Always The Last Word

As soon as Carolyn's trial ended, the San Diego County Sheriff's Department wasted no time making the necessary arrangements to have their most annoying and irritating prisoner placed into the state penal system. It had been almost ten months since Sam's arrest in July 1991 for raping Karen. During that time, everyone who worked at the jail had an opportunity to become familiar with Sam. He had been demanding; never failing to offer his opinions on a variety of subjects. He had demanded law books, ordered pizzas delivered to his cell and argued with jailers and sheriff's deputies when they wouldn't let him keep it. He argued with the staff, always complaining that he was having problems with other prisoners. He complained of illness, and sought special favors over and over as a result of his "pro per" status. With his special status, he continued to intimidate his victims and witnesses by calling them from the free phone provided him by the County of San Diego. Now, Sam was facing a total of 54 years in prison and no one at the San Diego County Jail seemed disappointed. "He's a big pain in the ass," one of the jailers remarked. "A regular jailhouse lawyer."

Sam was taken by bus, crowded with other prisoners, to the California Correctional Facility in Donavan, a temporary stopover, en-route to his new permanent home. Sam no longer enjoyed the same privileged status as he had inside the San Diego County Jail. "The service at this one star motel really sucked," Sam, said. "No cigarettes, coffee, soap, toothpaste, deodorant. They even run short of toilet paper occasionally."

A few days later, Sam arrived at his new home, the State Prison in Calipatria, California. It wasn't long, though, before Sam had his color television, stereo with headphones, an electric typewriter, and a supply of coffee, tobacco and stamps. "It just doesn't get any better than this," Sam said. "The only thing I don't have is pussy and I'm in the process of taking care of that. I just sent a letter off to the Warden requesting permission to utilize one of the local escort services for conjugal visits." What Sam didn't realize, was that while California did indeed allow inmates conjugal visits, there existed a requirement that the inmate be married. Sam was certain he could find a way to satisfy this prerequisite.

While Sam was exploring ways to overcome this obstacle to receiving conjugal visits, Jan Stiglitz, appointed by the court to represent Sam on his appeal, was busy preparing a Petition for Writ of Habeas Corpus, and an appeal on Sam's conviction of raping Karen.

On June 16, 1992, Stiglitz wrote to Carolyn Chapman, the attorney who had appeared briefly with Neal Gibbons when Sam appeared for sentencing in the Karen trial. Chapman had refused to represent Sam, telling the court that she had information that perjury had been committed in the case. In his letter, Stiglitz explained that he had an obligation as appellate counsel to investigate whether Sam had been denied effective assistance of counsel. Stiglitz asked Chapman if she had consulted with Sam prior to appearing in court and if she had agreed to represent him. He also asked about the information she provided the court indicating perjury had been committed and what steps she took to verify these accusations. Eight days later, according to Stiglitz, Chapman wrote back declining to answer his questions.

On October 2, 1992, Stiglitz received a sworn statement from a Dr. Michael N. Oxman, a physician and professor of medicine and pathology at the University of California, San Diego. Dr. Oxman had been the chief of the infectious diseases section of the Veterans Administration Medical Center in San Diego, and had published extensively on the subject of herpes or herpes simplex. In court, he would be considered an expert on the subject of herpes.

In his sworn statement, Dr. Oxman claimed that in his expert opinion, "visual examination, by itself, is not reliable in the diagnosis of this disease." Oxman claimed that there are two types of herpes simplex virus, HSV-1 and HSV-2. HSV-1 causes sores around the mouth and HSV-2 causes sores in the genital area. But because HSV-1 may also cause genital sores, it is impossible to determine the type of herpes simplex virus causing a given genital infection by visual examination. Dr. Oxman also claimed, "the frequency of recurrences, the harm, and the discomfort caused by the disease vary greatly from individual to individual." Dr. Oxman was prepared to argue that transmitting herpes did not necessarily constitute great bodily harm.

On October 8, 1992, Stiglitz filed a Writ of Habeas Corpus with the State of California's Office of Attorney General. In his introduction, Stiglitz wrote, "This case involves a rape that could not have happened when and where the complaining witness (Karen) said that it did. But trial counsel failed to effectively protect and defend his client. As a result, the jury found him guilty.

"The prosecution maintained that petitioner, (Sam Consiglio), raped Karen on the evening of July 2, 1991, at Wells Park in El Cajon. Karen's testimony indicated that the rape occurred some time around 8:00 p.m. There were no witnesses to the event and no evidence, other than the testimony of (the victim) which showed that any rape had occurred or that Consiglio was the rapist."

Sam admitted knowing Karen but testified that he was not with her that evening. Wava Howley had verified his defense. "She testified that she was on the telephone with Consiglio from approximately 8:00 to 9:00 p.m. that evening. Telephone records supported testimony about the call.

These records indicated both the times of the call and the fact that it was made from Consiglio's apartment in Clairemont, miles from the scene of the alleged crime. Telephone records were also introduced to show that Consiglio made other calls from Clairemont at 7:13, 7:40 and 9:12 p.m."

"Despite the weak case and the strong defense evidence, petitioner was convicted and sentenced to thirty years in jail. This was the product of a failure by counsel to conform to minimum professional norms. The ways in which counsel failed to be an effective and conscientious advocate are fully detailed and supported in the Points and Authorities, which follow. They include the failure to object to damaging testimony about petitioner; the failure to investigate and present any defense to a very questionable great bodily injury enhancement allegation; allowing the jury to learn (through sheer inadvertence) about petitioner's criminal history. It also includes the failure to present and buttress significant alibi testimony, and the violation of fundamental standards of ethical conduct by voluntarily disclosing damaging (and inaccurate) information to the trial court and the prosecution."

Using many of the same arguments in the original Writ, Stiglitz filed a Brief with the California Court of Appeals.

In a California criminal case (People v. Pope) decided in 1979, the Supreme Court of that State held that criminal defendants, at the time of trial, have a right to adequate and effective assistance of counsel. The ruling is based on the Sixth Amendment of the United States, which guarantees every citizen a right to a speedy, public, and fair trial. In order to demonstrate that Sam was denied "reasonably competent assistance," Stiglitz had to demonstrate first, that Neal Gibbons' defense of Sam at trial fell below an objective standard of reasonableness under prevailing professional norms. And two, that if he had, it is "reasonably probable" that the result of the trial would have been different. It is with this foundation, and judicial requirements, that Jan Stiglitz began his written argument as he attempted to have Sam's conviction of raping Karen overturned.

Stiglitz's first argument attacked Gibbons for failing to object to the admission of the "highly emotional and graphic letter" written by Karen and read by the prosecution's first witness, Jackie Thomas. Thomas had testified that two or three days after the alleged rape, she suggested to Karen that she write about the incident to release it from her system.

"Trial counsel could have and should have objected to it on two bases," Stiglitz wrote. "First, it was hearsay and did not fall within any of the exceptions to the rule against hearsay. Second, because the description was particularly powerful in its emotional content, any possible probative value was outweighed by its prejudicial effect."

Stiglitz maintained that Neal Gibbons should have objected before the letter was read, not after. Stiglitz compared it to someone trying to close the barn door after the horse had escaped.

The California Supreme Court has held that when evaluating the performance of an attorney during trial, tactical errors made by counsel are not deemed reversible because the decisions of counsel in the "midst of trial" cannot be second-guessed by the hindsight of an appellant court. Lilia E. Garcia, a deputy attorney general in San Diego, arguing for the People of the State of California, responded to Stiglitz's first allegation, claiming that even if Neal Gibbons should have objected, his failure to do so did not demonstrate prejudice. "The letter never identified appellant (Consiglio) as the rapist," Garcia wrote. "The letter merely expressed the victim's feelings of helplessness as she was being raped. Second, the victim at trial later testified to Karen's fear and helplessness expressed in the letter. Thus, the letter in that sense was cumulative, but harmless, since it merely reiterated the victim's feelings about the rape."

Next, Stiglitz attacked Gibbons' failure to cross-examine Karen regarding discrepancies in background information that she (Karen) provided to the prosecution. During the trial, Przytulski informed the court that there were some aspects of the victim's background that did not check out. Stiglitz asserted that defense counsel did not explore this issue on cross-examination. Since the case was primarily one of a credibility contest between Karen and Sam, that absent some strategic purpose, the failure to use any inconsistencies to impeach her amounted to ineffective assistance of counsel.

Garcia argued that on the second day of trial, Przytulski informed the court that the D.A.'s office needed additional time to further investigate the case but were unable to do so because Sam demanded that the trial begin immediately. Supporting her argument, Garcia cited Gibbon's comments to the court during the trial when he said:

"On numerous occasions I advised him (Consiglio) that a continuance would be in order so that I could fully prepare his case. At all times, Mr. Consiglio insisted that I not continue the case and that I proceed as rapidly as possible. Mr. Consiglio advised me of his alibi defense and at all times, demanded the case be tried immediately."

Next, Stiglitz disputed Gibbons' failure to object to testimony by a psychologist, which suggested that a rape had in fact occurred. In two criminal cases decided in 1984, People v. Bledso and People v. Stanley, the California Supreme Court condemned the use of "rape trauma syndrome" testimony because it went beyond the realm of legitimate scientific expert testimony and invaded the province of the jury as the trier of fact.

Stiglitz centered his argument around Belkis Bottfeld's testimony at trial when she testified that she did not have "any doubt" something had occurred after meeting with Karen the following morning after being told that Karen had been raped. "Bottfeld was not specifically qualified as an expert," Stiglitz wrote. "Her initial information about the alleged rape came from a co-worker. Yet, trial counsel failed to object to a series of questions which allowed the witness to testify that, in her opinion, the rape had in fact occurred and that Karen was telling the truth."

Garcia attacked Stiglitz's argument claiming that Przytulski had never asked Bottfeld whether she believed Karen had been raped. "The transcript reveals Bottfeld merely testified about her observations of Karen's condition. Since Bottfeld only related her observations, there is simply no reason to view her testimony as an expert opinion on the issue of whether Karen had been raped."

Next, Stiglitz attacked Gibbons for failing to investigate and defend against the claim that Sam had transmitted herpes to Karen during the alleged rape. Herpes simplex II or genital herpes is incurable. At sentencing, the court added six years to Sam's sentence for infecting Karen with the disease under the theory that the transmission of herpes constituted great bodily injury under the California Penal Code, allowing for the enhancement of the sentence. Neither the prosecution nor the defense, presented much evidence regarding the transmission of herpes. Instead, Gibbons stipulated that Karen had herpes and that Sam had tested positive for the virus. Gibbons also stipulated that, "the transmission of herpes during a rape constituted great bodily injury." Stiglitz claimed that Gibbons failed to adequately investigate the nature of the disease and its transmission. Had he done so, Gibbons could have presented a viable defense to the charge of inflicting great bodily injury.

According to Stiglitz, "in order for the prosecution to successfully prove the enhancement allegation, it first had to show that Karen had herpes. It then had to prove that she first contacted the disease after intercourse with petitioner (Consiglio). Finally, the prosecution had to convince the jury that the disease constituted the infliction of great bodily injury. The record fails to disclose whether any laboratory test was used. Karen's testimony suggests that the diagnosis was merely made by visual observation and that no clinical test was ever performed."

If Sam did in fact rape or have sexual intercourse with Karen, some proof would normally be required that Sam transmitted the virus to allow the court to enhance the sentence based on the theory that he inflicted great bodily injury and not that Karen was simply experiencing a recurrence of a previous infection.

According to Garcia, Stiglitz's argument was flawed. First, prior to stipulating to the great bodily injury claims, Gibbons and Sam consulted the same medical expert that the prosecution had. This, Garcia alleged, "undermines petitioners claim that counsel failed to conduct an investigation regarding the transmission of herpes before entering into the stipulations."

At trial, Karen had testified that 10 to 12 days after the trial, she experienced an outbreak of blisters in her genital area. After a medical examination, she was diagnosed as having herpes. In her testimony, she claimed that she had never had such an outbreak and that she had not had sex with anyone between the time she was raped and the time she was examined for herpes.

But the stipulation stated only that Sam had the herpes virus. Medical testing could not establish that it had been Sam that inflicted Karen with Herpes; it could only demonstrate that Sam could not be "excluded as a possible donor." The jury would have to make its own decision on this issue whether or not the stipulation had been entered into.

Stiglitz next addressed the issue of Gibbons' failure to adequately prepare the defendant's key witness, Wava Howley, for her testimony. As a result of that lack of preparation, Sam's prior criminal history was revealed to the jury. Except in certain situations, evidence of a defendant's prior criminal conduct is inadmissible character evidence.

Wava Howley testified that she had met Sam through the prison ministry and that she had visited Sam while he was in prison in Michigan. Gibbons did not object to Howley's testimony. Once this information was leaked to the jury, the court agreed to play the taped interview Sam made on July 17, 1991, with Harn and Przytulski.

Garcia rebutted this argument claiming that Howley's testimony did not open up Sam's entire criminal history. She alleged that the disclosure was harmless since Sam eventually took the stand and testified that he had a prior conviction and that he served a prison term in Michigan. Garcia argued that even if Sam had not disclosed information about his prior criminal record during direct examination, the jury would have nonetheless learned of it when Przytulski sought to impeach Sam's credibility during cross-examination.

Stiglitz continued to focus his argument for appeal on the testimony of Wava Howley, Sam's key defense alibi witness. Howley testified that she had been on the telephone with Sam for almost an hour during the time Karen claimed she had been raped. Telephone records showing that such a one-hour call had indeed been made supported Howley's testimony. But Przytulski, during his cross-examination asked Howley if her answering machine would stay on until the caller terminated the call. She answered that it would. This, Przytulski theorized during his summation to the jury, would provide Sam with an alibi while he went to El Cajon with Karen.

But Gibbons never asked Howley if she ever found such a long blank message. "After the trial, (Sam) was able to quickly find out that tapes on some answering machines are limited to thirty minutes. Similar research (by Gibbons) could well have established what kind of machine Wava Howley had and the limits of its capacity to record and keep a telephone line open. This was not done," Stiglitz argued.

Garcia responded to Stiglitz's claim that Gibbons should have asked Howley about a blank tape. This being the case, Howley's answer would have been "no."

One of the most critical issues in this case, according to Stiglitz, related to the time the rape allegedly occurred. Sam's defense rested on the argument that he (Sam) was in his apartment in Clairemont, between 7:00 and 9:15 p.m., talking on the telephone. Karen testified that it was during this time that Sam raped her in Wells Park. Karen also testified that she specifically remembered that the lights in the parking lot of Wells Park were on at the time. "To show that Sam was not at the park at that time, Gibbons needed to establish when the lights went on. But he failed to do this," Stiglitz claimed.

But Gibbons did question Ted Schroeder, the director of recreation for the City of El Cajon, about the time the lights were turned on. Schroeder testified that the lights were on a timing device but that he did not know when or even if the lights had been turned on at the park that night.

Garcia argued that simply because there was no witness available to establish or testify as to the time the lights were on or even turned on that night, does not render counsel as being incompetent or ineffective.

Stiglitz next attacked Gibbons' competency for failing to protect Sam by not objecting to "numerous improper questions" solicited by Przytulski during cross-examination; questions designed to destroy Sam's credibility. It is here, that Stiglitz offers his severest indictment of Gibbons' conduct during the trial. "Trial counsel (Gibbons) failed to object to a lengthy series of questions about whether and why petitioner (Sam) told Carolyn not to speak with the police. (At the time of the trial, Consiglio was facing seven felony sex offenses relating to crimes he allegedly committed on Carolyn.) Although petitioner's decision to take the stand waived his Fifth Amendment right against self-incrimination with regard to relevant cross-examination, it was not a waiver of any objection to improper cross-examination.

"Much of this cross-examination was an attempt to introduce improper character evidence. It would have been a simple matter for trial counsel to have made a limited motion to preclude this area of inquiry, so that petitioner would not face the choice of either answering or having to invoke his Fifth Amendment right in front of the jury.

"The trial court noticed that defense counsel (Gibbons) was not objecting and, after a lunch break, discussed this with counsel. The trial court delicately characterized counsel's failure to object as a willingness on the part of the defense to be totally open and forthright and frank. At this point, trial counsel seemed to indicate that his strategy had changed because Wava Howley had spilled the beans. After the trial court was assured that counsel's failure to object was allegedly based on strategy, the examination continued."

Stiglitz argued that he could see no explanation for the strategy used by Gibbons for failing to object to Przytulski's so-called badgering of Sam about his relationship with Carolyn especially since Sam's relationship with her had no direct bearing on the case involving Karen. Yet the prosecution kept "hammering away" at Sam, and Gibbons did not object.

Here too, is where Garcia offers her strongest rebuttal arguing that, Gibbon's decision to restrain his objections during Przytulski's cross-examination was based on Sam's express consent, and pursuant to his strategy, to "open the case up" to the jury. She said that out of the presence of the jury, judge Frank Brown provided Gibbons and Sam an opportunity to explain, on the record, why Sam elected to testify and open himself up to cross-examination. Gibbons told judge Brown that contrary to his advice, Sam had decided to testify. "He wants to tell his story," Gibbons told the court.

Garcia said that Gibbons' minimal objections during Sam's cross-examination by Przytulski was a tactical decision and consistent with the defense's strategy to be open with the jury in order to gain their confidence.

When Stiglitz focused his attack on Mike Przytulski for what was perceived as "his improper personal character on attacks" on Sam and, Gibbons' failure to object to these attacks, he cited case law, which holds that a prosecutor commits misconduct during the trial when he makes derogatory personal comments about the character of the accused. Although hinting but not actually accusing Przytulski of prosecutorial misconduct, Stiglitz cited Przytulski's closing remarks to the jury when the district attorney called Sam a, "liar who manipulated people around him to lie on his behalf." Gibbons' failure to object, stressed Stiglitz, constituted nothing less than ineffective assistance of counsel.

"It is hard to imagine any strategic reason for counsel giving the prosecutor free reign to wage an improper attack on Sam's character and credibility. Since Sam's credibility was matched against Karen's, a reasonably competent attorney, acting as a conscientious advocate, would have objected," Stiglitz claimed.

Garcia claimed that since Przytulski's remarks were appropriate, and based on well-supported evidence, there was no basis for Gibbons to object. Each of Przytulski's remarks, Garcia wrote, was supported by testimony provided during the trial. Garcia also cited several examples, including the instance when Sam, still in the San Diego jail, telephoned Carolyn and warned her not to tell the police that she was a prostitute and that he was a client.

According to California case law, (People v. Sassounian; 1986) a prosecutor is given wide latitude during closing arguments. The argument may be vigorous as long as it is fair and based on the evidence presented at the time of trial.

In her response to this argument, Garcia wrote, "The prosecutor's comments, including the portrayal of petitioner (Sam) as a liar, was well supported by the record." The California courts have held, (People v. Mora, 1956) that, "when a witness tells one story when arrested and another story at trial, one of the stories is untrue, i.e. a lie. And the person who tells such conflicting stories can properly be characterized as a liar."

Stiglitz also said that Sam was denied effective assistance of counsel when Carolyn Chapman and Neal Gibbons made representations that Wava Howley had committed perjury. On December 6, 1991, the day Sam was scheduled to be sentenced, Gibbons made a motion to withdraw as Sam's attorney. Gibbons told the court that Carolyn was going to substitute for him. It was then, that Carolyn made the statement in open court about having learned that perjured testimony had been given during the trial. An accusation, that Stiglitz, on behalf of Sam, claimed was untrue.

Stiglitz argued that while Chapman had no duty to represent Sam, by virtue of her appearing in court because Sam had consulted her, imposed a duty on her not to betray him. Sam, Stiglitz insisted, had, "every right to expect that when he consulted Ms. Chapman, that his statements to her would be within the attorney-client privilege. Gibbons made it quite clear that he did not even attempt to get the full story from Ms. Howley. Without that, he could not have had an intelligent discussion about it with Sam. Moreover, there is no indication that he ever discussed it with Sam. Similarly, Chapman's statements indicate that she only discussed it with Gibbons, who she had just met, and the district attorney. Thus, there did not appear to have been any effort on the part of either attorney to discuss the matter with Sam."

California law states that a defendant is entitled to effective assistance of counsel at every stage of a criminal prosecution, including sentencing. By virtue of Gibbons and Chapman's disclosure, they essentially told the court that was about to sentence Sam, that he was indeed a liar. Stiglitz took the position that Gibbons and Chapman's conduct was outrageous and that Chapman's, "gratuitous disclosure was reprehensible." Such action, Stiglitz believed could only result in prejudice at the time of sentencing.

In Garcia's response, she wrote, "Petitioner's sole contention was that contrary to counsel's representations, Howley had called counsel during and not after the trial. There is no demonstration that counsel's (Gibbons') disclosure improperly influenced the trial court's sentencing of petitioner."

Stiglitz claimed that errors made by Gibbons prejudiced the jury and prevented Sam from obtaining a fair sentencing hearing. Stiglitz began his argument by reminding the court that there were no witnesses to the crime itself, and almost no circumstantial evidence to support Karen's claim that a rape had occurred. The prosecution's case, rested on the issue of credibility; Karen's versus Sam's. Stiglitz seized every opportunity to attack Gibbons' failure to take significant opportunities to undermine Karen's credibility, such as presenting evidence as to the time the lights in the parking lot of Wells Park came on, and failing to investigate and call expert witnesses on the herpes issue.

"Even if Karen had herpes, the jury could not have found that Sam inflicted great bodily injury unless she got the disease from him. An expert was available to testify that many people with the disease wrongly identify recurrences as an initial outbreak. This, alone, would have raised reasonable doubt as to whether Sam transmitted the disease to Karen. Gibbons' actions here amounted to the withdrawal of a meritorious defense."

Garcia disagreed. Her response to Stiglitz's most recent argument was short and direct. "Petitioner (Sam) ignores that his credibility was completely impeached as a result of the numerous inconsistent statements he gave before and during trial. In contrast, the victim's credibility was solid and her account of the events leading up to and during the rape was credible. The jury had an opportunity to judge both (Sam's) and the victim's credibility. It chose to believe the victim and reject his alibi."

Stiglitz argued that early in the trial, Sam made a Marsden Motion to have Gibbons removed as his attorney, a motion that was denied. "Sam had nothing to do with Gibbons' failure to object to Karen's letter describing the rape, or Gibbons failure to cross-examine Karen regarding questions about her background, or his failure to prepare Wava Howley for her testimony, or to object to the prosecutor's improper character attacks during closing arguments." Stiglitz cited a 1989 California case, People v. Hamilton, as his source to support his argument.

"When the accused exercises his constitutional right to representation by professional counsel, it is counsel, not the defendant, who is in charge of the case. By choosing professional representation, the accused surrenders all but a handful of fundamental personal rights to counsel's complete control of defense strategies and tactics."

Garcia was quick to attack Stiglitz on this issue, as she had on each of the previous ones. "The record shows that petitioner participated in the trial strategy and attempted throughout the trial to control the proceedings. It is clear, from the evidence, that throughout the trial, petitioner was confident his alibi witness and the telephone records would exonerate him. It is this over confidence that was the basis for petitioner's strategy to open up the case to the jury, as he felt that jury would acquit him. Moreover, at no time did petitioner complain about his attorney or ask the court to substitute his counsel because he was not satisfied with his representation. At the Marsden hearing (Sam) did in fact tell the court he had no complaints regarding counsel and the only reason he made a Marsden Motion was to be allowed to cross-examine the victim."

Federal Constitutional Law requires that the accused, in a criminal trial, have a right to examine all evidence that is favorable to his/her defense. This is commonly referred to as discovery. This rule, while in existence for years, did not become famous until 1957 in the landmark

Supreme Court case, Jencks v. United States. Jencks was a labor union official who, had been convicted of allegedly filing a false affidavit claiming that he had never been a member of the Communist party. During the two-week trial, witnesses working with the FBI testified that they observed Jencks engaging in Communist party activities. The witnesses claimed they made reports about Jencks' activities to the FBI. Jencks, through his attorney, filed a motion to have those reports produced for their examination. But the trial judge denied the request, claiming there were no inconsistencies between the reports made to the FBI and the testimony of the witnesses. The U.S. Supreme Court overturned Jencks' conviction. The court ruled that Jencks had been denied due process because the government failed to produce the reports requested. The Supreme Court's decision in the Jencks case requires that a defendant in a criminal trial is entitled to inspect all reports in the hands of the government which touch on matters about which witnesses might testify. While there was no testimony given during the trial of Karen, the prosecution did allegedly have in its possession information that Carolyn had herpes. That information was allegedly not given to Gibbons as discovery. Here, Stiglitz argues that Sam was denied due process because of the states' failure to provide this information during discovery.

"If Carolyn had genital herpes and (Sam) had sex with her, she could have given the disease to him after any contact with Karen. Thus, information that Carolyn had herpes was relevant exculpatory evidence that should have been provided to the defense."

Garcia argued that Stiglitz's declaration rebutted Sam's claim that he had no knowledge about Carolyn. She also claimed that this information was made available during trial and that the prosecution had indeed complied with all discovery. "Petitioner (Sam), who was acting pro per in the Carolyn case, was given full discovery and was personally aware of the prosecution's evidence that Carolyn had herpes. At the preliminary hearing, Carolyn testified that she had herpes and that she informed (Sam) of this prior to having oral and anal sex. Since the preliminary hearing occurred on September 5, 1991, a month prior to his trial, (Sam) can hardly claim ignorance. Moreover, whether or not he (Sam) had sex with Carolyn after the rape was of little significance because he could have contracted herpes from another woman prior to the rape."

Stiglitz next argued that the court erred in sentencing Sam to three, full term, consecutive sentences for three rapes. Under California Law, the standard for evaluating the applicability of the law as it relates to rape, is articulated in the case of People v. Corona in 1988;

"Whether, between the commission of one sex crime and another, the defendant had a reasonable opportunity to reflect upon his or her actions and nevertheless resumed sexually assaultive behavior."

According to Stiglitz's argument on this issue, "Karen's testimony shows there was a break in time between the three rapes. Karen's description of the events indicates three insertions but does not indicate any break in time or reasonable opportunity to reflect. Since the record fails to show any reasonable opportunity for reflection, the trial court erred in imposing consecutive sentences under the (California) Penal Code." Stiglitz's argument was not that Sam hadn't committed the rape, but if he had, the rape was one continuous action, not three as determined by the court.

But Garcia argued that the court's sentence was proper under existing California law since, "the rapes were three separate and distinct sexual acts, not one continuous action." California law uses as its test for determining whether the crimes are separate, language stated in the 1988 case of People v. Corona. In the Corona case, the defendant, after raping a victim in an automobile, left the car for one or two minutes and then returned raping the victim a second time. In deciding the case on appeal, the California Appellate Court held that, "the state court had properly found that the defendant committed two rapes of the victim on separate occasions."

Supporting her argument, Garcia cited a 1989 California case, People v. Harrison. In that case, the California Court of Appeals held that, "a defendant who committed three rapid, identical sex acts of digital penetration of the victim's vagina, each lasting only a few seconds and the entire incident lasted only a few minutes" had been convicted of three counts of rape. On appeal, the Supreme Court upheld the three separate convictions and sentences for penetration of the victim's genital area.

Finally, Stiglitz argued that the court failed to state its reasons for sentencing Sam to consecutive full-term sentences. The trial court, Stiglitz maintained, concluded that Sam was a menace to all women and decided to lock him up for as long as possible. Stiglitz not only appealed this issue, but demanded that this matter must be remanded to a new judge if Sam were to be re-sentenced. He based this on the trial court's prejudice; a result of Sam's alleged lies and Gibbons and Chapman's improper disclosure.

Garcia countered stating that the trial court did indeed address the question of whether to impose consecutive sentences. "The court gave three separate reasons for choosing consecutive sentences: the victim's particular vulnerability; the existence of planning, sophistication, and showing premeditation; and (Sam's) criminal history which demonstrated he was a danger to society."

Stiglitz, Garcia, and Sam would now wait for the case to be reviewed by a panel of judges. Stiglitz would continue to teach while Garcia continued her work in the Attorney General's Office. Sam waited, not always patiently, inside the Calipatria State Prison. He was satisfied with the work done on his behalf by professor Stiglitz. He had little grounds to complain since the taxpayers of the State of California were paying for Stiglitz's services. But Sam couldn't relax; he had another brief to prepare, or at least assist in preparing dealing with his conviction of raping Carolyn.

Chapter 18

Help Me Joan, Please Help Me

On September 30, 1992, Sam, while sitting in his cell inside the Calipatria State Prison, wrote a 19 page, single spaced typewritten letter to Joan Isserlis, an attorney in San Francisco, California. In his letter, Sam described his anger and how he had tried so hard to turn his life around, wanting to lead a better life. But all of this was impossible now that he had been wrongly convicted of two rapes; crimes he swore he did not commit.

In his letter, Sam acknowledged that he had "no business messing around with an unattractive hooker and manipulating her into free sex." But Sam contended that in his heart he was truly a good person who was just a little lonely in a new city. Sam explained that he had found a way to compensate for that loneliness by taking advantage of someone who was easy to manipulate. These actions, Sam told her, "Were not something one would expect from someone who professes to be a Christian."

Sam took great care in presenting Joan Isserlis with his version of the "true details" surrounding his relationship with Karen and Carolyn. Never once did Sam hint that he had raped either one of these women. Describing his alleged dinner engagement with Karen, Sam wrote: "I asked Karen to have a spaghetti dinner with me and she agreed. I was planning to break the news to her gently (that we did not get the job). I learned that food always puts people in better moods. That night, I was calling all my friends and family bragging about my new job. I kept trying to get a hold of Karen to find out why she never showed for dinner as she had promised. After leaving her several messages, she finally called me after 10:00 p.m. I asked why she didn't show up and she said she had to go to her aunt's house in Lemon Grove, a city next to El Cajon."

Sam attacked everything and everybody in his letter to Isserlis. He attacked Neal Gibbons, Mike Przytulski, and P. J. Harn. He attacked the judge for trying him in prison clothes. He attacked Logan McKechnie, who Sam claimed did absolutely nothing to prepare for trial. Sam described how he considered ending his life the night he was convicted of raping Carolyn, but reconsidered while sitting in his private cell on his bed, watching Country Music videos. "I watched Reba McEntire sing *"For My Broken Heart"* and related to that song, thinking that if I could just hold out a little longer, the sun would start shining for me again."

Sam, as he had so often done in his life when trying to persuade someone to help him, brought religion into the picture, telling Isserlis that he kept trying to figure out exactly what God's purpose was for allowing all this to happen to him. Sam pleaded for Joan to help him. "I am scared," Sam told her.

Joan Isserlis did agree to help Sam. With Sam's letter and copies of the trial transcripts, she began to prepare a brief to the California Court of Appeals, in an attempt to get Sam's conviction of raping Carolyn overturned.

Isserlis' first argument focused on what she contended was a violation of Sam's Fifth Amendment guarantees against self-incrimination. The Fifth Amendment to the U.S. Constitution provides that, "no person shall be compelled in any criminal case to be a witness against himself." According to Isserlis, Sam, while free on bail on charges related to Karen, received an invitation from Harn to come to the district attorney's office to discuss the case. Sam volunteered to discuss the allegations and freely went to the district attorney's office for that purpose. Prior to the interview, P. J. Harn placed a tape recorder on the table where Sam could easily see it. The conversation with Sam would be tape recorded and transcribed. Harn then advised Sam of his Miranda rights.

Miranda rights or warnings, were made famous from the landmark court case, Miranda v. Arizona decided by the U.S. Supreme Court in 1966. It is seen as one of the most significant decisions impacting on law enforcement in the past 50 years. Miranda generally provides that if at the time police interrogate someone, the person is not considered by the police to be a suspect, then the police are then only in the investigating stage. They do not have to advise the person of their constitutional rights. During this stage, any incriminating statements made by such a person can be used against them. If however, the police consider that person to be a suspect, and there is what is considered "custodial interrogation" that is, the person's freedom of movement is curtailed, or that person is in custody or has otherwise been deprived of his freedom of movement in any way, then the accusatory stage has been reached. Then, that person must be advised of their right to remain silent. If they give up that right, anything they say can be used against them in court, and that they have a right to counsel. In short, the Supreme Court's ruling dealt with the rights of an accused person having the assistance of counsel during a custodial interrogation. It was an abuse of Sam's Miranda rights that Joan Isserlis began her brief to the California Court of Appeals.

Isserlis wrote that during his interview of Sam, Harn took four or five breaks. During each break, Harn turned off the recorder. He read him his rights again and re-mirandized Sam when the recorder was turned back on after the break, and prior to Harn asking him any additional questions. On each occasion, Sam was eager to continue the questioning and claimed that he understood his rights. After the questioning concluded, Harn, based on a warrant obtained from judge Larry Stirling, arrested Sam. This warrant resulted in Sam's bond being raised to $1 million. While putting Sam in jail, Harn asked Sam how many people he had slept with during his time in California. It is during that time, that Sam told Harn about the prostitute, "Sue" that thought he was a cop.

Isserlis argued that Sam was in custody when he told Harn and Przytulski about his sexual relations with Carolyn. Isserlis also argued that by virtue of the fact that Sam was being arrested, Harn's asking Sam the question, "how many people had he slept with…" continued the interrogation. Sam's statements concerning Carolyn, Isserlis argued, "were indisputably the result of a custodial interrogation by law enforcement officers. The only question this case presents is whether appellant (Sam) understood the rights he had at the time he spoke of Carolyn and, with such understanding, validly waived those rights."

Isserlis went on to argue that the conduct taken by Przytulski and Harn "strongly suggests" that Sam no longer had the same rights he had prior to his arrest. These rights included the right to walk away from the interrogation, the right to answer questions, and the right to call or have an attorney furnished to him, free of charge.

Next, Isserlis argued that the evidence obtained from Sam as a result of his being questioned about Carolyn, after being arrested, should have been barred under the theory that it was, "the fruit of the forbidden tree."

The Miranda decision also reemphasized that not only will any statements made by the accused be excluded when their rights have been violated, but so will any evidence obtained as a result of such statements. The Supreme Court has held that if a confession is improperly obtained or poisonous, then any evidence discovered from that confession is considered "fruits of the poisonous tree" and will subsequently be excluded. If the confession is inadmissible, so is the evidence obtained from that confession.

Isserlis argued that there was no evidence presented during the trial indicating that Sam had not been forced to speak to Harn. Claiming that Carolyn, a prostitute who, by her own admission, was afraid to talk to the police, in all probability, never would have revealed her relationship with Sam.

Sara Gros-Cloren, a deputy attorney general of the State of California, responded to Isserlis' claim that Sam's Miranda rights had been violated. Gros-Cloren concurred with judge Thompson's ruling during the trial when he rejected the argument that Sam had been lulled into thinking his statements could not be used against him because he had not been re-informed of his rights after the recorder was turned off and he was placed under arrest. Judge Thompson ruled that Sam's statements to Harn had been voluntary. The fact that Sam was no longer free to leave, Gros-Cloren wrote, did not demonstrate that Sam could not invoke his Miranda rights.

Isserlis next argued that the court erred when Logan McKechnie's motion for a mistrial was wrongly denied after the jury heard testimony from Carolyn that Sam had committed identical crimes; that is, impersonating a police officer for the purpose of obtaining sex. Instead, the court sought to remedy the harm done by Carolyn's testimony.

Gros-Cloren countered Isserlis' argument claiming that judge Thompson had properly exercised his discretion by denying the motion for a mistrial, "Because there was no incurable prejudice resulting from Carolyn's statement." Gros-Cloren disagreed with the argument that the remedy allowed by the court was too narrow. "Harn's testimony and the stipulation (that Sam had not committed similar offenses) contradicted Carolyn's testimony. Since Carolyn (was) a very credible witness, despite her mental impairment, the prosecutor correctly noted that contradicting Carolyn might not only neutralize her statement but also actually benefit (Sam) by showing her testimony was not true. Thus, the remedy not only cured any potential prejudice, but additionally afforded appellant a net benefit."

Isserlis next argued that Sam was denied effective assistance of counsel and that the court erred when it denied Sam's Marsden Motion. Her argument was based on Sam's informing the court that he was dissatisfied with Logan McKechnie's representation and that he wanted a different attorney. Once Sam notified the court that he filed a complaint against McKechnie with the California Bar Association, the court was obligated to grant his Marsden Motion. Although the state bar had not initiated an investigation of McKechnie, McKechnie acquired, "an inordinate interest in conducting the defense in a manner calculated to minimize any opportunity for post hoc criticism of his efforts. This is particularly true in light of the fact that Mr. McKechnie had, in the last 18 months, expended

$30,000 fighting what he deemed to be spurious claims by clients. His personal and pecuniary interest in being extremely cautious conflicted with appellant's interest in receiving zealous representation."

Isserlis cited one example of McKechnie's cautiousness, which she argued was a crucial error on the part of the defense, as being McKechnie's failure to impeach Carolyn with her former testimony when she admitted that on the 4th of July, she did not believe Sam was a cop. During the trial, Carolyn testified that she thought Sam was a cop, but that later, as she continued to meet with him, she became suspicious of his true identity. Isserlis contended that had McKechnie impeached Carolyn's testimony on this issue, he would have accomplished two things. First, he would have impeached Carolyn's credibility, which would have helped Sam in his effort to combat all the charges against him, and second, McKechnie would have supplied evidence that on the 4th of July, Carolyn did not believe Sam was a police officer. These issues, together, Isserlis argued would have raised a reasonable doubt in the jury's mind to acquit him on all charges.

The decision to grant or deny a Marsden Motion is normally the responsibility of the trial court. In this case, whether or not to grant Sam's motion rested within the discretion of judge Thompson. Gros-Cloren, maintained that McKechnie's comments to the court after Sam's first Marsden hearing that Sam's filing of the complaint had an effect on him, is not well placed. "Such comments do not rise to the level showing an actual conflict of interest. Under these circumstances, (Sam's) Marsden Motions appear to be nothing more than a delaying technique to avoid facing trial and judgment."

Gros-Cloren attacked Isserlis' argument that Sam had been denied effective assistance of counsel because McKechnie had failed to finish impeaching Carolyn with her preliminary hearing testimony. "The failure to complete the impeachment does not rise to the level of deficient performance." Carolyn, Gros-Cloren reminded the Appeals Court, "suffered from serious memory problems and was not even able to remember appearing at the preliminary hearing." Gros-Cloren also disagreed with Isserlis' claim that McKechnie had not tried to impeach Carolyn. "At one point, McKechnie asked Carolyn if she remembered testifying at the preliminary hearing that she did not think (Sam) was a police officer but instead thought he was a snitch. Carolyn responded 'I believed he would snitch me off.' McKechnie pursued this line of questioning and Carolyn responded she believed Sam was both a police officer and a snitch. McKechnie failed to complete the impeachment on this point by reading Carolyn's preliminary haring testimony as he did with other points of impeachment. His oversight with respect to this one point does not establish a performance falling short of a reasonably competent attorney acting as a diligent advocate. Since the issue of impeachment is a matter for trial counsel's discretion, McKechnie was not required to impeach Carolyn's on every point."

Isserlis next sought to have Sam's conviction remanded on the theory that judge Thompson, had committed prejudicial error in instructing the jury that a witness is presumed to speak truthfully. This presumption, Isserlis asserted, worked in Carolyn's favor and to the detriment of Sam. "Without the presumption in Carolyn's favor, the jury would have doubted the truth of many of her assertions. Carolyn was brain damaged. Her memory was unreliable. She could not even remember that she had testified against (Sam) at his preliminary hearing. Because of her intellectual disabilities, it is not unlikely that Carolyn sometimes confused what one man did or said to her with what another man did or said to her."

Isserlis claimed that Sam was paying the price for Carolyn's confused memories and for her, "anxiety to cooperate with law enforcement."

Instructions to the jury are normally discussed with both members of opposing counsel prior to a judge issuing the jury guidelines by which it is to consider the case before it.

Gros-Cloren argued that the defense in this case did not object to this instruction prior to it being issued to the jury. "First, the error in telling the jury that a witness is presumed to speak the truth was immediately counteracted to some degree by the court's recitation of factors which could over-come that presumption. Second, the jurors were instructed that they (were) the sole judges of the believability of a witness and the weight to be given the testimony of each witness. Appellant's (Sam's) contention that he was con-victed because his statements denying culpability were not afforded the same presumption of credibility as Carolyn's testimony is nothing short of unreal-istic speculation and is unsupported by the record."

Isserlis next argued that Sam was prejudiced when he was made to appear before the jury in a pair of pants emblazoned with the label "San Diego Jail" written on the side. Isserlis said that compelling (Sam), an incarcerated defendant, to wear jail "garb" in front of the jury, "violates (a defendant's) federal rights to due process and equal protection because it tends to undermine the presumption of innocence. It also places the accused at a disadvantage in relation to defendants who can afford bail."

Isserlis contended that had McKechnie asked for a short continuance to try and get Sam a plain pair of trousers to go with the plain white shirt, and had effectively impeached Carolyn's testimony, it was "reasonably probable" the jury would have returned verdicts in the case more favorable to Sam. Regardless of whose fault it was for forcing Sam to be tried in jail clothing, be it McKechnie or judge Thompson, Isserlis argued, the judg-ment in this case should be reversed.

But Gros-Cloren argued that Sam was not forced to wear jail clothing because he did not object to wearing jail pants. She supported her argu-ment citing additional language in Estelle v. Williams and People v. Taylor. In those cases, the court states, "the constitutional right not to be compelled to wear jail garb at trial will be deemed waived by the failure to timely object or otherwise bring the issue to the court's attention." Gros-Cloren argued that McKechnie was not, "overly concerned" with Sam's attire and if he were, he certainly did not pursue the matter."

Count one of the indictment against Sam relating to charges that he raped Carolyn, read that he was charged with, "accomplishing an act of sexual intercourse on July 4, 1991 by means of force, violence, and fear of immediate and unlawful bodily injury." In count two, Sam was charged with, "accomplishing an act of sexual intercourse by threatening to incarcerate or arrest a woman who reasonably believed that the perpetrator was a public official." This was the official charge as opposed to Sam's version of "oral copulation by trickery." Citing these two counts, Isserlis next attempted to argue that there was insufficient evidence presented at trial to convict Sam of forcible rape, as well as insufficient evidence to prove that Carolyn reasonably believed him to be a police officer on the 4th of July. In what may be Isserlis' weakest argument of all her challenges, she contended that there was insufficient evidence to find Sam guilty of forcible rape as charged in count one. Carolyn had testified that Sam threatened to "beat her up" prior to committing sodomy but did not make a similar threat prior to the act of oral copulation and sexual intercourse, which took place later that night. Carolyn, Isserlis asserted, may for a short period of time have, "genuinely believed (Sam) was a police officer." But believing Sam to be a police officer for any length of time was not something a reasonable person could do. "A reasonable person would have deduced from the words and conduct Carolyn attributed to (Sam) that he was merely a bully seeking to intimidate a vulnerable person."

Gros-Cloren's opposition to this argument centered on the uncontested testimony that Sam had first sodomized Carolyn after threatening her with bodily harm. "A trier of fact," she wrote, "could reasonably conclude the threat would be repeated to accomplish the subsequent offenses if Carolyn refused."

Gros-Cloren also argued that there was ample evidence to prove that Sam had posed as a police officer and that Carolyn believed him to be a police officer that could have had her arrested. Sam had told Carolyn on several occasions that he was a police officer, and if she were ever arrested, he would get her out of jail. She also described how Sam picked Carolyn up while she was soliciting herself and argued that it is, "common knowledge the police frequently arrest prostitutes this way" all of which tended to reinforce Carolyn's belief that Sam was a police officer.

Both Isserlis and Gros-Cloren's briefs were filed with the California Court of Appeal, Fourth Appellate District in April 1993, and one month after the briefs in Karen's case had been filed. Like Jan Stiglitz and Lilia Garcia, Isserlis and Gros-Cloren went back to work dealing with other clients and other judicial issues. Sam had successfully achieved what he had set out to do; that is, have both cases sent up for review to the court of appeals. His fight now rested in a new arena. All he could do was wait for a decision by the judges. Confident that both cases would be overturned on appeal, Sam refused to accept any type of work while inside the prison at Calipatria. Had he agreed to take some type of job, Sam would have been able to obtain credit toward time off of his sentence. Instead, he sat in his cell, continued to draft writs, both for himself and other prisoners, watched television, ate and gained weight. He would simply let the system dictate what his next legal move would be. As far as his personal interests, Sam was always vigilant in his efforts to continue to portray himself as something other than what he actually was. Sitting inside his cell, Sam had a great deal of unoccupied time to contend with. He spent much of it watching television, letting his mind wonder as he viewed the instant news events from around the world. Sam watched as the war in Bosnia dragged on, revealing the suffering of thousands of innocent people. He watched as a religious sect in Waco, Texas, burned itself to the ground killing its leader, David Koresh and many of his followers along with their children. He also followed stories of gay parades in the nations capital.

"I've been really depressed the past couple weeks," Sam said. "It really upset me to watch the slaughter in Bosnia. No one seems to want to do anything about it. If they'd let me, I'd go over there in a moments notice. Those Serbs are real tough guys beating up on all the little kids suffering the way they did."

Sam also took time to write to Janet Reno, the U.S. Attorney General. "I wrote Jane Reno and asked her to investigate my case," Sam said. "But now that they've got her driving tanks. It may be a while before she finds time for me. I don't fault the government, except they should have launched their initial assault differently. They should never have lost four ATF agents. Koresh is a real idiot. I even wrote him a letter a couple weeks ago telling him so. I guess I should give up waiting for a reply back from him."

But it was television that Sam enjoyed most and it was through television that Sam explored new opportunities to exploit anything and anyone who would bring him some gratification. It was through this medium, that he next ventured, allowing his tentacles to reach outside the prison walls of Calipatria.

Chapter 19

Everyone Gets 15 Minutes Of Fame

Her appearances on the "Jenny Jones Show", one of the many television tabloid talk shows that exploit every imaginable topic, and capitalizing on the misery of others, could easily have been interpreted as a cry for help. It may also have been just another opportunist looking for their fifteen minutes of fame. Whatever her reason, Karron hoped to regain some of her lost self-esteem while perhaps gaining the strength needed to escape from an abusive environment.

Karron Thompson was born in August 1957 in Frankfurt, Germany, where her father was stationed with the U.S. Army. She was the sixth of seven children. After leaving the Army, Karron's father took up the ministry, moving Karron and her three brothers and three sisters throughout the south before settling in Texas. At 16, Karron, looking for any opportunity to leave a house where her father had turned to drinking, married Earl. At 18, Karron gave birth to her first daughter. Two years later at 20, Karron gave birth to her second daughter. When they first married, Karron said Earl appeared "sweet" and attentive. In less than a year, the physical abuse started. After five years of marriage, Karron and Earl divorced.

In February 1993, when she first appeared on the Jenny Jones Show, Karron was 35 years old. Her long light colored hair and youthful figure certainly did not reveal the fact that she was thirty-five and the mother of two teenage daughters. In 1993, Karron had been divorced from Earl for

14 years. During those 14 years, Earl continued to rape and beat her. It's unclear why Karron and Earl chose the Jenny Jones Show to discuss their lifestyle, but they did.

The "Jenny Jones Show" advertised the segment as one about women who stay with men who are abusing them physically and sexually. Jones introduced Karron as a woman who lived in fear of her ex-husband. For the entire one-hour segment, taped on February 12, 1993 in Chicago, Illinois, Karron described the brutal sexual assaults her ex-husband Earl, a carpenter, had committed against her. She described how Earl had broken three of her ribs on her birthday several years prior, and how he had cracked her collarbone and given her a concussion. Karron explained how Earl, for 14 years, had continually assaulted her, sodomized her and forced her to accommodate him by performing a variety of sexual acts, including anal intercourse. She was unable to get a restraining order, explaining that the police were of little help because of the laws in her community. Her only option, she claimed, was to have Earl charged with trespassing.

The audience reaction was one of absolute outrage. Earl did not deny the allegations. In fact, he readily admitted to his host, the audience, and the viewers that what Karron described was true. Earl tried to explain some of his actions, claiming Karron wanted to have sex with him. That often, she was drunk and didn't really know what she was doing.

Jenny Jones asked her guest why he just didn't get out of Karron's life. Earl responded to Jones question with a question of his own. He wanted to know where he was to go if he did leave. His response drew the ire of the audience, some of whom told Earl that he should be shot. Others said death would be too easy and suggested that Earl be castrated, while the rest advised Karron to get out, to move away, and find a man that loved her.

Karron told the audience that she believed Earl did love her and she still loved him. Nonetheless, she wanted help getting away from him.

Earl said that he wasn't sure how he felt after raping his ex-wife. He just didn't' think about it was all he said. Karron's daughters, aged 15 and 17 appeared on the show and begged their father to leave. An audience member asked Earl what would he do if someone did to his daughters what he had been doing to his ex-wife. Earl indicated that he would probably kill them.

Before the show concluded, in a sincere gesture of compassion for her guest, Jenny Jones offered to help Karron and her daughters' relocate, to get away from Earl. Karron, to the applause of the audience, agreed to accept the offer of help; an offer she subsequently failed to take.

The producers of the Jenny Jones show received hundreds of letters and telephone calls from around the country wanting to know if they had helped Karron. They hadn't. Karron had not taken advantage of Jenny's offer. Jenny Jones thought so often about Karron that she brought her and Earl back on the show to follow up on her progress. The second show featuring Earl and Karron was taped on July 29, 1993.

At the beginning of the second show, Karron explained that she had moved, found a new place to live, but that Earl continued to come to her home. In fact, things had gotten worse after the first show, Karron told Jones and the audience. The first night after returning to Texas, Karron claimed to have woken up one morning to find Earl in her bed trying to sodomize her. Earl explained that the only time he could have Karron was in her sleep. She didn't want anything to do with him when she was awake.

Jones presented excerpts from the first telecast, highlighting those segments in which Karron graphically described Earl's physical sexual assaults. Jones demanded to know why Earl had not kept his promise, a promise he made on the first show to leave Karron alone.

Earl told the audience he couldn't leave, claiming they only had one car and that the kids needed to get to school and that he had to get to work. The audience, in virtual total unison, exhibited a loud, distinguished roar demonstrating their disgust at Earl's transparent excuses.

Once again, Jones offered to help Karron relocate, and extended the offer of aid further with financial help. And once again, Karron told Jenny Jones that she would accept her offer of help to get away from Earl. This time, the audience gave her a standing ovation.

Toward the end of the show, Charlotte Watson, the Vice-President of the National Council for Safe Families and a battered women's advocate, appeared on the show alongside Karen and Earl. Watson said men battered women because they believed they have a right to batter them. It's when women leave violent domestic situations, that they are at their greatest risk, she told her host. During the taping of the show, Watson told the viewers that every year, between 2,000 and 4,000 women are murdered by their male partners. Husbands or boyfriends kill about 40% of all women murdered in the U.S. every year.

Watson tried to convince Earl that he needed to take responsibility for his behavior and that he needed medical treatment. Watson told the audience that what Earl was doing was not about sex. It was about a man who believed he has a right to control and dominate his partner.

Sitting alone in his cell inside the Calipatria State Prison, Sam turned off the television. He had seen enough.

"I was furious to see him (Earl) go on like that, even admitting what he'd done," Sam said. "The guy should be locked up for all he did to her."

Sam took a few moments to assemble his thoughts. When he did, he composed a short letter to Karron and sent it to her in care of the "Jenny Jones Show." The "Jenny Jones Show", as they did with so many other letters they received about the show, forwarded Sam's letter to Karron.

"I received dozens of letters, but his was different," Karron said. "He seemed so sincere, so nice. Something about his letter stood out from the others. His was the only one I responded to."

On August 4, 1993, Karron penned a short note to Sam in response to his letter.

Dear Sam:

I am responding to your letter sent to Jenny Jones on May 21. My name is Karron, not really Kate. We had our names changed for the show.

I wanted to write and tell you I received your letter. It took awhile but I got it. Your letter was very impressive. You seem to be a man with morals and a big heart. I would take great pride in having you for a friend or as my brother. You may write me at:

Karron gave Sam her home address and signed the letter, sincerely, Karron. P.S. I hope to hear from you soon. God Bless you Sam.

Sam was ecstatic. Karron had not only responded to his letter, she wanted to hear back from him. Immediately, Sam sat down in his cell, and typed a three-page letter to Karron. It was August 10, 1993.

Dear Karron:

It certainly was a nice surprise receiving your letter yesterday, especially since it was so unexpected. I've been praying very hard for you the past couple months and maybe your letter was a sign from God to let me know he was hearing my prayers.

As I write this letter, I'm not too sure if it's safe for you to be receiving letters from another man. Even though I clearly remember at the end of Jenny's show, that you agreed to take her up on her offer of safe haven from the one who was abusing you. I'm not sure if you followed through with it. I hope and pray that you did. You are such a great woman, you're pretty, you're intelligent, and you have a very good personality, and you certainly don't deserve the kind of treatment you were receiving. As I recall, you have two young teenage daughters and I remember feeling so bad I wished I could have put my arms around all three of you and give you a big hug.

Not only do I want to be your friend; I'd be honored, someday in the near future, to be considered one of your best friends. I hope you don't think I'm being too forward, but in a few months, hopefully by Christmas time, I would very much like to meet you and the kids in person and take you out to dinner to a nice restaurant. I would do it sooner if I could, but I just won't be able to. I'll give you plenty of advance notice and I can either fly to Texas or I can fly all of you out here, it's entirely up to you. If you've never been to California, it would probably be better for you to come here. That way, I can give you a grand tour and show you what a beautiful state this is. It's immaterial to me, whether we meet here or there. I'd just be honored to get the chance to meet you in person.

I've enclosed a photo of myself with this letter. It was taken a couple of years ago and just so you don't think I was anorexic, it was taken when I was running 10 miles a day. I've put a few pounds on since then but that's because of all the stress in my life the past two years, which I'll explain briefly in a moment. This photo is special to me because I found it in my mom's bible after she died in March 1991, but you can have it. I would like a photo of you and your kids but don't want you to send me one because you feel you're obligated to do so. If you want to send me one, that'll be great.

Since we are starting a new friendship, I guess I should tell you a little bit about myself, then you can do the same. If the Post Office does their job properly, you should receive this by the 13th and if so, please write me back right away or at least by the 20th. Late this month, I'm going to be all over this state and I don't want any of your letters to get lost. To make sure we don't lose contact, let me give you an address where you can always get word to me. It's my secretaries address. Her name is Cathy Showers. She used to work for me full time, but lately, she's only working part time. Her husband is a very good friend of mine. Any mail you send there will get to me promptly.

Now, let me tell you a little about myself. I was born in Detroit, Michigan on May 17, 1951, but by the time I was 5 years old, we moved to one of the upper-middle class suburbs of Detroit. There were seven kids, including me, plus my mom and dad and grandpa, all living in one house, and to most people, we appeared to be the perfect all-American family, but that simply was not the case. My father worked with Jimmy Hoffa, during the time the Teamsters Union began to grow. My father was a very violent man, and the memories I have of him, which stand out the most are of him constantly beating my mother. The most painful memory I have, which just won't go away, and one which I'll probably take with me to my grave, was watching him punch my mom with his fists and hearing my mom begging me to go call the police. I was about 8 years old at the time and instead of doing what she begged me to do, I was so frightened, I froze in my tracks and didn't do a thing. She damn near died because of me. After my father died in 1978, my biggest regret was never having the courage to tell him how badly he hurt me as a child. I loved my father very much, but I despised him for the way he treated my mom and I should have told him that before he died.

So that should tell you why I couldn't stand it when I hear of any man abusing a woman. To me, women are to love and be loved and no man has a right to abuse any woman.

I got married and divorced at a very young age, but it was more of a marriage of convenience than anything else. It was my way of getting away from my violent father. As it turned out, it was a blessing, because I ended up going to college at the University of Michigan, and in 1978, I graduated with a law degree.

I've never taken a Bar exam and became a licensed attorney, but that's because I got involved in Property Management, and I've done pretty good for myself in that field, and probably even better than most attorneys.

After my dad died, I tried to ease my guilt by taking care of my mom. I thought that would make me feel better and in some ways it did. I became very close to my mom, and even though she never came right out and said it, I know she forgave me for not going for help when she begged me to back when I was 8 years old. I hoped to keep her around for a long time, but in 1991, she had a heart attack and died suddenly. I took some comfort in believing I was her favorite and she sort of proved as much when she left me her entire estate and excluded everyone else. I didn't have to but since she left behind so much, I still shared it with the rest of my brothers and sisters.

I planned to come out here to California, find a nice woman to settle down with, and open up an Italian Restaurant with the money she left me, but so far, none of that's been accomplished yet. I'm still young yet, so there is really no rush.

I have a lot more to tell you and I could go on and on, but this is already turned into a short novel. So I will close for now, and give you a chance to respond to it. I'm still worried about you and your kids. Please get back to me soon and let me know what's going on in your life. Even though we've never met in person, Karron, I really do care about you, and I will help you in any way I can. All I ask is that you be patient for a few months until I get some of my very important busi-

ness out of the way. Take good care of your-self, and since I'm unable to do it myself, please give your beautiful children a hug for me.

I'm looking forward to hearing from you real soon.

Sam signed the letter, "Very Sincerely Yours." While the return address identified a Post Office Box in Calipatria, there was no indication that Sam was confined in a state prison there. Sam also added a short postscript to this letter; "You may want to consider sending me an address of a close friend or relative, just in case, so we never lose contact."

After mailing the letter, Sam waited anxiously for a response. He didn't have to wait long. On August 18, Karron answered Sam's letter.

Dear Sam:

I'm sorry for taking so long to answer your letter. Do you know how con-fused I am? Your first letter said you were married and your second letter con-tradicted the first. I'm not angry with you; I don't understand your motive. Your letters were so nice. You seem to be a true soul. You know you'll tell me so why not put the cards on the table? I don't mean to sound bold but this is the 6th letter I've written to you and I can't get it right. I tell myself not to push you into telling me; you'll do it in your own time. Please let it be now.

I hate writing about myself so I hope you aren't self absorbed with me, as I am you. I know you could be anyone. I know you have a secret; why Sam? You know how bad I've been hurt. What do I have to say to earn your trust? I can't say I trust you yet, but you will learn to trust me. Actually, I don't know if I'll ever trust anyone again. Not just because of Earl, my-ex but other factors.

Karron went on to explain about her brothers and sisters, her father dying, and how she never planned to visit his grave because of the unpleasant past. She asked Sam to hand write his future letters, not to type them. She wanted to study his handwriting. She thought this would give her a better chance to get to know him. Karron ended her letter telling Sam that he was special to her. She told him to keep himself safe and prayed that he would get through the difficult emotional period he was experiencing. "Be strong and positive," Karron wrote. "After all, we have a new friend, each other." She signed the letter, love Karron.

For the next four months, Sam and Karron engaged each other in a massive letter writing campaign. They sent letters back and forth to each other as quickly as the Postal Service could deliver them. In late August, Sam finally told Karron that he was in prison. It was, "just a big misunderstanding," he told Karron. Sam alluded to a former girlfriend that had fabricated charges against him as the reason for his being in jail. He convinced Karron that he would be out soon and the two of them would be together. Sam told Karron about his interests in music, his love of Reba McEntire while Karron talked about Patricia Carlisle being one of her favorites. In her first letter to Sam after learning that he was in prison, Karron told Sam she was dedicating a Patricia Carlisle song to him, "Leave the Light on For Me." Sam kept pleading for Karron to send him a photograph, but Karron procrastinated, always finding some excuse not to send a picture.

Sam asked about Karron's two daughters, what they liked, and what would make them happy. Karron interpreted Sam's inquisitiveness as a genuine interest in her daughters. Sam even asked Karron if she was still capable of having babies. Karron told Sam that she had always wanted a boy but that if she ever conceived again, it would have to be out of love. Sam sent Karron photographs of his daughter Kimberly and his son, Sam Jr. By early September, Karron was telling Sam that she was convinced he was innocent. She begged him to try and telephone her, hoping to talk to Sam, to hear his voice. They discussed their future together and talked about presenting both their stories and the turnaround in their lives, and how they found each other, on the Jenny Jones Show.

"I am shocked about how much we truly are alike," Karron wrote. *"Like I've always said, God has a master plan. It's not for us to question, why, what or how? Go with the flow, have faith in Him and he will deliver us to each other when the time is appropriate."* Karron finally told Sam that she loved him. With that statement, Sam could not have been happier.

"For the first time in my life, I found myself deeply in love with a woman," Sam said. "I had planned to go to Texas to pick her up just as soon as I got out of prison."

But Sam's euphoria was short lived. On September 14, 1993, the California Court of Appeals, Fourth Appellate District, rejected Sam's appeal on the conviction relating to Carolyn. The court, in its decision, addressed each of the major issues presented in the appeal. Sam, as he had done so often, sat in his cell reading the court's decision. As Sam read the Courts findings, he fought to hold back the tears.

Chapter 20

Game Tied

The Court 1; Sam 1

The first issue addressed by the appellate court dealt with the alleged Miranda violations. After being interviewed by P. J. Harn, Sam was placed under arrest. While Harn was taking Sam to jail, he asked Sam, without reminding him of his Miranda rights, how many people he had sex with since coming to California. Sam made an incriminating statement that he had engaged in sex with a prostitute. This statement, ultimately lead the police to Carolyn. The court ruled that:

"When a suspect has been properly advised of his Miranda rights and expressly waives those rights, the admonishments need not be repeated at a later interview if circumstances establish the suspect understands his rights. In making the determination, courts examine the totality of the circumstances, including the amount of time that has passed since the waiver. Any change in the identity of the interrogator or the location of the interview, any official reminder of the prior advisement, the suspect's sophistication or past experience with law enforcement, and any indicia that he subjectively understands and waives his rights. Thus, re-advisement is unnecessary where the subsequent interrogation is reasonably contemporaneous with the prior knowing and intelligent waiver."

The court ruled that in viewing the totality of the circumstances, no Miranda violation had occurred.

In count 1 of the indictment, Sam had been charged with raping Carolyn by means of force, violence, or fear of immediate and unlawful bodily injury. In his appeal, Sam conceded that he had threatened to beat Carolyn if she refused to engage in sodomy, but argued that there was insufficient evidence to establish a nexus between that threat and his threatening physical violence with the sexual intercourse that took place later that evening.

The appellate court ruled that, "the fact that (Sam) Consiglio did not repeat the threat of physical violence immediately before the sexual intercourse did not preclude the jury from finding a relationship between the earlier threat and Carolyn's later submission to the intercourse. The jury could reasonably decide Carolyn submitted to the intercourse based on the threat of physical violence and on the later threat he would arrest her."

The court ruled that there was sufficient evidence to support the charge in Count 1 of the indictment.

In Count 2 of the indictment, Sam was charged with raping Carolyn by threatening to use the authority of a public official to incarcerate, arrest, or deport the victim or another.

The appellate court found that there was indeed, sufficient evidence supporting the jury's conclusion that Carolyn believed Sam was a police officer.

On the issue of Sam's motion for a mistrial when Carolyn testified that Harn had told her Sam had been arrested for doing this to other girls, the court ruled that the trial court's approach to remedying the harm was appropriate. In it's ruling, the Appellate Court wrote:

"Taken together, Harn's testimony and the parties stipulation established Carolyn's statement was false. Although the court failed to additionally admonish the jury to disregard Carolyn's testimony, Harn's denial and the parties' stipulation accomplished the same goal. Moreover, Harn's denial was more beneficial to the defense than a judge's statement to ignore the testimony since, unlike an admonishment, the evidence directly contradicted Carolyn's testimony and forcefully called into question her credibility."

In his appeal, Sam raised two claims of ineffective assistance of counsel. First, was his allegation that there was a conflict of interest. He had filed a complaint with the California State Bar about Logan McKechnie's performance. McKechnie had failed to impeach Carolyn with a statement she had made earlier during the preliminary hearing when she testified that after the first time, she didn't think Sam was a police officer but knew he was a snitch.

The appellate court rejected the rule that a, "criminal defendant creates a conflict requiring new counsel every time the defendant files a state bar complaint against defense counsel."

In this case, the court was not persuaded by Sam's argument that McKechnie's remarks to the judge that the state bar complaint affected him. "Counsel (McKechnie), made the comment immediately after learning of the complaint and based on the mistaken impression he was actually being investigated for alleged improprieties. After further reflection and learning that the state bar had not responded to the complaint, counsel demonstrated his readiness to represent (Sam)."

The appellate court ruled that the trial judge did not err in denying Sam's Marsden Motion because Sam had failed to point to anything, which would indicate McKechnie's representation was, "Adversely affected by the purported conflict of interest or that any such conflict resulted in prejudice."

Regarding Sam's allegation that his attorney failed to impeach Carolyn based on her testimony at the pre-trial hearing, the appellate court agreed that McKechnie erred. But the error was insignificant and did not prejudice Sam's case, the judges wrote. Explaining their position, the court said: "Counsel, (McKechnie) effectively impeached Carolyn on numerous other points, establishing she could not remember many important events and she had previously made numerous conflicting and inconsistent statements."

The court next addressed Sam's argument that the trial court erred when it instructed the jury that a witness is presumed to speak the truth. Sam maintained the instruction was prejudicial because without the presumption (in Carolyn's favor), the jury would have doubted the truth of many of her assertions. But Sam had not objected to the court's instruction to the jury.

Addressing this issue, the appellate court stated, "a single instruction to a jury may not be judged in artificial isolation, but must be viewed in the context of the overall charge. And, it is not prejudicial if the jury had a correct concept of the law viewing the instructions as a whole. Immediately after the court told the jury it was to presume the witnesses told the truth, it listed several factors which could rebut that presumption, including a witness's inconsistent statements or contradictory testimony. It is undisputed Carolyn made numerous inconsistent and contradictory statements, thus easily overcoming the presumption in this case. Viewing these instructions as a whole, it is reasonably likely the jury understood it was not compelled to presume Carolyn was telling the truth and instead that it was free to reject any testimony or witness it did not find trustworthy or plausible. Thus, there was no prejudicial instructional error."

The appellate court next addressed Sam's allegation that his constitutional rights were violated because he was compelled to wear pants with the words "San Diego Jail" on them. While it is indeed a violation of an accused's federal and state constitutional rights to equal protection and due process to not be forced to stand trial in jail attire, such a right, however, may be waived by a defendant's failure to timely object to this issue. On this record, the court ruled that Sam, "waived his right to assert error by failing to timely object to his wearing the jail pants."

When Sam finished reading the appellate courts decision, he sat on his bunk, angry and dumbstruck. He was fatigued; feeling like the last ounce of life had been sucked from him. That night, nothing mattered to Sam, not Karron, his new found love, not his family, not Carolyn or Karen. Nothing whatsoever mattered. Sam was at a loss for eloquence when he described his feelings after learning the court had denied his appeal, "life really sucks," was all he said.

The next morning, Sam telephoned Karron. It was a normal conversation, the two talked about being together as soon as Sam was freed. But Sam never told Karron that his appeal had been denied. He couldn't bring himself to tell her that the appeal had been denied or that he had been convicted of rape.

The next day, Sam's thoughts focused on his "relationship" with Karron Thompson. He wanted desperately to be with Karron and believed that she too, wanted to be with him. The California prison system allows some of its prisoner's conjugal visits, at least under certain conditions, one of which requires that the inmate be legally married. To Sam, this was simply a minor obstacle.

Sam was able to obtain a blank copy of a California License and Certificate of Marriage; complete with the license number and signature of a state employee in Sacramento that had allegedly performed the marriage ceremony. On his prison typewriter, Sam filled in the personal data requiring his name and date of birth. Sam listed his residence as 222 West C. Street in San Diego, and indicated that he had six years of college and that his occupation was that of a property supervisor.

Sam next typed in the required information for Karron Thompson, the bride. He listed her occupation as a secretary. Just for laughs, he wrote that Karron's mother's maiden name, required for the certificate, was Opal McEntire, since both he and Karron love Reba McEntire. After signing both his name in the groom's signature block and Karron's name in the bride's, Sam had what appeared to be, a valid California marriage certificate. Two days later, Sam took out a marriage announcement in the local Calipatria newspaper.

"Sam Consiglio of Calipatria and Karron Thompson of Temple, Texas were married September 25 in a private informal ceremony officiated by the Reverend Velma Austin in San Diego, County. The bride, a lifetime resident of Texas, is a 1975 graduate of Temple High School. The bridegroom, former resident of Detroit, Michigan graduated from LakeShore High School in 1969 and went on to receive a degree in law from the University of Michigan in 1978. The newlyweds plan to settle down soon in Muskegon, Michigan with the bride's two daughters from a previous marriage."

Karron Thompson had no idea that she had just gotten married.

In early October 1993, Sam had $3,618.02 in a bank in Mt. Clemens, Michigan. He originally had about $4,800 from his share of the sale of his mother's home but his sister Virginia had previously written a check to Wava Howley for $1,000. Since the estate had not settled until after Sam had left Michigan and was arrested for raping Karen, his sister Virginia put the money in a joint account bearing her and Sam's name. The $1,000 paid to Wava Howley was supposedly for having testified for Sam at trial. Howley told Virginia that Sam had promised to cover her expenses and lost wages during the trial and sent her a copy of an agreement Sam signed stipulating to that arrangement.

Howley estimated that she had been earning about $124 a day. "I missed 11 days," Wava said. "Sam did pay me the $450 I had loaned him when he went to California and he did pay me $150 of what he owed me towards lost wages. But a whole year passed and I didn't hear any more from him. I know he's going to be angry because he thought he was going to get away without paying me obviously, or he would've paid me."

When Sam learned that Virginia had paid Howley the money, his money, he became furious. He accused Virginia of stealing his money and demanded that she return it. But Virginia refused. She accused Sam of taking advantage of Howley, telling her brother that she stood by her decision. Sam then telephoned Howley's son and sister, telling them that Howley had stolen his money. He wrote Virginia convincing her that he was going to "get that old witch school teacher."

On October 5, 1993, Sam contacted the bank in Michigan and arranged to have $400 sent to Karron in Texas. Sam told Karron to use the money to have a telephone installed in her trailer and to put the listing in his name. As soon as Karron did that, Sam obtained a telephone calling card. Once again, he was able to make long distance telephone calls.

A month later, Sam contacted the bank again and withdrew another $500. He wrote a short note asking that they make a check out for $500 payable to Karron. "She needs it as soon as possible so she can fly here to spend a few days with me," Sam told the bank. Sam was continuing to make plans for Karron's visit, a visit solely designed for conjugal purposes. Sam had made temporary arrangements with the prison to have this "visit" with Karron in just ten days.

"I had agreed to visit him, but I never agreed to a conjugal visit. And, I never agreed to marry him," Karron said.

Four days after sending Karron $500, Sam learned that the Superior Court of California for the County of San Diego had granted his Writ of Habeas Corpus as it pertained to ineffective assistance of counsel during Karen's trial. The writ was denied in all other aspects, but that was irrelevant. Sam conviction for having allegedly raped Karen was overturned. He was getting a new trial.

Superior Court Judge Robert E. May, in his opinion granting Sam's writ, said that, "Sam was denied effective assistance of counsel. It is reasonably probable, the results of the trial would have been different had (Sam) had a good attorney."

"That's one down and one to go," Sam said. While Sam was thrilled with the court's decision, he was concerned that he would be transferred to the San Diego County Jail the following week jeopardizing his planned conjugal visit with Karron. And whatever else Sam was thinking that day sound financial planning was not something he gave considerable time to. Sam quickly sent a letter to the bank in Michigan asking that all the money in his account be sent to his wife in Texas. Sam provided the bank with Karron's name and address and asked that they rush the check before he got "ripped off anymore."

Sam was referring to the money he claims was stolen by his sister Virginia and Wava Howley.

Karron had received over $3,600 from Sam in just over a month. "He had me install a telephone in his name," Karron said. "And, he had three credit cards sent to me in the name of Karron Consiglio. The cards were from Mobile, Exxon and Robinson May, a department store." Just after receiving a check for $2,728 from Sam's account, Karron received a telephone bill for the long distance charges initiated by Sam. "Sam had run up telephone charges well over a thousand dollars," Karron said. Karron felt obligated to pay the telephone bill and used the money Sam had sent her for that purpose. When she did, there was little money left for her to travel to California. When Sam learned that Karron had used his money to pay the telephone bill, a bill he never intended to pay, he became frantic. But he had little time to deal with his anger. While pacing in his cell contemplating his next move as to how he would retrieve his money, Sam's other fear came true. He was being sent back to the San Diego County Jail to await a new trial on charges that he raped Karen. While he was excited about getting a new trial, Sam knew that any chance of a conjugal visit was now void.

As soon as he arrived at the jail, Sam filed a motion with the court seeking pro-per status. Sam not only wanted to represent himself; he wanted an attorney appointed by the court to assist him in his defense. The court granted his request. Once again, Sam was pro-per with all the rights and privileges associated with it including private television, telephone, access to a fax machine and law books; all at the expense of the taxpayers of California.

As soon as Sam settled into his new cell inside the San Diego County jail, he started calling Karron, demanding his money back. "He got very emotional," Karron said. "He was bad, he just turned hard like." Karron started to fear for her safety and for the safety of her daughters. The man she had corresponded with for almost five months, the man who had written so many "beautiful letters" had suddenly revealed a dark, violent side that she was convinced, did not exist. "His letters were so entertaining," Karron said. "He appeared intelligent. I wasn't going to condemn him the courts had already done that. I received about 80 letters from him; the last few were very threatening." In addition to the threatening letters, Sam, with almost unlimited use of a telephone, continued to call Karron, scarring her with his demands and "insinuations." Realizing that she no longer could tolerate Sam's abuses, Karron contacted the San Diego Sheriff's Department and lodged a complaint against him for his alleged threatening telephone calls. After filing the complaint, Karron contacted the telephone company and got a new unlisted telephone number.

As soon as they received Karron's complaint, the deputies at the San Diego Jail removed the telephone from Sam's cell. The biggest perk of his pro per status was gone, at least temporarily. Sam had no way to telephone Karron. She had a new phone number and his "free" phone had been removed. On December 8, 1993, Sam wrote Karron another letter:

Karron:

I lost my pro per status because the Sergeant said you told them I was harassing you. I don't know why you'd do such a thing when all I did was ask for my $3,600 back.

You go right ahead and fuck over me right now as much as you like, but I will get my money back one way or another. You better think about your girls.

Starting Monday, 12/13/95, for each day you keep my money, I'm adding 10% compounded daily, and if you think this is a joking matter, just keep laughing.

Its really not worth it Karron to have to worry every time there's a knock at the door, or everytime (your daughters) are late coming home.

I want my money and all my property now and I'm not waiting much longer. You may consider this a threat if you like but on the phone, all I told you is I was going to get…. If you still want to call my bluff, go ahead. You have till Tuesday, 12/14/93.

After sending the letter to Karron, Sam petitioned the court to have his telephone privileges returned. He argued that Karron had stolen $3,600 from him and that he was just trying to get his money back to help offset his legal expenses. The court complied with Sam's request. As soon as the telephone was installed back in his cell, Sam called a local pizzeria near Karron's home. He ordered a large pepperoni pizza and had it sent to Karron's trailer just to let her know that he was thinking of her.

Chapter 21

No Remorse

Leaving a Sociopath can be the worst experience of all. Many times they are so resentful of their rejections that they will muster a vengeful attack on the very things that one loves. They believe that you should be punished for their rejection no matter what it does to one's family, children, finances, or health.

Damian

Karron Thompson wasted no time calling the San Diego Jail. She was frightened. She told the deputy who answered the phone, that Sam had threatened her and her two daughters during a series of phone calls that he was placing from his cell. Karron also told the deputy that in addition to the phone calls, Sam had written a letter threatening her and her daughters and offered to send a copy of the letter to the district attorney's office.

When the sheriff deputies learned of Sam's latest impropriety, they suddenly not only revoked his pro per privileges; they also placed him in solitary confinement. Sam immediately filed a motion with the Superior Court in San Diego to have his pro per privileges restored. On December 10, 1993, Sam appeared before judge John M. Thompson, in San Diego Superior Court. Once again, Mike Przytulski represented the people of California. Representing himself, Sam began by telling judge Thompson, "Karron was my fiancée. She has absolutely nothing to do with my pro per status because my calls to her have been ongoing for quite some time and I've only been pro per for about a week now. When the Sergeant asked me to stop calling, I did. I haven't called since. There was no reason for the court to order me into segregation yesterday. I didn't do anything to deserve that."

Thompson was not pleased with Sam's accusation. "Let me get one thing clear for the record. I never ordered you into solitary confinement. What I did, was tell you your phone privileges would be suspended."

Sam told Thompson that he thought the removal of his phone privileges was unfair, especially since Karron had been his girlfriend and fiancée. Thompson told Sam that he had suspended the phone privileges because he had been notified by the jail that he (Sam) was calling Karron and threatening her and her two daughters with death. And for telling them he would get to them when he got out of prison if she did not accept the calls and that the calls were occurring at the rate of 50 to 60 times a day resulting in phone bills close to $4,000.

"She's not my fiancée," Sam told judge Thompson. "When we spoke as of the 8th (December), she was. But we had our argument. But I did not threaten her. But yes, we broke up on the evening of the 8th. At the time, she was my fiancée. But now, she isn't. But I haven't abused my pro per privileges, your honor. I have been working really hard. I had a little problem with my fiancée that's all. That would have happened wherever I was at. I apologize for whatever inconvenience, I mean it probably is unfortunate that it happened."

Przytulski told Thompson about Sam's previous telephone threats to Carolyn and the details of his threats to Karron. Przytulski also told the court that he had been told by other people that Sam had harassed them during phone calls placed from his cell.

"Quite frankly, the phone privileges that are allowing him to prepare the case at this point in time are being abused," Przytulski said. "This court is not without the power to protect citizens of Mr. Consiglio's abuse, threats, and manipulations."

Sam was furious. He wasn't afraid of this judge or anyone else at this moment. "Everything he is talking about is strictly hearsay," Sam said, almost yelling. "Let's have a full hearing on who I have threatened," he demanded. "I haven't threatened anybody. He is talking about a year and a half ago. I'm talking about only what happened between my fiancée and me. One incident; nothing else. And to deny me pro per status at this time, you're denying me of my 6th and 14th amendment rights."

"I'm not about to take away your pro per status, Mr. Consiglio. I'm not going to do that. You want to go pro per you are entitled to go pro per. What you're deserving now is me denying your phone privileges."

Thompson ordered Przytulski to draft an order limiting Sam's phone privileges to one hour a day for the purpose of conducting his own investigation in preparation of his defense. Przytulski was eager to comply with Thompson's instruction.

Al Arena was raised in Bayville, New York, a small community on Long Island. Like Sam, Al grew up in a strong Italian home and eventually made his way to California. Unlike Sam, Arena actually did go to law school studying under Jan Stiglitz, and graduated from Cal Western in 1983. Arena spent seven and half years prosecuting cases for the San Diego District Attorney's Office after graduating from law school. On December 14, 1993, 37-year-old Arena, who had been in private practice for less than two years, was appointed by the San Diego Superior Court to act as "advisory counsel" for Sam. One week later, on December 21, Arena appeared for the first time alongside his new client as Sam filed yet another motion regarding his pro per status.

"Your honor," Sam said, after judge Thompson opened the proceeding; "I have the Supreme Court decision on pro per privileges, Wilson versus Superior Court of Los Angeles decided in 1978. One of the things they require is that we should be afforded due process. This is very serious and shouldn't be taken lightly. I was never afforded proper due process by the jail or this court. And, that's all I'm asking for, a fair and impartial hearing on all the facts in this case. And, if the court would do that, they would restore my privileges I believe."

Arena listened patiently as he sat next to Sam. Dressed in a dark conservative colored suit that highlighted his dark complexion and fit as if it had been specially made for him, Arena looked like one of those fortunate few who kept a year round tan and belonged in his adopted state of California far more than he did on Long Island. But while he listened patently, Arena was not unimpressed by Sam's representation. Nonetheless, he knew that eventually he would take on a more prominent role in this case and would be ultimately responsible for defending Sam. With that in mind, Al Arena wasted no time being heard on Sam's latest motion.

"Your honor, I've been appointed as advisory and standby counsel. And, I may have actually try this case. In addition, as advisory counsel, I should be standby at all times in order for Mr. Consiglio to prepare his case. It's my understanding that the phone privileges at this time are between 1:00 and 2:00 in the afternoon. I believe, your honor, that given any normal schedule of any working attorney, that would provide inadequate access to his advisory counsel, save me going to the jail every day and seeing him."

"I believe that the removal of the phone privileges was a result of a phone call placed to a fiancée in Texas. Well, judge, I think that this is a little different than abusing the phone in the sense of intimidating people. They got in a fight. It was his fiancée. I think we can put appropriate constraints on the phone in the future so that he will be allowed the due process in which he requests."

Thompson was not impressed with Arena's argument. He told Arena that Sam was afforded due process and that a hearing had been held on the issue after he had been notified by deputies at the San Diego jail of Sam's threats made over the telephone. Thompson did, however, modify his previous order and allow Sam two hours of telephone use, twice a day, once in mid morning and another two hours in late afternoon.

Sam was, of course, less than pleased with the decision. Sam was not satisfied with having his access to a telephone limited to strictly talking to potential witnesses and Al Arena. In spite of the new restrictions, he still found opportunities, especially through three way calling, to contact "friends" and family. On Christmas Eve, Sam called his brother, Louie. Louie was living near his parents old home in St. Clair Shores when Sam called. Louie and Sam had not been close for years. Louie believed that Sam had threatened their sister Virginia, and for that, there was no forgiveness.

Sam had left several short messages over several days, wishing his brother a Merry Christmas. On Christmas Eve, when Louie heard his brother's voice through the speaker on the answering machine, he picked up the phone.

"Hi Lou. What are you doing, taping me?" Sam asked. Unbeknown to Sam, that's exactly what Louie was doing.

"You're crazy," Louie said, denying the accusation.

Sam told his brother that he was positive he would win his upcoming trial involving Karen and that the appeal of his other case involving Carolyn would soon be overturned. But Louie wasn't impressed. He told Sam that, regardless, he was still wrong for what he had done.

"Oh, I know I'm wrong," Sam said. "I don't care. I'm not going to spend no fucking twelve years for getting a blow job, fucking not."

"Well, you told her you were a cop, man," Louie said.

"No, I didn't correct her," Sam told his brother.

Louie was angry with his brother and did nothing to mask his indignation. "Talk to me, man. Talk to me," Louie yelled into the receiver. "Don't play with me. Why did you hurt the other girl, Sam? Why would that other girl say you did those things?"

"Because she's a homeless broad and I promised her a job." Sam told his brother that Karen was devastated over learning that she was not going to get the job he promised her and that saying he had raped her was Karen's way of getting back at him.

Louie wasn't buying Sam's story but he listened as his brother tried to justify each of his actions. "What about the girl in Florida?" Louie asked.

"That's Jamiss," Sam said. "I shacked up with her in Florida. I manipulated the shit out of her, but there was no force. I just kept pretending like I was going to give her a job. She was married to this guy…"

Louie interrupted his brother, screaming into the phone, "You threatened her, you threatened her, you threatened her."

"No. There was no threat to kill. Listen; listen to the story Lou, Sam interjected. "She was going with this guy in the Navy and they were getting married. She shacked up with me and I manipulated her. Then she decided to cut it off and I said no, you can't cut it off, and I blackmailed her. I didn't blackmail her, I just made her think that I was going to tell her old man, but I never came out and said it."

"So why did you send Karron (Thompson) threatening letters?" Louie asked.

"I just blew up," Sam said. "It didn't have anything to do with her, it had a lot to do with my disappointment."

Sam told his brother that he would be acquitted of raping Karen explaining that Wava Howley was going to be his key witness.

"I'm acquitted with Wava," Sam said. "Wava is coming to testify and we got it all set up. We are going to make her look fucking stupid in that courtroom. We are going to make her look terrible. She, in fact, is going to get charged with perjury before she leaves there."

"You're scaring her man," Lou told Sam. "There is another person inside of you that's done all the crimes, you know. You got a fucking split personality, man; you're like fucking three faces of Eve. I believe that. There is one side of you that you are so good at, you can manipulate people."

"I never scared Wava, she scared out on her own. I told Wava she owes me a thousand dollars and I'm going to get it. Is that a threat? I kept asking Virginia about my money, where is my thousand dollars. She didn't say a word until I found out about it from the bank."

"Virginia is not going to do that man, nobody wants your money Sam." Sam was still angry that his sister, Virginia, had paid Howley for traveling to California and testifying at his trial in 1991.

"You know, you had your whole family behind you as much as you were wrong, you had your whole family behind you, you had everyone else fucking baffled, except for me."

"I don't know what you are talking about," Sam told his brother. "Who was behind me?"

Louie was loosing control. His anger grew as he shouted into the phone. "Your mother for one thing," he told Sam. "Your mother put up with your fucking shit, man, that's what happened. You think I'm going to forgive you for what you did to her. I ignored a lot of shit because she was still alive. Now that she is not, I'm not. You put her in an early grave."

"Not any more than what the rest of you have done," Sam yelled back.

"I don't think so Sam. I think you caused more fucking stress than anybody could ever go through. I've seen your evidence. You think you're fucking slick but I know you better than that, cause all you did is call and talk to the girls answering machine."

Sam laughed and told his brother that he would give him all of his money if he could prove that allegation. "So, you think I committed a crime, huh?" Sam asked.

"Committed a crime. Sam, man, this isn't once or twice. I would give you the benefit of the doubt you know, this is fucking thirty, and and forty times you've hurt somebody. Don't try to think I'm stupid now, you know, I mean, when you fucking start facing the fact that you've got a problem maybe you'll wake up one day but until you fucking keep on bull shitting to yourself or lying to yourself, you know. I don't want you calling Virginia no more, she don't want to talk to you. I don't want you hassling her, I don't want you writing to her no more cause if I have to, we will get a hold of the warden, make sure your fucking privileges are all fucking gone."

Louie continued as he tried punishing Sam with his verbal assault. "You fucking ended up just like dad was. All you did was end up like dad, taking advantage of women. That's not cool, man, what you did. Your whole fucking life you cause nothing but grief. If you want to call me that's fine, you're going to be getting this fucking kind of abuse from me, you know."

Sam was still laughing. "Louie you are not abusing me, but you are wrong."

"Did you pay that fucking lady Sam? You didn't pay her. You were going to fuck that religious lady over, you scum bag," Louie screamed as he accused his brother.

"I paid her a thousand dollars," Sam said.

"You didn't pay her nothing."

"She ruined my case," Sam said.

"Ruined your case because she told the truth," Louie claimed.

"Yeah, that I was in prison. That's what ruined the case."

"That's the problem with the fucking system, Sam. The system is fucked up. They let fucking criminals like you out on the street because of technicalities. They should keep your fucking ass, and fucking electrocute you mother fuckers. That would be the way to go, you know. I'd like to see it man. I want to see you fucking soon, believe me. I'd like to see you out because I'm going to fuck you up. I'm telling you right now, you write any more letters, you're going to get fucking hurt. Don't fuck with my sister; she's been a good person all her life. She's done nothing wrong."

Sam tried to reassure his brother that he meant no harm to anyone, especially their sister, Virginia. All he wanted, he told Louie, was his $1,000 back that Virginia had given to Wava Howley. But Louie didn't believe his irritating brother. He had heard all of Sam's excuses far to many times before. And Louie wasn't shy about telling his brother exactly how he felt about him. But in spite of Louie's violent and accusatory attacks, Sam listened; he had no one else to talk to, and it was, Christmas Eve. At that moment, Louie despised his brother; but he was still family and the whole episode disturbed him. Wanting desperately to end the conversation, Louie finally told Sam he had to go. He was fed up with his brother;

he'd heard enough of what he perceived as "Sam's lies" and simply said "later" as he hung up the phone.

The following day, Christmas, Sam called Louie again. Sam knew that he was rapidly approaching a point in his life when he would be truly alone. The last thing he wanted to do was lose what little contact he had left with some of his brothers and sisters. But Louie wasn't home. All Sam heard was the same recorded greeting he had heard several times before when he tried to call his brother. "I just called to wish you a Merry Christmas Lou. I know it hasn't been very good but maybe some day things will get better, I don't know. No matter what you think, no matter what Virginia thinks, what anybody thinks, I don't care. I know in my heart, that I haven't done anything wrong in California and I'll be acquitted soon. In spite of all that, I just want to wish you a Merry Christmas and say I love you. I tried to call Virginia and patch things up but I guess that isn't going to work. Maybe you want to tell Virginia I love her, it's up to you. Take care."

Two days later, Sam called Louie again. This time, Louie was home. "What do you want," Louie asked. What Sam wanted most, was to talk to someone, especially someone who might be sympathetic towards him. Who better than a family member? But Louie wanted no part of Sam's lies and deception. He and his brothers and sisters had been hurt far too often. Still, Louie asked his brother for the truth, begging him to be honest with him about what he had done to both Karen and Carolyn.

"I have never laid a finger on Karen, never touched her anywhere. I wasn't with her that night," Sam told his brother.

"I didn't think you'd be truthful with me, I really didn't," Louie said.

"I am truthful," Sam insisted. "I never touched the bitch."

"Even if you were innocent Sam, it wouldn't matter to me because of all the other crimes you've committed all your life. I'm going to hold those against you until you're dead."

"I can't tell you I did something I didn't do, Lou. I just want you to be my brother, Lou, that's all I want you to be."

"You're fucking lying to me, man. Why should I be your brother when you're lying to me?"

Sam told Louie that he got the idea of getting a woman from the homeless shelter from a secretary at a local church. He told his brother that he couldn't get hired managing apartments unless he was part of a "couple". "At first I thought, that's a good idea, find yourself some strange piece of ass, have some strange pussy all the time; that was my first thought. When I see this girl, well, Karen is not an attractive girl at all; she's kind of a dikish person. So, I think, no, I need this fucking job."

Louie was furious. "Something happened man. I don't know what it is but, you know, I know you're wrong. Why would the girl take you to court? You did something."

Louie told Sam that he didn't believe anything he said, and suggested he not call him anymore. "If it wasn't for my past, I could probably convince you that I'm innocent right now. But, its my past that is preventing that," Sam said.

For once, Louie agreed with Sam. "You're right," he said. "And it always will."

After hanging up the phone, Louie removed the tape from the answering machine. He had the tapes copied onto a standard cassette and mailed it to Mike Przytulski in San Diego.

On Tuesday, December 30, 1993, judge Thompson, on his own motion, convened a hearing to investigate new allegations that Sam had, once again, abused his telephone privileges. Sitting in the courtroom for the second time in a week, Sam listened as Thompson told him that he had read the threatening letter that Sam had sent Karron Thompson in Texas. "I took the lead suggested by you in your correspondence and contacted Karron Thompson," the judge told Sam. "She confirmed each and every allegation set forth in the (district attorney's) investigative report." Without allowing Sam an opportunity to respond, Thompson terminated his telephone privileges.

During the first week of January 1994, the People of the State of California versus Sam Consiglio in the case involving Karen was assigned to the court of judge Bernard E. Revak. In his early 50's, Revak looked every bit the authoritarian who, off the bench, could have been anyone's grandfather. On January 20, Revak met Sam for the first time. Sitting next to Sam was Arena. Opposite them, as he had so often before, sat Mike Przytulski.

"This matter has been assigned here, Mr. Consiglio, for all purposes, with a trial date anticipated for March the 6th, 1994," Revak said.

Sam rose from his chair and like a seasoned trial lawyer said, "I have a motion to present your honor. For the past month, I have been denied my pro per privileges and my case has been at a complete standstill since then. I want to go to trial as soon as possible but because of my lack of communication for the past six weeks, I haven't had contact with anyone; none of my witnesses.

"On December 8th, I had an argument with my fiancée over the telephone. She is not a witness in this case. She has nothing to do with this case.

"On December 10th, I appeared before judge Thompson. Based solely on the hearsay evidence of my fiancée, my phone was reduced from twelve hours per day to one hour per day. On December 21, judge Thompson increased my phone time to four hours. That was not enough time as far as I'm concerned.

"On December 24, I did call her (Karron) and I talked to her up through December 29th. As far as I'm concerned, I thought everything was fine between us. I wasn't aware that she was stabbing me in the back at the same time."

"On December 30th, without any prior notice or warning, I had to appear before judge Thompson. Without any hearing at all, he revoked my phone completely. That made it impossible for me to represent myself. In 1978, the California Supreme Court addressed this issue. In Wilson versus Los Angeles Superior Court, the court held that pro per privileges should be protected by due process and that the privilege initially granted would not thereafter be restricted or terminated except for cause. The court further held that the nature of an inmate's interest in the exercising (of) those privileges was such that, except in emergency situations, they may be restricted only after notice and hearing. In this case, I was never afforded a hearing. This incident should have been handled internally by the jail, and the jail was in the process of doing that when I was written up. The recommendation was loss of phone privileges for two weeks. I did have an argument with my fiancée. I admit that I was wrong. I did lose my temper. But under the circumstances, I felt that at the time I was justified. But she, again, has nothing to do with this case, your honor."

Revak had sat patiently listening to Sam as he pretended, once again, to demonstrate that he was a seasoned trial lawyer. "Well, that brings up a point that I want to talk to you about Mr. Consiglio. And, I want to deal with your pro per privileges. If she has nothing to do with this case, then you are not calling her as your own attorney to deal with matters involving this case. It appears to me that it's strictly private. And I don't think you should have any greater privileges in private conversations that have nothing to do with this case than any other inmate in the county jail."

"I would stipulate on the record to having no more further contact with Karron Thompson from this day forward if my phone privileges are restored," Sam told Revak.

Przytulski told Revak about Sam's prior arrests and the fact that the district attorney's office had received numerous complaints about threats made from the telephone inside the jail cell. Przytulski also explained that Sam had friends in the San Diego area and that he would use those friends to make third party telephone calls. "It should be noted, that Mr. Consiglio has demonstrated, during the course that I have known him, an ability to manipulate people. He represented himself as being in the Mafia and that he had a Godfather, again a Mafia connection. So he apparently had or indicated that he had the capability of carrying out these threats," Przytulski said. "Judge Thompson was concerned. He had to balance the pro per status and privileges and his (Sam's) right to represent himself against these threats. When Mr. Consiglio promised he wouldn't call her anymore, the phone privileges were extended to four hours. Within a matter of days, just a few days, Karron Thompson again reported that Mr. Consiglio was threatening her."

Revak listened to all the arguments, both from Sam and Przytulski. Finally, he had heard enough. Looking directly at Sam and Arena, Revak said, "You will have a telephone. Your telephone however, is going to be limited. I am not going to have any repetition of what Mr. Przytulski has indicated to the court. I want you getting ready for trial. You have a lawyer that you can contact. The phone calls will not be monitored. However, when you want to make a phone call, I will order that the sheriff's deputy place the phone call to the telephone number, give the phone to you and they will leave the room."

"I made one mistake your honor. I had an argument with my fiancée. It doesn't justify losing my pro per status."

"You are not losing your pro per status," Revak told Sam. "I am granting your motion to have pro per telephone privileges as I have now limited them. Beyond that, I think it is totally unnecessary for you to have unlimited phone use to call anybody you want to." With that, Revak had had enough of Sam. Court was adjourned for the day. To Sam, the adjournment was nothing more than the short rest provided fighters between rounds. Sam went to his corner located inside the San Diego County Jail to prepare for the next round. And, he didn't have to wait long. The following morning, at 9:07 a.m., Sam, Revak and Mike Przytulski faced each other again.

"Your honor, I have a motion regarding my representation," Sam said as he made his opening remarks. "I'd like to have an in camera hearing. I don't think the district attorney has the right to be present during my discussion on my representation."

"Judge, I submit that unless this is a Marsden Motion, that everything in here is adversary in nature," Przytulski said.

Revak was confused. He told Sam that he didn't understand his motion and that unless he (Sam) was making a Marsden Motion, there was no justification for removing the district attorney from the courtroom. Sam told Revak that he wanted to address the court's decision made the day prior regarding his telephone privileges. "I had hoped to be treated fairly by this court. But obviously, that's not going to happen. So, I would ask this court, I would like to go to trial on Monday. But if the court refuses that, I would ask that Mr. Arena be taken off my case as advisory attorney."

"You want me to relieve Mr. Arena as your stand-by-counsel for all purposes, is that what you are asking me to do?" Revak asked.

"Yes. I want the court to understand why I'm doing that, Sam said."

"Okay. You no longer want him as advisory or stand-by counsel. I want you to understand what that means. Come April the first, we will proceed with this trial. You understand that? You will be representing yourself without stand-by counsel."

"I have no alternative your honor," Sam said. "I wanted pro per status and I wanted to prepare my case. The court is preventing me from doing that as long as I have Al Arena as my attorney. So, the court is in effect forcing me to get rid of him."

They had all been in court for a matter of minutes, but in that short period of time, Sam had shocked Arena, confused Przytulski, and angered judge Revak. "That's your interpretation of it. I disagree with you. I'm not forcing you to do anything," Revak told Sam. Revak, now focusing his attention on Al Arena, said, "I'm going to relieve you from any further responsibility in this case as stand-by or advisory counsel."

Sitting in the courtroom behind Sam and Al Arena was Dennis Sesma; a private investigator assigned to assist Sam in preparing his defense. Sesma worked for the Office of Alternate Defense Counsel for the County of San Diego. Revak turned his attention to Sesma and said, "You weren't here yesterday, Mr. Sesma. I'm going to order that Mr. Consiglio have telephone privileges at the county jail for local calls only between the hours of 10:00 a.m. and noon and 3:00 p.m. and 6:00 p.m. I am advising you, and you are hereby ordered that you are not to connect him to a third person if and when he calls you so that he may have communications with a third person. If he desires for you to get into contact with a third person, you may do so as his investigator. Do you understand that?"

Sesma's answer was short and direct, "Yes, your honor."

Sam was frantic. He wasn't sure what Revak was doing to him. He accused the judge of taking away his phone privileges and forcing him to make all of his calls through Sesma. "I have a list of 44 regular people that I need to talk to in order to prepare this case," Sam told Revak.

"You may discuss it with Mr. Sesma. You need not show it to me. He is authorized to act on matters pertaining to your representing yourself as your own attorney in this case."

"So he is authorized to make the calls but I'm not?" Sam asked.

"That's correct," Revak said.

"Can I go to trial on this Monday your honor," Sam asked.

"No sir, you may not."

Sam was shocked at Revak's position. He had been certain that he would have been able to convince him to restore his full telephone privileges after making a motion to have Arena removed as advisory counsel. And, Sam was certain that Revak did not want to do anything to jeopardize his "rights" giving the higher courts cause to have his case overturned again. But again, Sam was wrong. Revak was not one to be easily convinced.

"I would like to withdraw my motion," Sam said, realizing quickly that he had gone to far with this judge.

"What motion?" Revak asked.

"Of asking for removal of Mr. Arena."

Revak was losing his patience. "Mr. Consiglio, you are vacillating a little bit here. I'm wondering what your true intentions are. Don't play fast and loose with me. This is not some type of a circus that we are running here. This is a serious criminal trial. If you want to represent yourself, which you indicated, you may do so. Mr. Arena is a very fine attorney and has been designated as your standby-advisory counsel. You are telling me this morning you want to fire him. Now you are telling me you want him back. I'm not going to go back and forth like this with you, Mr. Consiglio. You have to understand that you are now an attorney before this court and I'm going to treat you like an attorney as well as like a defendant. Don't be like the cabin boy trying to take over the ship. I'm running this court."

"I just want to be treated fairly, your honor," Sam said.

"Well, I think you are. You may disagree with me, but I think you are. That's the last I'm going to hear of this."

"Well, the court of appeals is still reviewing the matter. So, I will just defer to their..."

Revak's anger was now apparent to everyone in the courtroom as he interrupted Sam. "Don't threaten me with the court of appeals. I understand the court of appeals and I understand my function. You may file anything you want to with the court of appeals. Don't threaten me with the court of appeals. I don't care. They have their job and I have my job."

Al Arena had been sitting patiently watching his "client" spar with the judge. Hoping to calm things down he asked Revak if the court was ordering him back on the case. "I couldn't slip a thread through my schedule," Arena told Revak. "I would like to know the court's final decision so I can prepare my future scheduling accordingly."

Revak told Arena that he was indeed back on as Sam's advisory counsel. He also told Sam, once again, that he was not to dial the telephone, that a sheriff's deputy would do that. With those instructions, Revak adjourned court for the day.

On March 11, judge Revak presided over a hearing to deal with a series of motions filed by Sam, as he prepared to defend himself at trial. What Sam hoped to have suppressed, was the transcript of the interview he gave Przytulski and P. J. Harn on July 17, 1991. Sam alleged that the statement had been taken illegally since the district attorney had planned on re-arresting him and had arranged to have his bond increased. Judge Revak asked Sam if he had any witnesses to present in defense of his motion. "I will give oral testimony and I would like to do it in narrative form," Sam said.

Sam remained sitting at the defense table as he raised his right hand and "swore" to tell the truth. With that, he proceeded to provide Revak with an historical overview of the facts surrounding his case. As he did, Arena sat patiently next to him.

"On July 12, 1991, I was arrested by the El Cajon Police. The only thing I was told at that time was that I was being accused of raping Karen. I was never given a date of the alleged rape or a place where the alleged rape occurred. On July 13th, I posted a $25,000 bond and was released from jail. On July 16th, I was given a message that Mr. Harn was at my apartment and wanted to speak to me. I called Mr. Harn that afternoon. We just talked briefly and I promised to call back the following day, which I did. On July 17, I, again, spoke with Mr. Harn and he wanted me to come in and talk about the Karen case. I was very reluctant to do so. I contacted an attorney. He advised me not to go. I just called any attorney out of the phone book. I don't even recall his name anymore. Because of the fact that I had not been arraigned, a public defender had not been appointed to me so I did not have an attorney out of the public defenders office that I could have contacted."

"I did contact an agent with the FBI to ask him what I should do because I felt my civil rights were being violated. After speaking with the agent, I decided to go in and cooperate and speak with Mr. Harn. The first person I ran into when I arrived was Mr. Przytulski. He escorted me to an office. I do not dispute the fact that they read me my rights and that I waived my rights. At the time, I felt that it was a voluntary interview. I always felt free to leave. Throughout the entire interview that lasted approximately three hours, I was never given the impression that I was under arrest or that I was not leaving there that day."

"Following that interview, I was placed under arrest by Mr. Harn and handcuffed. Then, Mr. Harn continued to question me without advising me that I still had the same rights. Had I known that Mr. Harn and Mr. Przytulski had a warrant for my arrest, I would not have talked to them that day or any day. And I believe that they knew that, that's why they didn't inform me. I think it was a violation of my Fifth and Sixth Amendment rights but my research says Sixth Amendment." After Sam concluded his testimony, Przytulski stood and proceeded to cross-examine his adversary.

"When you talked to him (Mr. Harn) he identified himself as an investigator with the district attorney's office, is that correct?" Przytulski asked.

"That's correct," Sam said.

"Did Mr. Harn tell you that the DA's office had filed a complaint against you charging you with rape?"

"Absolutely not," Sam said.

"You don't remember the conversation with Mr. Harn on the 16th, do you?"

"Not entirely, no."

"So, are you telling this court that did not occur or are you telling the court that you don't remember what the entire conversation was on the 16th?"

"I'm telling the court that Mr. Harn never advised me that he had a formal complaint against me," Sam said.

Przytulski asked the same question, changing its variation each time he asked it. Every answer was the same; Sam denied ever knowing or being told that a warrant had been issued for his arrest or that Harn had told him he would be arrested if he came in and spoke to him. Przytulski then changed the direction of the questioning, introducing a four-page letter that Sam had written to Wava Howley on May 18, 1992. Sam testified that the handwriting in the letter was his and that he had indeed sent the letter to Howley.

"Did you write quote: it is very apparent that I appeared to be very dishonest throughout the whole trial and it was because I was trying to protect myself regarding other stuff. But I didn't tell any lies about the Karen case except whether or not I talked to her on the phone on the evening of July 2nd. I did talk to her that night but I denied it at trial only because I testified previously I had only talked to her on July 3rd. Did you write that?" Przytulski asked.

"Yes," Sam replied.

"So, you did lie at Karen's trial?"

"I made a mistake in my testimony," Sam answered.

"Well wait a minute. Didn't you just write in this letter that you did lie?"

"This is not testimony. I'm giving you testimony today. I did not lie in my trial. I made a mistake as far as the day." Sam's appearance of confidence was eroding.

"You wrote Wava Howley a letter saying you had been dishonest throughout the whole trial. Tell us what other matters you were dishonest about."

Sam objected to Przytulski's line of questioning. He told Revak that the district attorney's questions were irrelevant.

Exhibiting a rare sense of humor inside the courtroom, Przytulski said, "Well your honor, if Mr. Consiglio will stipulate that he has no credibility, I will accept that. If not, I think I am entitled to inquire about his credibility."

But Revak wasn't finding any of this funny and agreed with Sam and sustained the objection. Przytulski would not be able to pursue the line of questioning as to what, if any, other lies Sam may have told during the previous trial.

"Is it true, Mr. Consiglio, that you are willing to testify to anything that you believe will help your case, regardless of whether it's true or not?" Przytulski asked.

"That's incorrect," Sam answered.

"Mr. Consiglio, did you want to talk to Patrick Harn on the 17th of July, 1991?"

"I would say no. Did I want to? The answer would be no. When I got there, the answer would be yes."

"So, you wanted to talk to him?"

"At the time that I was at that interview, yes, I wanted to talk to him."

"You were eager to speak to him?"

"Yes sir."

"Wild horses couldn't have kept you from talking to him at this time?" Przytulski asked.

Sam objected to the district attorney's question, telling Revak that he thought it was argumentative. Revak agreed, and again, sustained Sam's objection. Przytulski continued to question Sam about his wanting to talk to Harn about Karen's allegations that he (Sam) had raped her. Sam kept telling the court that had he known the district attorney had a warrant for his arrest, he would not have come in on his own and voluntarily submitted to a series of questions. When Przytulski completed his cross-examination, Sam asked to be heard on re-direct.

"I just wanted to point something out that is really important here, that is the letter to Wava Howley was sent following my conviction and I had just got sentenced to a total of 54 years in prison and I was upset. Take it for what it's worth."

"Do you want to argue or do you want to give evidence?" Revak asked.

"I want to give testimony to show how I felt. At this time, I would like to call P. J. Harn," Sam said.

P. J. Harn had been sitting in the courtroom during the entire morning proceeding. He had witnessed Sam's rhetoric as he tried desperately to demonstrate to Revak that his constitutional rights had been violated. Harn certainly had not expected to be called to the witness stand and be cross-examined by Sam.

"When I came to the interview on the 17th, did you have a warrant for my arrest at that time?" Sam asked.

"Yes," Harn responded.

"Did you advise me that you had that warrant?"

"Sam, I told you that you were in custody any time you talked to me or any law enforcement officer and you should consider that you were in custody anytime that you talked to me or any other law enforcement officer."

"Why did you not advise me that you had a warrant for my arrest on the afternoon of the 17th?"

"You were in custody the minute you started talking to me, Sam."

"Is it your practice not to advise people that you have a warrant for their arrest? Is that your normal practice?"

It was now Przytulski's turn to object. He argued that Sam had not demonstrated that the question was relevant. But Revak disagreed, once again, ruling in Sam's favor. Harn was instructed to answer the question.

"I asked you if on the 16th of July, if you had that warrant and you said no. Then I asked you on the 17th and you said that's when you had the warrant, the warrant you got on the 16th. So, when did you advise me that you had the warrant for my arrest?"

"On the 16th, Sam," Harn said.

"Did you ever advise me that you had a signed order from the judge ordering my arrest?"

"Yes," Harn said.

"When did you advise me of that?"

"The 17th."

"After the interview; isn't that correct, Mr. Harn?"

"Correct."

"Why did you wait until after the interview was concluded to advise me that you had the warrant? Why did you not advise me prior to the interview?"

"Well, prior to the interview, I looked at your jacket and you have an escape rap that is from Michigan. You were gone for two years before you were captured. It's in your nature to run, Sam, that's why I didn't tell you on the phone that morning because I knew you would run."

Sam asked Harn why he didn't tell him about the warrant after he had gone into the interview room with him and Mike Przytulski. Harn's answer was the same as it had been. He told Sam that he was in custody whenever he spoke to him or other law enforcement officers and that he chose to conduct the interview prior to informing him of the warrant.

When Sam had finished questioning Harn, he told Revak that he had no further evidence to present. Sam began his summation by telling Revak that, "had I known prior to going to that interview that he had a warrant for my arrest, I would not have been so cooperative and I don't believe I would be sitting here today. I still say it's a Fifth Amendment violation but everything I've found, says it's a Sixth Amendment not a Fifth Amendment.

"And in my opinion, your honor, he violated the law. They knew it all along. Mr. Harn testified that I was in custody and it was a custodial interrogation. It doesn't matter what he thinks it is. It matters what the defendant feels. And, at the time, I felt free to leave at any time." Sam apparently didn't know it, but by explaining that he felt free to leave at anytime, he had just defeated his own argument.

"Had Mr. Harn informed me of the warrant and that I was in custody and not free to leave, I would have either asked for counsel or I would not have spoken to him period. I only cooperated because I felt that I was going to go there, tell my side of the story, and go home. I didn't know I was going to stay. And based on that, your honor, I would ask that the interview be excluded from the trial, and all evidence that he confiscated that day should also be excluded."

Mike Przytulski argued that the people had not violated Sam's Fifth or Sixth Amendment rights. The courts had found that if a defendant was aware that a case had been filed against him, that in itself was enough and that Sam certainly knew that he had been arrested on a charge of rape.

Revak had heard both sides of Sam's motion. He had sat patiently while Sam, once again, played the role of attorney in his courtroom. This time, Sam had done an admirable job. After listening to both Sam and Przytulski, Revak told the two adversaries that he would render his decision the following Monday. With that, he adjourned court for the weekend.

On Monday, March 14, 1994, at 10:00 a.m., Revak greeted Przytulski, Al Arena, and Sam, as he opened court. He asked Sam if he had anything else he wished to present regarding his motion to have the statement he made to P. J. Harn suppressed.

"Yes, your honor," Sam said. "The thing that troubles me about it is, if I don't post bond, I stay in the county jail and I probably would have got arraigned. Instead, I got released on Saturday night. I probably would have got arraigned on Monday or Tuesday. So, I am being penalized because I posted bond and by posting bond, they put your arraignment off so you can't get an appointment with counsel. I was never formally arraigned, never formally charged.

"In short, your honor, they took advantage of me. I think of myself as being intelligent, but I was manipulated. As much as it hurts me to admit that, I was manipulated by the district attorney and his investigator."

Przytulski had the next word on the subject. "Your honor, when Mr. Consiglio came in he was Mirandized, I believe, four times. He was advised of his right to an attorney. He waived those rights and he chose to talk and then he was taken into custody. Mr. Harn told him a case had been filed against him. He waived his rights under Miranda, being advised of his right to counsel; understanding those rights, and waived them. Secondly, he was under arrest for this offense by Mr. Hicks and, subsequently, by Mr. Harn. So, I don't think there is any doubt that, certainly, the people have carried their burden, and the defendant was advised properly, and made knowing and intelligent waivers."

Revak didn't waste time rendering his decision. He told Sam that it was clear from his own testimony that he wanted to talk to the district attorney's office. "You knew that a citizen complaint had been made against you, namely, that you had raped somebody. It is clear to me that you wanted to talk to Mr. Harn when you went to the district attorney's office. He (Harn) has indicated the reason he didn't tell you on the telephone that he had a warrant for your re-arrest, was that he was concerned that you would flee the jurisdiction. And, it wasn't designed just to get you down to an interview. But, he wanted to talk to you, to hear your side of the story. And, I think you willingly, voluntarily went to the district attorney's office to give that interview. So, I'm going to deny the motion to suppress the interview between you and Mr. Harn. Right or wrong, that's my ruling."

The decision devastated Sam. He had convinced himself that the interview would be suppressed, forcing the district attorney to possibly dismiss the charges against him. Still, Sam had other issues he wanted the court to deal with, like, purchasing clothes for him to be worn during trial. Sam requested that the court purchase "adequate" clothing for him to wear while on trial and indicated he would need $300 for that purpose. However, he had yet to receive any clothes. But Revak was not about to authorize the purchase of a small wardrobe for Sam and ordered that the jail provide Sam with clothes they had in stock for that purpose. Revak did authorize the purchase of two dress shirts and two ties that Sam could wear during the course of the trial. The next issue Sam presented Revak with was his getting a haircut.

"Look at this," Sam said, as he ran his hand through his long, shaggy hair. "I've been trying to get this cut since December. The only time you are allowed to get a haircut is right now." Sam explained that the only time a prisoner could get a haircut was during "roof call" and that he had been in court during "roof call" the last couple of months. "I mean, it's like every two or three weeks you get roof. If the court was to order me to have a haircut, I will get a haircut right away."

Revak thought he had heard it all. And while he had indeed experienced most everything and every type of person a judge can encounter during his many years on the bench, he had rarely come across anyone like Sam. Sam was a defendant who was quickly demonstrating to everyone around him, that the judicial system could easily be manipulated to benefit the accused. Now, as it had so often, the system was proving that it was unprepared to deal with someone like Sam.

"Put it in the minute order that he is to have a haircut," Revak ordered, instructing the district attorney to see that Sam's hair was trimmed in time for trial.

Arena had sat patiently over the last several days as Sam made his motions to the court. While Sam had certainly demonstrated a limited knowledge of the law, and appeared to be at ease in the courtroom, Arena knew that Sam could not properly defend himself against someone like Mike Przytulski. Still, he continued to allow Sam to have his day in court since Sam insisted on arguing on his own behalf. Sam presented a variety of motions to the court including one to appoint a runner that he would have access to, and a motion for approval to contact several attorneys and psychologists, all necessary, he claimed, to aid him in preparing for his defense. Arena would meet with Sam each evening inside the jail to assist in that preparation.

Sam kept telling Arena that Karen had lied about him raping her and that she was a lesbian. What the two had in common, Sam did not explain. What Arena wanted most, was to talk to Karen. In fact, so did the district attorney. As the trial date approached, neither Arena nor Przytulski could locate Karen. Mike Przytulski had checked everywhere. What he didn't do, was check with Sam. From inside his jail cell, Sam had made a series of telephone calls, which lead him to information that Karen was living in Colorado Springs, Colorado. "I decided to go out there myself," Arena said. "I knew we had to find out all we could about Karen, so I flew to Colorado with our investigator, Mike Black."

Arena had little information to go on other than Sam's insistence that Karen had been living in the area and that she was a lesbian. Over the next several days, armed with that information and a photograph of Karen, Arena and Mike Black, who was a former deputy sheriff in Riverside, California, began canvassing bars catering to gays and lesbians, in hopes of finding witnesses that might contradict Karen's claims that she had been raped by Sam. It was tedious work, but Arena had the energy of a young child and the personality of a seasoned politician, both of which aided him in establishing an excellent rapport with the local bar patrons in Colorado Springs.

"We actually got to know some of the women very well," Arena said. "They were actually very friendly towards us." It took only two days before Al Arena found someone who knew Karen. He and Black had been to two bars before going to True Colors, a local nightspot in the Colorado Springs community. It was there that they met a woman who introduced them to Stacy Knutson, a friend of Karen's.

Stacy had lived in Colorado Springs for about two years. She worked in the hardware section of Design Laminates, a company that produces lamination surfaces for commercial fixtures, cabinets, and counter tops. Stacy told Arena that she knew Karen as Kasey and that she had met Kasey (Karen) about a year earlier when Karen had helped her get the job at Design Laminates. Stacy also told Arena that Karen had told her that she had to go back to San Diego to testify at a trial; that she had been raped on a boat while living in San Diego, and that she had sent a man to prison for doing that. Stacy also told Arena that Karen was perceived as a liar among people in the community. Arena was convinced his trip was a success, especially after Stacy agreed to come to San Diego and testify for the defense.

Arena was even more convinced, that if Sam had any chance of being acquitted, he would have to take over the defense of this case himself. He was determined to convince Sam to accept him as his attorney of record prior to trial. What convinced him most to take on the defense of this case, was the strong feeling that Sam was innocent.

On April 11, 1994, trial was set to begin in San Diego Superior Court in the case of the People versus Sam Consiglio. Sam and Arena appeared together as Revak opened the court. As soon as Revak asked if everyone was ready to begin, Sam indicated that he would like an "in camera" or private audience with his honor regarding his representing himself. Although Przytulski objected, Revak granted Sam's request and instructed the district attorney to leave the courtroom and to step out into the hallway.

"What I would like for this court to do is appoint Mr. Arena to take control of the case. But, I would like to be kept as co-counsel so that I can stay involved and assist him any way that he needs me. But I will defer to whatever he does. I mean he is the boss. He runs the show and I have complete confidence in him. The people cannot be prejudiced by me being co-counsel because, if anything, one who is co-counsel is, in effect, waiving his right to argue ineffective assistance of counsel. I can't raise that issue by being co-counsel. And, I don't have that problem with Mr. Arena. He is very competent. I'm certain he is going to do a remarkable job. I'm not concerned about ineffective assistance of counsel as I was previously. The only thing I have ever wanted for the past three years, your honor, is a fair trial. And, I think with this court and with Mr. Arena as my attorney, I'm going to get my fair trial." Sam had articulated his position exactly as he had been instructed to do by Arena. The argument had been rehearsed and finely tuned, resulting in a flawless presentation that, under different circumstances, might have actually brought Sam that Academy Award nomination he bragged about receiving regarding his courtroom antics.

"What do you perceive to be your privileges as co-counsel?" Revak asked. "What do you foresee as your participation in this case?"

Sam told judge Revak that nothing would change with regard to his pro per privileges. What he wanted to do, was to keep in constant contact with Arena during the course of the trial but let Arena conduct all of the cross-examination of the witnesses. "I really want to be thought of as a quiet co-counsel, your honor. I just want to assist my attorney. And while I'm at it, this is a sex case, your honor. It will be a very high profile case. Where I'm at right now, I'm very safe. I'm in a cell by myself. I want to remain there for my safety's concern. The jail will not remove me from there as long as I am co-counsel." The pattern was always the same, Sam begging for help but flouting the rules.

"Well, if that's your desire, that's fine with me, Mr. Consiglio. But I want you to understand that once that's done, henceforth, you are going to remain silent and Mr. Arena is going to do all the talking in this court-room," Revak told Sam.

"You have my word, your honor," Sam said. Revak was not totally convinced of anything that Sam said, especially if the statement involved the phrase, "you have my word". At that point, Revak called Przytulski back into the courtroom telling him that Arena would be the attorney of record and that Sam would act as "silent" co-counsel. When he did, Sam asked, "I want to know at what point do I shut up. Right now?"

Arena quickly stood up and told his co-counsel and client, "right now." Almost simultaneously, Revak said, "yes."

This was now Al Arena's show. Sam was delighted that a lawyer of Arena's reputation had been assigned to represent him. At least now, Sam felt like he had someone he could talk to; someone he could trust, and certainly someone who had the talent to have him acquitted. What Sam liked most of all was that Arena said he believed him when he said that he had not raped Karen.

As soon as Arena took over as lead attorney, he presented the court with a series of motions, all dealing with issues relating to the presentation of evidence during the upcoming trial. One motion sought to deny the district attorney from calling Sam's brother Louie to the stand to testify about Sam's phone calls to him, while another motion sought to have Karen fingerprinted in order to have her identity checked with the FBI. Judge Revak eventually denied both motions. The trial would be delayed eight days while Przytulski responded to all of the motions filed by his new adversary, who, just two years prior, had been one of his colleagues.

Chapter 22

Round 2; In the Arena with Arena

Those that live a false self to such an extent, will fight, to defend their own act and actually evolve to believe their own lies. The lies that they generate are usually full of emotions and exaggerations that they tend to pull in the unsuspecting.

Damian

On April 18, 1994, the state of California was ready to present evidence, for the second time in three years, that Sam Consiglio had raped Karen. Judge Revak was presiding. Sitting next to Sam and wearing a dark pinstripe suite that looked as if it had been tailored especially for him, was Al Arena. Across the aisle, were Mike Przytulski and P.J. Harn. As soon as Revak went on the record, informing both attorneys that it was time to select the jury, Przytulski stood and told the court that he had received an important phone call.

"Your honor, I received a phone call last Thursday from a woman, Sandra Delehanty, who, in 1991, was a intern counseling therapist out of San Diego State University. Mr. Consiglio was able to get counseling through a therapist during that time. He developed an acute fondness for Ms. Delehanty during those four months or so that she worked with him."

"In May of 1992, the defendant wrote a letter to Wava Howley where he relates a dream that he has about Sandra Delehanty and I will read into the record as it ties in to what I'm about to say. It's entitled The Dream:

'I'm not sure of the time frame but I knocked on the apartment door and Sandra opened it. She was startled to see me standing there holding a gun. I told her I wasn't there to hurt her but she said she was finding it hard to believe under the circumstances. I went into the apartment and let her into the bedroom. She was shaking very badly and this really bothered me. This is the worst part of my dream. So, please bear with me. I laid down on the bed with her and told her I was not going to rape her: I only wanted to hold her in my arms as long as I could. Her shaking took a long time to stop and I felt terrible. I kept assuring her that I only needed to hold her.

'I told her then that I decided to give up the rest of my life just as long as I would be able to hold her in my arms for just one night. I also told her that there would be no trial and that I planned to plead guilty. Probably out of pity, she started to relax. It was such a great feeling even in the dream to hold her close to me for what seemed like an eternity. It even appeared she was getting somewhat comfortable and even started to hold me tightly. When morning came, I got up and proceeded to leave. Before going out to turn myself in to the waiting SWAT team, she ran to me with outstretched arms right into my arms. It was a fitting end to the most beautiful dream I ever had.'

Przytulski told Revak that Delehanty claimed that another psychiatrist who had treated Sam had informed her after she had that he considered Sam to be a danger to her. Delehanty had taken great care to cover up her personal "transactions" moving to the East Coast and back to Arizona so that Sam would not be able to locate her. But Sam did locate her, and on April the 8th, from inside his jail cell, he called her at the Federal Prison in Arizona where she was working. Przytulski explained to judge Revak that Sandra did not accuse Sam of threatening her but that, because of his ongoing fantasies, she was terrified of him.

"Your honor, I'm going to object," Arena said. "I didn't object to this before because I didn't know where it was going. That's a very nice letter that Mr. Przytulski read. But if he wants to prosecute Mr. Consiglio based on his dreams, I would like to know that right now so we may do relevant research concerning that. At this point, what is the relevance of this besides character assassination by way of the bench prior to beginning of trial?"

"Your honor," Przytulski responded, "this court has allowed Mr. Consiglio virtually unlimited phone privileges, for several months now. I know that great efforts have been made to make him keenly aware of the unlawful or the unreasonable use of the phone." Przytulski tried to tell Revak that Sam had made other threatening phone calls to Karen Thompson and other witnesses. But again, Arena objected, telling Revak that there was no evidence that Sam had made those threatening calls and that Mike Przytulski's allegations were, "unfounded, unwarranted and unsubstantiated suspicions."

"Judge, he is abusing those privileges. I wish that you would reconsider. He is abusing that phone to a point where people are literally afraid of Mr. Consiglio. It's your decision. It's your call. But this is an intolerable situation. The public, the people out there, these victims, these witnesses, people that had contact with him, they have a right to expect (that) when a fellow is in jail, they are not going to be intimidated, threatened and coerced by him, directly or indirectly. Reconsider what the status and situation is here and take the appropriate steps," Przytulski pleaded.

"Your honor," Arena said, "the prosecution is bent out of shape because Mr. Consiglio has the phone. He is utilizing the phone in an appropriate manner for his defense. He has been most helpful in his defense in utilizing that phone. And, he has not abused that privilege period. Because he attempts to contact someone who never told him not to do so in the past, is not an abuse of the phone privilege."

Revak was curious to know how Sam had located Delehanty if she had left San Diego and gone to work in Arizona. Arena explained that it was not difficult to track someone down if they have a certain type of training or posses a particular area of expertise or if they work in a particular field.

"I'm just wondering, Mr. Arena, why Mr. Consiglio should not be similarly situated with other defendants who are facing trial?" Revak asked.

"Well, this judge," Arena said, reminding judge Revak that it was he, "who agreed he (Sam) could be co-counsel on this case. This court has made that determination."

"Well, I can't imagine what legitimate purpose some therapist who he saw after a conviction for this crime, would be relevant as a witness in this case. I'm going to let things slide temporarily and I'm going to think about this. If I hear anything about this telephone, I mean calling witnesses, defense witnesses, I don't mind that. But this woman has absolutely nothing to do with this case. But I want to warn you, if I hear anything about that telephone, I'm going to cancel his status. He is no more than any other individual who is facing trial and is held in custody. I think he's, quite frankly, abused many of these privileges," Revak said.

Once again, Sam avoided the loss of his pro-per privileges. And once again, the court, for reasons that are not totally clear, failed to impose sanctions; sanctions that would have prevented a prisoner from reaching out from inside the restraints of a jail cell to intimidate, harass, and frighten people who had either nothing to do with the pending trial or, who were prospective witnesses.

"We had a very interesting relationship," Arena said. "He would call me several times a day. It seemed like every time I tried to help him, he would pull some type of rear guard action on me creating a new obstacle for us."

With his decision made, Revak impaneled a jury of 14 people, seven men and seven women; two of which would serve as alternate jurors, to hear the case of Sam Consiglio charged with the rape of Karen.

The first witness called by the prosecution was Gloria Chase, who had been a receptionist at St. Vincent De Paul's shelter in July, 1991. Gloria testified that on the evening of July 2, 1991, sometime between 9:35 and 9:45 p.m., while riding the trolley home after work, she saw Karen standing at the Massachusetts Street stop looking dazed and holding her shoes in her hand. Chase told the court she was use to seeing Karen smiling most of the time but the look on Karen's face that evening was contrary to her normal demeanor. On cross-examination, Chase denied telling anyone at St. Vincent's, the following morning, that Karen had seemed fine when she saw her the night before. It was also Chase's testimony that when she saw Karen that night, her clothes did not appear to be wrinkled, ripped or disheveled.

Andre Kennedy, the next witness called by the prosecution, testified that he had known Karen for about two months, having met her at St. Vincent's where he, too, lived. He claimed they had dated several times and were very good friends but the friendship did not include a sexual relationship. Kennedy told the court that he escorted Karen to the Trolley stop at 12th and Imperial, three blocks from St. Vincent's, between 4:30 and 5:00 p.m., on the afternoon of July 2, 1991. Kennedy swore that Karen told him she was going to have dinner with her soon to be new boss. "She seemed excited, happy, and energetic; anxious actually," Kennedy said.

The next witness, Jackie Thomas, who had resided in the room next to Karen at St. Vincent's, in July, 1991, testified that she loaned Karen a black and white jump suit to wear on a job interview with a man named Sam Consiglio. "She was very upbeat because she had smaller jobs in the past that didn't amount to a whole lot. She seemed very exuberant, very excited. She was very pleased to have something nice to wear," Thomas said.

Thomas also testified that later that night, after Karen had showered, she (Karen) invited her out onto the balcony for a cigarette. While they were on the balcony, Karen broke down and started crying. Thomas told the court that Karen told her Sam Consiglio had raped her.

Belkis Bottfeld, who had been a counselor and an instructor in the lifestyles program at St. Vincent's, was the next witness called by the prosecution. As soon as Przytulski called Bottfeld to the stand, Arena stood and asked to approach the bench. With Przytulski by his side, Arena, in a soft low voice so that the jury could not hear, told Revak, "Your honor, as background, she has some type of degree in counseling. She was either a junior psychologist or wannabe. Or, she has some kind of master's degree. At the first trial, she testified under examination by Mr. Przytulski that, in her opinion, a rape had occurred based on her examination of Karen. We would ask the court to admonish Mr. Przytulski to refrain from that line of questioning. I think it's not admissible." Revak agreed and instructed the aistrict attorney to refrain from asking that type of question.

Bottfeld testified that she had first met Karen sometime in the middle part of June 1991, after being assigned to her as a counselor. Bottfeld told the court that she had a counseling session scheduled with Karen at 9:30 on the morning of July 3, 1991. "It did not turn out to be the session I had expected. I found out from her case manager earlier that morning that she had been raped the night before and so she was evidently traumatized. And, that's the state I fond her in when I saw her that morning."

"Describe to the jury those observations that you made that would support that state that you just referred to?" Przytulski instructed his witness.

"She wouldn't talk. She was very quiet. She couldn't talk. She was obviously in a state of shock. It seemed obvious to me she had gone through some kind of trauma because she…"

Arena jumped up from his seat not allowing Bottfeld to finisher her statement. "I'm going to object as to the statement she obviously went through some type of trauma as calling for a conclusion," Arena said. "I believe she can testify to her observations but not offer a conclusion at this point."

Again, Revak agreed with Arena and instructed the jury to disregard Bottfeld's statement.

When Przytulski resumed his questioning of Bottfeld, he asked, "Was her attitude or demeanor consistent with being traumatized?"

"Yes. It was in my estimation," Bottfeld answered.

On cross-examination, Bottfeld refused to answer Arena's question as to why Karen needed therapy in the first place, citing therapist confidentiality. Arena politely said he understood her response and asked for another sidebar conference with Revak. This time, Revak allowed the jury to take a short recess, suspecting exactly what Arena's argument was going to be.

"Your honor," Arena began, his voice no longer in a whisper now that the jury had been allowed to leave the courtroom, "the prosecution has opened the door. They have basically indicated that she (Karen) was in counseling, and in need of a therapist. Mr. Przytulski has taken great pains to describe to this jury, a woman that was traumatized. I think that the defense should have a right to go into that counseling to ascertain whether in fact it could have been other reasons for her acting in the manner in which she was acting."

Przytulski argued that Bottfeld was correct in claiming the privilege and told the court that his witness had never revealed what that privileged material was. "We did not breach any confidentiality material or open the door because that strictly isn't accurate. The fact that she was in counseling and had a counselor is accurate. That does not open the door to what the patient/client privilege is," Przytulski contested.

"Ms. Bottfeld testified that in her opinion, this girl was traumatized," Arena countered. "Now, she also is of the opinion that this girl was involved in counseling sessions and was in need of a therapist obviously prior to something that purportedly happened on July 2nd. We have a right to go into that; perhaps present to the jury the alternative explanation for her being traumatized. She could have been a time bomb waiting to explode. The littlest thing could have set her off. I can assure the court, Mr. Przytulski is going to be arguing that this witness, Ms. Bottfeld, a trained therapist, is telling you ladies and gentlemen, that she was traumatized. This is a trained person telling you this. Well, that prohibits and handcuffs the defense from offering an alternative explanation, especially when it's coming from this type of witness."

"Judge," Przytulski pleaded, "this witness was not called as a therapist, only a person who happened to be a therapist who witnessed an event."

Again, Revak had heard enough. He told the district attorney that Arena had made a stronger argument and would instruct the jury to strike Bottfeld's testimony. "What she is telling this jury is, Mr. Consiglio raped that woman the night before," Revak said. "And, the defense does not have an opportunity to try to show that this is a pre-existing condition and maybe it was just the straw that broke the camel's back and she went over the edge and made up this allegation, which they have a right to show. I'm not saying it's true and I'm not saying she wasn't raped. But the impression is that you've got a professional witness who is now in effect becoming an advocate for Karen. But the defense can't adequately cross-examine to show that maybe there is something else that was there in the makeup of Karen that caused her to point the finger at Mr. Consiglio and maybe outwardly manifest this maybe psychological problem."

Przytulski was shocked. He certainly wasn't prepared to journey into an area opening up Karen's past revealing problems which may have contributed to her "traumatized" appearance. Rather than breach the counselor/client privilege, Przytulski agreed to have Revak strike Bottfeld's testimony.

After the jury returned to the courtroom, Revak instructed them to disregard Bottfeld's testimony about her observations of July the 3rd of 1991. "You are to totally disregard it. Treat it as though you had never heard that testimony," he told them.

Arena then continued his cross-examination of Bottfeld. He only had a few questions focusing on whether or not she had seen Karen between 4:00 p.m. and 4:30 p.m. on July 2, 1991. Bottfeld testified that to the best of her recollection, she had, indeed, seen Karen during that time frame. After completing his brief cross-examination, Arena asked for another side bar conference with the court. "For the record, your honor, I am requesting a mistrial at this time. I feel that the information offered by Ms. Bottfeld, although the court has admonished the jury to disregard it, is of such prejudicial nature that the only thing they are going to basically remember is that this woman was traumatized because of the rape. Although they have been told to disregard it, they know she was in therapy for other things but that this counselor apparently did not attribute her trauma to those particular problems. I feel that it's damaging. It's prejudicial and it cannot be rehabilitated."

Revak told Arena and Przytulski that he would consider the motion for mistrial. But first, he wanted to ask the jurors if any of them would have a problem with disregarding Ms. Bottfeld's testimony. If any of them did, he would dismiss them. When none of the jurors indicated that would be a problem for them, Revak instructed Przytulski to call his next witness. The motion for mistrial was denied.

The next witness, Robert Knott, testified that in July 1991, Sam had told him that he owned several pieces of property in the San Diego area, and was looking for a woman, preferably between the ages of 18 and 35, to work as a residential manager and do light accounting and bookwork. Knott told the court that he put Karen in contact with Sam for that purpose.

During cross-examination, Arena asked about the initial intake forms applicants such as Karen would complete or have completed upon making an application for shelter at St. Vincent's. Knott explained what was referred to as the "Homeless Employment Linkage Program Registration Form" which is the initial registration form that a person completes when they enter the federally funded "Help" program for homeless and unemployed people. Arena had the form identified as defense exhibit A and asked Knott to examine it.

"And what basically does the registration form do?" Arena asked.

"It just gives some general demographics; what the client had previously done, what kind of employment history was indicated, previous income sources, how long the person had been homeless, et cetera," Knott explained.

Arena had set the stage for his cross-examination of Karen regarding the information she had provided to St. Vincent's when she completed her application for entry into the Help program. It was then that Revak decided to adjourn for the day.

Prior to the jury being seated when court resumed on Thursday, Przytulski told Revak that his office and P. J. Harn had done everything possible to locate Rosalind Bell, Karen's former roommate at St. Vincent's. After a prolonged and extensive search, Rosalind Bell was nowhere to be found. Her testimony, however, was critical to the prosecution. So, Przytulski offered to have Bell's former testimony read into the record. Arena objected, arguing that the reason they were trying this case again was because of the incompetency of counsel. According to Arena, questions posed to Rosalind Bell during the first trial should have been objected to, and, now, by reading her prior testimony into the record, Sam lost his right to effective cross-examination. Revak listened as both attorneys debated the merits of reading Bell's former testimony into the record. When he had heard enough, Revak agreed to the testimony being read into the record.

Rosalind Bell testified in October 1991, that she was Karen's roommate at St Vincent De Paul's the night of July 2, 1991. That night, sometime after dark, she received a telephone call from a man identifying himself as Sam Consiglio. Sam had indicated that he was looking for Karen and wanted to know if she had made it home yet. When Bell told him no, Sam said that he was at his hotel room and that it was necessary for her to call him when she got in. Bell also testified that Sam sounded agitated and anxious. After Karen had returned home, she appeared distraught. Around midnight, Karen allegedly told Bell that she had been raped. "After that, she just started crying and bent over, sobbing."

"Did she ever have a name?' Przytulski had asked in 1991.

"Yes," Bell had answered. But Mike Przytulski could not have that name, which was Sam Consiglio, read into record. Revak had limited Bell's former testimony to that point. When the reading was completed, Przytulski called Karen to the witness stand.

Karen testified that after the July 2nd meeting in Carlsbad where Sam had tried to get a job managing an apartment complex, they had stopped briefly at a restaurant to talk about the interview. "He was really mad because he felt like he blew it," Karen said. Karen told the court that Sam drove her back to St. Vincent's and asked Bob Knott for a tour of the facility. While there, Sam used the pay phone in the lobby to make a telephone call. "While he was on the phone talking, he asked me if I liked spaghetti. I said yes, and he asked me if I wanted to come over for dinner that night. At first, I said no, but he told me that he wanted me to look at an apartment complex in El Cajon. So I said yes. He said he had some errands to run and I offered to meet him up at 32nd and Imperial where the trolley stops so that he wouldn't have to come back to St. Vincent's," Karen said.

Karen testified that she met Sam sometime between 4:30 p.m. and 5:00 p.m. and that the two of them drove to El Cajon. On the way, Sam stopped to use a pay phone. After making the call, they drove to an apartment complex but they didn't speak to anyone, nor did they go inside any of the units. "He said this place needed too much work and that he had a lot of changes to make," Karen whispered, her voice growing softer as she asked Revak for a drink of water. Karen began to weep.

Drying the tears from her eyes, Karen told the court that after leaving the apartment complex, Sam drove to a side street and made a phone call. Afterwards, they got into Sam's car and drove a short distance when Sam told her that he needed to make yet another phone call. After driving a couple of more blocks, Sam drove into a park, claiming that he had to make still another call.

Karen told Przytulski and the jury that Sam disappeared around a building in the park and was gone for several minutes. While Sam had gone to make his phone call, she got out of the car to stretch her legs. It was a few moments later when she saw Sam return. "He walked up on my side of the car and grabbed me by the throat. He pushed me against the hood of the car. He told me not to scream and said he didn't want to hurt me. Then he told me to take my clothes off. He leaned me back against the hood of the car and put his penis inside of me," Karen said.

"How many times did his penis actually fall out of your vagina and he re-penetrate?" Przytulski asked.

"Three times that I remember," Karen answered. "Afterwards, he told me to put my clothes back on and he took me to the trolley stop in El Cajon. He told me not to tell anyone, that he knew where I lived."

"Karen, are you a lesbian?" Przytulski asked.

"Yes," Karen said.

"Are you also bisexual? Have you had sex with men?"

"Yes."

Karen continued with her testimony telling the court that after she arrived back at St. Vincent's, she went directly to her room and took a shower and that she douched. "I felt filthy. I wanted to get him off of me." After showering, Karen was told that her boss had called and that she was to call him right away. "I called him and he wanted to know where I had been and why it took me so long to get home. He wanted to know if I had said anything to anybody and I told him no. Then he offered me a job at the El Cajon apartment complex. He said it would only be one bedroom and a hundred dollars a month and that I would have to stay with him. But, that would be better than my staying at St. Vincent's."

Karen also testified that nine days after being raped, she noticed an outbreak of blisters in the area of her vagina. Karen claimed that she had never had such an outbreak before and after being examined by a doctor at Sharp Hospital in San Diego, she was told that she had herpes. Przytulski then showed a photograph of a white jump suit to Karen and asked her if she recognized the jump suit as the one she wore the night she was raped. Karen said that it was.

After the lunch recess, Przytulski told Revak that he had several motions relating to Arena's proposed cross-examination of Karen. Revak ordered all of the witnesses excluded from the courtroom while the district attorney made his presentation.

Przytulski told Revak that there were certain areas of cross-examination that he considered irrelevant and should not be inquired into. Those issues involved Karen's alleged false employment applications and her history of drug use. But Arena had a different opinion and considered both issues relevant to Karen's credibility.

"Your honor, credibility is always relevant," Arena argued. "Karen filled out an application on or about the time that she indicates this purported rape had occurred. The information that she filled out was false. She lied. Sort of almost like the same thing that Mr. Przytulski is trying to do with (Sam's) resume.

"Now, concerning her drug use, again, it has come to my attention during the late part of this trial, that Karen was doing drugs on or about the time that she was traveling to San Diego. Mr. Przytulski told me that when she was in Houston and the Seattle area and Las Vegas area, that she was ingesting illegal narcotics. That was two months before the alleged rape. And, she told Mr. Consiglio's last counsel, that she had a fourteen year met amphetamine habit. I always find myself forced to divulge trial strategy, but I have no other choice given the offers by Mr. Przytulski. I'm of the opinion, that if she went to 30th and Imperial, she went there to buy drugs. 30th and Imperial is well known by just about everyone who uses illegal narcotics in the San Diego area that it's a place where you can readily find drugs. Because of her insatiable appetite derived from 13 or 14 years of drug use, she went somewhere and consumed those drugs. That would explain the blank stare on her face, the nervousness, and the agitation. She had consumed drugs."

"Now, if we can't go into that particular area, which I believe is relevant to prove the defense position, then we can't put forth the defense position while Mr. Przytulski gets to argue this is a nice person who had never done anything wrong in her life. That certainly doesn't give the jury the right to gauge her credibility."

Revak told both attorneys that he thought it was relevant what Karen was doing on the day of the incident, but it was not relevant what she had done 10 and 15 years before the incident. Arena couldn't believe what he was hearing. Revak was tying his hands, not in front, but behind his back. And while some suggest that Arena has a knack for the dramatic, he is basically just an Italian. He raises his voice when in full rhetorical battle and gestures with intense enthusiasm. He prides himself on being able to argue either side of an issue, often quoting the phrase that he can whistle Dixie or sing the Battle Hymn of the Republic with equal enthusiasm. And no one present thought he lacked enthusiasm as he continued with his argument.

"Judge, what Mr. Przytulski has failed to tell you, is that she told Mr. Harn that she stopped using drugs in 1988 and she said she stopped using drugs in 1988 in that first trial. Now we come to find out that she lied to P. J. Harn about that. So, she gave false information to an investigating officer relative to this case. That goes right to her credibility. We are indicating that she has given additional false information to this investigating officer, that being the rape allegation against Mr. Consiglio," Arena pleaded.

"Well, the fact that she gave false information to P. J. Harn about her drug usage, does that in itself tell you that because she lied she must have been taking drugs at about the time of this alleged incident?" Revak asked.

"How about the fact that she lied, period," Arena said, answering judge Revak's question with a question of his own.

"What does that have to do with this case?" Revak responded. "I mean, you can put on reputation evidence of Karen, she is a liar. Everybody lies. But what are you proving? You don't bridge the gap. Because she lied to P. J. Harn about drug usage, she is lying to this jury about being raped?"

Revak rejected Arena's argument. The defense would not be allowed to question Karen about her past drug use, nor could they question her about the fact that she falsified her application for admission to St. Vincent's. "Because she lied to St. Vincent De Paul to get shelter doesn't mean she is a liar before this jury when she claimed she was raped. Do it right. You can call character witnesses. You can put on what she told P. J. Harn that is inconsistent with her testimony," Revak told Arena. Revak had indeed heard enough. He ordered the jury brought back into the courtroom and for trial to resume.

Arena, who had come to do battle, had argued for almost thirty minutes, virtually to no avail. He would now try and question Karen under what he considered harsh restrictions imposed upon him by the court.

"Prior to coming to San Diego in 1991, had you ever used illegal controlled substances?" Arena asked.

"Yes," Karen said.

"What was your relationship with Barry Vance?"

"Friend," Karen answered.

"Do you remember ever indicating to St. Vincent De Paul that he was your brother?"

"Yes."

"But he really wasn't was he?"

"No."

"Did you ever tell them (St. Vincent's) that you had been working for Mission Bay Cabinets?"

"Yes."

"But that was a lie, correct?"

"No."

"Were you working for Mission Bay Cabinets?"

"Yes."

"Where was Mission Bay Cabinets located? Do you remember?"

Karen said she never went to the shop, explaining that she worked at MacDonalds Shipyard doing refurbishing for a man named Roger Sullivan. Karen told Arena that she would work three or four days a week for anywhere between six to ten hours a day.

Most of Arena's questions centered on Karen's alleged employment with Roger Sullivan, how she met Sam, and how she felt about becoming a bookkeeper. Then, Arena asked Karen about having had a cast on her foot the first time she met Sam.

"I had sprained my ankle playing volleyball," Karen said. It was then, that Revak adjourned court for the day.

When court resumed on Friday, April 22, Arena resumed his argument to expand the scope of his cross-examination of Karen. "Judge, I know that you limited my access to certain parts of Karen's history, but she has testified to something we believe is untrue. She said she left Seattle in 1988. We believe she left in 1990. She told P. J. Harn that she stopped consuming narcotics in 1988. We have come to learn that was a lie. I mean, it's all relative to her credibility. Everything is. She lied about the drug use. We think she went to 30th and Imperial to buy drugs."

Revak told Arena that he could ask Karen about her drug usage at the time of the alleged rape and if she did indeed go to 30th and Imperial to buy drugs. Arena told Revak that it was an act of futility because Karen would deny using drugs during that time.

"See the problem is, the way you want to prove she is lying is you want to bring in all these extraneous things and say, therefore ladies and gentlemen, she must have been at 30th and Imperial to buy drugs. If she was at 30th and Imperial to buy drugs, she made up this story about Mr. Consiglio raping her. The two don't connect. I don't see the logical connection," Revak said.

"It's not a question of connection," Arena argued. "It has to do with credibility."

Revak had lost his patience. "It's always an issue. You don't have to remind me of that, Mr. Arena," Revak said as he began a stern lecture on the law. "I have been doing this for 30 years. I understand the issue of credibility. But there are certain ways you can do it and there are certain ways that you can't do it. You can't just attack a person and assassinate a person's character. You can present evidence through witnesses that she is a pathological liar as far as I am concerned. That is her reputation. That's their opinion of her. You may do that," Revak said. The court's position on the subject was clear. Judge Revak was not going to change his mind.

Due to scheduling conflicts, the prosecution called Dr. Lawrence W. Schenden to the stand before Arena continued his cross-examination of Karen. Schenden had graduated from the University of Notre Dame and gone on to finish medical school at the University of Michigan. In July 1991, he had been a doctor for just over four years when he examined Karen at Mercy Hospital in San Diego. Schenden, relying on information contained in a medical report that he had signed, testified that he diagnosed Karen as having genital herpes. He based his conclusion after finding of a vesicular lesion in the area of her perineum, which is between a woman's vagina and her rectum. When Dr. Schenden was excused, Karen took her place back on the witness stand.

For almost an hour, Al Arena questioned Karen about how she had met Sam. He asked how the two of them went on the job interview, how she went about borrowing the dress to wear, what type of shoes she had on, how she had hurt her foot. He asked nothing that she had not already testified to. Then, Arena began to question her about the alleged assault. Again, Karen answered each question as to how Sam approached her, grabbed her by the neck and pushed her back against the car, told her that he didn't want to hurt her, and ordered her to take off her clothes.

"Now, you told us then at that point, that Mr. Consiglio had dropped his pants. Do you remember that happening?" Arena asked.

"I don't know what he did," Karen answered.

"Okay. You told us that you remember at least three times that Mr. Consiglio had removed himself and then placed his penis back in your vagina again. Was there any time that you say you felt Mr. Consiglio not pressing his body against you? Having not done so during the course of this assault?"

"I don't remember a lot of the assault."

"Could you be mistaken then about the amount of times that you say that Mr. Consiglio exited and re-entered?"

"I remember the pain," Karen said, not answering the question.

"You really don't remember then if, in fact, it could have happened or he could have removed his body from you and then put his body back on you?"

Przytulski objected, claiming the question was ambiguous. Revak agreed.

Arena then shifted the focus of his cross-examination, asking Karen about how she got to the trolley station, what trolley she took, and what time she arrived back at St. Vincent's. Still trying to demonstrate to the court and the jury that Karen lied more often than she told the truth, Arena asked about her ankle injury, an injury she had testified she received playing volleyball. He showed her a copy of a medical report where Karen had allegedly told people at Mercy Hospital that she had injured herself after falling twenty feet down a cliff. But Karen claimed that she could not recall what she told the people at the hospital at the time of her injury.

Revak ordered Arena to show him what he had just presented to Karen. Both attorneys approached the bench and whispered so that the jury could not hear.

Arena explained that he had shown Karen a medical report taken at the time of the injury, which indicated she was unemployed at the time. "We don't believe she was working the amount of hours that she said she was working at the time. The other thing, those records indicate patient history; 30-year-old patient states that she fell down a cliff. She fell 20 feet down a cliff and that's how she injured her ankle.

"The significance behind that, is that in fact, she was examined by a doctor on July 3rd and noted that she had certain bruises and she felt sore in certain spots. That could be a result of a fall down a cliff. The residual effects of falling down a cliff." Revak agreed to allow Arena to pursue his line of questioning.

"Do you remember telling them on June 21st of 1991 when you had that soft cast put on, telling the hospital that you were unemployed?"

"Yes. That's what the record shows," Karen answered.

"Had you ever been tested for herpes before this July 11, 1991 date?"

"Not specifically for herpes. No."

"Do you remember testing for herpes in 1983?"

"I remember having venereal tests run on me in 1983 which would include herpes."

"Karen, I need to ask a few questions of a personal nature because of the allegation of the herpes. The court needs to know, we need to know, exactly how many sexual partners that you have had prior to July of 1991. Do you remember?"

Przytulski interrupted Arena's question. "Your honor, is that male and female?"

"Both," Arena answered.

"Seven," Karen said.

"I believe you were married at one time?" Arena asked.

"No." Karen said.

"Now, in 1993 you were working at Design Laminates. Do you remember telling people that you had to go to San Diego to testify at a rape trial?"

"Yes. I told my boss, Bunny."

"Do you remember having a conversation with a person by the name of Del La Bre? Do you know who that person is?"

"No," Karen said.

"Do you remember telling Del La Bre that you were coming to San Diego to testify at a rape trial? That you were working on a boat doing cabinetry work and that you had to go back to finish some work, and when you got there, your boss raped you on the boat? Do you remember telling Del that?"

"I don't know Del. So, how can I tell someone something like that when I don't know that person?"

Arena tried momentarily to get Karen to admit knowing Del La Bre but she insisted that she had never met her. He would call Del to the witness stand later. For now, he had no further questions of Karen.

Przytulski knew that on his redirect examination, he had to minimize whatever damage Al Arena had inflicted on Karen's credibility.

"Karen, when you came to San Diego in May of 1991, you came with Barry and Virginia Vance; is that correct?" Przytulski asked on his redirect.

Karen testified she had indeed arrived in San Diego with Barry and Virginia and that they had fabricated a story indicating that Barry was her brother hoping that would help all of them obtain shelter at St. Vincent's. Karen also told Przytulski that Roger Sullivan did not rape her; Sam Consiglio did. Karen said she made up the name of Lyle Vance, indicating he was her former husband and that he had abused her while living in Seattle. This was all done, Karen said, for the purpose of gaining entry into St. Vincent's and having a roof over her head.

Przytulski then called Wava Howley to the witness stand. Before Przytulski could question his witness, Arena had some issues he wanted addressed prior to Howley testifying, especially about the letters Sam had written to her.

"I don't want that letter coming out because I don't think this jury needs to know there was a previous trial," Arena argued.

"Judge that's what needs to be addressed because the relevance at this point in time is in Mr. Consiglio's own handwriting. He says that he lied at the previous trial. I think the court remembers the content of that, which goes towards a consciousness of guilt," Przytulski told Revak.

Al Arena argued that by having Howley testify to the letter Sam had written her, the jury would learn about the previous trial and use that as a catalyst to finding him guilty.

Revak offered to admonish the jury but Arena argued that, "Admonishments are like trying to undo the gun blast that just went off next to somebody's ear; telling them all your eardrums are about to be destroyed. Just regard that it didn't really happen. They hear it. Once they hear it, the damage is done."

Revak agreed with Arena's argument. "It almost requires this jury to know what he testified to at the other trial. I understand the argument of consciousness of guilt. I agree with you. I'm going to allow the part about Karen, the telephone call and I'm going to reserve the rest of it." With Revak's decision made, Przytulski called Wava Howley to the witness stand.

Wava testified that Sam had telephoned her prior to October, 1991 and told her that he had taken Karen to his apartment in Clairemont the day she said he had raped her, but that she did not go inside with him. While on the witness stand, Howley told the court that Sam had told her about having invited Karen to dinner the night of the alleged rape, but that Karen had never showed up. "He said he called the shelter to see why she hadn't come to meet him; that they were supposed to have spaghetti together later that evening," Wava said. Wava also testified that Sam had written her a letter claiming to have lied about talking to Karen that night.

When Howley finished testifying, Przytulski had Sam's previous testimony given at a preliminary hearing on July 31, 1991 read into the court record. The jury heard the transcript being read and Sam's testimony claiming that he had not spoken to Karen the night of July 2, 1991. After Sam's previous testimony was read, Revak adjourned court for the day.

When trial resumed, the first witness called to the stand was Dr. Dwight Lemon. Lemon testified that he was a physician at Sharp Cabrillo Emergency Room in Point Loma on July 3, 1991, and that he examined Karen in connection with an alleged rape.

"Now, did you find anything inconsistent with her being raped during your vaginal inspection?" Przytulski asked.

"No," Dr. Lemon reported.

"Now, Doctor, let's assume for a second that a man ejaculates into a vagina, there would be semen present; is that correct?"

"Yes."

"If a woman showers and douches, what happens to that sperm and semen?"

"A shower would have no effect. A douching would have the effect of washing out semen and sperm from the vagina."

"Is it common for women, based on your experience to douche after being raped?"

"Yes. In my experience, approximately half of the women shower and/or douche before submitting for an examination."

During Lemon's testimony, he constantly referred to his notes made at the time he examined Karen.

On cross-examination, Arena asked, "I noticed in the entire inspection that you did involving Karen, that there was no indication of any visible bruising; is that correct?"

"That's correct," Lemon said, again, referring to his notes.

Arena was able to demonstrate that Lemon did not observe any bruising or see anything visible on Karen that supported her allegation of being raped. "In this particular instance, she says she's tender in certain areas, although you cannot visibly verify it, you accept her word for it. You don't know if someone was lying to you under the circumstances like that, would you?"

"No," Lemon said.

"You did indicate, however, that the patient, Karen, complained of tenderness to the back of the neck?"

"Correct."

"Would those injuries be the type of injury that could have come about by, say, someone rolling 20 feet down a cliff or something? Would that be consistent with that type of happenstance?"

"I would say yes. I would expect other additional complaints. If those were the only complaints, I would be surprised."

"Now, you indicated on direct examination, that the report was not inconsistent with the person being raped. Are you stating that because of the history that was given by Karen?"

"Yes. I'm tender in this area, anything that would have indicated otherwise. Her examination was a typical rape exam. There were minor to zero findings. All you have is the story to deal with and the findings of the tenderness we spoke about already. But the hard, direct evidence of sexual assault is rarely found."

"You didn't see any in this particular case, did you?" Arena asked.

"I didn't see any visual evidence, hard evidence of definite sexual assault."

Arena thanked the witness for his testimony and sat down next to Sam who sat at the defense table trying hard not to look like the cat that just ate the canary. Przytulski tried hard not to look like the canary being chased by the cat as he stood and walked to the podium, hoping to neutralize Arena's cross-examination of the prosecution's witness.

"Doctor, would it be fair to say that in many of your rape examinations, there is no tearing in the vaginal area?" Przytulski asked.

"I would guess less than 10% of the women I examine have had hard evidence of sexual assault and wherever they were allegedly, you know, penetrated."

Przytulski thanked the witness and called Louie Consiglio, Sam's brother, to the witness stand. Arena quickly asked for another bench conference. Whispering so the jurors couldn't hear, Arena argued that the testimony of Louie Consiglio was not relevant to the current proceedings, and that the conversation, to which he would testify, took place two years after the alleged attack. Arena requested a hearing to establish the relevancy of Louie's testimony. But first, he asked Revak for a short recess. "I have to use the facilities," Arena said.

But Revak wanted to continue before taking a recess. "I have to use the facilities sometime soon, judge," Arena pleaded. Przytulski wanted to have P. J. Harn read another portion of Sam's testimony from his preliminary hearing into the record prior to Louie testifying. "How long will it take?" Revak asked.

"About 20 minutes," Przytulski said.

"Can you wait that long?" Revak asked Arena.

"Yeah," Arena said. "If my eyes start to water, it's not because I'm bored."

After reading another portion of Sam's testimony from his preliminary hearing, Przytulski called Louie Consiglio to the witness stand. Once again, the jury was escorted from the courtroom while Arena and Przytulski argued what the witness would be allowed to testify to. Arena's concern, other than the relevancy of Louie's testimony, was that nothing be introduced during his testimony that would indicate Sam had been in prison. Arena also argued that Louie had made an illegal intercept of the conversation with his brother Sam and that the entire taped recording should be suppressed. Revak disagreed. He would allow portions of the taped calls to be read into the court record but would not allow any testimony that would indicate Sam had been in prison.

Again, the jurors were brought back into the courtroom while Louie Consiglio took the witness stand. Przytulski asked his witness to begin reading from the transcript made of the telephone calls between he and his brother Sam.

Sam: *"When I was talking to the church secretary, I was telling her that I needed a girl because they won't hire people unless you're a couple. So the lady said, go to the shelter. My first thought, to be honest with you, was that's a good idea. Find yourself, pick some strange piece of ass and get some strange pussy all the time. That was my first thought."*

Louie: *"So already, you were thinking of it."*

Sam: *"At first, yeah. But on the way there I thought, no, I need this fucking job. I can't fucking wait. I'm just going to pick her up and take her to the apartment house where we are going to try and get the job."*

"Now, from 1980 to 1991, Mr. Consiglio, were you aware that your brother was in the state of Michigan for approximately eight of those years?" Przytulski asked.

"Yes," Louie answered.

"Were you aware that he was not employed in the property management business for those eight years?"

"That's right. I am certain of that."

Przytulski had limited Louie's testimony to two critical issues. Louie had introduced Sam's state of mind prior to meeting with Karen at St. Vincent's and, without revealing that his brother had been in prison during those eight years in Michigan, demonstrated that Sam had lied on his resume.

On cross-examination, Arena asked, "During this phone conversation you had with your brother, would it be a correct statement that there was some animosity between the both of you at that time?"

Louie admitted that there was in fact animosity between he and Sam but that all he wanted his brother to do was tell the truth.

"And you were aware that your brother, at the time that you had this conversation, had certain feelings for a particular person, correct?"

"That is correct."

"And I believe you indicated that if your brother didn't tell you the truth, that you were going to hop on a plane and go see that person, correct?" Arena was alluding to Karron Thompson. Louie had threatened Sam with going to Texas and seeing Karron himself in an effort to disrupt his brother's relationship with her, if Sam did not tell him the truth about assaulting Karen.

"That is correct," Louie said.

"Your brother said, I can't do that Lou. I can't lie to you. I just didn't do this. Is that correct?"

"That is correct."

"And you said to him, if you don't tell me, I'm going to go and see that person or hop on a plane and see that person, that girl that he liked. And notwithstanding such indication, Mr. Consiglio, your brother still told you, he didn't do it. Is that correct?"

"That is correct," Louie said.

Louie did go to Texas after talking with Sam and met with Karron Thompson. He felt he had an obligation to tell her about his brother Sam before he victimized her any further.

"He invited me to his hotel room," Karron said later. But Karron refused Louie's offer. She suspected that he wanted the same thing his brother Sam had wanted. Regardless of Louie's intentions, Karron Thompson wanted nothing to do with the Consiglios.

When trial resumed the next day, Przytulski called Dr. Michael N. Oxman, a professor of medicine pathology at the University of California

San Diego and Infectious Diseases, to the witness stand. Dr. Oxman explained that herpes was the lay term for herpes simplex virus.

"Genital herpes is an infection caused by herpes simplex virus when it is inoculated into the skin or mucous membranes in the genital area. Characteristically, 75 - 80% of those initial infections cause so little trouble that we don't recognize them. But even if we don't recognize them very early on, the virus from the skin or the mucous membranes enters the ends of the sensory nerves and travels up to the nerve body in the sensory ganglii and goes to sleep. These diseases then are in the nerve cell for the rest of our life. Periodically, it wakes up, comes back down the nose and gets back into the skin or the mucousmembranes in the genital area," Oxman said.

"If a person makes a visit to a doctor after not going to a doctor before for herpes, would that be an indication that this is their first outbreak or at least they believe that was their first outbreak?" Przytulski asked.

"A lot of people who come to physicians with genital herpes, believe it's their first outbreak, and in fact, it is often their first recognized outbreak, although a lot of the time, probably most of the time, it's not their first exposure to the virus."

"Their first exposure happens sometime earlier, perhaps years earlier, without symptoms or without recognized symptoms. The virus has been latent. And most people, when this happens, of course, think they have just gotten infected when in fact, they were infected perhaps years ago," Oxman testified.

"Would you tell the jury what the incubation period is for herpes virus to be transmitted?" Przytulski asked.

"That's a period between when the encounter; personal contact, occurs which gives you the virus and when you're going to have a symptom. It can vary from as short a period as one day to as long an interval of 20 days. But most of the time it's in the range of three to seven days after the encounter."

"You indicated that herpes virus does relatively little harm physically?" Arena asked on cross-examination.

"I indicated that in most people, most of the time, the infection is silent; it's not recognized."

"If Mr. Consiglio had herpes type one and Karen was determined to have herpes type two, could Mr. Consiglio have given her the infection?"

"No," Dr. Oxman said.

"Can the transmission of herpes from one person to another be done through heterosexual contact?"

"Yes."

"Can that also be done through homosexual contact?"

"Yes."

When Arena finished questioning Dr. Oxman, Revak had a few questions of his own for the witness.

"If the male has genital herpes and in order to pass it on to a female, must he have an outbreak of some kind at that time?"

"No. He can be asymptomatically shedding the virus. When it's transmitted, someone who is infected often doesn't know it."

"Is it visible on the skin, then, of the male like it is on the female?" Revak asked.

"No."

When Oxman finished testifying, Przytulski called Roger Sullivan to the witness stand. Sullivan testified that in the spring of 1992, he was the foreman on a job working for McDonalds Yards in San Diego, refurbishing a boat called the "Liberated Lady", and that he had hired Karen during that time. Sullivan claimed that he did not know Karen in 1991.

When Roger Sullivan completed his limited testimony, the prosecution found itself waiting on Karen to return to the courtroom. She had not returned from the court's lunch recess. Przytulski agreed to allow the defense to begin presenting its case instead of delaying the proceedings.

For his first witness, Arena called Toni Lenhart, a manager with AT&T corporate security to the witness stand. Arena questioned Lenhart about subscriber numbers and how the cards are issued.

Lenhart testified that a non-subscriber card is one that is issued to a customer who does not have a residential or business telephone number, and, that if a person used a non-subscriber telephone card, the charges would be recorded where the calls originated. The computer then generates a bill and identifies what calls are charged to that card number, the date, and time.

Arena displayed a large blown up photograph of a telephone bill revealing a series of telephone calls made on a non-subscriber telephone card issued to Sam Consiglio. Lenhart testified that according to the bill, the calls originated at a phone number belonging to Steve and Lauren Skye and physically located inside their apartment on Clairemont Drive.

On cross-examination, Lenhart said that anyone with Sam's card number could have placed the calls.

When Lenhart had finished testifying, Karen returned to the courtroom and took her place back on the witness stand.

"Karen, prior to coming to San Diego, you had a drug problem, didn't you?" Przytulski asked.

Karen testified that she'd had a bad drug problem and had actually overdosed in Houston, Texas. Karen also testified that she was no longer taking drugs when she arrived in San Diego.

On cross-examination, Arena asked Karen what other types of drugs she had been using.

"Acid, speed, marijuana, cocaine," Karen said.

"Did you consume narcotics on or about June, July of 1991?"

"No."

"After June, July of 1991?"

Przytulski jumped from his chair, yelling objection. Again, Przytulski and Arena were whispering to the judge so that the jurors could not hear.

"Judge, for the life of me, I don't know why Mr. Przytulski brought it up, but he did. She's got like a 15-year drug history, heavy drug usage before she comes to San Diego. I've got a witness that is going to testify she was doing cocaine in late 1993. And, I think I should be allowed to go into that. If I show she's got a 15-year drug history, that she has used drugs right before San Diego, and she's used drugs after San Diego, this could explain her presence at 32nd and Imperial. Basically, you can buy drugs anywhere, but drugs are prevalent in that area and we can show a pattern."

Revak disagreed. "What is the relevance of recent usage? They don't want to know whether she's using it in San Diego," Revak told Arena. Before Arena could answer, Revak denied the request. Revak was not going to reverse his ruling. He ordered Arena to continue his questioning.

"When you said to Mr. Harn during your interview with him that you stopped consuming narcotics in 1988, you were not being truthful with him, correct? Just yes or no, that's all I'm asking," Arena pleaded.

"No, I was not being truthful," Karen, answered.

When Karen had finished testifying, the defense continued presenting its case. Arena called Lauren Skye to the witness stand.

Skye testified that Sam had arrived in San Diego in late May 1991 and was living with her and her husband, Steve, while Sam looked for work. On cross-examination, Przytulski asked if she ever assisted Sam in making three way phone calls. Lauren told the court that she had not.

Steve Skye was the next to testify. His testimony was the same as it had been in October 1991; Sam had used the phone in his apartment extensively, and was housesitting for him when he and his wife went on vacation on July 2, 1991. Steve Skye also testified that he never helped Sam set up any three-way calls.

Lori Beliveau, the director of recreation for the city of El Cajon, testified her records indicated that on the night of July 2, 1991, adult softball games were scheduled from 6:30 p.m. to 9:30 p.m. While the games were being played, most people would park near the ball fields, which were in the proximity of the parking area where Sam allegedly raped Karen. Beliveau also testified that the park was staffed with two people the night of July 2.

When Beliveau completed her testimony, Revak adjourned court for the day. He told the jurors that they would have to be in court the following day in spite of the fact that the nation was in mourning and would be observing the funeral of former President Richard Nixon. While the federal courts and government were shut down, Pete Wilson, the governor of California, had not declared it a state holiday. Revak did indicate that he would adjourn court at 3:00 p.m. the following afternoon to give anyone who wanted, an opportunity to participate in the funeral of President Nixon.

When trial resumed on Wednesday, April 27, Arena called Wava Howley to the stand. Arena wanted one thing out of this witness; he wanted Howley to identify her phone number of July 2, 1991. Arena showed Howley the blow up poster of Sam's telephone charges for July 1991. Wava quickly identified her telephone number as one called for approximately 52 minutes on the night of July 2, 1991. Howley did not, however, testify that she had spoken to Sam that night. The question was not asked.

Next, Arena called David Sieffert to the witness stand. Sieffert testified that the telephone number of his father Tom Sieffert, who lived in Muskegon, Michigan, was also on the phone bill for the night of July 2, 1991.

Frances Marygold, the former manager of the Valley House Apartments in El Cajon, testified that she was leaving her job as the manager of the Valley House Apartments to move to San Jose. "I had first met Sam on July 2, 1991. It was about 4:00 in the afternoon. I had left work early to meet Skip and Marie Beaman at the complex because I had to take a microwave over to apartment 6 which was the new managers apartment," Marygold said.

"Did you notice whether Mr. Consiglio was with anyone at that time," Arena asked.

"Yes, he was with Mr. Beaman, the owner of the complex."

Marygold testified that she did not see anyone else with Sam at that time.

On cross-examination, Przytulski asked, "Did you ever help Mr. Consiglio make any three-way phone calls?"

"Yes, I did."

"When did you do that?"

"Various times when he was here in the jail."

Again, Arena objected asking for Przytulski to define a time frame.

"June and July, 1991," Przytulski said.

Marygold testified that she had helped Sam place three way calls during June and July 1991. According to Marygold, Sam had the phone installed in her apartment. "It appeared to be a regular phone. He had a special thing set up from the phone company. I don't know; I'm not an engineer."

"Was there any conversation with you and Mr. Consiglio about using the code name Utah?"

"Yes."

"And did he tell you that unless he used the word Utah, that you weren't to do anything for him so that you would know that it was him that you were actually talking to? Did he tell you that?"

"Not that I recall. All I know about Utah was his name. That is all I know."

"What was the code for?"

"I don't remember. It was a nickname."

Przytulski knew he was going nowhere with the witness and quickly ended his cross-examination. Next, Arena called Stacy Knutson to the witness stand.

Knutson testified that Karen had told her that she had a business doing cabinetwork while living in San Diego. A man who owned a boat had called her to prepare a bid on reworking the cabinetry on the boat. According to Knutson, Karen went back to the boat the day after working up a bid proposal. That's when this man had raped her. Stacy also told Arena that she considered Karen to be a liar and she didn't believe a word Karen said.

Arena next called Del La Bre to the witness stand. La Bre testified that Karen had told her she had to go back to San Diego to testify at a rape trial. "She went to do some work on a boat. I guess there was a room underneath it and some gentleman attacked her at that point is what she told me," La Bre said.

"Did you ever talk about her with your co-workers?" Arena asked.

"Yes we did," La Bre answered.

"Was there an opinion as to what her propensity for truthfulness or veracity was? Was there an opinion amongst the co-workers?"

"Yeah, a very strong one."

"What was that opinion?"

"She was full of it," La Bre said.

"Are you saying that she was a liar?"

"Yes, a chronic liar, habitual," La Bre claimed.

Arena next called Christina Cassidy, a bartender at the True Colors Lounge in Colorado Springs. She testified she had observed Karen on several occasions and had heard other patrons refer to her as a liar and a manipulator. Cassidy also testified that Karen had told her she had been married and had been living in Seattle until her husband began abusing her. Cassidy identified two bank checks that Karen had cashed at True Colors, both of which were returned for insufficient funds.

Przytulski began his cross-examination of Cassidy by asking if she ever received a phone call from an individual.... But before he could identify who that person was, Arena jumped from his seat and yelled "Objection." Arena and Przytulski approached Revak and, again, outside the hearing of the jury, argued their position.

"Your honor," Arena began, "this area of inquiry has to do with her receiving a phone call from a person who identified himself as a private investigator by the name of Bill Johnson; Bill Johnson being Mr. Consiglio. I don't know the relevance of it except to point out to the jury that Mr. Consiglio was representing himself as another individual."

"Your honor," Przytulski argued, "this witness received a phone call from an individual who identified himself as Bill Johnson who I believe will be identified as Mr. Consiglio. Bill Johnson told her that Karen had lied, gave her a series of instances where she had lied. He asked for her opinion as to her being truthful in the past. I want to know if she relied on that opinion for the relevant period of time in connection with that. And it becomes relevant if Mr. Consiglio is called back in and that Mr. Consiglio was threatening to have Karen arrested if she came back to California for perjury. That goes to a consciousness of guilt because he's trying to get her not to come back."

"Judge," Arena argued, "may I ask, what is the purpose of that? What is the relevancy of that?"

"Maybe she can identify the voice of Mr. Consiglio as being the person who says, I'm Bill Johnson. Don't you think that shows consciousness of guilt?" Revak said and overruled his objection.

Przytulski played a taped recording of Sam's voice for Cassidy. Cassidy testified that the voice on the recording sounded like the man who identified himself as Bill Johnson, but she couldn't be positive. Cassidy told Przytulski and the jury that "Bill Johnson" had called her three or four times while she was working. She also testified that "Bill Johnson" had told her that if Karen came back to San Diego to testify, she would be arrested for perjury.

When trial resumed on Thursday morning, Al Arena had just one more significant witness to present, Michael Black, a private investigator. Black testified that he had driven several traffic routes, all at Arena's request, and recorded the distances and times of each of the trips. According to Black's testimony, he drove from 3133 Clairemont Drive, the home of Steve and Lauren Skye, to Wells Park. The distance between the two locations was 20.1 miles. Black testified that it took 23 minutes and 48 seconds to travel that route while staying within the speed limit. Exactly what Arena was preparing for with Black's testimony would have to wait until his summation. When Black finished testifying, Arena told judge Revak that he had no more witnesses to present. The defense was resting.

Przytulski was prepared to present rebuttal witnesses to dispute whatever evidence Arena had presented to the jury. But before calling any witnesses, both he and Arena stipulated to the testimony of Gary Harmor a senior forensic serologist with the Serological Research Institute in Richmond, California. Revak told the jurors that had Harmor testified he would have told them that no semen was detected on the vaginal swabs taken from Karen and that no semen was detected on the black and white jumpsuit.

Przytulski then called Virginia Kukuk, Sam's sister, to the witness stand.

"Did you have a conversation with the defendant, your brother, regarding access codes on your answering machine?" Przytulski asked.

"Yes. I had my answering machine on a lot. Sam called me quite frequently. I was very busy. I could not take the calls to talk to him. He said he was tired of talking to the damn machine. He said he was going to go break that S.O.B. I said, what do you mean? And he said, 'I'm going to break into that thing one day. You know, if I call the company, they will give me the access code'."

On cross-examination, Arena asked Virginia if she had given anyone her personal access code to her answering machine and if there was some animosity between her and her brother Sam. Virginia answered no to both questions and was excused. She had been subpoenaed by the prosecution to testify at the trial; flown to San Diego from Detroit and lodged at a local motel for almost one week, all at the expense of the taxpayers of San Diego County, before testifying for less than five minutes. During that week, Virginia experienced as much emotional trauma as she ever had in her life. She loved her brother and had stood by him when most members of her family refused to acknowledge his existence. Virginia had strong religious convictions. It was her sense of right that caused her to reimburse Wava Howley for her expenses when Howley testified for Sam in 1991. And, it was her sense of right that brought her to San Diego to testify for the prosecution. No longer, could she mask her brother's behavior. To her, Sam had become a true disappointment. Her parents had expected more and believed in him. They always held out hope. But Virginia no longer held out any hope for Sam. She had convinced herself that her brother had raped Karen, and it was her strong belief in Jesus Christ that dictated she tell the truth, especially if it would prevent her brother from ever hurting another woman again.

Przytulski then called Wava Howley back to the witness stand. Howley told the jurors that in October 1991, she had testified that she had engaged in a 53 minute phone conversation with Sam beginning around 10:00 p.m. Arkansas time, on the night of July, 2, 1991. Howley testified that after giving testimony in the case, she thought that she might have been confused about the time and date of Sam's call and notified Sam's attorney, Neal Gibbons of her concerns. Howley told the court that she had received a letter from Sam prior to her testifying in October 1991 reminding her of his telephone call to her. Mike Przytulski then introduced the contents of the letter into the record.

"I called you in the afternoon on the 26th of June and left a message on your machine. Looks like I'll get that job in El Cajon as apartment manager of a 25-unit building. Then, on June 28, I talked to you for over 15 minutes and in that conversation, I told you that I indeed got that job in El Cajon but didn't know how soon I could move in. In the meantime, I am going to check out a better opportunity in Carlsbad. Then on the evening of July 2, around 8:00 to 9:00 p.m. in a phone call, I told you that I had decided to take the job in El Cajon. That was my reason for calling you that night to let you know I had signed a contract and could move in right away. I want you to think very hard on this. This might help you a little. I remember making you laugh on July 2, when I shared with you that my AID's test on July 1 was negative. You laughed at first because you thought I was joking. But when you realized I was serious, you gave me a lot of encouragement that I could do it. That is, go without sex until Christmas. Don't laugh, but you have done a pretty good job so far. I'm telling you all this to prepare you for trial."

"I didn't remember talking to him on the 2nd," Howley testified. "I remember that I had received a phone call during that time span but not on that date. When I testified first in court, I said that, yes, I was home that evening. There was no doubt in my mind then."

"Prior to this time, had you ever had a phone conversation with Mr. Consiglio where he asked you the make and model of your answering machine?" Przytulski asked.

"Yes he did. I thought it was strange at the time. He said he could call the company that manufactured the answering machine and get the access code and retrieve my messages."

"He also told you he could call the machine and keep it running, isn't that true?"

"Yes he did," Howley said.

On cross-examination, Arena asked Howley about her previous testimony during which she claimed she had almost a one-hour conversation with Sam on the night July 2, 1991. "You truly believed that you had a conversation with Mr. Consiglio at that time?"

"Well, only because he had a phone bill that said so. I really didn't remember having the conversation. But he had the phone bill. So, I thought that was proof that couldn't be refuted," Howley said.

Przytulski waited until the following morning to call the prosecution's chief rebuttal witness; Mark Foster, an engineer who had owned his own company servicing and designing telecommunications equipment. Foster had spent over eight years working with various law enforcement agencies designing special surveillance equipment for clandestine operations. On this very morning, Foster had examined the telephone hookup at 3133 Clairemont Drive.

Foster testified that the phone system was a simple system found in most homes. There were two phone lines per apartment. The lines were wired into the apartment through an open central junction box located on the outside of the building. "You have access in the box to all lines coming into that apartment building. You also have access to all lines going to each apartment. That's where the phone company makes the decision to route the calling telephone numbers from their central office. You could route secondary lines in by simple jumpers across and/or by moving simple pairs of wires around to suit your needs," Foster said.

"So, it's possible for anybody to actually work up and switch phone service phone lines from apartments?" Przytulski asked.

Foster told Przytulski that a person could bootleg the line connection, call into that line using a telephone credit card from another location, and it would appear on the phone bill that the call was placed from the fixed location, in this case, 3133 Clairemont Drive.

"Is there anything complicated about doing this?" Przytulski asked.

"Not really. It's fairly simple. It's simple basic circuits in electronics. It doesn't take much to do it, a simple screwdriver and moving two wires."

Arena was stunned. He had not prepared for Przytulski introducing what he referred to as last minute "high tech" star wars technology. As such, Arena did what he knew best to counter the damage inflicted on his client by the district attorney's witness; he put on a show. 'Mr. Foster, I never knew how to do this. This is amazing. So, I...," Arena began as he walked promptly toward the witness, waiving his arms and gesturing around the courtroom. But Revak was getting tired. He was not about to lose control of his courtroom and stopped Arena cold. "Ask a question, please," Revak demanded as he stared directly at Arena.

"All right. How did you determine that two lines go into each apartment?"

"I opened the junction box and looked at the lines going out of the junction box. They are hermetically sealed wire cables with four wires. It's basic common knowledge that that's normal in how most residences are wired. Same with apartment buildings."

"When you say that's basic common knowledge, is that basic common knowledge among people in your industry?"

"I should say within the industry, yes," Foster answered.

"You wouldn't expect the milkman who delivers the milk to Clairemont Drive to know?" Arena asked.

Przytulski objected to Arena's question, claiming that it called for speculation on the part of the witness. Revak agreed.

Foster said he had a degree in electrical engineering, but learned about telephone wiring from practical experience. Foster told the jurors that wiring the phone lines was easy and that the telephone lines come in pairs with the lines being color coded, red and green being one, and normally yellow and black being the other. While there were four wires and two lines, there is normally only one telephone number listed for each two wires. What Foster could not answer, was whether or not any such bootlegging had been done to the phone lines leading into apartment 3 located at 3133 Clairemont Drive. He did testify during re-direct, that he found two of the phone lines inside the junction box to have been wrapped very tightly backward around the sheath. "In other words, to keep them from shorting out. For some reason, the wires were left straight open hanging out as if at one time possibly they were being used for something." Foster could not explain whether or not this had happened a week ago or three years ago because of the dirt around the wires and inside the junction box.

On Monday, May 2, 1994, closing arguments in the case of the People of the State of California v. Sam Consiglio, who, this time, never took the witness stand. Przytulski, as he had done in October 1991, addressed the jury first. He told the jury that Sam went looking for a woman at St. Vincent De Paul's because it is a homeless shelter and the homeless are vulnerable people because they are down and "not sharp". He pleaded for the jury to consider just how lucky Karen was to guess that Sam had no alibi during the time she claimed to have been raped.

"She doesn't know he doesn't have a human being that can give him an alibi. Mr. Consiglio could have been with ten people. He could have been at the police station having his car towed. How could Karen know that he did not have somebody that could say he was with me that night? What a lucky guess," Przytulski told the seven men and five women sitting on the jury as he reviewed the evidence, trying to put into some reasonable order, the sequence of events surrounding Sam and Karen's relationship during the first two days in July 1991.

"Most of what Karen had testified to, actually happened, but not everything," Arena told the jury as he began his summation. "Let me start off by saying to you, that rape is a human tragedy. It's the type of tragedy that brings out the very best in people. We saw that. All Karen had to say to St. Vincent De Paul, is, I've been raped. All of a sudden, people help you. They stop doing the things that they are doing. They may stop having expectations of you. They help you. That's a good thing, because rape is truly a tragedy. And, by no means, do we, by putting on a defense, condone rape, because I don't. I do not condone it. But understand something, because equally as tragic as what rape is, is the false accusation of rape," Arena told the jury.

Arena explained that there was no solid evidence that they could hang on to in this case. Everything they heard, from each of the witnesses, P. J. Harn, Jackie Thomas, Rosalind Bell, all testified as to what Karen had told them. "None of them were there. None of them were in Mr. Consiglio's apartment that night. None of them were in Wells Park that night. Their entire testimony is simply based on her version."

Arena was trying to convince the jury that Karen had falsely accused Sam of raping her. He was also trying to portray Karen as a pathological liar. He reminded the jury that Karen had lied on her application to St. Vincent's, telling them she was an abused wife in Seattle. She had lied to the police about her use of illegal drugs, even overdosing in Houston. She had lied about her physical injury and the reason she had to wear a cast. While Al Arena was portraying Karen as a devious liar, he was trying to depict Sam as someone who was proud and looking for work.

"The guy wanted to work," Arena said. "He is not limping into the Carlsbad apartment with a cast on his right ankle saying he fell down a cliff 20 feet. He was unemployed. Did he check unemployment benefits? No sir. He's a proud man. So, he stretches his resume a little bit. My God, he stretches his resume. That doesn't make him a rapist. If everyone who stretched their qualifications so they could get a job, I submit, all members of the Congress should be thrown in jail. They all stretched their qualifications."

Arena asked why someone who was planning to rape Karen would ask for a tour of St. Vincent's so that a number of people would be able to see his face, when prior to that, he had picked Karen up and dropped her off without anyone seeing him. As for the phone records, Arena explained that the prosecution didn't believe that the purported attack took place in 53 minutes, the time of the so-called telephone call to Wava Howley. That's why Przytulski had to explain that Sam was in another location. "All of a sudden, we have this star wars technology that Mr. Consiglio apparently had to have a tremendous amount of electronic information, like Mr. Foster who is gifted and was born with it," Arena said.

"What it really comes down to ladies and gentlemen, when all is said and done, it comes down to a 53 minute phone call. Mr. Consiglio made it. It appears on this long distance credit card." Arena concluded his summation telling the jury that it was his decision that Sam, not testify during the trial. "I'm the attorney. I made the decision. You're not to consider that at all. You will get an instruction as to that," he told them.

As soon as both attorneys had concluded with their summations, Revak instructed the jury as to the law in this case and, to what was expected of them. "You must base your decision on the facts and the law," Revak told the jury before sending them into deliberations. "You have two duties to perform. First, you must determine the facts from the evidence received in the trial and not from any other source. Second, you must apply the law that I state to you to the facts as you determine them." As soon as the jurors left the courtroom, Przytulski had one more piece of business for Revak to consider.

"Judge, this morning I had a call from Louis Consiglio. He indicated that the defendant had called him last night and threatened to kill him, to kill Virginia, to kill Wava Howley and their other brother as well. I haven't heard the defendant's version of what happened or anything, but at this point in time, these threats are serious; they have occurred before. We're asking that the court reconsider the defendant's phone privileges at this time."

"Well, they are revoked. The trial is over. He has no need for a telephone," Revak said. "I'm not even going to consider these allegations to be true. He is now no different than anybody else in the county jail. He doesn't need a telephone." Arena's response to Revak was short. "I understand that judge," was all he said.

It was Friday, May 6th at 11:15 a.m., two and half days since the jury had first begun its deliberations, when they instructed judge Revak that they had reached a verdict.Sam, as he had in October 1991, stood, this time alongside Al Arena, as the verdict was read.

"We the jury in the above entitled cause find the defendant, Sam Consiglio, guilty of the crime of forcible rape in violation of penal code second 261 (2) as charged in count one of the information; first penetration. We further find that in the commission of the above offense, said defendant did not personally inflict great bodily injury upon Karen within the meaning of the penal code."

As to counts two and three of the information, the jury found Sam not guilty. He had been convicted of only one count of rape as opposed to three in 1991 and, was found not guilty of inflicting great bodily injury upon Karen. The jury did not believe that Sam had inflicted Karen with herpes. To everyone but Sam, the outcome had been expected. When it did come, it generated no joy or anger for Karen. She felt only relief that the tragic soap opera Sam had cast her in was now over.

Revak thanked the jurors and asked them to wait outside before dismissing them. Afterwards, he asked Sam if he did indeed wish to stipulate that he had been in prison prior to being charged with raping Karen and that he had been out of prison less than five years. This fact would possibly enhance Sam's prison sentence; therefore, he was entitled to a hearing on that issue before these same jurors. Sam stipulated that he had in fact been in prison previously. With that, Revak dismissed the jury.

"I spoke to several of the jurors after the verdict was rendered," Arena said. "They told me they thought both Sam and Karen had lied but that Sam did have sex with her. I too, think he had sex with her but inside his apartment and I think it was consensual. I think she got mad when he told her she wasn't getting the job managing the apartment complex with him. I don't think she wanted to have sex with him but did, hoping to get the job, and fabricated the allegations afterwards. I don't believe he ever raped her. But, we got his exposure (the time he could be sentenced on these charges) down from 30 years to 9. To me, that was in itself, a victory."

On July 13, 1994, Sam and Al Arena appeared once again before judge Revak. This time, the only thing left for Revak to do, was sentence Sam to prison. But first, Arena and Sam wished to be heard. Arena spoke briefly, knowing that his efforts were in vain as he tried to persuade Revak to refrain from sentencing his client to the maximum number of years in prison. "Now this court has indicated that the court believes a rape had occurred. Perhaps not in the manner in which Karen indicated, but this court was satisfied that there was a rape. But I think out of that statement, one could find that perhaps it was a rape in Karen's mind and not actually or legally a rape as a rape is defined. Perhaps it was a situation where Mr. Consiglio had made certain promises to Karen for sexual favors. Those promises were not realized. As far as Karen was concerned, it was rape. Your honor, there is still a doubt as to whether that happened," Arena argued.

When Arena had finished his discussion, it was time for Sam to address the court.

"This has been going on now for three years, your honor," Sam began. "I have never touched Karen. I have never committed a crime in this city. But I have been locked up ever since July 17th of 1991. The first thing I want to do is thank the court for making sure that I had excellent representation this time. I don't think I could have gotten any better. And, I would like to thank the court and all your staff for all the respect they have given me throughout the course of these proceedings."

"Let me address the past first. I will stipulate that up to 1978, I was a bad person. People change. So, on April 26, 1981, I made a vow never to assault anyone again. To this day, I've kept that vow. Karen has never been with me to El Cajon. She fabricated the whole story. There is no evidence showing that I'm guilty. I think it's a lot easier for everyone to pretend that I'm guilty and sentence me under that pretense rather than for the district attorney or someone else to stand up and say okay, we screwed up. We made a mistake. We are sorry, Mr. Consiglio. I would really hope the court would be fair in the sentence. Thank you your honor."

The formalities over, Revak looked at Sam and said, "It seems Mr. Consiglio, that I've known you for a long time. You know, one to one, man to man, you don't seem to be a bad person to me. You communicate well. You are articulate. I think you are a bright person. You are personable. You are outgoing. You even wrote me a letter telling me you had tickets to see Reba McIntyre in Las Vegas this July and asked me to release you so you could go see her. The more I think about it, you are really a charlatan. I read sometime ago, that the earnestness of a charlatan is only a profounder kind of charlatan. And, I think that fits you. I'm not convinced beyond all possible doubt that it happened the way Karen said it happened. I am convinced, beyond a reasonable doubt that a rape happened. And, that's as far as I think I need to go."

"I'm also mindful of the statement you made to your brother on the telephone about going to the home for the downtrodden. I can't remember the exact quote, but it was something about it being an opportunity to get a piece of ass. That's what you had in mind. This case involved violence. So, based on those reasons, your record and the amount of sophistication, I think the upper term is clearly justified in this case."

Revak sentenced Sam to eight years in the state prison for raping Karen and one extra year for having been out of prison less than five years before committing another crime. Revak then told Sam that he would serve those nine years consecutive to the 24-year sentence being served for raping Carolyn. Revak adjourned the court and, Sam was taken back to his cell inside the San Diego County jail faced with serving a total of 33 years in prison. He had, however, been incarcerated for almost three years, leaving him only 30 more to serve; less, if he started to work once he returned to prison. Less than a week later, he was sent back to the California State Prison in Calipatria.

Epilogue

On August 17, 1994, the Department of Alternative Defense Counsel for the County of San Diego revealed that between Logan McKechnie and Al Arena, along with witness fees, air fare, lodging, investigative services, and phone calls, most of which were made by Sam, they had expanded $62,084.07 of their budget for Sam's defense. This did not include the costs associated with the district attorney's office to prosecute Sam.

In November 1994, Paul Pfingst, a former assistant district attorney, was elected as the new district attorney for the County of San Diego. On November 22, Sam wrote Pfingst congratulating him on his victory and asked him to look into his convictions. "I do hope and pray you will keep your word and clean up that office. There's a lot of corruption in it and for the past few years, some of the assistants in that office have deliberately prosecuted and, in some cases, convicted people they knew were innocent. You cannot let that go on." Sam pleaded for Pfingst to investigate what Harn and Przytulski had done to him. If he did, Pfingst would discover that Sam was completely innocent of the charges. "Once you correct it, all I want is an apology, reimbursement for all my lost wages, and assurances from you that those responsible for what's happened to me will be held accountable for their actions and never given an opportunity to do this to someone else."

In 1995, the administration of Governor Pete Wilson prepared regulations for the California legislature to deny conjugal visits to thousands of state prisoners who fell within a certain category of crime, including those found guilty of murder, statutory rape, spousal rape, incest, oral copulation, child abuse, and other types of lewd and lascivious acts on a child. The California Department of Corrections estimated that the new regulations would exclude about a fifth of California's 125,000 inmates from the visitation program. Francisco Lobaco of the American Civil Liberties Union was quoted as saying, "It's just mean-spirited and totally unjustifiable to do this type of action."

On January 16, 1995, Joan Isserlis, who had unsuccessfully represented Sam on his appeal from his conviction in the Carolyn case, also, at Sam's request, wrote Paul Pfingst requesting that his office look into the conviction. Because she believed there had been a miscarriage of justice in this case, Isserlis acceded to Sam's request.

"Mr. Consiglio had sexual relations on numerous occasions in 1991 with a prostitute named Carolyn. He never paid Carolyn and the reason she did not withhold her favors was the main factual question in dispute at Mr. Consiglio's trial. Carolyn claimed Mr. Consiglio told her he was a cop and would arrest her if she did not have sex with him; she believed these representations.

"Carolyn did not go to the police to complain of the harassment to which Mr. Consiglio was subjecting her. Instead, it was Mr. Consiglio himself who brought his relations with Carolyn to the attention of Patrick Harn. At trial, Mr. Consiglio's attorney failed to present crucial exculpatory evidence in that Carolyn's preliminary hearing testimony that she did not believe Mr. Consiglio was a police officer after the first time they had sex. Found guilty of coercing Carolyn into sex acts on three occasions, Mr. Consiglio was sentenced as harshly as he would have been had he brutally raped three children.

"Rape and other sex offenses are crimes deserving of severe punishment chiefly because of the outrage the acts ordinarily do to the feelings and dignity of non-consenting victims. In this case, however, the victim was not unwilling to engage in sex with Mr. Consiglio. Indeed, the two met when Carolyn offered Mr. Consiglio sexual services for money. Instead of paying, Mr. Consiglio took tawdry advantage of her gullibility. His conduct, while reprehensible, constituted what was essentially an annoyance to Carolyn. It caused her worry and monetary loss, not trauma and humiliation. Surely this matters.

"I am concerned not only for Mr. Consiglio. I am concerned that if we give lengthy prison sentences to men who do not use physical force or threats of physical force but con or pressure women into sex, our society will become increasingly cynical about the gravity of sex offenses. It will, in time, rationally regret its harshness in cases such as Mr. Consiglio's and it will in an overreaction, cease to impose substantial punishment even in cases where heinous sex crimes are perpetrated. Then women will have no protection."

Sincerely,
Joan Isserlis.

I received a copy of this letter from Sam shortly after Joan Isserlis sent it to Paul Pfingst. Attached to the letter was a short handwritten yellow stick-em note from Sam. It read, "This woman has realized what most of you son of a bitches take years to learn. That is, to know Sam is to love him; deal with it."

Mike Przytulski continues to prosecute cases for the San Diego County District Attorneys Office.

Al Arena maintains a successful law practice in San Diego handling a variety of defense work.

Wava Howley continues to live in Arkansas and has recently gone back to teaching. She is far more reluctant to get involved in corresponding with prisoners and has limited her association with prison ministries.

The whereabouts of Karen and Carolyn are unknown.

Karron Thompson is believed to be residing in Texas. She is no longer appearing on tabloid talk shows.

Gerard Griesbeck and Paul Carey have since retired from the Sterling Heights Police Department.

Tom and Loretta Sieffert still live in Muskegon, Michigan. Both are still active in the prison ministry and pray for Sam's recovery. They claim there are many people in the Muskegon area that would be willing to help Sam adjust to life outside of prison if he made Muskegon his home when he is released.

None of Sam's three ex-wives agreed to be interviewed in connection with this book.

In March 1997, Sam headed a fundraiser among prison inmates. He was photographed in a ceremony with the Chief Deputy Warden at the Calipatria State Prison handing over a check made out to a women's shelter.

On May 22, 1998, Sam married Yolanda Romero, ten years his junior in a civil ceremony at the Calipatria State Prison. Yolanda speaks almost no English, and has four children from previous unions. She is his fourth wife.

On May 21, 2000, Jan Stiglitz wrote Lisa Weinreb, one of his former students currently working for the San Diego District Attorney's Office. He asked Weinreb if the dress worn by Karen was still available for testing since no DNA testing was ever done during the investigation. Stiglitz told Weinreb that, "I remain convinced that he (Sam) didn't rape Karen that night." On this same day, Stiglitz wrote Sam telling him that the San Diego District Attorney's Office is reviewing pre 1992 cases to see if there are any, where DNA testing might prove innocence.

Sam is currently residing in the State Prison at San Diego in California. He continues to file briefs and appeals to the State and Federal Courts in an effort to have both of his convictions overturned and looks forward to someday receiving conjugal visits from his wife, Yolanda.

One can never change a sociopath through care, love, attention, communication, or money. DO NOT TRY! These are the things that they have no true respect for or do not understand. Therefore, they will drain the victim until there is no more thrill, challenge, money or ego to satisfy. These people are control freaks. Let go of the desire to help these lost people before they control you out of your life.

Damien

About The Author

Ernie Dorling has spent over 20 years in federal law enforcement. He has taught and lectured on various Criminal Justice courses in Germany and the U.S. He is the author of the short story, "Where's the Crime." in the anthology *Cop Tales 2000*. He lives in Connecticut.